Artificial Intelligence

Springer
Berlin
Heidelberg
New York
Barcelona
Budapest
Hong Kong
London
Milan
Paris
Santa Clara
Singapore
Tokyo

V.S. Subrahmanian
Sushil Jajodia (Eds.)

Multimedia Database Systems

Issues and Research Directions

With 104 Figures and 9 Tables

Springer

Prof. V.S. Subrahmanian
University of Maryland
Computer Science Department
College Park, MD 20742
USA

Prof. Sushil Jajodia
George Mason University
Dept. of Information and Software
Systems Engineering
Fairfax, VA 22030
USA

Catalogue in Publication-Data applied for

ISBN-13: 978-3-642-64622-5 e-ISBN-13: 978-3-642-60950-3
DOI: 10.1007/978-3-642-60950-3

Die Deutsche Bibliothek - CIP-Einheitsaufnahme
Subrahmanian, V.S.: Multimedia database systems: issues and research directions/ V.S. Subrahmanian, Sushil Jajodia;. - Berlin; Heidelberg; New York; Barcelona; Budapest; Hong Kong; London; Mailand; Paris; Santa Clara; Singapore; Tokyo: Springer, 1996 (Artificial Intelligence) NE: Subrahmanian, V.S:

Softcover reprint of the hardcover 1st edition 1996

Cover Design: Künkel+Lopka, Ilvesheim Printing: Druckhaus Beltz, Hemsbach
Typesetting: Camera ready by authors
Printed on acid-free paper SPIN 10486907 45/3142 - 5 4 3 2 1 0

Foreword

With the rapid growth in the use of computers to manipulate, process, and reason about multimedia data, the problem of how to store and retrieve such data is becoming increasingly important. Thus, although the field of multimedia database systems is only about 5 years old, it is rapidly becoming a focus for much excitement and research effort.

Multimedia database systems are intended to provide unified frameworks for requesting and integrating information in a wide variety of formats, such as audio and video data, document data, and image data. Such data often have special storage requirements that are closely coupled to the various kinds of devices that are used for recording and presenting the data, and for each form of data there are often multiple representations and multiple standards – all of which make the database integration task quite complex. Some of the problems include:

- what a multimedia database query means
- what kinds of languages to use for posing queries
- how to develop compilers for such languages
- how to develop indexing structures for storing media on ancillary devices
- data compression techniques
- how to present and author presentations based on user queries.

Although approaches are being developed for a number of these problems, they have often been ad hoc in nature, and there is a need to provide a principled theoretical foundation. To address that need, this book brings together a number of respected authors who are developing principled approaches to one or more aspects of the problems described above. It is the first book I know of that does so.

The editors of this book are eminently qualified for such a task. Sushil Jajodia is respected for his work on distributed databases, distributed heterogeneous databases, and database indexing. V. S. Subrahmanian is well known for his work on nonmonotonic reasoning, deductive databases and heterogeneous databases – and also on several different media systems: MACS (Media Abstraction Creation System), and AVIS (Advanced Video Information System), and FIST (Face Information System, currently under development). It has been a pleasure working with them, and I am pleased to have been able to facilitate in some small way the publication of this book.

Dana Nau, College Park, MD

Preface

With the advent of the information superhighway, a vast amount of data is curently available on the Internet. The concurrent advances in the areas of image, video, and audio capture, and the spectacular explosion of CD-ROM technology has led to a wide array of non-traditional forms of data being available across the network as well. Image data, video data, audio data, all perhaps stored in multiple, heterogeneous formats, traditionally form the "core" of what is known today as multimedia data.

Despite the proliferation of such forms of media data, as well as the proliferation of a number of commercially available tools to manipulate this data, relatively little work has been done on the principles of multimedia information systems. What common characteristics do all these different media-types have in common? Can these characteristics be exploited so as to provide a "common core" skeleton that can be used as a platform on which other multimedia applications can be built? If so, how can this be accomplished? These, and other questions arise in the context of such multimedia systems.

In this book, we bring together a collection of papers that address each of these questions, as well as a number of other related questions.

The first paper, by Marcus and Subrahmanian, provides a basic theoretical foundation for multimedia information systems that is independent of any given application. The authors identify core characteristics common to a variety of media sources. They then show that these core characteristics can be used to build indexing structures and query languages for media data. They argue that query processing can be used as a way of specifying media presentations.

The paper by Gudivada et al. studies a specific kind of multimedia information system – those dealing only with image data. The authors describe various kinds of operations inherent in such systems (e.g. retrieving objects based on shape similarity). They then provide a unified framework, called the AIR model, the treats all these different operations in a unified manner.

The paper by Arya et al. describes the design and implementation of the QBISM system for storing and manipulating medical images. In contrast to the paper of Gudivada et al., in this paper, the authors study issues of logical database design by including two special data types – `VOLUME` and `REGION` to represent spatial information.

In the paper by Sistla and Yu, the authors develop techniques for similarity based retrieval of pictures. Their paper is similar in spirit to that of Gudivada et al. – the difference is that whereas Gudivada et al. attempt to develop a unified data model, Sistla and Yu formalize the process of inexact matching between images and study the mathematical properties resulting from such a formalization.

The paper by Aref et al. studies a unique kind of multimedia data, viz. handwritten data. The authors have developed framework called *Ink* in which a set of handwritten notes may be represented, and queried. The authors describe their representation, their matching/querying algorithms, their implemented system, and the results of experiments based on their system.

In the same spirit as the papers by Gudivada et al. and Sistla and Yu, the issue of retrieval by similarity is studied by Jagadish. However, here, Jagadish develops algorithms to index databases that require retrievals by similarity. He does this by mapping an object (being searched for) as well as the corpus of objects (the database) into a proximity space – two objects are similar if they are near each other in this proximity space.

Belussi et al.'s paper addresses a slightly different query – in geographic information systems, users often want to ask queries of the form: "Find all objects that are as close to (resp. as far from) object O as possible". The authors develop ways of storing GIS data that make the execution of such queries very efficient. They develop a system called Snapshot that they have implemented.

The paper by Ghandeharizadeh addresses a slightly different problem. Once a query has been computed, and we know which video objects must be retrieved and presented to the user, we are still faced with the problem of actually doing so. This issue is further complicated by the fact that video-data must be retrieved from its storage device at a specific rate – if not, the system will exhibit "jitter" or "hiccups". Ghandeharizadeh studies how to present video objects without hiccups.

The paper by Ozden et al. has similar goals to that of Ghandeharizadeh – they too are interested in the storage and retrieval of continuous media data. They develop data structures and algorithms for continuous retrieval of video-data from disk, reducing latency time significantly. They develop algorithms for implementing, in digital disk-based systems, standard analog operations like fast-forward, rewind, etc.

The paper by Marcus revisits the paper by Marcus and Subrahmanian and shows that the query paradigm developed there – which uses a fragment of predicate logic – can just as well be expressed in SQL.

Cutler and Candan study different multimedia authoring systems available on the market, evaluating the pros and cons of each.

Finally, Kashyap et al. develop ideas on the storage of metadata for multimedia applications – in particular, they argue that metadata must be stored at three levels, and that algorithms to manipulate the meta-data must traverse these levels.

The refereeing of the papers by Marcus and Subrahmanian, Jagadish, Ozden et al., Marcus, and Kashyap et al. was handled by Sushil Jajodia. The refereeing process for the other papers was handled by V.S. Subrahmanian. In addition, all but three papers (Ozden et al., Kashyap et al., and Jagadish) were discussed for several hours each in Subrahmanian's Multimedia Database Systems seminar course at the University of Maryland (Spring 1995). We are extremely grateful to those who generously contributed their time, reviewing papers for this book. Furthermore, we are grateful to the authors for their contributions, and for their patience in making revisions. Finally, we are grateful to Kasim Selcuk Candan for his extraordinary patience in helping to typeset the manuscript, and to Sabrina Islam for administrative assistance.

We would like to dedicate this book to our parents.

V.S. Subrahmanian
College Park, MD

Sushil Jajodia
Fairfax, VA

September 1995

Table of Contents

Towards a Theory of Multimedia Database Systems
Sherry Marcus and *V.S. Subrahmanian* 1

1. Introduction 1
2. Basic Ideas Underlying the Framework 3
3. Media Instances 4
   3.1 The Clinton Example 5
   3.2 Examples of Media-Instances 8
4. Indexing Structures and a Query Language for Multimedia Systems 12
   4.1 Frame-Based Query Language 12
   4.2 The Frame Data Structure 15
   4.3 Query Processing Algorithms 21
   4.4 Updates in Multimedia Databases 22
5. Multimedia Presentations 24
   5.1 Generation of Media Events = Query Processing 24
   5.2 Synchronization = Constraint Solving 27
   5.3 Internal Synchronization 28
   5.4 Media Buffers 28
6. Related Work 29
7. Conclusions 31

A Unified Approach to Data Modelling and Retrieval for a Class of Image Database Applications
Venkat N. Gudivada, *Vijay V. Raghavan*, and *Kanonluk Vanapipat* 37

1. Introduction 37
2. Approaches to Image Data Modeling 39
   2.1 Terminology 40
   2.2 Conventional Data Models 40
   2.3 Image Processing/Graphics Systems with Database Functionality 41
   2.4 Extended Conventional Data Models 42
   2.5 Extensible Data Models 42
   2.6 Other Data Models 43
3. Requirements Analysis of Application Areas 43
   3.1 A Taxonomy for Image Attributes 43
   3.2 A Taxonomy for Retrieval Types 46

3.3 Art Galleries and Museums ... 48
3.4 Interior Design ... 48
3.5 Architectural Design ... 49
3.6 Real Estate Marketing ... 49
3.7 Face Information Retrieval ... 50
4. Logical Representations ... 51
5. Motivations for the Proposed Data Model ... 52
6. An Overview of AIR Framework ... 53
6.1 Data Model ... 53
6.2 The Proposed DBMS Architecture ... 57
7. Image Database Systems Based on AIR Model ... 58
8. Image Retrieval Applications Based on the Prototype Implementation of AIR Framework ... 61
8.1 Realtors Information System ... 61
8.2 Face Information Retrieval System ... 62
9. Research Issues in AIR Framework ... 64
9.1 Query Interface ... 64
9.2 Algorithms for RSC and RSS Queries ... 67
9.3 Relevance Feedback Modeling and Improving Retrieval Effectiveness ... 68
9.4 Elicitation of Semantic Attributes ... 69
10. Conclusions and Future Direction ... 70
A. Image Logical Structures ... 74

The QBISM Medical Image DBMS
Manish Arya, William Cody, Christos Faloutsos, Joel Richardson, and *Arthur Toga* ... 79

1. Introduction ... 79
2. The Medical Application ... 81
2.1 Problem Definition ... 81
2.2 Data Characteristics ... 82
3. Logical Design ... 83
3.1 Data Types ... 83
3.2 Spatial Operations ... 83
3.3 Schema ... 84
3.4 Queries ... 85
4. Physical Database Design ... 86
4.1 Representation of a VOLUME ... 87
4.2 Representation of a REGION ... 88
4.3 Conclusions ... 89
5. System Issues ... 89
5.1 Starburst Extensions ... 89
5.2 System Architecture ... 90
6. Performance Experiments ... 93

6.1 Experimental Environment 93
6.2 Single-study Queries 94
6.3 Multi-study Queries 96
6.4 Results from the Performance Experiments 97
7. Conclusions and Future Work 97

Retrieval of Pictures Using Approximate Matching
A. Prasad Sistla and *Clement Yu* 101

1. Introduction 101
2. Picture Representation 102
3. User Interface 103
4. Computation of Similarity Values 105
4.1 Similarity Functions 105
4.2 Object Similarities 106
4.3 Similarities of Non-spatial Relationships 107
4.4 Spatial Similarity Functions 108
5. Conclusion 111

Ink as a First-Class Datatype in Multimedia Databases
Walid G. Aref, *Daniel Barbarà*, and *Daniel Lopresti* 113

1. Introduction 113
2. Ink as First-Class Data 114
2.1 Expressiveness of Ink 115
2.2 Approximate Ink Matching 116
3. Pictographic Naming 117
3.1 Motivation 118
3.2 A Pictographic Browser 120
3.3 The Window Algorithm 121
3.4 Hidden Markov Models 122
4. The ScriptSearch Algorithm 124
4.1 Definitions 125
4.2 Approaches to Searching Ink 126
4.3 Searching for Patterns in Noisy Text 128
4.4 The ScriptSearch Algorithm 129
4.5 Evaluation of ScriptSearch 132
4.6 Experimental Results 134
4.7 Discussion 136
5. Searching Large Databases 137
5.1 The HMM-Tree 137
5.2 The Handwritten Trie 149
5.3 Inter-character Strokes 160
5.4 Performance 160
6. Conclusions 160

Indexing for Retrieval by Similarity
H. V. Jagadish ... 165

1. Introduction ... 165
2. Shape Matching ... 166
   2.1 Rectangular Shape Covers ... 167
   2.2 Storage Structure ... 169
   2.3 Queries ... 171
   2.4 Approximate Match ... 172
   2.5 An Example ... 177
   2.6 Experiment ... 178
3. Word Matching ... 180
4. Discussion ... 181

Filtering Distance Queries in Image Retrieval
A. Belussi, *E. Bertino*, *A. Biavasco*, and *S. Rizzo* ... 185

1. Introduction ... 185
2. Spatial Access Methods and Image Retrieval ... 187
   2.1 Query Processor ... 187
   2.2 Image Objects and Spatial Predicates ... 189
3. Snapshot ... 191
   3.1 Regular Grid with Locational Keys ... 192
   3.2 Clustering Technique ... 194
   3.3 Extensible Hashing ... 195
   3.4 Organization of Snapshot ... 198
4. Filtering Metric Queries with Snapshot ... 201
   4.1 Search Algorithm ... 202
   4.2 Min Algorithm ... 205
5. Optimization of Spatial Queries ... 210
6. Conclusions and Future Work ... 211

Stream-based Versus Structured Video Objects: Issues, Solutions, and Challenges
Shahram Ghandeharizadeh ... 215

1. Introduction ... 215
2. Stream-based Presentation ... 217
   2.1 Continuous Display ... 218
   2.2 Pipelining to Minimize Latency Time ... 224
   2.3 High Bandwidth Objects and Scalable Servers ... 225
   2.4 Challenges ... 226
3. Structured Presentation ... 227
   3.1 Atomic Object Layer ... 229
   3.2 Composed Object Layer ... 231
   3.3 Challenges ... 232
4. Conclusion ... 235

The Storage and Retrieval of Continuous Media Data
Banu Özden, *Rajeev Rastogi*, and *Avi Silberschatz* 237

1. Introduction 237
2. Retrieving Continuous Media Data 238
3. Matrix-Based Allocation 240
   3.1 Storage Allocation 241
   3.2 Buffering 243
   3.3 Repositioning 243
   3.4 Implementation of VCR Operations 244
4. Variable Disk Transfer Rates 245
5. Horizontal Partitioning 247
   5.1 Storage Allocation 248
   5.2 Retrieval 250
6. Vertical Partitioning 250
   6.1 Size of Buffers 252
   6.2 Data Retrieval 255
7. Related Work 257
8. Research Issues 257
   8.1 Load Balancing and Fault Tolerance Issues 257
   8.2 Storage Issues 258
   8.3 Data Retrieval Issues 259
9. Concluding Remarks 260

Querying Multimedia Databases in SQL
Sherry Marcus 263

1. Introduction 263
2. Automobile Multimedia Database Example 265
3. Logical Query Language 269
4. Querying Multimedia Databases in SQL 270
5. Expressing User Requests in SQL 274
6. Conclusions 276

Multimedia Authoring Systems
Ross Cutler and *Kasım Selçuk Candan* 279

1. Introduction 279
2. Underlying Technology 280
   2.1 ODBC 280
   2.2 OLE 281
   2.3 DDE 281
   2.4 DLL 281
   2.5 MCI 282
3. Sample Application - "Find-Movie" 282
4. Multimedia Toolbook 3.0 283

5. IconAuthor 6.0 287
6. Director 4.0 289
7. MAS's and Current Technology 290
   7.1 How to improve MAS's? 291
   7.2 How to Benefit from MAS's in Multimedia Research 294
8. Conclusion 295

Metadata for Building the Multimedia Patch Quilt
Vipul Kashyap, *Kshitij Shah*, and *Amit Sheth* 297

1. Introduction 297
2. Characterization of the Ontology 300
   2.1 Terminological Commitments: Constructing an Ontology 301
   2.2 Controlled Vocabulary for Digital Media 302
   2.3 Better understanding of the query 304
   2.4 Ontology Guided Extraction of Metadata 305
3. Construction and Design of Metadata 306
   3.1 Classification of Metadata 307
   3.2 Meta-correlation: The Key to Media-Independent Semantic Correlation 309
   3.3 Extractors for Metadata 312
   3.4 Storage of Metadata 314
4. Association of Digital Media Data with Metadata 315
   4.1 Association of Metadata with Image Data 315
   4.2 Association of Symbolic Descriptions with Image Data 316
   4.3 Metadata for Multimedia Objects 316
5. Conclusion 317

Contributors 321

Towards a Theory of Multimedia Database Systems

Sherry Marcus[1] and V.S. Subrahmanian[2]

[1] 21st Century Technologies, Inc. 1903 Ware Road, Falls Church, VA 22043.
E-mail: marcus@nego.umiacs.umd.edu

[2] Institute for Advanced Computer Studies, Institute for Systems Research
Department of Computer Science, University of Maryland, College Park, Maryland 20742.
E-mail: vs@cs.umd.edu

Summary. Though there are now numerous examples of multimedia systems in the commercial market, these systems have been developed primarily on a case-by-case basis. The large-scale development of such systems requires a principled characterization of multimedia systems which is independent of any single application. It requires a unified query language framework to access these different structures in a variety of ways. It requires algorithms that are provably correct in processing such queries and whose efficiency can be appropriately evaluated. In this paper, we develop a framework for characterizing multimedia information systems which builds on top of the implementations of individual media, and provides a logical query language that integrates such diverse media. We develop indexing structures and algorithms to process such queries and show that these algorithms are sound and complete and relatively efficient (polynomial-time). We show that the generation of media-events (i.e. generating different states of the different media concurrently) can be viewed as a query processing problem, and that synchronization can be viewed as constraint solving. This observation allows us to introduce the notion of a media presentation as a sequence of media-events that satisfy a sequence of queries. We believe this paper represents a first step towards the development of multimedia theory.

1. Introduction

Though numerous multimedia systems exist in today's booming software market, relatively little work has been done in addressing the following questions:

- What are multimedia database systems and how can they be formally defined so that they are independent of any specific application domain ?
- Can indexing structures for multimedia database systems be defined in a similar uniform, domain-independent manner ?
- Is it possible to uniformly define both query languages and access methods based on these indexing structures ?
- Is it possible to uniformly define the notion of an update in multimedia database systems and to efficiently accomplish such updates using the above-mentioned indexing structures ?
- What constitutes a multimedia presentation and can this be formally defined so that it is independent of any specific application domain ?

In this paper, we develop a set of initial solutions to all the above questions. We provide a formal theoretical framework within which the above questions can be expressed and answered.

The basic concepts characterizing a multimedia system are the following: first, we define the important concept of a **media-instance**. Intuitively, a media-instance (e.g. an instance of video) consists of a body of information (e.g. a set of video-clips) represented using some storage mechanism (e.g. a quadtree, or an R-tree or a bitmap) in some storage medium (e.g. video-tape), together with some functions and/or relations (e.g. next minute of video, or who appears in the video) expressing various aspects, features and/or properties of this media-instance. We show that media-instances can be used to represent a wide variety of data including documents, photographs, geographic information systems, bitmaps, object-oriented databases, and logic programs, to name a few.

Based on the notion of a media-instance, we define a **multimedia system** to be a set of such media-instances. Intuitively, the concatenation of the states of the different media instances in the multimedia system is a snapshot of the global state of the system at a given point in time. Thus, for instance, a multimedia system (at time t) may consist of a snapshot of a particular video-tape, a snapshot of a particular audio-tape, and segments of affiliated (electronic) documentation. In Section 4., we develop a **logical query language** that can be used to express queries requiring multimedia accesses. We show how various "intuitive" queries can be expressed within this language. Subsequently, we define an **indexing structure** to store multimedia systems. The elegant feature of our indexing structure is that it is completely independent of the type of medium being used – in particular, if we are given a *pre-existing* representation/implementation of some information in some medium, our method shows how various interesting aspects (called "features") of this information can be represented, and efficiently accessed. We show how queries expressed in our logical query language can be efficiently executed using this indexing structure.

Section 5. introduces the important notion of a media presentation based on the notion of a **media-event**. Intuitively, a media-event reflects the global state of the different media at a fixed point in time. For example, if, at time t, we have a picture of George Bush on the screen (i.e. video medium) and an audio-tape of George Bush saying X, then this is a media-event with the video-state being "George Bush" and the audio-state being "George Bush saying X." A **media presentation** is a sequence of media-events. Intuitively, a media-presentation shows how the states of different media-instances change over time. One of the key results in this paper is that any query generates a set of media-events (i.e. those media-events that satisfy the query). Consequently, the problem of specifying a media-presentation can be achieved by specifying a sequence of queries. In other words,

Generation of Media Events = Query Processing.

Finally each media-event (i.e. a global state of the system) must be "on" for a certain period of time (e.g. the audio clip of Bush giving a speech must be "on" when the video shows him speaking). Furthermore, the next media-event must come on immediately upon the completion of the current media-event. We show that this process of synchronizing media-events to achieve a deadline may be viewed as a constraint solving problem, i.e.

Synchronization = Constraint Solving.

2. Basic Ideas Underlying the Framework

In this section, we will articulate the basic ideas behind our proposed multimedia information system architecture. For now, we will view a media-source as some, as yet unspecified, representation of information. Exactly how this information is stored physically, or represented conceptually, is completely independent of our framework, thus allowing our framework to be interface with most existing media that we know of.

Suppose $\mathcal{M}$ is a medium and this medium has several "states" representing different bodies of knowledge expressed in that medium – associated with this data is a set of "features" – these capture the salient aspects and objects of importance in that data. In addition, there is logically specified information describing relationships and/or properties between features occurring in a given state. These relationships between features are encoded as a logic program. Last, but not least, when a given medium can assume a multiplicity of states, we assume that there is a corpus of state-transition functions that allow us to smoothly move from one state to another. These are encoded as "inter-state" relationships, specifying relations existing between states taken as a whole. As the implementation of these inter-state transition functions is dependent on the medium, we will assume that there is an existing implementation of these transition functions. As we make no assumptions on this implementation, this poses no restrictions. Figure 2.1 shows the overall architecture for multimedia information systems.

The ideas discussed thus far are studied in detail in Section 4. where we develop a query language to integrate information across these multiple media sources and express queries, and where we develop access structures to efficiently execute these queries.

All the aspects described thus far are independent of time and are relatively static. In real-life multimedia systems, time plays a critical role. For instance, a query pertaining to audio-information may need to be synchronized with a query pertaining to video-information, so that the *presentation* of the answers to these queries have a coherent audio-visual impact. Hence, the data structures used to represent information in the individual media (which so far,

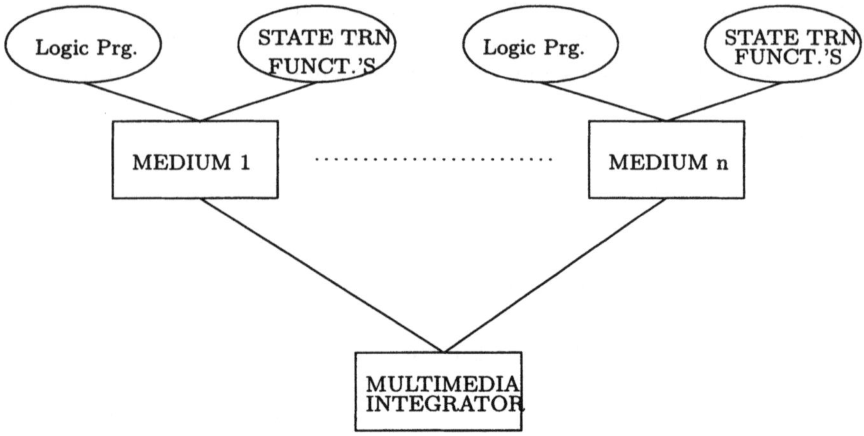

Fig. 2.1. Multimedia Information System Architecture

has been left completely unspecified) must satisfy certain efficiency requirements. We will show that by and large, these requirements can be clearly and concisely expressed as constraints over a given domain, and that based on the design criteria, index structures to organize information within a medium can be efficiently designed.

3. Media Instances

In this section, we formally define the notion of a media-instance, and show how it can be used to represent a wide variety of data stored on different kinds of media. Intuitively, a medium (such as `video`) may have data stored on it in many formats (e.g. `raster`, `bitmap`, `vhs_format`, `pal`, `secam`, etc.). Thus, raster is an example of an instance of the medium `video` because video information may be stored in raster format. However, in addition to just storing information, media instances, as defined below contain information on how to access and manipulate that information.

A *media-instance* is a 7-tuple $\mathbf{mi} = (\mathbf{ST}, \mathbf{fe}, \lambda, \Re, \mathcal{F}, \mathbf{Var}_1, \mathbf{Var}_2)$ where $\mathbf{ST}$ is a set of objects called *states*, $\mathbf{fe}$ is a set of objects called *features*, λ is a map from S to $2^{\mathbf{fe}}$, $\mathbf{Var}_1$ is a set of objects called *state variables* ranging over states, $\mathbf{Var}_2$ is a set of objects called *feature variables* ranging over features, $\Re$ is a set of *inter-state relations*, i.e. relations (of possibly different arities) on the set $\mathbf{ST}$, and $\mathcal{F}$ is a set of *feature-state relations*. Each relation in $\mathcal{F}$ is a subset of $\mathbf{fe}^i \times \mathbf{ST}$ where $i \geq 1$.

3.1 The Clinton Example

We will try to explain the intuitions underlying the definition of a media-instance by considering three media (video, audio and document) representing various political figures. This example will be a "running example" throughout the paper.

Example 3.1. **(A Video-Domain)** Consider bitmapped photographs of various high-ranking US government officials shown in Figure 3.1.

Fig. 3.1. Two Picture Frames

Intuitively, a media instance $\mathbf{mi} = (\mathbf{ST}, \mathbf{fe}, \Re, \mathcal{F}, \mathbf{Var}_1, \mathbf{Var}_2)$ depicting the above two photographs contains:

1. a state $s \in \mathbf{ST}$ captures a certain structure used to store information. For example, in Figure 3.1, the set **ST** is the set of all possible bitmaps of the appropriate dimensions. The two photographs shown in Figure 3.1 represent two specific states (i.e. bitmaps) in **ST**. By just looking at a state, it is impossible to say anything about the objects of interest in that state.
2. A *feature* is a piece of information that is thought to be an item of significance/interest about a given state. For instance, the features of interest in our bitmapped domain may include `clinton, gore, bush, nixon, reno, reagan, kissinger`. (The fact that only some of these features appear in the two pictures shown in Figure 3.1 is irrelevant; the missing features may occur in other pictures not depicted above).
3. λ is a map that tells us which features are possessed by a given state. Thus, for instance, suppose s_1 and s_2 denote the two states depicted in Figure 3.1. Then

$$\lambda(s_1) = \{\texttt{bush}, \texttt{clinton}, \texttt{nixon}\}.$$
$$\lambda(s_2) = \{\texttt{clinton}, \texttt{reno}\}.$$

The first equation above indicates that the features possessed by state s_1 are **clinton, nixon,** and **bush**.

4. Relations in $\Re$ represent connections between states. For instance, the relation
delete_nixon$(\mathtt{S}, \mathtt{S}')$ could hold of any pair of states $(\mathtt{S}, \mathtt{S}')$ where S contains **nixon** as feature, and $\mathtt{S}'$ has the same features as $\mathtt{S}$, with the feature **nixon** deleted. As implementation of inter-state relations is fundamentally dependent upon the particular medium in question, we will develop our theory to be independent of any particular implementation (though we will be assuming one exists).
5. Relations in $\mathcal{F}$ represent relationships between features in a given state. Thus, for instance, in the photograph of Clinton and Reno shown in Figure 3.1(b), there may be a relation $\mathtt{left}(\mathtt{clinton}, \mathtt{Reno}, \mathtt{s}_2)$ specifying that Clinton is standing to the left of Reno in the state $\mathtt{s}_2$.

◇◇

A *state-term* of a media-instance $\mathbf{mi} = (\mathbf{ST}, \mathbf{fe}, \Re, \mathcal{F}, \mathbf{Var}_1, \mathbf{Var}_2)$ is any element of $(\mathbf{ST} \cup \mathbf{Var}_1)$. A *feature-term* of media-instance $\mathbf{mi} = (\mathbf{ST}, \mathbf{fe}, \Re, \mathcal{F}, \mathbf{Var}_1, \mathbf{Var}_2)$ is any element of $(\mathbf{fe} \cup \mathbf{Var}_2)$.

If $R \in \Re$ is an n-ary relation in media-instance $\mathbf{mi} = (\mathbf{ST}, \mathbf{fe}, \lambda, \Re, \mathcal{F}, \mathbf{Var}_1, \mathbf{Var}_2)$ and $t_1, \ldots, t_n$ are terms, then $R^*(t_1, \ldots, t_n)$ is a *state-constraint* in media instance **mi**. This constraint is solvable iff there exists a way of replacing all variables occurring in $t_1, \ldots, t_n$ by states in **ST** so that the resulting n-tuple is in relation R. Here, R^* is a symbol (syntactic entity) denoting the relation R (semantic entity). If $\phi \in \mathcal{F}$ is an n-ary relation in media-instance $\mathbf{mi} = (\mathbf{ST}, \mathbf{fe}, \lambda, \Re, \mathcal{F}, \mathbf{Var})$ and $c_1, \ldots, c_{n-1}$ are features terms and s is a state-term, then $\phi^*(c_1, \ldots, c_{n-1}, s)$ is a *feature-constraint.* This constraint is solvable iff there exists a way of replacing all variables in $c_1, \ldots, c_{n-1}$ by features in **fe** and replacing s (if it is a state variable) by a state in **ST** so that the resulting n-tuple is in relation ϕ. Here, $\phi*$ is a symbol (syntactic entity) denoting the relation ϕ (semantic entity).

The concept of a media-instance as defined above is extremely general and covers a wide range of possibilities. Below, we give a number of examples of media-instances, specifying different areas of applicability of this framework.

Example 3.2. Let us return to the Clinton-scenario depicted by the two pictures shown in Figure 3.1. It may turn out that some relevant audio-information is also available about that particular cast of characters, i.e. **clinton, gore, bush, nixon, reno, reagan, kissinger**, as well as some other entities e.g. **who, unesco, world_bank**. This, then, may be the set of features of a (restricted) audio media-instance. For instance, we may have a set of audio-tapes a_1, a_2, a_3 where a_1 depicts Clinton speaking about the WHO (World Health Organization), a_2 may be an audio-tape with Clinton and Gore having a discussion about unesco, while a_3 may be an audio-tape in which Bush and Clinton are engaged in a debate (about topics too numerous to mention). The feature assignment function, then is defined to be:

$$\lambda(a_1) = \{\texttt{clinton}, \texttt{who}\}.$$
$$\lambda(a_2) = \{\texttt{clinton}, \texttt{gore}, \texttt{unesco}\}.$$
$$\lambda(a_3) = \{\texttt{clinton}, \texttt{bush}\}.$$

There may be an inter-state relation called `after` defined to be the transitive closure of $\{(a_1, a_2), (a_2, a_3)\}$ saying that a_2 occurs after a_1 and a_3 occurs after a_2. Feature-state relations specify connections between features and states. For instance, the relation `topic` may contain the tuples $(\texttt{who}, \texttt{a}_1)$, $(\texttt{unesco}, \texttt{a}_2)$ specifying the topics of a_1 and a_2, respectively. Likewise, the relation `speaker(i,person,frame)` may specify that the i'th speaker in a particular frame is `person` so and so. Thus, with respect to the audio-frame a_2, we may have the tuples:

$\texttt{speaker}(1, \texttt{clinton}, \texttt{a}_2)$
$\texttt{speaker}(2, \texttt{gore}, \texttt{a}_2)$
$\texttt{speaker}(3, \texttt{clinton}, \texttt{a}_2)$
$\texttt{speaker}(4, \texttt{gore}, \texttt{a}_2)$

specifying that Clinton speaks first in a_2, followed by Gore, followed again by Clinton, and finally concluded by Gore. ◇◇

A more detailed scenario of how audio-information can be viewed as a media-instance is described later in Example 3.9. The following example revisits the Clinton-scenario with respect to document information.

Example 3.3. Suppose we have three documents, d_1, d_2 and d_3 reflecting information about policies adopted by various organizations. Let us suppose the set of features is identical to the set given in the previous example. Suppose document d_1 is a position statement of the World Health Organization about Clinton; document d_2 is a statement made by Clinton about the WHO and document d_3 is a statement about UNESCO made by Clinton. The feature association map, λ is defined as follows:

$$\lambda(d_1) = \{\texttt{who}, \texttt{clinton}\}.$$
$$\lambda(d_2) = \{\texttt{who}, \texttt{clinton}\}.$$
$$\lambda(d_3) = \{\texttt{unesco}, \texttt{clinton}\}.$$

Note that even though d_1 and d_2 have the same features, this doesn't mean that they convey the same information – after all, a WHO statement about Clinton is very different from a statement made by Clinton about the

WHO. Hence, let us suppose we have a feature-state relation in $\mathcal{F}$ called $\mathtt{contents}(\langle\mathtt{author},\mathtt{topic},\mathtt{state}\rangle)$, and that this relation contains the following triples:

$\mathtt{contents}(\mathtt{who},\mathtt{clinton},\mathrm{d}_1)$
$\mathtt{contents}(\mathtt{clinton},\mathtt{who},\mathrm{d}_2)$
$\mathtt{contents}(\mathtt{clinton},\mathtt{unesco},\mathrm{d}_3)$.

The set $\Re$ of inter-state relations is left empty for now. ◇◇

A more detailed scenario of how documents can be viewed as a media-instance is described later in Example 3.10. Above, we have described a scenario containing information pertaining to certain objects (e.g. `clinton, gore,`, etc.) and shown how this information can be represented using `video, audio` and `document` media-instances. We will refer to these three particular scenarios as the "Clinton-example" in the rest of this paper.

3.2 Examples of Media-Instances

The following examples show how the notion of a media-instance is very general and can be used to describe a wide variety of media types (and data representations on that medium) that are likely to be encountered in practice.

Example 3.4. (**2 × 2 Matrices**) Consider the set of 2 × 2 matrices whose values can be in the set { red, blue, green }. This forms the set, **ST**, of states of a media-instance **LM**. We can define several inter-state relations on this media-instance. For instance, we may define:

1. M_1 similar M_2 iff matrices M_1 and M_2 have the same color in at least 2 pixel entries. In figure 1, matrices A and B are similar, but A and C are not.
2. M_1 have the same colors M_2 iff the set of colors in M_1 and the set of colors in M_2 are the same. In figure 1, A and C have the same colors, but A and B do not, and B and C do not either.

Note that A, B, C shown in Figure 3.2 are state-terms in the matrix media-instance. In this example, we assume that the feature set is empty, and hence, the function λ is empty and $\mathcal{F}$ is empty. ◇◇

Example 3.5. (**Quad-Tree Media-Instance**) Consider any elementary record structure called `INFO`, and suppose we consider the space of all quad-trees [17] that can be constructed using this record structure as the information field(s) in a node. In addition, there are four fields, `NW, SW, NE, SE` denoting the four quadrants of a rectangular region. Then we can define a media-instance called QT $= (\mathbf{ST}, \mathbf{fe}, \lambda, \Re, \mathcal{F}, \mathbf{Var}_1, \mathbf{Var}_2)$ where **ST** is the set of all such quadtrees (this set may be infinite). The variables in $\mathbf{Var}_1$ can be instantiated to specific quadtrees. $\Re$ may contain a bunch of relations of (possibly) different arities. Some examples of such relations are:

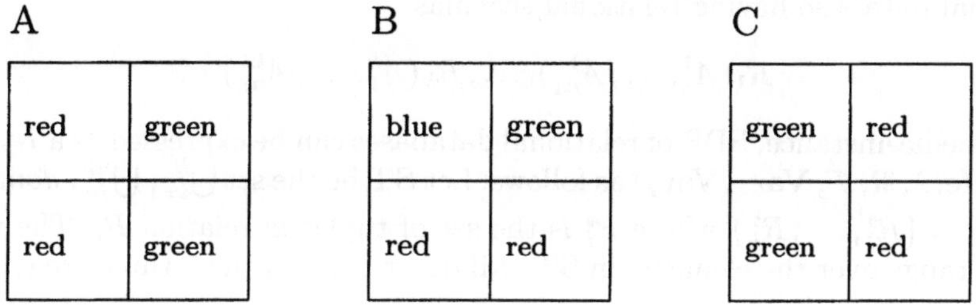

Fig. 3.2. Example for the Matrix Media-Instance

- nw_empty is a unary relation such that nw_empty(V) is true of quad-tree V iff the NW-link of each node in quadtree V is empty.
- V_1 same_num V_2 iff quad-trees V_1 and V_2 have the same number of nodes (even though both quadtrees may be very different).
- V_1 same V_2 iff V_1 and V_2 are identical.
- between(V_1, V_2, V_3) iff V_1 is a subtree of V_2 and V_2 is a subtree of V_3.

Suppose the quadtrees in question describe the geographical layout of Italy. Then some of the features of interest may be: `Rome, Venice, Genoa, Milan`. There may an inter-feature relationship called `larger_than` such that:

```
larger_than(milan,genoa,S)
larger_than(rome,venice,S)
... etc.
```

Above, `S` is a state-variable and the above constraints reflect the fact that Milan is larger than Genoa in all states. However, there may state-specific feature constraints: for instance, in a specific quad-tree instance showing a detailed map of Rome, we may have a constraint saying:

$$\texttt{in(rome, colosseum, s}_1\texttt{)}.$$

However, in a full map of Italy, the constraint

$$\texttt{in(rome, colosseum, fullmap)}$$

may not be present because the Colosseum may be a feature too small or too unimportant to be represented in a full map of Italy. The feature assignment function would specify precisely in which states which features are relevant. ◇◇

Example 3.6. **(Relational Database Media-Instance)** Consider any relational database having relational schemas

$$R_1(A_1^1, \ldots, A_{n_1}^1), \ldots, R_k(A_1^k, \ldots, A_{n_k}^k).$$

The media-instance, RDB of relational databases can be expressed as a 7-tuple $(\mathbf{ST}, \mathbf{fe}, \lambda, \Re, \mathcal{F}, \mathbf{Var}_1, \mathbf{Var}_2)$ as follows. Let **ST** be the set $\bigcup_{i=1}^{k} \bigcup_{j=1}^{n_k} dom(A_j^i)$. Let $\Re = \{R_1^b, \ldots, R_k^b\}$ where R_i^b is the set of tuples in relation R_i. The variables range over the elements in **ST**. All other parts of the 7-tuple are empty. ◇◇

Example 3.7. **(Deductive Database Media-Instance)** Suppose we consider definite Horn clause logic programs [14] over a given alphabet. Then we can define a media-instance DDL as follows: **ST**, the set of states, is the set of ground terms generated by this alphabet. $\mathbf{fe} = \emptyset$ and so is λ. $\mathbf{Var}_1$ is simply the set of variable symbols provided in the alphabet (and, as usual, these variables range over the ground terms in the language). For each n-ary predicate symbol p in the alphabet, there is an n-ary relation, R^p in $\Re$; $\Re$ contains no other relations. (A logician might recognize that DDL is, intuitively, just an Herbrand model [14]). All other components of the media instance are empty. ◇◇

Example 3.8. **(Object-Oriented Media-Instances)** Suppose we consider an inheritance hierarchy containing individuals $i_1, \ldots, i_n$, classes $c_1, \ldots, c_r$, methods $m_1, \ldots, m_s$, and properties $p_1, \ldots, p_k$. Let H be the hierarchy relationship, i.e. $H(x, y)$ means that individual/class x is a member/subclass of class y. Then we can define a media-instance, OOL as follows: the set of states, **ST**, is $\{i_1, \ldots, i_n, c_1, \ldots, c_r, m_1, \ldots, m_s\}$. Variables range over individuals, classes and methods. Each property p_j is a unary relation in $\Re$.

Some additional examples of relations that could be in $\Re$ are:

- subclass(V_1, V_2) iff V_1 is a subclass (resp. individual) of (resp. in) class V_2.
- same_num(V_1, V_2) iff V_1 and V_2 are both classes containing the same number of individuals.
- An important relation is the applicability of methods to classes. This could be encoded as a special relation, applicable(m_j, c_w) saying that method m_j is applicable to class c_w. All other components of the 7-tuple are empty.

◇◇

Example 3.9. **(Audio Media-Instances)** Suppose we consider audio input. It is well-known that voice/audio signals are sets of sine/cosine functions[1]. Let VL be the language defined as follows. The set, **ST**, is the set of all

[1] Technically, it would be more correct to say that it is possible to approximate any audio signal with sine and cosine waveforms (using Fourier series) as long as the signal is periodic. The reason is that you need the fundamental frequency (or time period) to decompose the signal into a series.

sine/cosine waves. Features may include the properties of the signals such as frequency and amplitude which in turn determine who/what is the originator of the signals (e.g. Bill Clinton giving a speech, Socks the cat meowing, etc.). State variables range over sets of audio signals. Examples of relations in $\Re$ are:

- same_amplitude(V_1, V_2) iff V_1 and V_2 have the same amplitude.
- Similarly, binary relations like higher_frequency and more_resonant may be defined.

Relations in $\mathcal{F}$ may include feature-based relations such as

`owns(clinton, socks, S)`

specifying that Socks is owned by Clinton in all states in our system. ◇◇

Example 3.10. **(Document Media-Instances)** Suppose we consider an electronic document storage and retrieval scheme. Typically, documents are described in some language such as SGML. Let DOCL be the media-instance defined as follows. **ST** is the set of all document descriptions expressible in syntactically valid form (e.g. in syntactically correct SGML and/or in Latex or in some other form of hypertext). State variables range over these descriptions of documents. Examples of relations in $\Re$ are:

- university_tech_rep(V) is true iff the document represented by V is a technical report of some university.
- cut_paste(V_1, V_2, V_3, V_4) iff V_4 represents the document obtained by cutting V_1 from document V_3 and replacing it by V_2.
- comb_health_benefits_chapter($V_1, \ldots, V_{50}, V$) iff V represents the document obtained by concatenating together, the chapter on health benefits from documents represented by $V_1, \ldots, V_{50}$. For example, $V_1, \ldots V_{50}$ may be handbooks specifying the legal benefits that employees of companies are entitled in the 50 states of the U.S.A. V, in this case, would be a document describing the health benefits laws in the different states.

Features of a document may include entities such as:

`dental, hospitalization, emergency_care.`

Feature constraints (i.e. members of $\mathcal{F}$) may include statements about maximal amounts of coverage, e.g. statements such as:

```
max_cov(dental,5000,d_1),
max_cov(hospitalization,1000000,d_1),
max_cov(emergency,100000,d_1).
```

Here, d_1 is a specific document describing, say, the benefits offered by one health care company. Conversely, d_2 may be a document reflecting similar coverage offered by another company, except that the maximal coverage amounts may vary from those provided by the first company. ◇◇

A *multimedia system* **MMS** is a finite set of media instances.

4. Indexing Structures and a Query Language for Multimedia Systems

Consider a multimedia system $\mathcal{M}^{\cdot} = \{\mathcal{M}_1, \dots, \mathcal{M}_n\}$ that a user wishes to retrieve information from. In this section, we will develop a query language and indexing structures for accessing such multimedia systems.

4.1 Frame-Based Query Language

In this section, we develop a query language to express queries addressed to a multimedia system $\mathbf{MMS} = \{\mathcal{M}_1, \dots, \mathcal{M}_n\}$ where

$$\mathcal{M}_i = (\mathbf{ST}^i, \mathbf{fe}^i, \lambda^i, \Re^i, \mathcal{F}^i, \mathbf{Var}_1^i, \mathbf{Var}_2^i).$$

We will develop a logical language to express queries. This language will be generated by the following set of non-logical symbols:

1. **Constant Symbols:**
   a) Each $f \in \mathbf{fe}^i$ for $1 \leq i \leq n$ is a constant symbol in the query language.
   b) Each $s \in \mathbf{ST}^i$ for $1 \leq i \leq n$ is a constant symbol in the query language.
   c) Each integer $1 \leq i \leq n$ is a constant symbol.
2. **Function Symbols:** `flist` is a binary function symbol in the query language.
3. **Variable Symbols:** We assume that we have an infinite set of logical variables $V_1, \dots, V_i, \dots$.
4. **Predicate Symbols:** The language contains
   a) a binary predicate symbol `frametype`,
   b) a binary predicate symbol, $\in$,
   c) for each inter-state relation $R \in \Re^i$ of arity j, it contains a j-ary predicate symbol R^*.
   d) for each feature-state relation $\psi \in \Re_2^i$ of arity j, it contains a j-ary predicate symbol ψ^*.

As usual, a term is defined inductively as follows: (1) each constant symbol is a term, (2) each variable symbol is a term, and (3) if η is an n-ary function symbol, and $t_1, \dots, t_n$ are terms, then $\eta(t_1, \dots, t_n)$ is a term. A ground term is a variable-free term. If p is an n-ary predicate symbol, and $t_1, \dots, t_n$ are (ground) terms, then $p(t_1, \dots, t_n)$ is a (ground) atom. A *query* is an existentially closed conjunction of atoms, i.e. a statement of the form

$$(\exists)(A_1 \,\&\, \dots, A_n).$$

Example 4.1. Let us return to the video-domain in the Clinton-example (Figure 3.1). Let us suppose that we have the following feature-state relations.

1. `running_mate(X,Y,S)`: `X`'s running mate is `Y`.

2. `appointed(X,Y,P,S)`: `X` appointed `Y` to position `P` in state `S`.
3. `with(X,Y,S)`: `X` is with `Y` in state `S`.

Observe that in the first two relations listed above, the state (i.e. the video-frame) does not actually matter – Clinton's running mate is Gore, independent of which picture is being looked at. Clinton appointed Reno as Attorney General, and this is independent of the picture being looked at. The third relation above is picture-specific, though. In picture frame 1 Clinton is with Bush and with Gore – this contributes the facts:

```
with(clinton, bush, 1).
with(clinton, nixon, 1).
```

while the fact

```
with(clinton, reno, 2).
```

is contributed by the second picture. In addition, we will allow background inference rules to be present; these allow us to make statements of the form:

$$\texttt{with(Y,X,S)} \leftarrow \texttt{with(X,Y,S)}$$

specifying that if `X` is `with` `Y` in state `S`, then `Y` is `with` `X` in that state.

A user of the multimedia system consisting of the picture frames may now ask queries such as:

1. $(\exists \texttt{X},\texttt{P},\texttt{S})\texttt{appointed(clinton,X,P,S)}\ \&\ \texttt{with(clinton,X,S)}\ \&\ \texttt{frametype}$ $(\texttt{video}))$: This query asks whether there is anyone who is a Clinton-appointee who appears in a picture/video frame with Clinton. The answer is "yes" with $\texttt{X} = \texttt{reno}$, $\texttt{P} = \texttt{Attorney General}$ and $\texttt{S} = 2$. (We are assuming here that atoms defining the predicate `appointed` are stored appropriately.)
2. $(\exists \texttt{X},\texttt{Y},\texttt{S},\texttt{S}_1,\texttt{S}_2)\texttt{president}(\texttt{X},\texttt{S}_1),\ \&\ \texttt{president}(\texttt{Y},\texttt{S}_2)\ \&\ \texttt{X} \neq \texttt{clinton}\ \&\ \texttt{Y} \neq \texttt{clinton}\ \&\ \texttt{X} \neq \texttt{Y}\ \&\ \texttt{with(clinton,X,S)}\ \&\ \texttt{with(clinton,Y,S)}\ \&\ \texttt{frametype(S, video)})$: This query asks if there is any picture in which which three Presidents of the USA (one of whom is Clinton) appear together.
3. $(\exists \texttt{S})(\texttt{clinton} \in \texttt{flist(S)}\ \&\ \texttt{horse} \in \texttt{flist(S)}\ \&\ \texttt{on(clinton,horse)}\ \&\ \texttt{frametype(S,video)})$: This question asks if there is a picture of Clinton on a horse.
4. $(\exists \texttt{S})(\texttt{clinton} \in \texttt{flist(S)}\ \&\ \texttt{socks} \in \texttt{flist(S)}\ \&\ \texttt{meowing\_at(socks, clinton)}\ \&\ \texttt{frametype(S,audio)})$: Is there an audio-frame in which both Clinton and Socks are "featured" and Socks, the cat, is meowing at Clinton ?
5. $(\exists \texttt{S}_1,\texttt{S}_2)\texttt{nixon} \in \texttt{flist}(\texttt{S}_1)\ \&\ \texttt{frametype}(\texttt{S}_1,\texttt{video})\ \&\ \texttt{X} \in \texttt{flist}(\texttt{S}_1)\ \&\ \texttt{X} \neq \texttt{nixon}\ \&\ \texttt{person(X)}\ \&\ \texttt{X} \in \texttt{flist}(\texttt{S}_2)\ \&\ \texttt{frametype}(\texttt{S}_2,\texttt{audio}))$: This query looks to find a person pictured in a video-frame with Nixon, who is speaking in an audio-frame elsewhere. ◇◇

In general, if we are given a media-instance

$$\mathcal{M}_i = (\mathbf{ST}^i, \mathbf{fe}^i, \lambda^i, \Re^i, \mathcal{F}^i, \mathbf{Var}_1^i, \mathbf{Var}_2^i),$$

then we will store information about the feature-state relations as a logic program. There are two kinds of facts that are stored in such a logic program.

State-Independent Facts: These are facts that reflect relationships between features that hold in all states of media-instance $\mathcal{M}_i$. Thus, for example, in the Clinton example, the fact that Gore is Clinton's vice-president is true in all states of the medium $\mathcal{M}_i$. This is represented as:

$$\texttt{vice\_pres(clinton,gore,S)} \quad \leftarrow$$

where S is a state-variable.

State-Dependent Facts: These are facts that are true in some states, but false in others. In particular, if $\phi \in \mathbf{fe}$ is a j-ary relation ($j \geq 1$), and tuple $\mathbf{t}, \mathbf{s} \in \phi$, then the unit clause (or fact)

$$\phi^*\texttt{(t,s)} \quad \leftarrow$$

is present in the logic program. Thus, for instance, in a particular picture (e.g. Figure 3.1), Clinton is to the left of Reno, and hence, this can be expressed as the state-dependent fact

$$\texttt{left(clinton,reno,}\mathtt{s}_2\texttt{)}$$

where $\mathtt{s}_2$ is the name of the state in Figure 3.1(b).

Derivation Rules: Last, but not least, the designer of the multimedia system may add extra rules that allow new facts to be derived from facts in the logic program. For instance, if we consider the predicate

$$\texttt{left(person1,person2,S)}$$

denoting that `person1` is to the left of `person2` in state S, then a designer of the media-instance in question (video) may want to add a derived predicate `right` and insert the rule:

$$\texttt{right(P1,P2,S)} \quad \leftarrow \quad \texttt{left(P2,P1,S)}.$$

A word of caution is in order here. The more complex the logic programs grow, the more inefficient are the associated query processing procedures. Hence, we advocate using such derivation rules with extreme caution when building multimedia systems within our framework; however, we leave it to the system designer (based on available hardware, etc.) to make a decision on this point according to the desired system performance.

4.2 The Frame Data Structure

In this section, we will set up a data structure called a *frame* that can be used to access multimedia information efficiently. We will discuss how frames can be used to implement all the queries described in the preceding section.

Suppose we have n media instances, $\mathcal{M}_1, \ldots, \mathcal{M}_n$ where

$$\mathcal{M}_i \quad = \quad (\mathbf{ST}^i, \mathbf{fe}^i, \lambda^i, \Re^i_1, \Re^i_2, \mathbf{Var}^i_1, \mathbf{Var}^i_2)$$

for $1 \leq i \leq n$. We will have *two* kinds of structures used, in conjunction with each other, to access the information in these n media instances.

1. The first of these, called an OBJECT-TABLE, is used to store information about which states (possibly from different media instances) contain a given feature. Thus, for each feature $f \in \bigcup_{i=1}^{n} \mathbf{fe}^i$, a record in the OBJECT-TABLE has as its key, the name f, together with a pointer to a list of nodes, each of which contains a pointer to a state (represented by a data structure called a `frame` described below) in which f occurs as a feature. As the OBJECT-TABLE is searched using alphanumeric strings as the keys, it is easy to see that the OBJECT-TABLE can be organized as a standard hash-table, where relatively fast access methods have been implemented over the years.
2. The second of these structures is a `frame`. It should be noted that the OBJECT-TABLE data structure and the `frame` data structure are closely coupled together. With each state $s \in \bigcup_{i=1}^{n} \mathbf{ST}^i$, we associate a pointer which points to a list of nodes, each of which, in turn, points to a feature in the OBJECT-TABLE (or rather, points to the first element in the list of nodes associated with that feature).

We now give formal definitions of these structures, and later, we will give examples showing how these structures represent bodies of heterogeneous, multimedia data.

Suppose $\mathcal{M}_i = (\mathbf{ST}^i, \mathbf{fe}^i, \lambda^i, \Re^i_1, \Re^i_2, \mathbf{Var}^i_1, \mathbf{Var}^i_2)$ and `framerep` is a data structure that represents the set, $\mathbf{ST}_i$, of states. Then, for each state $s \in \mathbf{ST}^i$, a *frame* in medium $\mathcal{M}_i$ is a record structure consisting of the fields shown in Figure 3.2 such that:

1. for each feature $f \in \lambda^i(s)$, there is a node in `flist` having f as the `info` field of that node, and
2. if f occurs in the `info` field of a node in `flist`, then $f \in \lambda^i(s)$, and
3. if $f \in \mathbf{fe}^i$ is a feature, then there is an `object` whose `objname` is f and such that the list pointed to by the `link2` field of this `object` is the list of all states in which f is a feature, i.e. is the list of all states $s \in \mathbf{ST}$ such that $f \in \lambda^i(s)$.
4. We assume that all `feature-state` relations are stored as a logic program as specified in Section 4.1.

```
frame = record of
   name:  string;  /* name of frame */
   frametype: string; /* type of frame: audio, video, etc. */
   rep:  ^framerep ; /* disk address of internal frame rep. */
   flist: ^node1  ; /* feature list */
   end record

node1 = record of
   info:  string ;  /* name of object */
   link:  ^node1 ;  /* next node in list */
   objid: ^object ; /* pointer to object structure named in
                       "info" field */
   end record;

object = record of
   objname:  string ; /* name of object */
   link2  :  ^node2 ; /* list of frames */
   end record

node2 = record of
   frameptr : ^frame ;
   next : ^node2
   end record
```

Fig. 4.1. Data Structure for Frame-Based Feature Storage

The above definition specifies frames independently of the medium (e.g. audio, video, latex file, quadtree, bit maps, etc.) used to store the specific data involved. The internal representation of the structures are specified using the data type `framerep` listed (and intentionally not defined) above. When several different data structures are being simultaneously used, we will use $\mathtt{framerep}_1, \ldots, \mathtt{framerep}_k$ to denote the different instantiated structures. Some examples of data representable as frames are the following:

- a "still" photograph;
- a video/audio clip;
- a Latex document
- a bitmap of a geographic region, etc.

In addition to the above, for any $\mathcal{M}_i$, we assume that there is an associated string, called the `frametype` of $\mathcal{M}_i$. Intuitively, this string may be "video," "audio," etc. Let us now consider a couple of very, very simple examples below to see how a collection of objects can be represented as a frame.

Example 4.2. **(Indexing for a Single Medium)** Let us return to the Clinton-example and reconsider the two video-clips v_1 and v_2 in Figure 3.1.

The first video clip shows three humans who are identified as George Bush, Bill Clinton, and Richard Nixon. The second clip shows two humans, identified as Bill Clinton and Janet Reno.

This set of two records contain *four* significant objects – Bush, Clinton, Nixon and Reno. Information about these four objects, and the two photographs may be stored in the following way.

Suppose v_1 and v_2 are variables of type `frame`. Set:

$$\begin{aligned} v_1.\mathtt{rep} &= 100 \\ v_2.\mathtt{rep} &= 590 \end{aligned}$$

specifying that the disk address at which the video-clips are stored are 100 and 590, respectively. Let us consider v_1 and v_2 separately.

- the field v_1`.flist` contains a pointer to a list of three nodes of type `node1`. There are *three* nodes in the feature list because there are three objects of interest in video-frame v_1. Each of these three nodes represents information about the objects of interest in video-frame v_1.
  - the first node in this list has, in its `info` field, the name `BUSH`. It also contains a pointer, `P1` pointing to a structure of type `object`. This structure is an object-oriented representation of the object `BUSH` and contains information about *other* video-frames describing George Bush (i.e. a list of video-frames `v` such that for some node `N` in `v`'s `flist`, `N.info` = `BUSH`.) The list of video-frames in which `BUSH` appears as a "feature" in the manner just described is pointed to by the pointer `P1.link2` = ((v_1`.flist`)`.objid`)`.link2`. In this example that uses only two video-frames, the list pointed to by ((v_1`.flist`)`.objid`)`.link2` contains only one node, viz. a pointer back to v_1 itself, i.e. ((v_1`.flist`)`.objid`)`.link2` points to v_1.
  - the second node in this list has, in its `info` field, the name `CLINTON`. It also contains a pointer, `P2` pointing to alist of video-frames in which `CLINTON` appears as a "feature." In this case, `P2.link2` points to a list of two elements; the first contains v_1, while the second points to v_2.
  - the third node in this list has, in its `info` field, the name `NIXON`. The rest is analogous to the situation with `BUSH`.
- the field v_2`.flist` contains a pointer to a list of two nodes of type `node1`. There are *two* nodes because there are two objects of interest in video-frame v_2.
  - the first node in this list has, in its `info` field, the name `CLINTON`. The `objid` field in this node contains the pointer *P2* (the same pointer as in item 4.2 above. The values of the fields in the node pointed to by `P2` have already been described in item 4.2 above.
  - the second node in this list has, in its `info` field, the name `RENO`. The `objid` field in this node contains a pointer, `P4`. The node pointed to

by P4 has the following attributes: `P4.objname` = `RENO`, while `P4.link2` points to the start address where v_2 is stored.

bush	P1
clinton	P2
nixon	P3
reno	P4

Figure 4.1 shows a diagrammatic representation of the storage scheme used to access the two video-frames described above. In this example, the `OBJECT-TABLE` is

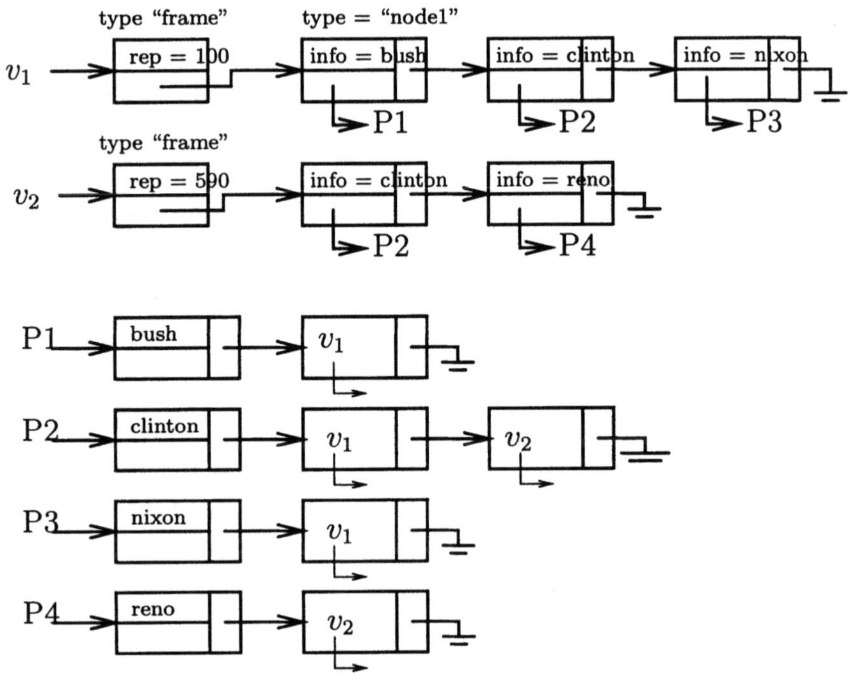

Fig. 4.2. Data Structure for the 2 Video-Frame Example

◇◇

The main advantages of the indexing scheme articulated above are that:

1. queries based both on "object" as well as on "video frame" can be easily handled (cf. examples below). In particular, the `OBJECT-TABLE` specifies where the information pertaining to these four objects is kept. Thus, retrieving information where accesses are based on the objects in the table can be easily accomplished (algorithms for this are given in the next section).

2. the data structures described above are *independent* of the data structures used to physically store an image/picture. For instance, some existing pictures may be stored as bit-maps, while others may be stored as quad-trees. The precise mechanism for storing a picture/image does not affect our conceptual design. In this paper, we will not discuss precise ways of storing the OBJECT-TABLE – any standard hashing technique should address this problem adequately.
3. Finally, as we shall see in Example 4.4 below, the *nature* of the medium is irrelevant to our data structure (even though Example 4.2 uses a single medium, it can be easily expanded to multiple media as illustrated in Example 4.4 below).

Example 4.3. Let us return to the Clinton-example, and the two video-frames shown in in Figure 3.1. Let $(\exists X, Y)$with(X, Y) denote the query: "Given a value of X, find all people Y who appear in a common video-frame with person X ?" Thus, for instance, when X = CLINTON, Y consists of RENO,NIXON and BUSH. When X=RENO, then Y can only be CLINTON.

Such a query can be easily handled within our indexing structure as follows: When X is instantiated to, say, CLINTON, look at the object with objname = CLINTON. Let N denote the node (of type object) with its objname field set to CLINTON. The value of N can be easily found using the OBJECT-TABLE. N.*link*2 is a list of nodes, N′ such that N′.frameptr points to a frame with Clinton in it. For each node N′ in the list pointed to by N.*link*2, do the following: traverse the list pointed to by (N′.frameptr).flist. Print out the value of ((N′.frameptr).flist).objname for every node in the list pointed to by (N′.frameptr).flist. Repeat this process for each node in the list pointed to by N.link2. ◊◊

The following example shows how the same data structure described for storing frames can be used to store *not only video data, but also audio data, as well as data stored using other media.*

Example 4.4. **(Using the Frame Data Structure for Multimedia Information)** Suppose we return to example 4.2, and add two more frames – one is the audio-frame a_1 from the Clinton-example, while the other is the structured document d_1 from the Clinton example. Note that in Example 4.2, the structure used to store a picture/video-clip did not affect the design of a frame. Hence, it should be (correctly) suspected that the same data structure can be used to store audio data, document data, etc.

We know that our audio-frame a_1 is a text read by Bill Clinton, and that it is about the World Health Organization (WHO, for short). Then we can create a pointer, a_1 (similar to the pointers v_1 and v_2 in Example 4.2). The pointer a_1 points to a structure of type frame. Its feature list contains two elements, CLINTON and WHO referring to the fact that this audio-clip has two objects of interest. The list pointed to by P2 is then updated to contain an extra node specifying that a_1 is an address where information about Clinton is kept. Furthermore, the pointer associated with the object WHO in the OBJECT-TABLE is P5 which points to an object called WHO. The list of frames associated with P5 consists of just one node, viz. a_1.

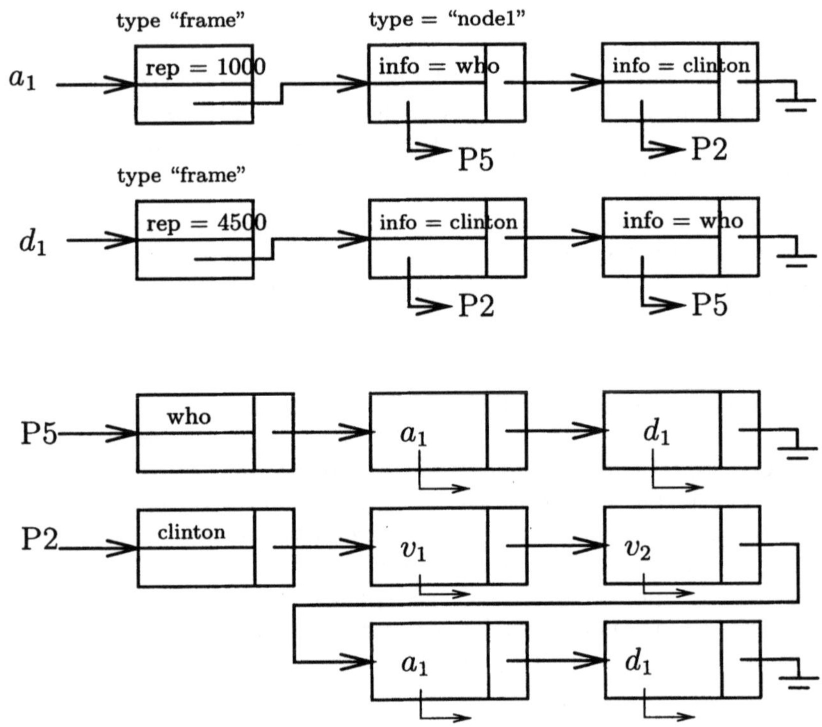

Fig. 4.3. Data Structure for Multimedia-Frame Example

We also know that the document d_1 is a position statement by the WHO about CLINTON. Then we have a new pointer, d_1 (similar to the pointers v_1 and v_2 in Example 4.2). The pointer d_1 points to a structure of type frame. Its feature list contains two elements, CLINTON and WHO referring to the fact that this audio-clip has two objects of interest. The list pointed to by P2 is then updated to contain an extra node specifying that d_1 is an address where information about Clinton is kept. Furthermore, the pointer list of frames associated with the entry in the OBJECT-TABLE corresponding to WHO, i.e., P5, is updated to consist of an extra node, viz. d_1.

Figure 4.3 contains the new structures added to Figure 4.2 in order to handle these two media. ◇◇

4.3 Query Processing Algorithms

In this section, we will develop algorithms to answer queries of the form described in Section 4.1. As queries are existentially closed conjunctions of atoms, and as atoms can only be constructed in certain ways, we will first discuss how atomic queries can be answered (depending on the kinds of atoms involved) and then show how conjunctive queries can be handled (just as a JOIN).

4.3.1 Membership Queries. Suppose we consider a ground atom of the form t $\in$ flist(s) where t is an object-name and s is a state. As the query is ground, the answer is either yes or no. The algorithm below shows how such a query may be answered.

```
proc ground_in(t:string; s:↑node1):boolean;
  found := false; ptr := s.flist;
    while (not(found) & ptr ≠ NIL do
      if (ptr.info = t) then found := true
      else ptr := ptr.link ;
    return found.
end proc.
```

It is easy to see that the above algorithm is linear in the length of flist(s).

Suppose we now consider non-ground atoms of the form t $\in$ flist(s) where either one, or both, of t, s are non-ground.

(Case 1: s ground, t non-ground) In this case, all that needs to be done is to check if s.flist is empty. If it is, then there is no solution to the existential query "$(\exists t)t \in$ flist(s)." Otherwise, simply return the "info" field of s.flist. Thus, this kind of query can be answered in constant time.

(Case 2: s non-ground, t ground) This case is more interesting. t is a feature, and hence, an object. Thus, t must occur in the OBJECT-TABLE. Once the location of t in the OBJECT-TABLE is found (let us say PTR points to this location), and if PTR.link2 is non-NIL, then return (((PTR.link2).frameptr).name). If PTR.link2 is NIL, then halt – no answer exists to the query "$(\exists s)t \in$ flist(s)." Thus, this kind of query can be answered in time O(k) where k is the length of the list PTR.link2.

(Case 3: s non-ground, t non-ground) In this case, find the first element of the OBJECT-TABLE which has a non-empty "link2" field. If no such entry is present in the table, then no answer exists to the query "$(\exists s,t)t \in$ flist(s)." Otherwise, let PTR be a pointer to the first such entry. Return the solution

$$t = \text{PTR}; \;\; s = (((\text{PTR.link2}).\text{frameptr}).\text{name}).$$

Thus, this kind of query can be answered in constant time.

4.3.2 Other Queries. The other three types of predicates involved in an atomic query can be answered by simply consulting the logic program. For instance, queries of the form $(\exists N, S)$**frametype**(N, S) can be handled easily enough because the binary relation **frametype** is stored as a set of unit clauses in the logic program representation. Similarly, queries involving feature-state relations can be computed using the logic program too. Queries involving inter-state relations can be solved by recourse to the existing implementation of those operations. As described earlier, inter-state relationships are domain dependent, and we envisage that the implementation of these relationships will be done in a domain specific manner.

Answers to conjunctive queries are just joins of answers to their atomic parts. Join queries can be optimized by adapting standard methods to work with our data structures.

4.4 Updates in Multimedia Databases

It is well-known that database systems need to be frequently updated to reflect new information that was not available before, or which reflect corrections to previously existing information. This situation will affect multimedia database systems in the same way current database systems are affected by it. However, *how* these updates are incorporated will change because of the nature of the indexing structures we use. Updates to an integrated multimedia system can be of two types:

1. **Feature Updates within States:** It may be the case that features in a given state were either not identified at all, or were incorrectly identified. For instance, a pattern recognition algorithm which extracts features from video may leave Jack Kemp unclassified simply because he was not on the list of features the system knew about. Am enhanced pattern recognition algorithm pressed into service later may wish to add a new feature, viz. `kemp`, to the list of features possessed by a certain video-frame. In the same vein, a Bill Clinton look alike may mistakenly be classified as Bill Clinton and later, it may become apparent that the feature `clinton` should be deleted from this video-clip (as Clinton is not in the video). We show, in Section 4.4.1 and 4.4.2 below, how features can be efficiently added and deleted from states.
2. **State Updates:** When new states arrive they need to be processed and inserted into the multimedia database system. For instance, new video-information showing Clinton speaking at various places may need to be added. In the same, deletions of existing states (that have been determined to be useless) may also need to be accomplished. Section 4.4.3 and 4.4.4 specify how these insertions and deletions may be accomplished.

4.4.1 Inserting Features into States. In this section, we develop a procedure called feature_add that takes a feature f and a pre-existing state s as input, and adds f to state s. This must be done in such a way that the underlying indexing structures are modified so that the query processing algorithms can access this new data.

proc feature_add(f:feature; s:state);
Insert f into `OBJECT-TABLE` at record R.
Let N be the pointer to state S.
Set R to N.
Add R to the list of features pointed to by node N.
end proc.

It is easy to see that this algorithm can be executed in constant time (modulo the complexity of insertion into the `OBJECT-TABLE`).

4.4.2 Deleting Features From States. In this section, we develop a procedure called feature_del that takes a pre-existing feature f and a pre-existing state s as input, and deletes f from s's feature list.

proc feature_del(f:feature; s:state);
Find the node N in s's `flist` having N.`info` $= f$.
Set T to N.`objid`.
Delete N.
Examine the list of states in $T.link2$ and delete the node whose `frameptr` field is s.
end proc.

It is easy to see that this algorithm can be executed in linear time (w.r.t. the lengths of the lists associated with s and f, respectively).

4.4.3 Inserting New States. Adding a new state s is quite easy. All that needs to be done is to:

1. Create a pointer S to a structure of type `frame` to access state s.
2. Insert each feature possessed by state s into S's `flist`.
3. For each feature f in s's `flist`, add s into the list of frames pointed to by f's `frameptr` field.

It is easy to see that the complexity of inserting a new state is linear in the length of the feature list of this state.

4.4.4 Deleting States. The procedure to delete state s from the index structure is very simple. For each feature f in s's `flist`, delete s from the list pointed to by f.`frameptr`. Then return the entire list pointed to by S (where S is the pointer to the `frame` representing s) to available storage. It is easy to see that the complexity of this algorithm is

$$length(\texttt{flist}(s)) + \sum f \in \texttt{flist}(s)\ell(f.\texttt{frameptr})$$

where $length(\mathtt{flist}(s))$ is the number of features s has, and $\ell(f.\mathtt{frameptr})$ is the length of the list pointed to by $f.\mathtt{frameptr}$, i.e. the number of states in which f appears as a feature.

In this section, we have made three contributions: we have defined a logical query language for multimedia databases, an indexing structure that can be used to integrate information across these different media-instances, query processing procedures to execute queries in the query language using the indexing structure, and database update procedures that use the indexing structure based on improved data.

5. Multimedia Presentations

The description of multimedia information systems developed in preceding sections is completely static. It provides a query language for a user to integrate information stored in these diverse media. However, in many real-life applications, different frames from different media sources must come together (i.e. be synchronized) so as to achieve the desired communication effect. Thus, for example, a video-frame showing Clinton giving a speech would be futile if the audio-track portrayed Socks the cat, meowing. In this section, we will develop a notion of a *media-event* – informally, a media event is a concatenation of the states of the different media at a given point in time. The aim of a media presentation is to achieve a desired sequence of media-events, where each individual event achieves a coherent synchronization of the different media states. We will show how this kind of synchronization can be viewed as a form of constraint-solving, and how the generation of appropriate media-events may be viewed as query processing. In other words, we suggest that:

$$\begin{aligned} \text{Generation of Media Events} &= \text{Query Processing.} \\ \text{Synchronization} &= \text{Constraint Solving.} \end{aligned}$$

5.1 Generation of Media Events = Query Processing

In the sequel, we will assume that we have an underlying multimedia system $\mathbf{MMS} = \{\mathcal{M}_1, \ldots, \mathcal{M}_n\}$ where $\mathcal{M}_i = (\mathbf{ST}^i, \mathbf{fe}^i, \lambda^i, \Re_1^i, \Re_2^i, \mathbf{Var}_1^i, \mathbf{Var}_2^i)$.

A *media-event* w.r.t. **MMS** is an n-tuple, $(s_1, \ldots, s_n)$ where $s_i \in \mathbf{ST}_i$, i.e. a media-event is obtained by picking, from each medium $\mathcal{M}_i$, a specific state. Intuitively, a media-event is just a snapshot of a medium at a given point in time. Thus, for instance, if we are considering an audio-video multimedia system, a media-event consists of a pair (a, v) representing an audio-state a and a video-state v. The idea is that if (a, v) is such a media-event, then at the point in time at which this event occurs, the audio-medium is in state a,and the video-medium is in state v.

Example 5.1. Suppose we return to the Clinton Example, and suppose we consider the video-frame shown in Figure 3.1(b). Let us suppose that this represents the state s_1 when Reno was sworn in as Attorney General, and let us suppose there is an audio-tape a_4 describing the events. Then the pair (s_1, a_4) is a media-event; intuitively, this means that state s_1 (video) and state a_4 (audio) must be "on" simultaneously. (We will go into details of synchronization in a later section. ◇◇

We now formally define the notion of "satisfaction" of a formula in the query language by a media-event.

Suppose $\mathbf{me} = (s_1, \ldots, s_n)$ is a media event w.r.t. the multimedia system $\mathbf{MMS} = \{\mathcal{M}_1, \ldots, \mathcal{M}_n\}$ as specified above, and suppose F is a formula. Then we say that $\mathbf{me}$ *satisfies* F (or $\mathbf{me}$ makes F true), denoted $\mathbf{me} \models F$ as follows:

1. if $F = \mathtt{frametype}(a, b)$ is a ground atom, then $\mathbf{me} \models F$ iff $a = s_i$ for some $1 \leq i \leq n$ and the frametype of $\mathcal{M}_i$ is b. (Recall, from the definition of the frame data structure, that associated with each $\mathcal{M}_i$ is a string called $\mathcal{M}_i$'s $\mathtt{frametype}$.)
2. if $F = (c \in \mathtt{flist}(b))$, and there exists an $1 \leq i \leq n$ such that c is a feature in $\mathbf{fe}^i$ and $b = s_i$, then $\mathbf{me} \models F$ iff $c \in \lambda^i(s_i)$.
3. if $F = \phi^*(t_1, \ldots, t_n, s)$ and for some $1 \leq i \leq n$, $t_1, \ldots, t_n \in \mathbf{fe}^i$ and $s \in \mathbf{ST}^i$, then $\mathbf{me} \models F$ iff $(t_1, \ldots, t_n, s) \in \phi \in \Re_2^i$.
4. if $F = (G \,\&\, H)$, then $\mathbf{me} \models F$ iff $\mathbf{me} \models G$ and $\mathbf{me} \models H$.
5. if $F = (\exists x)F$ and x is a state (resp. feature) variable, then $\mathbf{me} \models F$ iff $\mathbf{me} \models F[x/t]$ where $F[x/t]$ denotes the replacement of all free occurrences of x in F by t where t is a state (resp. feature) constant[2]

If F cannot be generated using the inductive definition specified above, then it is the case that $\mathbf{me} \not\models F$.

A *multimedia specification* is a sequence of queries $Q_1, Q_2, \ldots$ to $\mathbf{MMS}$. The intuitive idea behind a multimedia specification is that any query defines a set of "acceptable" media-events, viz. those media-events which make the query true. If the goal of a media specification is to generate a sequence of states satisfying certain conditions (i.e. queries), then we can satisfy this desideratum by generating any sequence of media events which satisfies these queries. Suppose $\mathbf{me}_0 = (s_1, \ldots, s_n)$ is the initial state of a multimedia-system, i.e. this is an initial media-event at time 0. Suppose $Q_1, Q_2, \ldots$ is a multimedia specification. A *multimedia presentation* is a sequence of media-events $\mathbf{me}_1, \ldots, \mathbf{me}_i, \ldots$ such that media-event $\mathbf{me}_i$ satisfies the query Q_i. The intuitive idea behind a multimedia presentation is that at time 0, the initial media-event is $(s_1, \ldots, s_n)$. At time 1, in response to query Q_1, a new media-event, $\mathbf{me}_1$ which satisfies Q_1 is generated. At time 2, in response to query Q_2, a new media-event, $\mathbf{me}_2$, in response to query Q_2 is generated. This process continues over a period of time in this way.

[2] The notion of a "free" variable is the standard one, cf. [19]).

Example 5.2. **(Multimedia Event Generation Example)** Let us suppose that we have recourse to a very small multimedia library consisting of five video-frames, and five audio-frames. Thus, there are two media involved, $\mathcal{M}_1$ (audio) and $\mathcal{M}_2$ (video), and there are five states in each of these media. The tables below specify the audio states and video states, respectively:

Audio Frame Name	Features	Video Frame Name	Features
a_1	clinton	v_1	clinton, gore, bush
a_2	clinton, socks	v_2	clinton, gore
a_3	gore	v_3	clinton
a_4	bush	v_4	gore, reno
a_5	clinton, gore	v_5	clinton, gore, reno

Let us now suppose that the initial media-event is some pair $\mathbf{me}_0 = (a_0, v_0)$ consisting of a blank, i.e. the feature lists for both media are initially empty (i.e. there is no video, and no audio at time 0). Suppose we consider the evolution of this multimedia system over three units of time. Let us consider the multimedia specification Q_1, Q_2, Q_3 where:

$$\begin{aligned}
Q_1 &= (\exists \mathtt{S}_1, \mathtt{S}_2)(\mathtt{frametype}(\mathtt{S}_1, \mathtt{video}) \,\&\, \mathtt{frametype}(\mathtt{S}_2, \mathtt{audio}) \,\&\\
&\quad \mathtt{clinton} \in \mathtt{flist}(\mathtt{S}_1) \,\&\, \mathtt{gore} \in \mathtt{flist}(\mathtt{S}_1) \,\&\, \mathtt{clinton} \in \mathtt{flist}(\mathtt{S}_2)).\\
Q_2 &= (\exists \mathtt{S}_1, \mathtt{S}_2)(\mathtt{frametype}(\mathtt{S}_1, \mathtt{video}) \,\&\, \mathtt{frametype}(\mathtt{S}_2, \mathtt{audio}) \,\&\\
&\quad \mathtt{clinton} \in \mathtt{flist}(\mathtt{S}_1) \,\&\, \mathtt{gore} \in \mathtt{flist}(\mathtt{S}_1) \,\&\, \mathtt{gore} \in \mathtt{flist}(\mathtt{S}_2)).\\
Q_3 &= (\exists \mathtt{S}_1, \mathtt{S}_2)(\mathtt{frametype}(\mathtt{S}_1, \mathtt{video}) \,\&\, \mathtt{frametype}(\mathtt{S}_2, \mathtt{audio}) \,\&\\
&\quad \mathtt{clinton} \in \mathtt{flist}(\mathtt{S}_1) \,\&\, \mathtt{gore} \in \mathtt{flist}(\mathtt{S}_1) \,\&\, \mathtt{bush} \in \mathtt{flist}(\mathtt{S}_1) \,\&\\
&\quad \mathtt{clinton} \in \mathtt{flist}(\mathtt{S}_2) \,\&\, \mathtt{gore} \in \mathtt{flist}(\mathtt{S}_2)).
\end{aligned}$$

Observe that query Q_1 can be satisfied by any substitution that sets S_1 to an element of $\{v_1, v_2, v_5\}$ and S_2 to an element of $\{a_1, a_2, a_5\}$ – thus there nine possible combinations of audio/video that could come up in response to this query at time 1. Had the user wanted to eliminate some of these nine possible s/he should have added further conditions to the query.

When query Q_2 is processed, S_1 can be set to any of $\{v_1, v_2, v_5\}$ as before, but S_2 may be set only to one of $\{a_3, a_5\}$. Thus, any of these six possible audio-video combinations would form a legitimate media event at time 2.

Lastly, to satisfy Q_3, S_1 must be set to v_1 and S_2 must be set to a_5; no other media-event would satisfy Q_3.

As a final remark, we observe that not all queries are necessarily satisfiable (and hence, for some queries, it may be impossible to find an appropriate media-event). For instance, consider the query

$$(\exists \mathtt{S})(\mathtt{frametype(S, audio)} \,\&\, \mathtt{reno} \in \mathtt{flist(S)}).$$

It is easily seen that there is no audio-frame in our library which has Reno in its feature list, and hence, this query is not satisfiable. ◇◇

5.2 Synchronization = Constraint Solving

In preceding sections, we have not considered the problem of synchronization. In particular, it is naive to assume, as done previously, that queries $Q_1, Q_2, Q_3, \ldots$ will be posed one after the other at times $1, 2, 3, \ldots$, respectively. Rather, experience with multimedia systems existing in the market suggests that a query may be "in force" for a certain period of time. In other words, the multimedia system (or the Multimedia Integrator shown in Figure 2.1) may be given the following inputs:

- a sequence $Q_1, Q_2, \ldots, Q_k$ of queries indicating that query Q_1 must be answered (i.e. a media-event that satisfies query Q_1 be "brought up"), followed by a media-event satisfying query Q_2, etc., and
- a deadline d by which the entire sequence of media-events must be completed, and
- for each query Q_i, $1 \leq i \leq n$, a *lower* bound $\mathtt{LB}_i$ and an upper bound $\mathtt{UB}_i$ reflecting how long the media-event corresponding to this query should be "on." $\mathtt{LB}_i$ and $\mathtt{UB}_i$ are integers – we assume discrete time in our framework.

The Multimedia Integrator's job is to:

- **(Task 1)** Answer the queries $Q_1, \ldots, Q_n$, i.e. find media events $\mathbf{me}_1, \ldots, \mathbf{me}_n$ that satisfy the above queries.
- **(Task 2)** Schedule the actual start time and end time of each media-event, and ensure that this time achieves the lower-bound and upper-bound alluded to earlier.

Task 1 has already been addressed in the preceding section; we now address task 2. We show that the scheduling problem is essentially a constraint satisfaction problem which may be formulated as follows.

Individual Media Constraints. Let s_i be a variable denoting the start time of media-event $\mathbf{me}_i$, and let e_i be a variable denoting the execution time of media-event $\mathbf{me}_i$ – it is important to note that the values of these variables may *not* be known initially. Then, as we know that media-event $\mathbf{me}_i$ must be "on" for between $\mathtt{LB}_i$ and $\mathtt{UB}_i$ time units, we know that:

$$\mathtt{LB}_i \leq e_i \leq \mathtt{UB}_i$$

is a constraint that must be satisfied within our framework. Furthermore, the constraints

$$s_i \geq 0\,;\; e_i \geq 0$$

must be satisfied as well.

Synchronization. The only remaining thing is to ensure that the media-event to query Q_{i+1} starts immediately after the media-event satisfying query Q_i. This may be achieved by the following constraint:

$$s_{i+1} = s_i + e_i$$

where $i < n$.

Deadline Constraint. Finally, we need to specify that the deadline has to be achieved, i.e. the completion-time of the last media-event must be achieved on, or before the deadline. This can be stated as:

$$s_i + e_i \leq d.$$

Together with the constraint that all variables (i.e. $s_1, \ldots, s_n, e_1, \ldots, e_n$) are non-negative, the solutions of the above system of equations specify the times at which the media-events corresponding to queries $Q_1, Q_2, \ldots, Q_n$ must be "brought up" or "activated".

5.3 Internal Synchronization

In the preceding section, we have assumed that though a media-event involves a multiplicity of participating media, all these different media-states are brought up simultaneously and synchronously. We call the problem of synchronizing the individual media-states participating in a particular media-event *internal synchronization* as this is related to the media-event generated by a specific query. An easy solution is to assume that while the media-event corresponding to query Q_i is "on," the system computes a media-event, $\mathbf{me}_{i+1}$, corresponding to query Q_{i+1} and stores the individual media-states in a buffer. Thus, there is a buffer, $\mathtt{BUF}_i$ corresponding to each media-instance, $\mathcal{M}_i$. In the next section, we discuss how these buffers can be organized and managed.

5.4 Media Buffers

Internal synchronization requires that at any given point in time, if the media-event $\mathbf{me}_i$ corresponding to query Q_i is "on," then the media-event $\mathbf{me}_{i+1}$ corresponding to query Q_{i+1} is ready and loaded in the buffers. Let

$$\begin{aligned} \mathbf{me}_i &= (s_1, \ldots, s_n) \\ \mathbf{me}_{i+1} &= (s'_1, \ldots, s'_n). \end{aligned}$$

Then, for each $1 \leq i \leq n$, it suffices to store the set of differences (this set is denoted δ_i) between state s_i and state s'_i. These two states reflect, respectively, the status of media-instance $\mathcal{M}_i$ when query Q_i is "on" and when query Q_{i+1} is "on." For instance, if media-event $\mathcal{M}_i$ is of frametype `video`, then s_i and s'_i may be pictures. Suppose, for instance, that we are discussing an audio-video presentation (say of some cowboys), and there are three differences between states s_i and s'_i, i.e. $\delta_i = \{d_1, d_2, d_3\}$ where:

1. d_1 represents a pistol which just appeared in a cowboy's hand,
2. d_2 represents a dog turning his head,
3. d_3 represents a leaf falling in the breeze.

Then it may be the case that d_1 is the "most important" of these changes, d_2 is the second most important, and d_3 is the least important of these differences. Hence, it may be critical, when bringing up state s'_i from the buffer, that d_1 be brought up first, then d_2 and only finally, d_3.

In general, we assume that associated with each medium $\mathcal{M}_i$, we have a *classification function*, $\mathtt{cf}_i$, which assigns, to each difference, a non-negative integer called that difference's classification level. The buffer, $\mathtt{BUF}_i$, associated with media-instance $\mathcal{M}_i$ is organized as a prioritized queue – all differences with priority 1 are at the front of the queue, all differences with priority 2 are next in the queue, and so on. Thus, when the queue is flushed (i.e. when the process of bringing state s'_i "up" is started), then the differences are brought up in the specified priority order. Note that if two differences are both labeled with the same classification level, then it is permissible to bring them up in any order relative to each other.

6. Related Work

There has been a good deal of work in recent years on multimedia. [29] has specified various roles that databases can play n complex multimedia systems [29], p.409. One of these is the logical integration of data stored on multiple media – this is the topic of this paper.

[27], [28] show how object-oriented databases (with some enhancements) can be used to support multimedia applications. Their model is a natural extension of the object-oriented notions of instantiation and generalization. The general idea is that a multimedia database is considered to be a set of objects that are inter-related to each other in various ways. The work reported here is compatible to that [27], [28] in that the frames and features in a media-instance may be thought of as objects. There are significant differences, however, in how these objects are organized and manipulated. For instance, we support a logical query language (Kim et. al. would support on object-oriented query language), and we support updates (Kim et. al. can do so as well but using algorithms compatible with their object-oriented model). We have analyzed the complexity of our query processing and update algorithms. Furthermore, the link between query processing and generation of media events is a novel feature of our framework, not present in [27], [28]. Last, but not least, we have developed a formal theoretical framework within which multimedia systems can be formally analyzed, and we have shown how various kinds of data representations on different types of media may be viewed as special cases of our framework.

[15] have defined a video-based object oriented data model, OVID. What the authors do primarily is to take pieces of video, identify meaningful features in them and link these features especially when consecutive clips of video share features. Our work deals with integrating multiple media and provide a unified query language and indexing structures to access the resulting integration. Hence, one such media-instance we could integrate is the OVID system, though our framework is general enough to integrate many other media (which OVID cannot). The authors have developed feature identification schemes (which we have not) and this complements our work. In a similar vein, [2] develop techniques to create large video databases by processing incoming video-data so as to identify features and set up access structures. Another piece of relevant related work is that of the QBIC (Query by Image Content) system of [3] at IBM, They develop indexing techniques to query large video databases by images – in other words, one may ask queries of the form "Find me all pictures in which image I occurs." Retrievals are done on the basis of similarity rather than on a perfect match. In constrast to our theoretical framework, [3] shows how features may be identified (based on similarity) in video, and how queries can be formulated in the video domain.

[5] have developed a query language called PICQUERY+ for querying certain kinds of federated multimedia systems. The spirit of their work is similar to ours in that both works attempt to devise query languages that access heterogeneous, federated multimedia databases. The differences, though, are in the following: our notion of a media-instance is very general and captures, as special cases, many structures (e.g. documents, audio, etc.) that their framework does not appear to capture. Hence, our framework can integrate far more diverse structures than that of [5]. However, there are many features in [5] that our framework does not currently possess – two of these are temporal data and uncertain information. Such features form a critical part of many domains (such as the medical domain described in [5]), and we look forward to extending our multimedia work in that direction, in keeping with a similar effort we have made previously [21] for integrating time, uncertainty, data structures, numeric constraints and databases.

[13] have developed methods for satisfying temporal constraints in multimedia systems. This relates to our framework in the following way: suppose there are temporal constraints specifying how a media-buffer (as defined in this paper) must be flushed. [13] show how this can be done. Hence, their methods can be used in conjunction with ours. In a similar vein, [16] show how multimedia presentations may be synchronized.

Other related works are the following: [10] develop an architecture to integrate multiple document representations. [6] show how Milner's Calculus of Communicating Systems can be used to specify interactive multimedia but they do not address the problem of querying the integration of multiple media. [7] study delay-sensitive data using an approach based on constrained block allocation. This work is quite different from ours.

Finally, we note that multimedia databases form a natural generalization of heterogeneous databases which have been studied extensively in [1], [8], [11], [12], [18], [20], [21], [22], [23], [24], [25], [26], [30]. How exactly the work on heterogeneous databases is applicable to multimedia databases remains to be seen, but clearly there is a fertile area to investigate here.

7. Conclusions

As is evident from the "Related Work" section, there is now intense interest in multimedia systems. These interests span across vast areas in computer science including, but not limited to: computer networks, databases, distributed computing, data compression, document processing, user interfaces, computer graphics, pattern recognition and artificial intelligence. In the long run, we expect that intelligent problem-solving systems will access information stored in a variety of formats, on a wide variety of media. Our work focuses on the need for unified framework to reason across these multiple domains. In the Introduction, we raised four questions. Below, we review the progress made in this paper towards answering those four questions, and indicate directions for future work along these lines.

- **What are multimedia database systems and how can they be formally/
  mathematically defined so that they are independent of any specific application domain ?**

  Accomplishments: In this paper, we have argued that in all likelihood, the designer of the Multimedia Integrator shown in Figure 2.1 will be presented with a collection of *pre-existing* databases on different types of media. The designer must build his/her algorithms "on top" of this pre-existing representation – delving into the innards of any of these representations is usually prohibitive, and often just plain impossible. Our framework provides a method to do so once features and feature-state relationships can be identified.

  Future Work: However, we have not addressed the problem of identifying features or identifying feature-relationships. For instance, in the Clinton Example (cf. Figure 3.1), Clinton is to the left of Nixon. However, from a bitmap, it is necessary to determine that Clinton and Nixon are actually in the picture, and that Clinton is to the left of Nixon. Such determinations depend inherently on the medium involved, and the data structure(s) used to represent the information (e.g. if the bitmap was replaced by a quadtree in the pictorial domain itself, the algorithms would become vastly different). Hence, feature identification in different domains is of great importance and needs to be addressed.

- **Can indexing structures for multimedia database systems be defined in a similar uniform, domain-independent manner ?**

  Accomplishments: We have developed a logic-based query language that can be used to execute various kinds of queries to multimedia databases. This query language is extremely simple (using nothing more than relatively standard logic), and hence it should form an easy vehicle for users to work with.

  Future Work: The query language developed in this paper does not handle uncertainty in the underlying media and/or temporal changes in the data. These need to be incorporated into the query language as they are relevant for various applications such as those listed by [5].

- **Is it possible to uniformly define query languages and access methods based on these indexing structures ?**

  Accomplishments: We have developed indexing structures for organizing the features (and properties of the features) in a given media-instance, and we have developed algorithms that can be used to answer queries (expressed in the logical query language described in the paper). These algorithms have been shown to be computable in polynomial-time.

  Future Work: Supporting more complex queries involving aggregate operations, as well as uncertainty and time in the queries (see preceding bullet) will require further work.

- **Is it possible to uniformly define the notion of an update in multimedia database systems and to efficiently accomplish such updates using the above-mentioned indexing structures ?**

  Accomplishments: We have defined a notion of an update to multimedia database systems that permits new features and states to be inserted into the underlying indexing structure when appropriate. Similarly deletions of old features and states are also supported. We have shown that these algorithms can be executed efficiently.

  Future Work: Of the update algorithms developed in this paper, the algorithm for deleting states is less efficient than the other three. In applications that require large-scale state deletions, it may be appropriate to consider alternative algorithms (and possibly alternative indexing structures as well).

– **What constitutes a multimedia presentation and can this be formally/mathematically defined so that it is independent of any specific application domain ?**

  Accomplishments: We prove that there is a fundamental connection between query processing and the generation of media-events. What this means is that a media presentation can be generated by a sequence of queries. This is useful because it may be relatively easy to specify a query articulating the criteria of importance – the system may be able to respond by picking any one of several media-events that satisfies this query. In addition, we show that synchronization really boils down to solving constraints.

  Future Work: A great deal of work has been done on synchronizing multimedia streams in a network[13], [16]. It should be possible to take advantage of these works to enhance the synchronization of answers to a query.

Acknowledgements

We are extremely grateful to Sushil Jajodia for many enlightening conversations on the topic of multimedia databases. We have also benefited from conversations with Sandeep Mehta, Raymond Ng, S. V. Raghavan and Satish Tripathi. We are grateful to C. Faloutsos for drawing our attention to [3].

References

[1] S. Adali and V.S. Subrahmanian. (1993) *Amalgamating Knowledge Bases, II: Algorithms, Data Structures and Query Processing*, Univ. of Maryland CS-TR-3124, Aug. 1993. Submitted for journal publication.

[2] F. Arman, A. Hsu and M. Chiu. (1993) *Image Processing on Compressed Data for Large Video Databases*, First ACM Intl. Conf. on Multimedia, pps 267–272.

[3] R. Barbet, W. Equitz, C. Faloutsos, M. Flickner, W. Niblack, D. Petkovic, and P. Yanker. (1993) *Query by Content for Large On-Line Image Collections*, IBM Research Report RJ 9408, June 1993.

[4] J. Benton and V.S. Subrahmanian. (1993) *Hybrid Knowledge Bases for Missile Siting Problems*, accepted for publication in 1994 Intl. Conf. on Artificial Intelligence Applications, IEEE Press.

[5] A. F. Cardenas, I.T. Ieong, R. Barket, R. K. Taira and C.M. Breant. (1993) *The Knowledge-Based Object-Oriented PICQUERY+ Language*, IEEE Trans. on Knowledge and Data Engineering, 5, 4, pps 644–657.

[6] S.B. Eun, E.S. No, H.C. Kim, H. Yoon, and S.R. Maeng. (1993) *Specification of Multimedia Composition and a Visual Programming Environment*, First ACM Intl. Conf. on Multimedia, pps 167–174.

[7] D.J. Gemmel and S. Christodoulakis. (1992) *Principles of Delay-Sensitive Multimedia Data Storqage and Retrieval*, ACM Trans. on Information systems, 10, 1, pps 51–90.

[8] J. Grant, W. Litwin, N. Roussopoulos and T. Sellis. (1991) *An Algebra and Calculus for Relational Multidatabase Systems*, Proc. First International Workshop on Interoperability in Multidatabase Systems, IEEE Computer Society Press (1991) 118-124.
[9] F. Hillier and G. Lieberman. (1986) *Introduction to Operations Research*, 4th edition, Holden-Day.
[10] B. R. Gaines and M. L. Shaw. (1993) *Open Architecture Multimedia Documents*, Proc. First ACM Intl. Conf. on Multimedia, pps 137–146.
[11] W. Kim and J. Seo. (1991) *Classifying Schematic and Data Heterogeneity in Multidatabase Systems*, IEEE Computer, Dec. 1991.
[12] A. Lefebvre, P. Bernus and R. Topor. (1992) *Querying Heterogeneous Databases: A Case Study*, draft manuscript.
[13] T.D.C. Little and A. Ghafoor. (1993) *Interval-Based Conceptual Models of Time-Dependent Multimedia Data*, IEEE Trans. on Knowledge and Data Engineering, 5, 4, pps 551–563.
[14] J. Lloyd. (1987) *Foundations of Logic Programming*, Springer Verlag.
[15] E. Oomoto and K. Tanaka. (1993) *OVID: Design and Implementation of a Video-Object Database System*, IEEE Trans. on Knowledge and Data Engineering, 5, 4, pps 629–643.
[16] B. Prabhakaran and S. V. Raghavan. (1993) *Synchronization Models for Multimedia Presentation with User Participation*, First ACM Intl. Conf. on Multimedia, pps 157–166.
[17] H. Samet. (1989) *The Design and Analysis of Spatial Data Structures*, Addison Wesley.
[18] A. Sheth and J. Larson. (1990) *Federated Database Systems for Managing Distributed, Heterogeneous and Autonomous Databases*, ACM Computing Surveys, 22, 3, pp 183–236.
[19] J. Shoenfield. (1967) *Mathematical Logic*, Addison Wesley.
[20] A. Silberschatz, M. Stonebraker and J. D. Ullman. (1991) *Database Systems: Achievements and Opportunities*, Comm. of the ACM, 34, 10, pps 110–120.
[21] V.S. Subrahmanian. (1994) *Amalgamating Knowledge Bases*, ACM Transactions on Database Systems, 19, 2, pp. 291–331, 1994.
[22] V.S. Subrahmanian. (1993) *Hybrid Knowledge Bases for Intelligent Reasoning Systems*, Invited Address, Proc. 8th Italian Conf. on Logic Programming (ed. D. Sacca), pps 3–17, Gizzeria, Italy, June 1993.
[23] G. Wiederhold. (1992) *Mediators in the Architecture of Future Information Systems*, IEEE Computer, March 1992, pps 38–49.
[24] G. Wiederhold. (1993) *Intelligent Integration of Information*, Proc. 1993 ACM SIGMOD Conf. on Management of Data, pps 434–437.
[25] G. Wiederhold, S. Jajodia, and W. Litwin. Dealing with granularity of time in temporal databases. In *Proc. 3rd Nordic Conf. on Advanced Information Systems Engineering*, Lecture Notes in Computer Science, Vol. 498, (R. Anderson et al. eds.), Springer-Verlag, 1991, pages 124–140.
[26] G Wiederhold, S. Jajodia, and W. Litwin. Integrating temporal data in a heterogeneous environment. In *Temporal Databases*. Benjamin/Cummings, Jan 1993.
[27] D. Woelk, W. Kim and W. Luther. (1986) *An Object-Oriented Approach to Multimedia Databases*, Proc. ACM SIGMOD 1986, pps 311-325.
[28] D. Woelk and W. Kim. (1987) *Multimedia Information Management in an Object-Oriented Database System*, Proc. 13th Intl. Conf. on Very Large Databases, pps 319–329.
[29] S. Zdonik. (1993) *Incremental Database Systems: Databases from the Ground Up*, Proc. 1993 ACM SIGMOD Conf. on Management of Data, pps 408–412.

[30] R. Zicari, S. Ceri, and L. Tanca. (1991) *Interoperability between a Rule-Based Database Language and an Object-Oriented Language*, Proc. First International Workshop on Interoperability in Multidatabase Systems, IEEE Computer Society Press (1991) 125-135.

A Unified Approach to Data Modeling and Retrieval for a Class of Image Database Applications

Venkat N. Gudivada[1], Vijay V. Raghavan[2], and Kanonluk Vanapipat[2]

[1] Department of Electrical Engineering and Computer Science
Ohio University, Athens, OH 45701, U.S.A.
[2] The Center for Advanced Computer Studies
University of Southwestern Louisiana, Lafayette, LA 70504, U.S.A.

Summary. Recently, there has been widespread interest in various kinds of database management systems for managing information from images. Image Retrieval problem is concerned with retrieving images that are relevant to users' requests from a large collection of images, referred to as the *image database*. Since the application areas are very diverse, there seems to be no consensus as to what an image database system really is. Consequently, the characteristics of the existing image database systems have essentially evolved from domain specific considerations [20]. In response to this situation, we have introduced a unified framework for retrieval in image databases in [17]. Our approach to the image retrieval problem is based on the premise that it is possible to develop a data model and an associated retrieval model that can address the needs of a *class* of image retrieval applications. For this class of applications, from the perspective of the end users, image processing and image retrieval are two orthogonal issues and this distinction contributes toward domain-independence.

In this paper, we analyze the existing approaches to image data modeling and establish a taxonomy based on which these approaches can be systematically studied and understood. Then we investigate a class of image retrieval applications from the view point of their retrieval requirements to establish both a taxonomy for image attributes and generic retrieval types. To support the generic retrieval types, we have proposed a data model/framework referred to as AIR. AIR data model employs multiple logical representations. The logical representations can be viewed as abstractions of physical images at various levels. They are stored as persistent data in the image database. We then discuss how image database systems can be developed based on the AIR framework. Development of two image database retrieval applications based on our implementation of AIR framework are briefly described. Finally, we identify several research issues in AIR and our proposed solutions to some of them are indicated.

1. Introduction

Recently, there has been widespread interest in various kinds of database management systems (DBMS) for managing information from images, which do not lend themselves to be efficiently stored, flexibly retrieved and manipulated within the framework of conventional DBMS. Image Retrieval (IR) problem is concerned with retrieving images that are relevant to users' requests from a large collection of images, referred to as the *image database*. There is a multitude of application areas that consider image retrieval as a principal activity [17]. Tamura and Yokoya provide a survey of image database systems that were in practice around the early 1980s [42]. Chock also provides a survey and comparison of functionality of several image database systems for geographic applications [9]. Recently, Grosky & Mehrotra [14], [13] and Chang & Hsu [8] discuss the recent advances, perspectives, and future research directions in image database systems. More recently, [20] provides a comprehensive survey and relative assessment of Picture Retrieval Systems.

Since the application areas are greatly diverse, there seems to be no consensus as to what an image database system really is. Consequently, the characteristics of the existing image database systems have essentially evolved from domain specific considerations. Though image database systems have been studied by researchers for quite sometime, tangible progress has not been realized. This is evidenced by the lack of a standard data model for image representation as well as a framework for image retrieval. The situation is attributable to several factors. Images demand enormous storage as well as faster processors for manipulating and retrieving image data. Until recently, the storage space required for image databases remained quite expensive. With the rapid advances in Very Large Scale Integration (VLSI) technology and the emergence of various types of storage media, both processor speeds and storage capacity continue to improve without a proportionate increase in the prices. It is expected that this trend will stimulate research in image databases and unfold several new application areas [33]. Also, due to the diverse nature of image database applications, it is intrinsically difficult to conceive a general image data model and operations on this data model so that it can be useful in many application areas. This renders the formalization of an image data model that can serve as a standard platform, on which other aspects of the image database system can be realized, an extremely difficult task.

In response to this situation, we have introduced a unified framework for retrieval in image databases in [17]. Our approach to the image retrieval problem is based on the premise that it is possible to develop a data model and an associated retrieval model that can address the needs of a *class* of image retrieval applications. These application domains are characterized by the need for efficient and flexible access to large image collections. Furthermore, retrieval is performed by naive and casual users. From the perspective of these end users, image processing and image retrieval are two orthogonal issues and the end users are interested only in retrieving images of relevance to their needs. Our approach to image database management aims at a reasonable degree of domain independence at the cost of a completely automated approach to image recognition/understanding task and is motivated by the methods employed in Bibliographic Information Systems [39]. In the latter, documents are uniformly represented by index terms in a domain-independent fashion. However, it should be noted that the indexing task itself is domain-dependent and complex and is usually performed in a semi-automated fashion in commercially successful Bibliographic Information Systems.

In this paper, we describe the data modeling and retrieval aspects of the framework for retrieving images from large repositories proposed in [17]. First, we analyze the existing approaches to image data modeling and establish a taxonomy based on which these approaches can be systematically studied and understood (Sect. 2). Then we investigate a *class* of image application areas from the view point of their retrieval requirements to establish both a taxonomy for image attributes and generic retrieval types (Sect. 3). This in turn enabled us to establish an image data model/framework to support these generic retrieval types. In Sect. 4, we introduce the notion of logical representations. The logical representations can be viewed as abstractions, of physical images, at various levels. The motivations for the proposed data model are discussed in Sect. 5. Sect. 6 describes the proposed data model which we refer to as *Adaptive Image Retrieval* (AIR) data model. The term "adaptive" is used to mean that the proposed framework can easily be adapted to a class of image retrieval appl ications. AIR employs multiple logical representations as an integral part of the data model. They are stored as persistent data in the image database. In Sect. 7, we discuss how image database systems can be developed based on the AIR framework. Development of two image database retrieval applications based on our implementation of AIR framework are briefly described in Sect. 8. Sect. 9 introduces some research issues in the context of AIR. More specifically, we address the query language/interface, algorithms for query processing, elicitation and modeling of user relevance feedback for improving retrieval effectiveness, and a knowledge elicitation tool known as Personal Construct Theory [27] as an image database design aid. Finally, Sect. 10 concludes the paper. With reference to the Medical Scenario described in the Introduction of the book, the work described herein is useful to model and retrieve images from the X-ray database.

2. Approaches to Image Data Modeling

Before we analyze the various existing approaches to image data modeling, first we introduce the terminology associated with data as used in advanced database applications vis-a-vis views of data. Approaches to image data modeling can be grouped on the basis of the view(s) of image data that the data model supports. Lorie classifies the data that exists in the current application areas of advanced database systems into the following categories: formatted data, structured data, complex data, and unformatted data [30]. *Formatted data* refers to the data that is found in traditional database applications. There are several situations where heterogeneous data about an object needs to be stored and retrieved together. Such data is referred to as *structured data* and is similar to the notion of structures or records in programming languages. Structured data that has variable number of components is referred to as *complex data*. Finally, *unformatted data* refers to string data whose structure is not "understood" by the DBMS. To support unformatted data, special methods/procedures that understand the semantics and perform operations on the unformatted data are provided. This usually requires the Abstract Data Type (ADT) facility either in the query language or in the host programming language of the DBMS. Unformatted data is also referred to as *byte string, long field*, and *BLOB* (Binary Long Object Box). When there is no need for distinction among the first three types of data, we collectively refer to them simply as formatted data. We now introduce some terminology to facilitate the discussion in the subsequent sections.

2.1 Terminology

An *Image Data Model* (IDM) is a scheme for representing entities of interest in images, their geometric characteristics and attribute values, and associations among objects in images and determines the view(s) of image data. Thus an IDM denotes various logical structures used in representing the above information. It should be noted that the term IDM is often used in the literature to refer to low-level schemes (i.e., the representations closer to the physical level representation (see Sect. 4)) used for representing images [36].

An *Image Retrieval Model* (IRM) encompasses the specification of the following: an IDM, a query specification language or scheme for expressing user queries, matching or retrieval strategies used for retrieving relevant images from an image database. An *Image Database Management System* (IDBMS) is a software system that provides convenient and efficient access to the data contained in an image database. It implements the IRM and provides additional services to insure integrity, security, and privacy of image data as well as mechanisms for concurrent access to image data.

We classify the users of an image database system into the following three categories: Naive, Casual, and Expert users. A *naive user* is one who is not well versed with the image domain characteristics. A *casual user* is one who is well versed with the image domain characteristics and performs retrieval only occasionally. An *expert user* is like a casual user with respect to the knowledge he/she has about the domain. However, the expert user performs retrieval quite frequently. In the next five subsections, we describe the existing approaches to modeling and retrieving image data.

2.2 Conventional Data Models

The database management systems that are based on one of the three classical data models (namely, hierarchical, network, and relational) are referred to as *Conventional Database Management Systems* (CDBMS). These systems are primarily designed for commercial and business applications where the data to be managed is of formatted type. However, the CDBMS have been used for modeling and retrieving images, especially the ones based on the relational data model. Image data is treated as formatted data and relational tables are used as the logical data structures for storing this data. Since the images are represented by a set of keywords or attribute-value pairs, the level of abstraction in image representation is quite high. The systems in this category are not "truly" IDBMS since the image data model, query specification language, and the retrieval strategy are essentially those of the underlying CDBMS and they are not convenient and natural to the image data. For example, a class of queries that are based on relative spatial relationships among the objects in an image is naturally specified using a sketch pad (see Figure 8.1) rather than using the relational query language SQL. The next section describes the data modeling and retrieval in image database systems in which an image processing/graphics system is at the core complemented by an advanced file system or database functionality.

2.3 Image Processing/Graphics Systems with Database Functionality

Systems under this category view images as unformatted data. However, the data about an image that is extrinsic to the image contents may be stored as formatted data in the header portion of the image data file. Furthermore, the results of image interpretation or image attributes derived through human involvement may also be stored as formatted data using a full-fledged CDBMS or a customized database system with minimal functionality. Therefore, there are two distinct data models associated with most of the systems in this category: one for the unformatted view of the data and the other for the formatted view of the data. The data model employed for unformatted view of data is primarily one of the two fundamental physical level representations: raster or vector. Representations such as topological vector representation, Geographic Base File/Dual Independent Map Encoding (GBF/DIME), and POLYgon conVERTer (POLYVERT) have also been used [36]. In systems where the formatted data is limited to that data that is derived external to the image contents, the data model used is simply a set of keywords that are integratedly stored as part of the header information. Such systems are not coupled with a CDBMS. In contrast, for systems which are coupled with a CDBMS, the data model employed for the data that is derived external to the image is usually that of the host CDBMS.

The query specification for both formatted and unformatted views of the image data is through user interaction with the system by using a set of commands. For example, in ELAS System [1], commands exist for retrieving LANDSAT images based on parameters such as date of image acquisition, geographic area represented by the image, spectral channel number, percentage of cloud cover, among others. Typically, a user expresses his retrieval need by a sequence of commands. A user may first execute a command to retrieve an image of a geographic area and then execute other commands to perform partitioning of this image into polygonal areas based on image features and to perform polygonal overlay with another image. The retrieval strategy employed for the formatted view of the data is that of the host CDBMS, if a CDBMS is coupled with the system. Otherwise, the file system of the underlying operating system is enhanced to store, edit, and retrieve formatted data that is stored as part of the header. Approaches to image data modeling based on various extensions to relational data model are described next.

2.4 Extended Conventional Data Models

There has been a great interest in providing several extensions to the relational data model to overcome the limitations imposed by the flat tabular structure of relations for geometric modeling and engineering applications [28]. The resulting data model is characterized by the addition of application specific components to an existing database system kernel. They include nested relations, procedural fields, and query-language extensions for transitive closure, among others. The primary objective of all these extensions is to overcome the fragmented representation of the geometric and complex objects in the relational data model. Image data is stored in the system as formatted data. However, to a database user this view of data is made transparent through these extensions. Image data is perceived as structured or complex data by the users.

The query specification language is essentially that of the relational DBMS. However, the expressive power of the query specification language is increased because a user can now specify procedure names for attribute values in formulating queries. However, the increased power of the language comes at the cost of performance penalty since a procedure name may implicitly specify several join operations. The retrieval strategy is exactly same as the one used by the host DBMS. Instead of providing a set of built-in extensions to the relational data model, some researchers have investigated extensible or customizable data models. This approach is discussed in the next section.

2.5 Extensible Data Models

The basic idea behind extensibility is to provide facilities for the database designers/users to define their own application specific extensions to the data model [2], [5], [41], [34]. An extensible data model must support at least the facility for abstract data types. Extensible data models provide most flexibility as far as the view(s) of image data is concerned. Image data can be represented as formatted, structured, complex, or unstructured data (new database features such as set-type attributes, procedural fields, binary large object boxes, and abstract data type facility accommodate these views of data). Query specification language of the host DBMS is extended to include these new features as well as for the inclusion of the user-defined operators in the formulation of queries. The retrieval strategy of the host DBMS is suitably modified to accommodate the new features in the query specification. In the next section we describe data models that are recent in origin.

2.6 Other Data Models

The data models that we include in this section are recent and are mostly in experimental stage. The goal here is to experiment with new image data models and retrieval strategies. Some systems perform spatial reasoning as a part of the query processing while other systems have attempted cognitive approaches to query specification and processing [6], [7], [12], [22], [23], [26], [29], [43]. In contrast with the other approaches we have discussed earlier, there are no full-fledged image database management systems built based on these data models. Detailed discussion on all of the above five approaches to image data modeling including representative systems can be found in [20]. The next section presents our retrieval requirements analysis of image application areas to establish a taxonomy for image attributes and to identify generic retrieval classes.

3. Requirements Analysis of Application Areas

A first step toward deriving a generic image data model is to identify and perform requirements analysis of the retrieval needs of a *class* of domains that seem to exhibit similar retrieval characteristics. Toward this goal, the application areas that we have studied to establish various types of attributes and retrieval are: Art Galleries and Museums, Interior Design, Architectural Design, Real Estate Marketing, and Face Information Retrieval. All these application areas are characterized by the need for flexible and efficient retrieval of archived images. Furthermore, from the perspective of the end users, image processing and image retrieval are two orthogonal issues. To facilitate the description of the individual application retrieval requirements using a consistent terminology, we first informally define some more terms. It should be noted that, however, the following terminology is established only after studying the retrieval requirements of the application domains.

3.1 A Taxonomy for Image Attributes

We begin by introducing the terminology associated with image attributes. A taxonomy for image attributes is shown in Figure 3.1. Image attributes are classified into two broad categories: objective attributes and semantic attributes. Objective attributes are further classified into two subcategories:

meta attributes and logical attributes. The attributes of an image that are derived externally and do not depend on the contents of an image are referred to as *meta attributes*[1]. These may include attributes such as the date of image acquisition, image identification number, and the modality of the imaging device, image magnification, among others. For example, the above meta attributes are used as the primary search parameters to locate relevant LANDSAT images to buyers' needs, at EROS data center. It is through these meta attributes we wish to model those characteristics of an image that relate the image with external "world." Intuitively, an image-object is a semantic entity contained in the image which is meaningful in the application domain. For example, in interior design domain, various furniture and decorative items in an image constitute the image-objects. At the physical representation (e.g., bitmap, see Sect. 4) level, an image-object is defined as a subset of the image pixels. Meta attributes that apply to the entire image are referred to as *image meta attributes* and the meta attributes that apply to constituent objects in an image are called *image-object meta attributes.*

The attributes that are used to describe the properties of an image viewed either as an integral entity or as a collection of constituent objects are referred to as *logical attributes.* In the former case they are referred to as *image logical attributes* while in the latter case they are named *image-object logical attributes.* Compared to semantic attributes (discussed below), logical attributes are more precise and do not require the domain expertise either to identify or to quantify them in new image instances. Furthermore, logical attributes are different from meta attributes in that the former are derivable directly from the image itself. Logical attributes manifest the properties of an image and its constituent objects at various levels of abstraction. For example, in real estate marketing domain, a house may be described by attributes such as number of bedrooms, total floor area, total heating area. These are image logical attributes since they describe the properties of the house image as a single conceptual entity. In contrast, attributes such as the shape, perimeter, area, ceiling and sill heights, number of doors and windows, accessories and amenities of a living room constitute the image-object logical attributes.

Simply stated, semantic attributes are those attributes that are used to describe the high-level domain concepts that the images manifest. Specification of semantic attributes often involves some subjectivity, imprecision, and/or uncertainty. Subjectivity arises due to differing view points of the users about various domain aspects. Difficulties in the measurement and specification of image features lead to imprecision. The following description further illustrates the imprecision associated with semantic attributes. In many image database application domains users prefer to express some semantic attributes using an ordinal scale though the underlying representation of these attributes is numeric. For example, in face image databases,

[1] This is similar to the concept of *media-instance* in [32], [31].

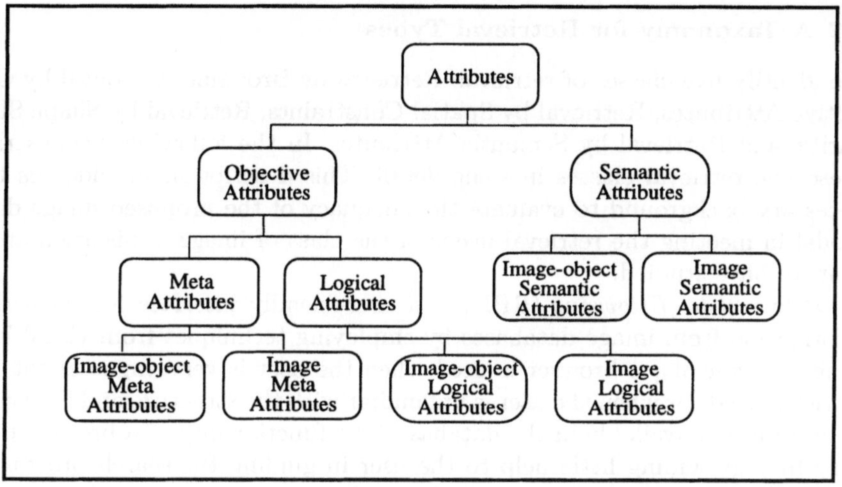

Fig. 3.1. A Taxonomy for Image Attributes

a user's query may specify one of the following values for an attribute that indicates nose length: *short*, *normal*, and *long*. The retrieval mechanism must map each value on the ordinal scale to a range on the underlying numeric scale. The design of this mapping function may be based on domain semantics and/or statistical properties of this feature over all the images currently stored in the database. Uncertainty is introduced because of the vagueness in the retrieval needs of a user. The use of semantic attributes in a query forces the retrieval system to deal with domain-dependent semantics and possibly differing interpretations of these semantics by the retrieval users. Semantic attributes can be identified in a semi-automated fashion using Personal Construct Theory [10], [27]. Semantic attributes may be synthesized by applying user-perceived transformations/mappings on meta and logical attributes of an image. A semantic attribute may be best thought of as the *consequent* part of a rule – the meta and logical attributes constitute the *antecedent* part of the rule. Thus, these transformations can be conveniently realized using a rule-base. Subjectivity and uncertainty in some semantic attributes may be resolved through user interaction/learning during query specification or processing [21], [25]. Thus the meaning and the method of deriving semantic attributes in a domain may vary from one user to another user. It is through these semantic attributes that the proposed unified model [17] captures domain semantics that vary from domain to domain as well as from user to user within the same domain. Semantic attributes pertaining to the whole image are named *image semantic attributes* whereas those that pertain to the constituent image objects are named *image-object semantic attributes.* In the following section, we provide a taxonomy for retrieval types.

3.2 A Taxonomy for Retrieval Types

We identify five classes of retrieval: Retrieval by Browsing, Retrieval by Objective Attributes, Retrieval by Spatial Constraints, Retrieval by Shape Similarity, and Retrieval by Semantic Attributes. In the following, we describe these five retrieval classes in some detail. This description provides us the necessary background to evaluate the adequacy of the proposed image data model in meeting the retrieval needs of the class of image application areas that we have studied.

Retrieval by BRowsing (RBR) is a user-friendly interface for retrieving information from image databases by employing techniques from visual languages. Typically, a browser is used when the user is very vague about his retrieval needs or when the user is unfamiliar with the structure and the types of information available in the database. The functionality of a browser may vary from providing little help to the user in guiding the search process to sophisticated filtering controls to effectively constrain the search space. It should be noted that, usually, advanced browsers are integrated with other types of retrieval schemes to constrain the search space. In this sense, browsing can also be thought of as an implementation technique for realizing other types of retrieval schemes. Browsing may be performed either on the actual physical images or on the "thumbnail" images[2].

In *Retrieval by Objective Attributes* (ROA), a query is formulated using meta attributes, logical attributes, or a combination of these attribute types. ROA is similar to the retrieval in conventional databases using SQL (Structured Query Language). Retrieval is based on perfect match on the attribute values.

Retrieval by Spatial Constraints (RSC) facilitates a class of queries that are based on relative spatial relationships among the objects in an image. In RSC queries, spatial relationships may span a broad spectrum ranging from directional relationships to adjacency, overlap, and containment involving a pair of objects or multiple objects. We partition the RSC queries into two categories: those that require retrieving all those database images that satisfy as many desired spatial relationships indicated in the query as possible and, those that require retrieving only those database images that precisely satisfy all the spatial relationships specified in the query image. The former are referred to as the *relaxed* RSC queries and the latter are referred to as *strict* RSC queries. When the number of objects involved in a query are few, then it may not be cumbersome to explicitly specify the desired spatial relationships. When this is not the case, a RSC query can be specified elegantly by borrowing techniques from visual languages. Under this scheme, the user specifies a query by placing the icons corresponding to the domain objects in a special window called the *sketch pad window* (see Figure 8.1 in Section 8.1.2).

[2] Thumbnail representation of an image is a low-resolution image with just enough resolution to reveal sufficient information content on display for the users to assess the image's relevance to their retrieval need.

The sketch pad window provides both the graphic icons of the domain objects and the necessary tools for selecting and placing these graphic icons for composing an RSC query. The spatial relationships among the icons in the sketch pad window implicitly indicate the desired spatial relationships among the domain objects in the images to be retrieved. For *relaxed* RSC queries, a function that provides a ranking of all the database images based on spatial similarity is desired. For *strict* RSC queries, however, spatial similarity functions are not appropriate. Rather an algorithm is required that provides a yes/no type of response. Though the algorithms for these two classes of RSC queries are different, however, the sketch pad window can be used as the query specification scheme in both the cases.

Retrieval by Shape Similarity (RSS) facilitates a class of queries that are based on the shapes of domain objects in an image. The Sketch pad window is enhanced to provide tools for the user to sketch domain objects. The user typically specifies an RSS query by sketching shapes of domain objects in the sketch pad window and expects the system to retrieve those images in the database that contain the domain objects whose shape is similar to those of the sketched objects. It should be noted that the combination of RSC and RSS queries is quite useful in medical imaging domain [24].

In *Retrieval by Semantic Attributes* (RSA), a query is specified in terms of the domain concepts from the user's perspective. The user specifies an exemplar image and expects the system to retrieve all those images in the database that are conceptually/semantically similar to the exemplar image. An exemplar image may be specified by assigning semantic attributes to the image and/or its constituent objects in the sketch pad window or by simply providing a set of semantic attributes in textual form.

The functionality of *Retrieval by BRowsing* in the proposed framework is two fold: to familiarize new or casual database users with the database schema and to act as information filter to other generic retrieval classes. A standard relational database query language such as ANSI standard SQL can be used to implement ROA. RSC, RSS, and RSA fundamentally affect the data model and the query language for image databases. Since it is not possible to explicitly store all the spatial relationships among the objects in every image in the database, the image data model must provide mechanisms for modeling spatial relationships in such a way that it enables the dynamic materialization of spatial relationships rather than explicitly storing and retrieving them. Robust shape representation and similarity ranking schemes are essential to support RSS queries. Techniques for modeling semantic attributes from individual user's perspective should also be an integral part of any image data model to incorporate RSA. It sh ould be recognized that it may be required to combine any of the above retrieval schemes in specifying a general query. Having established the terminology for the types of attributes and retrieval, next we describe the retrieval requirements of five image application domains in the following subsections.

3.3 Art Galleries and Museums

With the recent impressive advances in storage media technology, there is a strong trend toward capturing and storing various forms of Visual Art exhibits in electronic form. These art forms include Paintings, Sculpture, Architecture, and Minor Arts. Semantic attributes such as artistic styles, artistic principles, and the themes the art portrays are most frequently used in retrieving the various art forms[3]. This type of retrieval is modeled naturally as RSA. Furthermore, meta and image logical attributes such as artist's name, place of origin, chronology, civilization, historical context, materials, and tools and techniques used in the construction of the art forms are also used in the retrieval process. ROA is the obvious choice for implementing this type of retrieval need. RSS is also frequently used to retrieve paintings that consists of objects with the specified shape. RSA implemented using a browser (i.e., RSA coupled with RBR) is the preferred retrieval scheme of naive and casual users. Meta and image logical attributes are also very useful in making the browser even more constrained. Expert users prefer RSA and specify an exemplar image by a set of semantic attributes in textual form. As with naive and casual users, a query is made more specific by adding meta and image logical attributes. There seems to be no need for RSC queries in this domain.

3.4 Interior Design

Interior Designers are primarily concerned with spatially configuring furniture and decorative items to enhance the functional utility and esthetic value of various types of rooms in the buildings. We limit our retrieval requirements analysis to only the 2D aspects such as the floor and wall layout designs. For example, in dealing with floor layouts, quite often an expert desires to retrieve the floor layout designs in the archive that are spatially similar to a floor design that the expert is currently working on. Interior designers are also interested in retrieving those layout designs that are translation, scale, and/or rotational variants of a given design. It is easy to see that RSC models such a retrieval requirement. Also, more frequently there is a need for retrieval based on the image- object attributes which can be modeled by using ROA. Image-object attributes, for example, include furniture class, manufacturer, dimensions, weight, color, among others. RSC is often used in conjunction with ROA.

In this domain, semantic attributes are essentially implied by the spatial configuration of the domain objects. In this sense, RSC and RSA are considered to be the same. A sketch pad window is used for the specification of RSC query whereas RSA query is specified through semantic attributes expressed in textual form. Naive users are very uncommon in this domain.

[3] Personal communication, 1992, Prof. Mary McBride, School of Art and Architecture, University of Southwestern Louisiana, Lafayette, LA, U.S.A.

Casual users are often the students in the interior design courses. Retrieval performed by the domain experts is rather the rule than an exception.

3.5 Architectural Design

Architectural Designers deal with a broad spectrum of activities ranging from the conceptual design through cost estimation and 3D visualization of the buildings. However, we are interested in the retrieval requirements of those aspects of the architectural design that promote the reusability of the existing designs. From this perspective, the retrieval requirements of the architectural design are very similar to those of the interior design. Image-objects are the various rooms in a building and their attributes include dimensions, number of doors and windows, sill and ceiling heights, floor area, and amenities. Image attributes include the type of the building, building style, number of rooms, total floor area, and heating space, among others. Meta attributes include the architect's name, company name, date of design, and the file name under which the design is stored. Often RSC and ROA are combined in a complementary way in the query specification. The types of users are same as those in the interior design domain.

3.6 Real Estate Marketing

In huge metropolitan areas having large number of houses for sale, it is almost beyond the abilities of a human being to remember the spatial configuration of various functional and esthetic units in all the houses. Realtors receive information on the houses for sale through a service known as *multiple listing service* and this information does not contain any details on the floor plan design. Often, Realtors may be able to display from a video disk, an image of the house taken from a vantage point. This only provides a general feeling for the quality of the neighborhood and the exterior of the house. However, it has been noted that some home buyers prefer a house with a bedroom having orientation facing east so that waking up to the morning sun is a psychologically pleasant experience. Yet some other people may prefer certain orientation for specific units in the house based on cultural and religious backgrounds. Though this type of retrieval need has existed in the domain for sometime, none of the current systems seem to be providing for such a type of retrieval. If RSC were to be available as an integral part of the retrieval system, then Realtors can quickly identify only those houses that closely match the spatial preferences of the potential buyers. Image-object attributes include all those that are specified for Architectural Design domain as well as additional attributes such as floor and wall covering types. Image attributes are essentially the same as those in the Architectural Design domain. Meta attributes include home owner's name, subdivision name, the type of neighborhood, distances to various services such as Schools and Airport, and the cost of the home. As in the case of Architectural Design, often, RSC and ROA are combined in a complementary way in the query specification. ROA by itself is also used quite frequently. Information provided by the multiple listing service is considered proprietary and as such the querying is limited to only expert users.

3.7 Face Information Retrieval

Law enforcement and criminal investigation agencies typically maintain large image databases of human faces. Such databases consists of faces of those individuals who have either committed crimes or suspected of involved in criminal activities in the past. Retrieval from these databases is performed in the context of the following activities: matching Composite Drawings, Bann File searching, and Ranking for Photo Lineup.

Composite drawings are used in identifying a potential suspect from an image database. The victim or an eye witness of a crime describes the facial features of the perpetrator of the crime to a forensic composite technician. There may be considerable imprecision and uncertainty associated with this description. The forensic composite technician then sketches a face from these descriptions. The retrieval system is expected to display those images in the database that match the sketch. *Bann File* searching is performed when a (suspected) criminal at hand does not disclose his legitimate identification information to enable a law enforcement/criminal investigator to retrieve the criminal's past history. Under such circumstances, the investigator visually scans the criminal's face to extract some features and uses them in performing the retrieval. In *Ranking for Photo Lineup*, person performing the retrieval provides a vague and often uncertain set of features of a face and expects the system to provide a ranking of those faces in the database that match the feature descriptions. Often, this type of retrieval is performed in an exploratory manner by emphasizing a combination of prominent features during a retrieval and then emphasizing a different combination of features during subsequent retrievals to assist the investigation process.

Retrieval involving matching of Composite Drawings can be viewed as RSA since considerable imprecision and uncertainty is associated with the attributes used in the retrieval. In Bann File searching, the person performing the retrieval has "live" access to the features of a face to be retrieved. Therefore, there is very little imprecision and uncertainty associated with the specification of the attributes. However, the assignment of a symbolic or a numeric value to a semantic attribute may vary from one user to another user. For example, assignment of a value *wide* to the semantic attribute *nose width* may considerably vary amongst the retrieval users. Hence, Bann File searching can also be viewed as RSA. Finally, in Ranking for Photo Lineup, the person performing the retrieval uses some features about which he is very certain and also other features with which a great deal of imprecision and uncertainty may be associated. In this sense, Ranking for Photo Lineup can be considered as both ROA and RSA complementing each other. The notion of logical representations assume a central role in the proposed image data model and are introduced in the following section.

4. Logical Representations

An image representation scheme is chosen based on the intended purpose of an image database system. The primary objective of a representation scheme may be to efficiently store and display images without any concern for the interpretation of their contents or to provide support for operations that are essential in an application. There are various formats available for the former case such as GIF and TIFF [4]. For the latter case, most of the current representations are at the level of pixels [36], which we refer to as *physical representations* or *physical level representations*. Among the physical level representations, *raster* and *vector* formats are ubiquitous.

There is always a trade-off between the level of abstraction involved in the representation of an image and the operations and inferencing it facilitates. If a representation is very low, such as raster representation, virtually no query can be processed without extensive processing on the image. On the other hand, if a representation is somewhat abstracted away from the physical level representation, then it lends itself to efficient processing of certain types of queries. We refer to the latter type of representations as *logical representations* or *logical level representations*. Logical representations are classified into two sub-categories: logical attributes (discussed in Sect. 3.1) and logical structures. Logical attributes are viewed as simple attributes whereas the logical structures are viewed as complex attributes. When there is no need for any distinction between the two, we simply use the term logical representation. Logical structures play a central role in the efficient processing of queries against the image database. As an example, suppose we want to ascertain whether or not two objects intersect. Two objects do not intersect unless the corresponding Minimum Bounding Rectangles (MBR) intersect. MBR is a logical structure (discussed in Appendix A.) which can be efficiently computed and serves as a necessary (but insufficient) condition for the objects to intersect.

It should be noted that while there is only one physical level representation, there can be several logical representations associated with an image. Also, it is useful to perceive the logical representations as spanning a spectrum with physical level representation being situated at one end of the spectrum. At the other end of the spectrum, we have the logical image that is an extremely abstracted version of the physical image. In between, we can conceive several layers of logical representations and the layers at lower levels embody more accurate representations of the image than the layers at the higher levels. The layers at the higher levels provide a coarser representation by suppressing several insignificant and irrelevant details (vis-a-vis certain class of queries). The relationships among the logical level representations are not completely hierarchical. Some highly abstracted logical representations may be derived directly from the physical level representation while others may be derived from other moderately abstracted logical representations in the hierarchy. In Appendix A., we briefly discuss the following logical structures: Minimum Bounding Rectangle, Plane Sweep Technique, Spatial Orientation Graph, $\Theta\Re$-String, 2D-String, and Skeletons. In the following section, we summarize the limitations of the existing data models/systems for image retrieval and provide the motivation for the proposed data model.

5. Motivations for the Proposed Data Model

Initial proposals for managing image data have resulted in extracting attribute information from the images and treating them as formatted data within the framework of relational database systems. A major problem with the attribute based retrieval is that the user queries are limited to the predetermined simple (or scalar) attributes and hence the users may experience difficulties in precisely formulating their queries. Recent attempts to improve this condition were aimed primarily at storing the geometric and attribute information about the images as formatted data in relational tables. These approaches force the user to view images as fragmented structures and thus introduces *semantic gap* between the user's conceptualization of a query and the query that is actually specified to the system. Even in the subsequent proposals that treated images as complex and unformatted data by introducing abstract data type facility, the image data continued to be perceived as secondary in importance to the formatted data that is traditionally managed by database systems. Approaches to image retrieval advanced by the image interpretation researchers involve formulating queries with features that are often too primitive to the end users.

Until recently, almost all the efforts at developing a query language for querying image databases were based on either the query language SQL or the query language QBE (Query By Example). These approaches to querying image databases are unsatisfactory since the query specification schemes used are not natural for querying about image data. These languages assume that the user is familiar with the database schema. However, the schema that is presented to the image database user represents a fragmented view of the image and is not close to the user's view of the image. Moreover, there are several classes of queries that can be posed against an image database and each query class may require a specification scheme that is most natural to its intrinsic nature. Despite recent advances in the database technology, CAD systems continue to use file-oriented representations and GIS rely on ad hoc database systems [30]. This situation is attributable primarily to the inherent limitations of the current data models and database systems to cope with the complexity of image data representation, diversity in the image query specification techniques, and range of domain specific operations required. Thus, most of the proposed approaches to the image retrieval problem have originated from the needs of specific applications and are thus limited in their applicability to a wide range of domains.

As will be seen later, the notion of logical representation of images assumes a central role in the efficient processing of image queries especially in very large image databases. However, the logical representations have not been fully and coherently explored and integrated into the image database systems. Various logical representations can be incorporated into the query processing strategy for efficient retrieval. Moreover, if the logical representations are computed and stored as a part of persistent image data, the query processing efficiency can be further increased.

To respond to some of these problems, we have proposed a unified framework/system for retrieval in image databases [17]. The framework provides a general image data representation and retrieval model in the sense that it can be easily adapted to any one of a *class* of application domains discussed in Sect. 3. The framework employs several logical representations for efficient query processing. Chosen logical representations of an image are computed at the time of its entry into the image database system and they are stored as persistent data. The system provides five types of retrieval discussed in Sect. 3.2.

Since the system facilitates various types of retrieval, several query specification schemes are provided so that, for a specific type of retrieval, a scheme that is most natural to that type can be (automatically) chosen. These query specification schemes are made available to the user under a consistent and uniform user interface. Next section describes our proposed framework for image retrieval.

6. An Overview of AIR Framework

In this section, we introduce a framework which addresses retrieval requirements of image application domains discussed in Sect. 3. We refer to this framework as Adaptive Image Retrieval (AIR) system. The term "adaptive" above is used to mean that the proposed framework can easily be adapted to a class of image retrieval applications. Firstly, we present the semantic data model description of the AIR system in Sect. 6.1. In Sect. 6.2, we discuss the AIR architecture.

6.1 Data Model

The proposed data model is referred to as Adaptive Image Retrieval (AIR) data model. A semantic data model diagram of the AIR system is shown in Figure 6.1. Our diagram and the formalism of the constructs that we use in the diagram are based on the semantic data model proposed in [44]. The oval shape symbolizes the *abstract class* and is used to represent objects of interest in an application. The relationships between classes are indicated by *properties*. Moreover, the double-headed arrow represents *multi-valued property*; it is a set-valued functional relationship. The cardinality of a *multi-valued property* can be greater than or equal to one. As an example, has-image-physical-rep describes the relationship between the Image and Image-Base-Rep, and it is a *multi-valued property*. Hence, each instance of the Image class can correspond to one or more instances in the Image-Base-Rep class. In addition, a property may be mandatory. A *required property* indicates that the value set of the property must have at least one value. The letter "R" is used in our diagram to indicate that the property is required. For example, the has-image-physical-rep is a *required property*; thus, an instance in the Image class must have at least one corresponding instance in the Image-Base-Rep class. Furthermore, the model is extended by the addition of a new modeling construct, referred to as *IsAbstractionOf*. *IsAbstractionOf* construct models transformations between image representations. Informally, Class1 *IsAbstractionOf* Class2 indicates that Class1 is derived from Class2. Specifically, Class1 represents Class2 at a higher level of abstraction and the semantics of the abstraction is possibly domain-dependent (indicated by the symbol // in the diagram). For example, in our model, Image-Logical-Rep class *IsAbstractionOf* Image-Base-Rep class and is derived by applying various domain-dependent image processing and interpretation techniques.

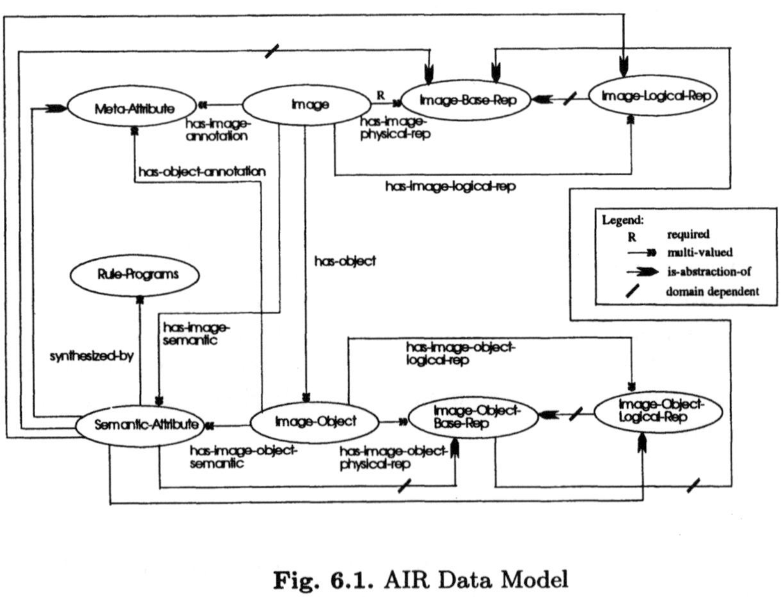

Fig. 6.1. AIR Data Model

There are two kinds of transformations which occur in the AIR model. The first transformation occurs when the unprocessed or raw images and image-objects are transformed to the logical representations, such as Spatial Orientation Graph, $\Theta\Re$-String. Another transformation involves the derivation of the semantic attributes. In the latter case, a set of user-defined rule programs is applied to meta attributes, logical attributes, and/or unprocessed images to derive the semantic attributes.

6.1.1 Image and Image-Objects. The AIR model facilitates the modeling of an image and the image-objects in the image. An image may contain many image-objects and the notion of an image-object is domain-dependent. The relevant image-objects are determined by the users at the time of image insertion into the database. For example, an image of a building floor plan may include various rooms of the building as the image-objects. As another example, an image of human face may include eyes, nose, mouth, ears, and jaw as image-objects.

6.1.2 Image-Base Representation and Image-Object-Base Representation. The Image-Base-Rep and Image-Object-Base-Rep provide persistent storage for raw or unprocessed images and image-objects. An image must have an Image-Base-Rep; thus, *has-image-physical-rep*[4] is a required property. Additionally, in many image application domains, multiple unprocessed representations are often provided to facilitate the handling of complex, 3-D phenomena. As an example, in biological studies involving microscopic images, multiple images of the same scene are produced at various magnifications. In such instances, the system may provide the same representation across all the magnifications of an image or may store each image magnification in a format that is intrinsically efficient for the types of features that are extracted at that magnification. Image-Object-Base-Rep facilitates the extraction of image-object features. Recall that we have intuitively defined an image-object as a semantic entity of an image that is meaningful in the application domain (Sect. 3).

Furthermore, the Image-Base-Rep and Image-Object-Base-Rep also provide storage structures for logical attributes. As mentioned previously, logical attributes manifest the properties of an image and its constituent objects at various levels of abstraction. Once these properties are abstracted, they are physically stored.

6.1.3 Image Logical Representation (ILR) and Image-Object Logical Representation (OLR). Modeling of logical attributes is similar to the data modeling in conventional DBMS. ILR and OLR model various logical attributes as well as logical structures of images and image-objects, respectively. In other words, the ILR describes the properties of an image viewed as an integral entity, while the OLR describes the properties of an image as a collection of constituent objects. The most important aspect of the ILR layer is the

[4] This is similar to the concept of *framerep* in [32], [31].

representation of an image using logical structures, such as Sweepline, $\Theta\Re$-String, for implicitly modeling the spatial/topological relationships. These representations are denoted as Image-Logical-Rep in Figure 6.1. Geometry-based logical structures, as shown in [19], [16], at the image level are used to model spatial/topological relationships among the image-objects. These structures effectively embody the requisite information to dynamically materialize spatial relationships among the objects in an image. ILR layer also models various properties of an image that are derived external to the image contents (i.e., meta attributes).

OLR for a new image is derived from the Object-Base-Rep by using automated domain-dependent image interpretation techniques, manual interpretation through human involvement, or a combination of both. However, once the image-objects are identified, their logical representations and those image-object attributes that can be derived from the object geometry are automatically generated. Geometry-based logical representation of image-objects include area, perimeter, centroid, MBR, among others. For example, a region in an image can be represented by its boundary or by its interior. Efficient algorithms for computing region features such as centroid and perimeter are available based on the boundary representation. Interior representation of a region may be efficient for computing certain other features, such as surface orientation. This kind of image-object representations are denoted as Image-Object-Logical-Rep in Figure 6.1. Image-object attributes that are not based on image-object geometry may include, for example, type, color, weight, and manufacturer of a piece of furniture in the interior design domain.

6.1.4 Semantic Attributes and Rule-Programs. The richness of the information content in the images leads to different interpretations of the same image by different user groups depending upon their information retrieval requirements and the level of the domain knowledge possessed. For example, the same image may be interpreted differently by novice and expert users. Semantic relationships between image-objects are explicitly modeled through *set-of*, *is-a* (generalization), and *composed-of* (aggregation) relationships. In addition, semantic attributes may be abstracted from the Image-Base-Rep, Image-Object-Base-Rep, Image-Logical-Rep, or Image-Object-Logical-Rep. Some semantic attributes may also be abstracted from the meta attributes.

The semantic attributes capture the high-level domain concepts that the image and image-objects manifest. A set of Rule-Programs is used to synthesize the semantic attributes. The Rule-Programs provide the transformation process at the semantic level. Semantic attributes can be derived by applying user-defined transformations on the Image-Base-Rep, Image-Object-Base-Rep, meta attributes, logical representations either in an automated fashion or with considerable human involvement.

6.1.5 Meta Attributes. As mentioned earlier, both image and image-objects may have meta attributes, which are derived externally and do not depend on the contents of the image or image-objects. For example, the meta attributes may include information such as the date of image acquisition, image identification number, or image magnification level. It is required that meta image-object attributes, for example, the cost of a piece of furniture object, be assigned through human involvement or through a table look up.

6.2 The Proposed DBMS Architecture

Through our observation of the AIR data model, the AIR framework can be divided into three layers: Physical Level Representation (PLR), Logical Level Representation (LLR), and Semantic or External Level Representation (SLR). The relationships between the layers is as shown in Figure 6.2. We refer to this three-layer architecture as Adaptive Image Retrieval (AIR) architecture.

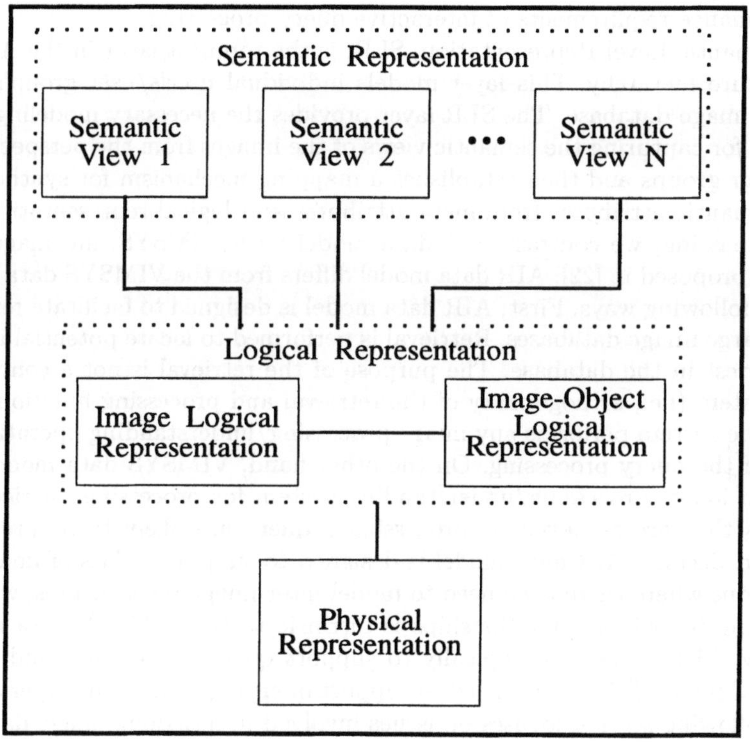

Fig. 6.2. AIR Architecture

The physical level representation, PLR, is at the lowest level in the AIR architecture. PLR layer consists of the Image-Base-Rep and the Image-Object-Base Rep classes. Hence, PLR layer provides persistent storage for unprocessed or raw images. Immediately above the PLR layer is the logical level representation, LLR. Image-Object Logical Representation (OLR) and Image Logical Representation (ILR) comprise the LLR. It should be emphasized that most commercial systems operate at the physical level representation and build ad hoc logical representations using domain-dependent procedures for answering certain types of queries. The ad hoc logical representations are transient and vanish as soon as the query is processed and the whole process starts all over when a similar query arrives subsequently. To avoid the exorbitant computational cost involved in building these logical representations repeatedly, some systems precompute and store important results that can be derived from such logical representations. However, it would simply be too voluminous and uneconomical to precompute and explicitly store all such data of interest. Hence, for practical and large image databases, multiple logical representations that are judiciously chosen are necessary to meet the performance requirements of interactive query processing.

Semantic Level Representation, SLR, is the topmost layer in the AIR architecture hierarchy. This layer models individual user's/user group's view of the image database. The SLR layer provides the necessary modeling techniques for capturing the semantic views of the images from the perspective of the user groups and then establishes a mapping mechanism for synthesizing the semantic attributes from meta attributes and logical representations.

In passing, we contrast AIR data model with VIMSYS, an image data model proposed in [22]. AIR data model differs from the VIMSYS data model in the following ways. First, AIR data model is designed to facilitate retrieval from large image databases. Retrieval is performed to locate potential images of interest in the database. The purpose of the retrieval is not a concern to the system (i.e., orthogonality of the retrieval and processing functions) nor does the system performs any image processing/understanding operations as part of the query processing. On the other hand, VIMSYS data model couples an image processing/understanding system for processing queries. The images that are retrieved by processing a query are likely to be processed further. Second, AIR data model is designed to support a class of image applications where there is no need to model inter-image relationships, whereas modeling inter-image relationships is intrinsic to the VIMSYS data model. Finally, AIR is designed typically to support querying by naive and casual users while VIMSYS is designed to support querying by domain expert users. The following section focuses on issues involved in designing image database systems for applications based on the AIR model.

7. Image Database Systems Based on AIR Model

We have implemented a prototype image database system on a UNIX workstation based on the AIR model. The underlying database management system for this implementation is POSTGRES [41]. The set of logical structures featured by the prototype are those that are essential for efficiently supporting the class of image retrieval applications described in Sect. 3. Furthermore, additional logical structures can be accommodated using the extensibility feature of our prototype implementation.

To develop image retrieval applications using database systems based on AIR model, images must be first processed to extract useful information and the latter are then modeled and utilized. In the AIR framework, the process to obtain useful information is modeled by *IsAbstractionOf* construct[5], and this information include image-objects, semantic attributes, and image logical representation (i.e., both logical attributes and logical structures). Image-objects are the *meaningful entities* that constitute an image (they can be viewed as "images within an image"). Each application typically defines its own set of meaningful entities and has its own interpretation of these entities. Therefore, image-objects are domain-dependent. For our current prototype, a user-system interaction is required to extract image-objects. For example, in face i nformation retrieval application, the designer must initially establish meaningful objects (such as eyes, nose, mouth, ears, etc.) in a human face. In most cases, the image-objects will be further processed to obtain logical and semantic attributes.

The AIR model captures the domain-dependent semantics associated with an image using the notion of "semantic attributes." The semantic attributes themselves and the methods for quantifying these attributes in image instances is domain-dependent. For example, in face information retrieval application, assignment of one of the values in the set {short, normal, long} to a semantic attribute named *"nose length"* is domain-dependent. However, AIR model provides a set of "rule programs" for applications to abstract the domain-dependent data semantics, which may be automatically derived or given by a domain expert. Algorithms to generate these rules (in case of automatic derivation) are built into the data model and can be applied to any image retrieval application.

The logical structure representation (e.g., minimum bounding rectangle, plane sweep, $\Theta\Re$-String) is the spatial/topological abstraction. It provides suitable data structures to represent the entities (viz., image and image-object), so that these entities can be easily managed and displayed. It also provides a set of methods associated with each data structure so that the structure is encapsulated and easily manipulated[6]. It is important to note that both the data structures and the associated methods are domain-independent. They are provided in our current AIR prototype as generic constructs (viz., classes in terms of object-oriented paradigm). Figure 7.1 illustrates our concept of logical structure representation for both the image and image-objects.

[5] IsAbstractionOf construct is unique to AIR model and formalism associated with other constructs used in the AIR model are as given in [44].

[6] This is the abstract data type (ADT) concept.

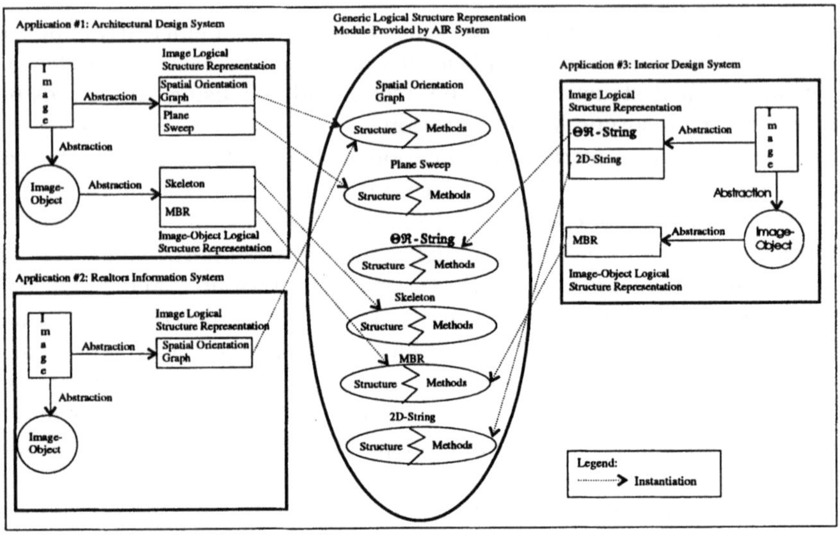

Fig. 7.1. Application-independent Logical Structure Representation in AIR

The *generic logical structure representation* module shown in Figure 7.1 is the component of the AIR system that contains all the application-independent logical structure representation. Each logical structure is modeled as a class which consists of a structure and a set of associated methods to manipulate the structure. In the example shown in Figure 7.1, we consider six classes of generic logical representations: Spatial Orientation Graph, Plane Sweep, $\Theta\Re$-String, Skeleton, Minimum Bounding Rectangle, and $2D$−String. Given an image, the structure to represent and methods to manipulate its (logical structures component of) image-logical representation (ILR) and image-object logical representation (OLR) can be instantiated from the generic logical structure representation. Through this instantiation, ILR and OLR become instances (viz., objects in terms of object-oriented paradigm) of the generic logical structure representation and both its structure and methods are inherited. Three applications are shown in the example: Architectural Design System, Realtors Information System, and Interior Design System. ILR and OLR of each of the three applications are instances of the generic logical structure representation; therefore, they are constructed out of generic data structures and manipulated through generic methods.

In summary, the data abstraction process in AIR can be possibly domain-dependent or domain-independent. We have discussed in this section some of the domain-independent constructs identified to be important for image database systems. Our current prototype implementation of the AIR model supports these domain-independent constructs and facilitates incorporating new constructs through its extensibility feature. In the following section, we describe the development of two image retrieval applications using our prototype implementation of the AIR Framework.

8. Image Retrieval Applications Based on the Prototype Implementation of AIR Framework

We have developed two image retrieval applications. The first application is a database system for real estate marketing and the intended users of this system are Realtors. We refer to this system as Realtors Information System and is described in Sect. 8.1. The second application is a face information retrieval system for campus law enforcement and the intended users of this system are police officers. This system is referred to as Face Information Retrieval System and is described in Sect. 8.2.

8.1 Realtors Information System

As noted in Sect. 3.6, current real estate marketing systems (e.g., multiple listing service system) are designed essentially to manage meta and simple logical attributes. Image data is treated as formatted data. We also observed that there is a need for Retrieval by Spatial Constraints queries in this domain. Furthermore, Retrieval by Spatial Constraints and Retrieval by Objective Attributes queries are often combined in a complementary way in querying the database. Therefore, the primary objective of the Realtors information system is to demonstrate the Retrieval by Spatial Constraints feature in conjunction with the Retrieval by Objective Attributes feature of the AIR framework. First, we describe the system design and implementation followed by query specification and processing.

8.1.1 System Design and Implementation. A set of 60 floor plans were selected from a residential dwellings design book. These plans are scanned and stored in digital form and constitute our database. Image meta attributes include style, price, lot size, lot type, lot topography, school district, subdivision name, and age of the house. Image logical attributes include number of bedrooms, number of bathrooms, total floor area, total heated area, foundation type, roof pitch, and utility type. The image-objects in this domain are various functional and esthetic units of the house such as bedrooms, porch. Dimensions and shapes of various image-objects constitute the image-object logical attributes. Only one logical representation (Spatial Orientation Graph) is required for the floor plan images. Of the two categories of RSC queries, only *relaxed* Retrieval by Spatial Constraints (i.e., retrieval by spatial similarity) queries are meaningful in this application.

8.1.2 Query Specification and Processing. Retrieval by Spatial Constraints queries are conveniently specified using a sketch pad. The query is specified by first spatially configuring the icons corresponding to the image-objects (Figure 8.1) and then assigning meta and logical attributes to these icons. The query is first processed by POSTGRES query processor as a Retrieval by Objective Attributes query by considering only the meta and logical attributes. The result is a set of database floor plans that satisfy all the meta and logical attributes specified in the query. Then the algorithm proposed in [19] is applied on this set of images to compute their spatial similarity with the query image. This application inherits Spatial Orientation Graph logical structure from our prototype implementation of AIR model (Figure 7.1). The images are then rank ordered based on the spatial similarity and are shown to the user using a browser (Figure 8.2).

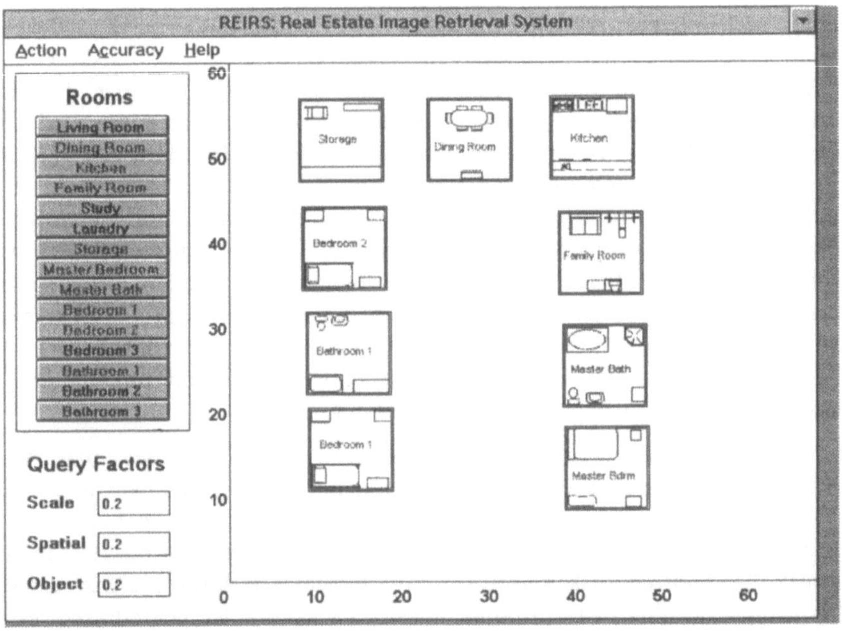

Fig. 8.1. Sketch Pad Window for Specifying RSC Queries

8.2 Face Information Retrieval System

Automated systems for human face identification and classification are useful in a multitude of application areas and the initial studies in this direction date back to last century. Samal and Iyengar provide a survey of work done in the automatic recognition and analysis of human faces [40].

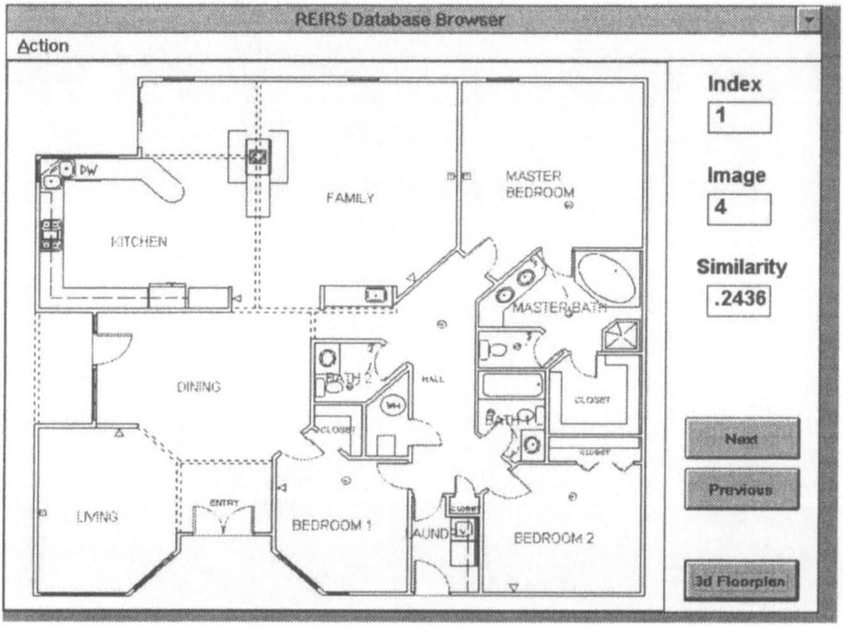

Fig. 8.2. Browser for Realtors Information System

8.2.1 System Design and Implementation. The primary objective of the face information retrieval system is to demonstrate Retrieval by Semantic Attributes feature of the AIR framework. The database consists of 93 human face images. Retrieval by Semantic Attributes is performed using the 19 semantic attributes (Figure 8.3). These attributes are elicited from a domain expert using Personal Construct Theory [10], [27].

8.2.2 Query Specification and Processing. Figure 8.3 shows Retrieval by Semantic Attributes query specification window of the prototype. A user specifies a Retrieval by Semantic Attributes query by selecting semantic attributes corresponding to a (small) subset of the 19 semantic attributes. The query is processed using the algorithm described in [21]. The window that is used to elicit user relevance feedback in the form of preference relation is shown in Figure 8.4. The initial testing indicates that the this algorithm is able to find the relevant images to queries within few iterations. Currently, we are conducting controlled experimentation of the algorithm to quantify its retrieval quality. In the following section, we enumerate the research issues that arise in the AIR Framework and summarize our research contributions in this direction.

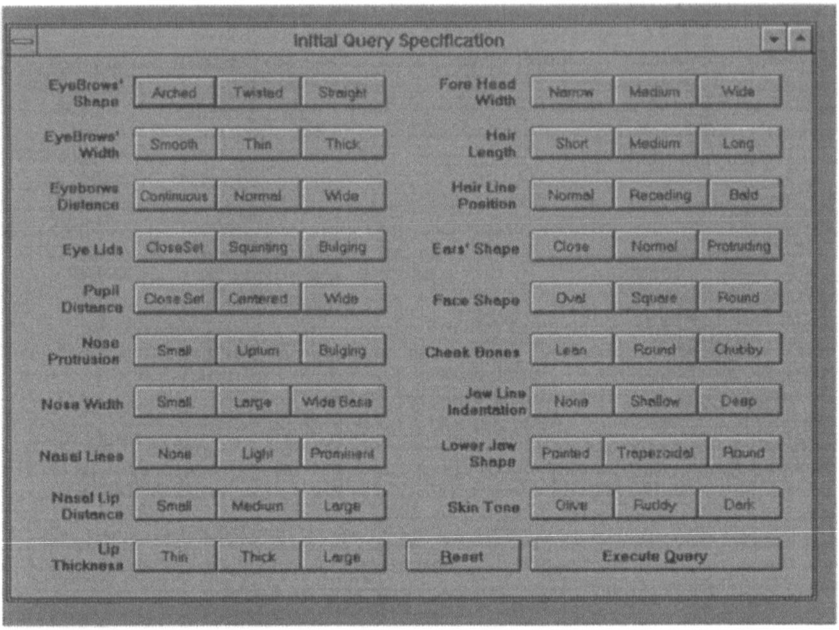

Fig. 8.3. RSA Query Specification Window

9. Research Issues in AIR Framework

We identify the following four major research issues in the context of AIR system: query language/interface, algorithms (based on logical representations) for processing Retrieval by Spatial Constraints (RSC) and Retrieval by Shape Similarity (RSS) queries, relevance feedback modeling and improving retrieval effectiveness, and tools for image database design. Sect. 9.1 briefly discusses the query interface design. Algorithms for RSC and RSS queries are discussed in Sect. 9.2. Relevance feedback modeling and its use in improving the retrieval effectiveness are discussed in Sect. 9.3. Personal Construct Theory (PCT) from the Clinical Psychology domain is outlined in Sect. 9.4 as a database design tool for eliciting semantic attributes.

9.1 Query Interface

Query language/interface for the AIR framework is essentially a sophisticated window-based graphical interface and we refer to this as the AIR Graphical Query Interface. It supports all the five classes of retrieval that we have introduced in Sect. 3.2. Query specification for each query class is based on schemes that are both natural and efficient for specifying queries in the class. However, all these specification schemes are uniformly integrated under

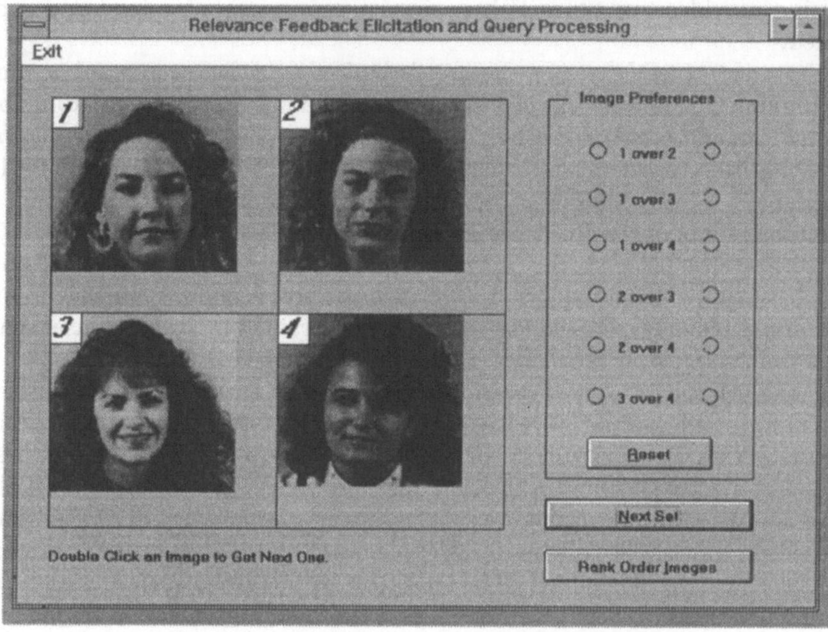

Fig. 8.4. User Preference Relation Specification

a windowing environment to provide a unified view of querying the image database. Retrieval strategies for Retrieval by Browsing and Retrieval by Objective Attributes have been intensely investigated in the recent years and these results have already been incorporated into several database systems. However, retrieval strategies for Retrieval by Spatial Constraints, Retrieval by Shape Similarity and Retrieval by Semantic Attributes are based on the algorithms and approaches that we have developed in [19], [21], [16], [25].

Retrieval by Browsing is designed primarily to provide the following functionality. First, it serves as a general query interface or as a gateway for the entire query subsystem. Second, it provides mechanisms for acquainting the new and casual users with the image database. Third, it provides limited querying based on non-semantic attributes. As a general query interface, Retrieval by Browsing provides options for choosing other types of retrieval. The facilities that Retrieval by Browsing provides for acquainting new and casual users with the database include a general on-line help facility, information on each of the image collections managed by the database system (e.g., interior designs, sculptures, fashion designs, paintings, etc.), and within an image collection information about various attributes. We assume that there is a unique identification (ID) number and optionally a symbolic name associated with each image. Also, there is an implicit logical ordering of images in the database and this ordering is implementation dependent. Retrieval by

Browsing provides two types of browsing/querying: unconstrained and constrained.

In *unconstrained browsing*, the user is limited to either sequential or random browsing of images. *Sequential browsing* allows a user to go from the "current" image to either the next or the previous image. *Random browsing* allows the user to select any image from the list of image ID numbers in the database. This is facilitated by displaying all the image ID numbers in a scrollable list box in the Retrieval by Browsing window. Once an image ID is selected from the list box, the browser displays the corresponding image and the values for predetermined attributes with the provision for inquiring about additional attributes. At anytime during unconstrained browsing, a user may switch from sequential browsing to random browsing and vice versa.

On the other hand, *constrained browsing* enables a user to specify queries by defining predicates on objective attributes and then logically combining these predicates. In specifying predicates on objective attributes, the user first selects an objective attribute, then an operator for the predicate, and finally a value for the objective attribute. Measurement of objective attributes may be based on any of the following scales: nominal, ordinal, interval, or ratio. Once an objective attribute (of an image or an image object) is chosen by the user, the system displays bounds (i.e., the minimum and the maximum values based on the actual images in the database) on that attribute provided that the attribute is measured using ordinal, interval, or ratio scale. The user then assigns a desired value for an attribute by indicating a position on the line joining the bounds for that attribute. However, specification of certain attributes such as color requires a method that involves interactively and visually composing a color by selecting three integer values for blue, green, and red components for the desired color (see Sect. 10.). If the objective attribute is measured on a nominal scale, the user assigns a value for that attribute by selecting one of the entries in a list box that contains various symbolic names comprising that nominal scale. Whenever a visual representation is possible for the specification of an attribute, that representation is always preferred over the textual representation. Options are provided to the user to switch from constrained browsing to unconstrained browsing and vice versa.

Once a predicate on an objective attribute is selected, it is added to a graphic pane within the Retrieval by Browsing window. The logical connectives *and*, *or* and *not* are used to connect these predicates in the graphic pane. Unlike SQL, the only operators allowed in formulating predicates on attributes are the relational operators (i.e., $<, \leq$, etc.). Retrieval strategies for implementing the browser are essentially those that are used for implementing a *subset* of SQL. A preprocessor translates a browser query into an SQL query.

Retrieval by Spatial Constraints queries are specified using the sketch pad window as discussed in Sect. 3.2. Specifying a Retrieval by Semantic Attributes query consists of selecting all the semantic attributes desired in a query. The procedure involved in specifying a semantic attribute is adapted from [23] and is as follows. First, the user selects a semantic attribute name from a list box. Immediately following this, three images from the database that contain this semantic attribute are displayed in an image pane. The image displayed at the left side of the image pane manifests one extreme value for the semantic attribute whereas the image displayed at the right side of the image pane manifests the other extreme value for the semantic attribute. The image displayed at the center of the image pane manifests the mean value of the semantic attribute. All the three images displayed are actual images in the database and the mean and extreme values are based on the image instances in the database. By observing the three images in the image pane, the user can visually see how the database images vary along this semantic attribute. By marking a position on the straight line that extends from the image on the left to the image on the right, the user can view an image in the database that manifests the semantic attribute to the degree indicated on the straight line. By experimentation, the user selects an appropriate position (thereby a value) on the line for the semantic attribute. The same procedure is repeated for selecting the other semantic attributes. When the user is very uncertain about which semantic attributes are suitable in specifying the (initial) query, an alternative query specification scheme is described in Sect. 8.2.2. Algorithms for Retrieval by Spatial Constraints and Retrieval by Shape Similarity queries are described in the next section.

9.2 Algorithms for RSC and RSS Queries

In [19], we have proposed an algorithm and a methodology for experimentally evaluating the performance of algorithms for retrieval by spatial similarity (i.e., relaxed RSC). The algorithm is robust in the sense that it can deal with scale, translation, and rotation variances in images. The proposed algorithm has quadratic time complexity in terms of the total number of objects in both the query and the database images. The retrieval results obtained by using the proposed algorithm are compared with the results obtained by using the algorithm of Lee et al. [29]. Lee et al.'s algorithm is based on a spatial data structure referred to as 2D-String and has exponential time complexity in terms of the total number of objects in the query image. Also, the proposed algorithm is contrasted with the algorithm of Chang & Lee [6]. Chang & Lee's algorithm is based on exhaustively enumerating and storing all the spatial relationships among objects in all the images in the database. M oreover, all the spatial relationships must be approximated to four directional and four diagonal relationships. Recently, we have developed a linear time algorithm for computing spatial similarity based on $\Theta\Re$-String representation [16]. An algorithm for spatial similarity in *3-D* image databases is reported in [18]. Currently, we are investigating algorithms for strict RSC queries (i.e., algorithms for adjacency, overlap, and containment). We are also developing algorithms for retrieval by shape similarity queries. Though shape representation and matching has been studied for quite some time by image interpretation researchers, the focus has been on exact matching. However, for image retrieval applications, we need algorithms that induce a rank ordering on the shapes in the database with respect to a query object shape.

9.3 Relevance Feedback Modeling and Improving Retrieval Effectiveness

As noted in Sect. 3.1, subjectivity, imprecision, and/or uncertainty are usually associated with the specification and interpretation of semantic attributes. Incomplete query specification and user relevance feedback elicitation on the (initial) retrieval results are used as a means to resolve the subjectivity and imprecision [21], [25]. The approach proposed in [21] is based on *preferences* and works as follows. First, a user specifies an (initial) query in terms of semantic attributes. The user may be uncertain about the accuracy or completeness of these attributes in precisely specifying his need. Second, the system retrieves and displays to the user a subset of the database images that exactly match the specified semantic attributes in the initial query. We denote this set of images as $\mathcal{F}$. Third, the system obtains user relevance preferences. It is assumed that each preference is of the form $f_r \cdot\!> \ f_s$ (that is, the user prefers image f_r over image f_s) and $f_s, f_r \in \mathcal{F}$. Fourth, using these preferences, the quality or the significance of all the semantic attributes for retrieval in the context of the present user need is evaluated. These quality assessments are quantified by assigning weights to semantic attributes. Fifth, using these weights, a numeric value is assigned to each image in the database. These values are referred to as Retrieval Status Values (RSV). Sixth, the database images are rank ordered using the RSV and are shown to the user in the decreasing order of relevance. If the user is not satisfied with this rank ordering, he may choose to provide additional preferences on few images placed at the top of this rank ordering. Again the quality of attributes is reevaluated, database images are rank ordered, and are shown to the user. This process continues until the user is satisfied with the retrieved images (i.e., the top few images in the rank ordering). The approach has been demonstrated on a collection of face images.

It should be noted that this method assumes independence among the semantic attributes.

On the other hand, the approach proposed in [25] is based on user relevance judgments. User's relevance judgments/feedback is obtained by asking the user to label the retrieved images as either relevant or non-relevant with respect to the query image. An inductive learning module is designed for providing facilities by which the user's relevance feedback is effectively utilized to incrementally/adaptively reformulate the query to improve the retrieval effectiveness. The query reformulation algorithm is based on the functional dependency between each image attribute and the user's relevance feedback using a theoretical framework referred to as Rough Set Theory [35]. The importance (or weight) of each semantic attribute in the reformulated query is modified based on the degree of such functional dependencies. Hence, the query reformulation algorithm is designed systematically, and the query reformulation process is both intuitive and easily understood. The method has been demonstrated on a hair-style image database. It should be noted that, in both the approaches, the user involvement in the relevance elicitation process is at a conceptual level. The following section introduces Personal Construct Theory (PCT) as a database design tool.

9.4 Elicitation of Semantic Attributes

In the context of the proposed framework, Personal Construct Theory [3], [10], [27] is viewed as a design/knowledge acquisition tool for identifying semantic attributes in an image database application. PCT was originally proposed by Kelly in the Clinical Psychology domain. This theory is viewed as a formal model of organization of human cognitive processes. Both animate and inanimate objects with which a person interacts in everyday life constitute that person's environment. According to PCT, the objects comprising a person's environment profoundly influence his decision making process. These objects are referred to as *entities* or *elements.* A property of an element that influences a person's decision making process is known as a *construct* or a *cognitive dimension.* In other words, PCT assumes that people typically use these cognitive dimensions in evaluating their experiences for decision making. An element may possess many constructs. The process of assigning a value for a construct on a linear scale to reflect the degree to which that construct is present in an element is known as *rating.* A matrix that shows the elements and the corresponding construct values is referred to as *repertory grid.* The rows are labeled with the construct names and the element names form the column labels. It is important to recognize that the repertory grid represents the knowledge of an expert and *not* the data. Several techniques are available for analyzing the knowledge in a repertory grid [3], [10]. We now briefly describe how Personal Construct Theory is used in eliciting semantic attributes in image database applications.

PCT experiment is carried out in two stages. During the first stage, a set of semantic attributes is discovered in the image database. The procedure for the first stage is as follows. Three randomly selected images from the image database are displayed in three quadrants of a computer display screen. The domain expert is asked to name the poles of a bipolar construct(s) vis-a-vis a semantic attribute by which images in the first and second quadrants are similar and maximally different from the image in the third quadrant. For the same set of images, the other two combinations are also considered. Then the next set of three images are shown to the domain expert and the same procedure is repeated. This process continues until the domain expert is unable to identify any more new semantic attributes. During the second stage, repertory grid is generated. The images in the database are shown to the domain expert in a sequence. The domain expert is asked to rate each of these images with respect to the semantic attributes identified in stage one. More details on the PCT experimental methodology can be found in [21].

In the context of images, the following interpretations are given to the constructs and the repertory grid. Constructs are viewed as cognitive dimensions of the image domain by which the images are judged to be similar or different from each other by an expert. Repertory grid generation is viewed as a complex sorting test in which the images are rated with respect to a set of constructs. The expert-provided constructs are considered same as the domain concepts hidden in the images. Hence, the terms concept, semantic attribute and construct are used interchangeably. We have successfully applied PCT for eliciting semantic attributes in two image database applications: Geometric Objects database [38] and Human Face database [21]. As noted earlier, in [21], we have developed an algorithm for Retrieval by Semantic Attributes queries based on the repertory grid. The next section concludes the paper.

10. Conclusions and Future Direction

The AIR Framework is unique in the sense that it is a first comprehensive and generic data model for a class of image database application areas that coherently integrates logical representations for efficient query processing. Our approach is motivated by methods used in bibliographic information systems where simple and generic representations are used for representing documents to achieve domain independence [39].

The success of the AIR framework depends upon finding solutions to the research issues that we have identified. Toward this goal, we have introduced Personal Construct Theory as a database design tool to systematically identify semantic attributes. We have successfully used this theory on two image database applications. Efficient and robust algorithms for processing *relaxed* Retrieval by Spatial Constraints queries have been developed. We are also developing algorithms for Retrieval by Shape Similarity queries. The two image retrieval applications we have developed demonstrated the practical utility of the AIR system.

The AIR framework addresses five major generic retrieval types. Currently, AIR does not support the modeling of inter-image relationships. Enhancements to AIR to incorporate inter-image relationships will increase its scope to image database applications involving spatio-temporal image sequences. Also, we are incorporating additional generic query classes including *Retrieval by Color*, *Retrieval by Texture*, *Retrieval by Volume*, *Retrieval by Text*, *Retrieval by Motion*, and *Retrieval by Domain Concepts*. *Retrieval by Color* and *Retrieval by Texture* queries facilitate retrieving images that have image-objects with the specified color and texture. *Retrieval by Volume* is an extension of *Retrieval by Shape* query class to 3*D* images. Some applications require retrieving images based on the text associated with the images. Such a need is modeled by *Retrieval by Text* query class. *Retrieval by Motion* queries facilitate retrieving relevant spatio-temporal image sequences that depict a domain phenomenon that varies in time or over a (geog raphic) space. Finally, complex queries formulated by using the other generic query classes are referred to as *Retrieval by Domain Concept* queries.

Acknowledgements

This research is supported by the U.S. Department of Defense under Grant No: DAAL03-89- G-0118. The authors are grateful to Prof. Mary McBride (Art Galleries and Museums), Officer Rose Latiolais (Forensic Art and Criminal Investigation), and Jay Melancon (Real Estate Marketing) for sharing their domain expertise.

References

[1] *Earth Resources Laboratory Applications Software.* Stennis Space Center, Bay St. Louis, MS., 1990.

[2] D.S. Batory et al. GENESIS: an extensible database management system. *IEEE Transactions on Software Engineering*, 14(11):1711–1730, 1987.

[3] J. Bradshaw et al. Beyond the repertory grid: new approaches to constructivist knowledge acquisition tool development. *International Journal of Intelligent Systems*, 8:287–333, 1993.

[4] C.W. Brown and B. Shepherd. *Graphics File Formats.* Prentice Hall, 1995.

[5] J.M. Carey et al. The architecture of the EXODUS extensible DBMS. In *IEEE/ACM International Workshop on Object-Oriented Database Systems*, pages 52–65, Pacific Grove, CA., September 1986.

[6] C. Chang and S. Lee. Retrieval of similar pictures on pictorial databases. *Pattern Recognition*, 24(7):675–680, 1991.

[7] S.K. Chang et al. An intelligent image database system. *IEEE Transactions on Software Engineering*, 14:681–688, 1988.

[8] S.K. Chang and A. Hsu. Image information systems:where do we go from here? *IEEE Transactions on Knowledge and Data Engineering*, 4(5):431–442, 1992.

[9] M. Chock. *A Database Management System for Image Processing.* PhD thesis, Department of Computer Science, University of California, Los Angeles, 1982.

[10] K. Ford et al. An approach to knowledge acquisition based on the structure of personal construct systems. *IEEE Transactions on Knowledge and Data Engineering*, 3(1):78–88, 1991.

[11] R. Gonzalez and P. Wintz. *Digital Image Processing.* Addison-Wesley, Reading, MA., 1987.

[12] J. Griffioen, R. Mehrotra, and R. Yavatkar. A semantic data model for embedded image information. In *Second International Conference on Information and Knowledge Management*, pages 393–402, Washington, D.C., November 1993.

[13] W. Grosky and R. Mehrotra. Image database management. In *Advances in Computers*, pages 237–291, Academic Press, NY, 1992.
[14] W. Grosky and R. Mehrotra. Image database management. *IEEE Computer*, 22(12):7–8, 1989. Guest Editors' Introduction.
[15] V. Gudivada. *TESSA*– an image testbed for evaluating 2-d spatial similarity algorithms. *ACM SIGIR Forum*, 28(2):17–36, 1994.
[16] V. Gudivada. *$\Theta\Re$-String: A Geometry-based Representation for Efficient and Effective Retrieval of Images by Spatial Similarity.* Technical Report, Ohio University, Department of Computer Science, Athens, OH, 1994. TR-19944.
[17] V. Gudivada. *A Unified Framework for Retrieval in Image Databases.* PhD thesis, University of Southwestern Louisiana, Lafayette, LA, 1993.
[18] V. Gudivada and G. Jung. Spatial knowledge representation and retrieval in *3-d* image databases. In *IEEE International Conference on Multimedia Computing and Systems*, 1995. in press.
[19] V. Gudivada and V. Raghavan. Design and evaluation of algorithms for image retrieval by spatial similarity. *ACM Transactions on Information Systems*, April 1995. In press.
[20] V. Gudivada and V. Raghavan. *Picture Retrieval Systems: A Unified Perspective and Research Issues.* Technical Report TR-19943, Ohio University, Department of Computer Science, Athens, OH, 1994.
[21] V. Gudivada, V. Raghavan, and G. Seetharaman. An approach to interactive retrieval in face image databases based on semantic attributes. In *Third Annual Symposium on Document Analysis and Information Retrieval*, pages 319–335, Las Vegas, April 1994.
[22] A. Gupta, T. Weymouth, and R. Jain. Semantic queries with pictures: the VIMSYS model. In *17th International Conference on Very Large Data Bases*, pages 69–79, 1991.
[23] F. Hirabayashi, H. Matoba, and Y. Kasahara. Information retrieval using impression of documents as a clue. In *ACM SIGIR Conference on Research and Development in Information Retrieval*, pages 233–244, 1988.
[24] T.-Y. Hou et al. A content-based indexing technique using relative geometry features. In *Storage and Retrieval for Image and Video Databases*, pages 59–68, SPIE, Vol. 1662, 1992.
[25] G. Jung and V. Gudivada. Adaptive query reformulation in attribute based image retrieval. In *Third Golden West International Conference on Intelligent Systems*, pages 763–774, Kluwer Academic Publishers, June 1994.
[26] T. Kato et al. A cognitive approach to visual interaction. In *International Conference on Multimedia Information Systems '91*, pages 109–120, McGraw-Hill, NY, 1991.
[27] G. Kelley. A mathematical approach to psychology. In B. Maher, editor, *Clinical Psychology and Personality:The Selected Papers of George Kelly*, pages 94–112, John Wiley, 1969.
[28] A. Kemper and M. Wallrath. An analysis of geometric modeling in database systems. *ACM Computing Surveys*, 19(1):47–91, 1987.
[29] S.Y. Lee, M.K. Shan, and W.P. Yang. Similarity retrieval of ICONIC image database. *Pattern Recognition*, 22(6):675–682, 1989.
[30] R. Lorie. *The Use of a Complex Object Language in Geographic Data Management.* Volume 525, Springer-Verlag, 1991. Lecture Notes in Computer Science.
[31] S. Marcus and V. Subrahmanian. *Foundations of Multimedia Information Systems.* Technical Report, University of Maryland, College Park, MD, 1994.
[32] S. Marcus and V. Subrahmanian. *Multimedia Database Systems.* Technical Report, University of Maryland, College Park, MD, 1994.

[33] A. Narasimhalu and S. Christodoulakis. Multimedia information systems: the unfolding of a reality. *IEEE Computer*, 24(10):6–8, 1991. Guest Editors' Introduction.

[34] J. Orenstein and F. Manola. PROBE spatial data modeling and query processing in an image database application. *IEEE Transactions on Software Engineering*, 14(5):611–629, 1988.

[35] Z. Pawlak. Rough sets. *International Journal of Information and Computer Sciences*, 11(5):145–172, 1982.

[36] D. Peuquet. A conceptual framework and comparison of spatial data models. *Cartographica*, 21(4):66–113, 1984.

[37] F. Preparata and M. Shamos. *Computational Geometry: An Introduction.* Springer-Verlag, NY, 1985.

[38] V. Raghavan, V. Gudivada, and A. Katiyar. Discovery of conceptual categories in an image database. In *International Conference on Intelligent Text and Image Handling*, pages 902–915, RIAO 91, Barcelona, Spain, 1991.

[39] G. Salton. *Automatic Text Processing.* Addison-Wesley, Reading, MA, 1989.

[40] A. Samal and P. Iyengar. Automatic recognition and analysis of human faces and facial expressions: survey. *Pattern Recognition*, 25(1):65–77, 1992.

[41] M. Stonebraker and L. Rowe. *The POSTGRES Papers.* Technical Report Mem. No.UCM/ERL M83/85, University of California, Berkeley, 1987.

[42] H. Tamura and N. Yokoya. Image database systems: a survey. *Pattern Recognition*, 17(1):29–43, 1984.

[43] M. Tanaka and T. Ichikawa. A visual user interface for map information retrieval based on semantic significance. *IEEE Transactions on Software Engineering*, 14(5):666–670, 1988.

[44] S.D. Urban. *Constraint Analysis for the Design of Semantic Database Update Operations.* PhD thesis, University of Southwestern Louisiana, Lafayette, LA, 1987.

Appendices

A. Image Logical Structures

In this appendix, we briefly discuss the following logical structures: Minimum Bounding Rectangle, Plane Sweep Technique, Spatial Orientation Graph, $\Theta\Re$-String, 2D-String, and Skeletons.

Minimum Bounding Rectangle

Minimum Bounding Rectangle (MBR) is the minimum size rectangle that completely bounds a given object. The MBR concept is very useful in dealing with image objects that are arbitrarily complex in terms of their boundary shapes. As we have seen earlier, MBR representation serves as an efficient test (a necessary but not a sufficient condition) to determine whether or not two objects intersect. Figure A.1 shows an example of MBR approximation for an image containing five image objects.

Fig. A.1. MBR Representation of Image Objects

Sweep Line Representation for Spatial Relationships

In Computational Geometry, there is an operation called *sweep*, that is natural and efficient for solving several geometrical problems [37]. Instantiation of the sweep technique for 3D geometrical problems is called *space sweep* and for 2D geometrical problems it is known as *plane sweep.* Plane sweep technique uses a horizontal line and a vertical line to sweep the image plane from top to bottom (horizontal sweep) and from left to right (vertical sweep). Both horizontal and vertical sweep lines stop at pre-determined points called the *event points.* Event points are selected in a way to capture the spatial extent of domain objects. For each stop position of the sweep line, the image objects intersect by the sweep line are recorded (i.e., the sweep line status). Therefore, the sweep line representation of an image consists of a set of event points, and for each event point, its sweep line status for both horizontal and vertical sweeps. Containment and overlap queries can be efficiently processed using this logical structure.

As an example, consider the image shown in Figure A.2. The spatial extent of each of the five domain objects is represented by their polygonal approximations. The vertices of these polygons constitute the event points for the sweep. The figure shows a snapshot of one stop of the horizontal sweep line (dotted line HH) and one stop of the vertical sweep line (dotted line VV). The sweep line status for the horizontal sweep line is: *tree* and *duck* and the same for vertical sweep line is: *plant* and *flower.*

Fig. A.2. Sweep Line Representation for Spatial Relationships

Spatial Orientation Graph

Spatial Orientation Graph (see Figure A.3) is a fully connected weighted graph. Each vertex in the graph corresponds to a domain object in the image and each vertex is connected to every other vertex in the graph. Associated with each vertex are the (x, y)-coordinates of the corresponding image object with reference to a Cartesian coordinate system. The weight of an edge connecting two vertices is the slope[7] of the line joining the corresponding image objects. Spatial Orientation Graph representation of an image has been used to compute spatial similarity between two images [19].

Fig. A.3. Spatial Orientation Graph Representation for Spatial Similarity

$\Theta\Re$-String

$\Theta\Re$-String representation of an image is a variation of the sweep line representation. While sweep line representation employs two lines (horizontal and vertical), $\Theta\Re$-String representation employs only one sweep line (i.e., radial sweep line). As shown in Figure A.4, the radial sweep line (line CH) is pivoted at the image centroid (point C). $\Theta\Re$-String representation is generated

[7] The weight of an edge connecting two objects o_1 and o_2 with centroid coordinates (x_1, y_1) and $x_2, y_2)$ is given by the expression $(y_2 - y_1)/(x_2 - x_1)$.

by concatenating the names of the image objects in the order intersect by the radial sweep line as it sweeps one full revolution about the pivot point. Assuming counterclockwise direction for the radial sweep, the $\Theta\Re$-String representation for this image is: *plant, sun_bird, tree, duck* and *flower.* This representation also has been used for computing spatial similarity between two images [16].

Fig. A.4. $\Theta\Re$**-String Representation for Spatial Similarity**

2*D*-String

2*D*-String can be viewed as a representation of the projections of the objects of an image along the x and the y axes. 2*D*-String is denoted by (U, V), where U and V are the projections of the objects of an image on the $x-$ and $y-$axes. Let R be the set $\{=, <, :\}$, where the symbol "=" denotes the spatial relation "at the same location as," the symbol "<" denotes the spatial relation "left of/right of" or "below/above," and the symbol ":" denotes the spatial relation "in the same set as." Consider the image shown in Figure A.4. The projection of the image objects on the $x-$axis gives the following string: (*tree* = *sun_bird* < *plant* = *flower* < *duck*). We have *tree* = *sun_bird* since the centroids of both *tree* and *sun_bird* project on to the same point on the $x-$axis and so is *plant* = *flower. sun_bird* < *plant* because *sun_bird* is to the left of *plant* and *fl ower* < *duck* for similar reason. Also, the projection of the image objects on the $y-$axis gives the following string: (*duck* < *tree* < *flower* < *sun_bird* = *plant*). Therefore, the $2D$-String representation of the image is: (*tree* = *sun_bird* < *plant* = *flower* < *duck*, *duck* < *tree* < *flower* < *sun_bird* = *plant*). In [29], $2D$-String representation has been used for computing the spatial similarity between two images.

Skeletons

The skeleton of a pictorial object is a logical representation of its structural shape. The skeleton can be obtained by using a thinning/skeletonizing algorithms [11]. Medial Axis Transformation (MAT) can be used to define the skeleton of a pictorial object. Let IO be the image object with border B. For each point $p \in IO$, find its closest neighbor in B. If p has more than one neighbor then it belongs to the MAT of the IO. Figure A.5 shows an image with two objects. The skeleton of the rectangular object is shown in dotted lines. The skeleton of the circle object is simply its center. Skeleton of an object can be regarded as its abstract representation in $1D$ preserving its overall structural shape. It should be noted that skeletal representation is based on considering the image objects in isolation whereas the sweep line representation is generated by considering all the image-objects.

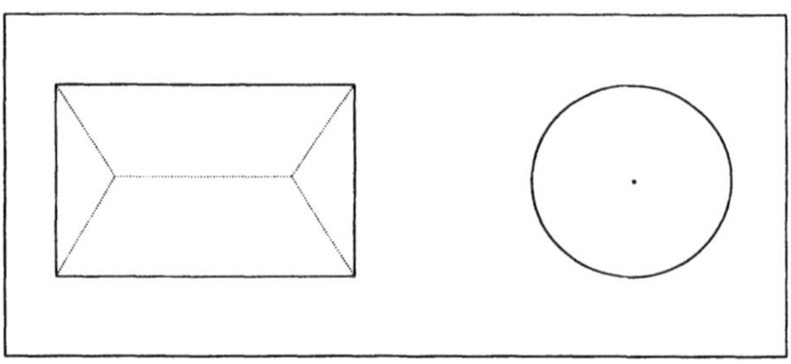

Fig. A.5. Skeletons of Image Objects

Design and Implementation of QBISM, a 3D Medical Image Database System

Manish Arya[1], William Cody[1], Christos Faloutsos[2], Joel Richardson[3], and Arthur Toga[4]

[1] IBM Almaden Research Center, San Jose, California
[2] Univ. of Maryland, College Park, Maryland 20742
[3] The Jackson Laboratory, Bar Harbor, Maine
[4] Dept. of Neurology, UCLA School of Medicine

Summary. We describe the design and implementation of QBISM (Query By Interactive, Spatial Multimedia), a prototype for querying and visualizing 3D spatial data. Our driving application is in an area in medical research, in particular, Functional Brain Mapping. The system is built on top of the Starburst DBMS, extended to handle spatial data types, and, specifically, scalar fields and arbitrary regions of space within such fields. In this paper we list the requirements of the application, discuss the logical and physical database design issues, and present timing results from our prototype. We observed that the DBMS' early spatial filtering results in significant performance savings because the system response time is dominated by the amount of data retrieved, transmitted, and rendered.

1. Introduction

The goal of the QBISM project is to study the extensions of database technology that enable efficient, interactive exploration of numerous large spatial data sets from within a visualization environment. In this work we focus on the logical and physical database design issues to handle 3-dimensional spatial data sets. We also present timing results collected from our prototype. As a first application area we have chosen the Functional Brain Mapping project. Our prototype serves as a tool medical researchers can use to visualize and to spatially query 3D human brain scans in order to investigate correlations between human actions (e.g., speaking) and physiological activity in brain structures. The spatial techniques presented here could also be applied to other medical applications involving anatomic modeling, such as surgery or radiation treatment planning.

Many other application domains involve access to and visualization of large spatial databases. In particular, Geographic Information Systems (GIS) [25] (e.g., environmental and archeological [24] applications); scientific databases (e.g., molecular design systems); and multimedia systems [19] (e.g., image databases [18]). In these classes of applications it is essential to provide accurate and flexible data visualization as well as powerful exploration tools [6] [12].

The **scalar field** is a data type common to several of these applications. In particular, a 3D scalar field is a collection of $(x, y, z, value)$ tuples. In a medical database, the 'value' could be a measure of glucose consumption at the (x, y, z) point in the brain as depicted in a PET study; in a meteorological database, the value could be the temperature at a given point in the atmosphere; and in a chemical database, the value could be the charge at a point in a molecular model. Scalar fields can have other dimensionalities as well; for example, the price history of a stock can be represented as a 1-d scalar field of <time, price> samples. Furthermore, fields can also represent non-scalar data, such as wind velocity. More generally, an n-d m-vector field is a field of samples in n-d where the value is an m-dimensional vector. The techniques presented in this paper can be extended to handle fields of dimensionalities other than 3 in a straightforward manner, and to handle vector fields by simply storing vectors in place of scalars in the appropriate data structures.

We believe our results on medical image databases will be useful in many of the above applications because they all share some basic traits: (a) the principal data objects have spatial extent, (b) the users would like to ask ad-hoc queries in an exploratory, interactive format, (c) the users need visualization tools to view 3D or higher dimensional data in a variety of ways, (d) the spatial data objects are large, and finally, (e) the number of spatial data objects over which the user wants to query is increasing. This last characteristic is especially important in our current work in which queries like '*display the PET studies of 40-year old females that show high physiological activity inside the hippocampus*' are essential for understanding structural and functional relationships in the brain over population groups.

To provide such a flexible query environment for non-traditional data, we utilized the extensibility features of the Starburst DBMS developed at IBM's Almaden Research Center and built an operational prototype. We added new data types and associated query processing operators. We studied compact representations for these data types and assessed their performance. We integrated IBM's Data Explorer/6000 into our prototype as a visual, query front-end. Finally, we populated our prototype with anatomic models and acquired human brain imagery from the Laboratory of Neuro-Imaging of the U.C.L.A. School of Medicine.

The remainder of the paper is organized as follows: Section 2. describes the particular medical research problem we studied and its query and data characteristics; Section 3. describes the logical database design; Section 4. analyzes compact representation schemes for the data; Section 5. describes our prototype implementation, concentrating on extensions to Starburst and Data Explorer/6000; Section 6. provides initial performance results derived from the prototype; and finally, Section 7. gives the project summary and future research directions.

2. The Medical Application

2.1 Problem Definition

As mentioned above, we have chosen the brain mapping project as a sample application for QBISM. The goal of the brain mapping research is to discover spatial correlations between activity in the brain and functional behavior, e.g. speaking or arm movement. Such activity in the brain is frequently characterized by localized, non-uniform intensity distributions involving sections or layers of brain structures, rather than uniform distributions across complete structures. Discovering the precise locations of brain activity, correlating it with anatomy, and constructing functional brain atlases is the goal of an ongoing major medical research initiative [29]. Ultimately, this understanding has clinical applications in diagnosis and treatment planning, as well as scientific and educational value.

Our system must support queries across multiple medical image studies. A study is actually a 'billing' term referring to a set of medical images collected for a single purpose on a single patient, such as a 50 slice MRI study or three x-rays of a fractured elbow. Querying across collections of these will enable the return of statistical responses and support the visualization of multiple data sets [8]. This will extend the power of medical visualization environments which today typically deal with a single study at a time. The system we envision will provide query capability over large image databases in a very investigative, interactive and iterative fashion. The following scenario illustrates a sample session with such a system in which each step generates a database query:

1. The medical researcher may start by selecting from a standard atlas [30] a set of brain structures for the system to render, for example those supporting the visual system.
2. After repositioning the scene to a desired viewing angle, structures may be texture mapped with a patient's PET study to highlight activity along their surfaces.
3. The intensity range may be histogram segmented and other regions in this PET study identified in the same range.
4. An arbitrary region may be compared with the same (or a nearby) region from a previous PET study.
5. Targeting electrodes or radiation beams to regions of interest may be calculated or simulated to visualize anatomical structures intersected.
6. An individual PET (or other study) may be compared with data from a comparable subpopulation of the same demographic group.

The above scenario is representative of the queries that medical researchers (i.e., those at the U.C.L.A. Laboratory of Neuro Imaging) would like to ask. To help provide a general classification of these queries, we use the concept of a scalar field: a study is represented as a collection of $(x, y, z, value)$

tuples, where 'value' is an intensity level in our application. We then have the following classification of queries:

1. Spatial queries specify a condition on the (x, y, z) part of a scalar field (e.g., *show the intensity values in a given query region of a particular MRI study*).
2. Attribute queries specify a condition on the value part of a scalar field (e.g., *show regions of high intensity in a PET study*).
3. Mixed queries involve both spatial and attribute specifications (e.g., *show the regions of high intensity in the right brain hemisphere*).
4. Data mining queries seek to discover patterns and 'association rules' [2] [3] in subpopulation groups (e.g., *find PET study intensity patterns that are associated with any neurological condition, such as focal epilepsy, in any subpopulation*).

The current prototype can handle the first 3 types of queries. Handling data mining queries is part of the future work.

2.2 Data Characteristics

Basically, the database will consist of a large, growing collection of static, 3-dimensional scalar fields and a collection of anatomic models (i.e., atlases) that describe the spatial extent of anatomical structures.

The 3-dimensional scalar fields correspond to the studies. These are collected via an assortment of medical imaging modalities used to capture structural (e.g., MRI, CT, histology) and functional / physiological (e.g., PET, SPECT) information about the human brain. Each of these studies results in a 3D 'volume' of intensity readings that can consume 1-100 megabytes of storage using current spatial resolutions and image depths. This volume is essentially a scalar field comprised of 3 spatial coordinates and an associated scalar intensity value. As a reference point, for clinical purposes a medium sized hospital (e.g., 500 beds) typically performs about 120,000 radiological image studies a year, including standard X-ray film studies. If all this imagery were stored in digital form (as hospitals are beginning to do [31]), the size of this hospital's yearly radiological data is estimated to be about 2 terabytes uncompressed, or 1 terabyte after lossless compression. In our work we must save the raw data volumes from the tomographic modalities as well as considerable amounts of derived data. The derived data is generated as a result of transformations to align and register the raw data, to create models suitable for surface and volume rendering of the data, and to build database representations that enable exploratory query.

As mentioned above, the database also contains atlases of reference brains for each demographic group. These models provide anatomical access to the acquired imagery via computed spatial transformations stored in the database and the spatial query operators. Their use is illustrated in the previous scenario by the step in which a structure in the visual system is used to select a particular patient's PET data. The spatial extent of that structure from the appropriate reference atlas is used to drive selective spatial extraction of the functional data.

An important point is that a PET study of a patient is not perfectly aligned with the corresponding atlas. To solve this problem, spatial and statistical warping techniques [23] [28] [27] are used to derive affine transformations that allow a study to be registered to an appropriate atlas. Thus, when a study is loaded into the database, warping matrices are computed and stored along with the original and warped study. The details of the warping techniques are outside the scope of this paper. However, these automatic or semi-automatic warping algorithms are extremely important for this application. It is precisely this technology that permits anatomic access to acquired medical images as well as comparisons among studies, even of different patients, that have been warped to the same atlas. Furthermore, it enables the database to grow, and be queryable, with minimal human analysis of the data. The coordinate system of the original study is called *patient space* while that of the atlas (and therefore, warped study) is called *atlas space.*

3. Logical Design

We discuss the logical data types, spatial operations, and database schema relevant to the medical application in this section. For implementation details, refer to Section 4. and Section 5..

3.1 Data Types

The data types REGION and VOLUME are of particular importance in this application; we store instances of these types, as well as other large objects, in long fields (see Section 5.1). A REGION encodes the spatial extent of an arbitrarily shaped entity, such as an anatomical structure. A VOLUME encodes all values from a 3D scalar field (e.g., a PET study) sampled on a complete, regular, cubic grid (e.g., 128x128x128 positions evenly-spaced along each axis corresponding to a 20x15x30 cm. real-world scalar field); the samples are stored in a linearized form in an implied order. We discuss these representations at length in Section 4..

3.2 Spatial Operations

To efficiently execute the queries discussed in Section 2., we need spatial operators to manipulate REGIONs and VOLUMEs. We defined and implemented the following useful subset:

- INTERSECTION(REGION r1, REGION r2) returns a REGION representing the spatial intersection of r1 and r2.

- CONTAINS(REGION r1, REGION r2) returns a boolean value indicating whether r1 is a spatial superset of r2.
- EXTRACT_DATA(VOLUME v, REGION r) returns a long field containing exactly those intensity values from v that are inside r.

Other spatial operations would be useful as well, such as UNION(r1, r2) and DIFFERENCE(r1, r2), and would be straightforward to implement.

3.3 Schema

In Figure 3.1 we present an E-R diagram capturing a subset of a full medical schema appropriate for our application. Each entity (in a rectangular box) corresponds to a table in our extended relational DBMS implementation of the system. The Neural System and Neural Structure entities capture various neuro-anatomic data and relationships common to all human brains, (e.g., which structures comprise the visual system). The Patient entity records information pertinent to each individual (e.g., name and age). The Raw Volume entity captures information pertinent to a particular study of a patient, including the actual study data stored in scanline order in a long field. We will not discuss these entities in any further detail.

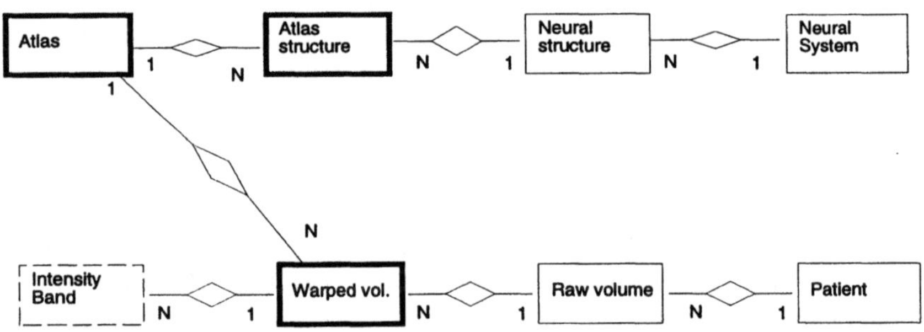

Fig. 3.1. An entity-relationship diagram of the medical database schema. Darker boxes represent the most important entities that support spatial operations.

The Warped Volume entity is particularly important for our current work; its most significant attribute is a long field VOLUME that stores the warped study. As mentioned in Section 2.2, a Raw Volume can be warped to one or more atlas reference brains; we generate and store the warped volume here at database load time (rather than query time) since the computation is expensive. Additional attributes of the Warped Volume entity include the actual warping parameters, the raw study id, and the atlas id, among others. For the rest of this paper, the term VOLUME implies warped VOLUME, unless explicitly specified otherwise.

Another key entity is the Atlas Structure entity. Its most important attribute is a long field REGION, storing the spatial representation of the interior of the given structure in the specified atlas space. A second long-field column stores a triangular mesh representing the surface of the structure to support faster rendering of the structure itself, optionally with study data mapped onto its surface.

The Atlas entity has several string and numeric attributes, describing the characteristics of the reference population it represents and the coordinate system it defines (e.g., resolution and voxel size in real world units).

Finally, the Intensity Band entity serves as an index on the Warped Volume entity that allows rapid access to VOLUME data based on intensity (it is shown in a dotted box because it is redundant). We define an intensity band as a REGION representing the subset of the voxels in a VOLUME that have intensities in a particular interval (with fixed width and uniform spacing in our current prototype), such as 0-31 or 32-63. The most important attributes of an Intensity Band are the intensity interval end-points and a long field for the associated REGION.

3.4 Queries

To demonstrate how we use the schema and the spatial operators (see Section 5. for more details), we show below two Starburst Structured Query Language (SQL) queries that the system generates in response to the user query '*retrieve the intensity values from study number 53 inside the putamen (a neural structure) from the Talairach atlas*':

```
select  a.n, a.x0, a.y0, a.z0, a.dx, a.dy, a.dz,
        a.atlasId, p.name, p.patientId, rv.date
from    atlas a, rawVolume rv,
        warpedVolume wv, patient p
where   a.atlasId = wv.atlasId and
        wv.studyId = rv.studyId and
        rv.patientId = p.patientId and
        rv.studyId = 53 and a.atlasName = 'Talairach'

select  as.region,
        extractVoxels(wv.data, as.region)
from    warpedVolume wv, atlasStructure as,
        neuralStructure ns
where   wv.studyId = 53 and
        wv.atlasId = <from first query> and
        as.structureId = ns.structureId and
        ns.structureName = 'putamen'
```

The first query checks that an appropriate warped study exists and obtains information about the atlas coordinate space and patient (necessary for rendering and annotation), while the second one retrieves the actual region and data values.

For a more complicated user query, such as '*retrieve the intensity values from some study inside some neural structure that are in the interval [100-200]*', the SQL is similar, but includes a call to `intersection()` in the select list and additional joins.

4. Physical Database Design

As mentioned before, there are two basic data types: VOLUMEs and REGIONs. A warped MRI study is an instance of a VOLUME, with intensity values defined over all the points of a 3D grid; an intensity band and an anatomical structure are instances of REGIONs. In the subsections that follow, we present methods of storing these data types so that the queries of interest can be answered efficiently.

In our discussion we present measurements from actual human brain data obtained from the Laboratory of Neuro Imaging at UCLA. The atlas was digitally extracted from the Talairach & Tournoux atlas and represented 11 neuro-anatomic structures as REGIONs in a 128x128x128 atlas space grid. The radiological data consisted of 5 PET studies (each with 51 128x128 8-bit deep image slices) and 3 MRI studies (each with 44 512x512 8-bit deep image slices). Each study was warped and re-sampled to produce a 128x128x128 8-bit per voxel VOLUME and banded with uniformly spaced intensity intervals 32 units wide covering the range 0-255 to produce 8 intensity band REGIONs.

We make heavy use of space filling curves and specifically, of the Hilbert curve. On a 4x4 grid, Figure 4.1 shows a 2-dimensional example of the Peano curve (dashed line, also known as the Z curve [21], bit-shuffling, or Morton key [25]) and Figure 4.2 gives an example of the Hilbert curve (solid line). The latter has been shown to have better spatial clustering properties [9]. Both curves require $O(n)$ complexity to convert between locations on the curve and Cartesian coordinates, where n is the number of bits used to store a position along the curve. A general algorithm for the Hilbert curve is presented in [4] and a simpler algorithm for 2 dimensions in [14].

Some terminology is necessary. Refer to Figure 4.1 and Figure 4.2 for examples. We give the definitions for the Z curve, using the prefix 'z-'; the same terms with the 'h-' prefix correspond to the Hilbert curve.

- The *z-id* of a voxel is its position in the Z ordering. Typically, it is considered as a binary string. In Figure 4.1, the z-id of the shaded 1x1 square is 2, or '0010'. Alternatively, one can compute the z-id by interleaving the voxel's x and y coordinates; for the same shaded 1x1 square, x_1x_0=01 and y_1y_0=00, so the z-id is $x_1y_1x_0y_0$ =0010 (in binary, or '2' in decimal).
- An *octant* is a cube of maximal size that is the result of the recursive decomposition of space, and entirely inside some REGION of interest (e.g., the shaded upper-left square in Figure 4.1 is a quadrant, or 2D octant). More generally, an *oblong octant* (or z-element) of rank r is the complete

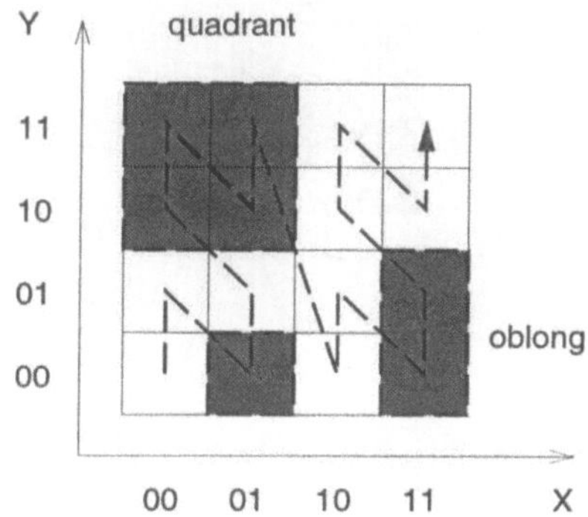

Fig. 4.1. Illustration of (oblong) quadrants in 2D on the Z curve.

set of 2^r voxels that have the same prefix in their z-ids, differing only in their r least significant bits (e.g., the shaded 1x2 rectangle in Figure 4.1). For a regular (cubic) octant in n-d, r must be a multiple of n.

- The *z-value* of an oblong octant is the common prefix of the z-ids of the constituent voxels (e.g., the upper-left quadrant in Figure 4.1 has '01**' as its z-value, where '*' stands for 'don't care'). Typically, the z-value is represented as a pair of the form (z-id, rank), using the smallest z-id of the constituent voxels. Using bit operations, the two components can be packed into 4 bytes for grids as large as 512x512x512.
- A *z-delta* is a maximal set of voxels with consecutive z-ids all either entirely inside or outside a REGION. When these voxels are inside, we call it a *z-run*; when outside, we call it a *z-gap*. For example, one z-run in Figure 4.2 stretches from z-id 1100 to 1101 (or, in decimal, from pixel 12 to pixel 13 (inclusive)).

4.1 Representation of a VOLUME

Our goal is to choose the best way to store a volume, with the following requirements:

1. efficient random access: spatial probes into a VOLUME should be fast and simple (e.g., '*what is the value at point (10, 10, 10)*').
2. good spatial clustering: neighboring grid points in 3D should be stored close to each other on disk to reduce the number of random disk accesses into a VOLUME during extraction queries.

The first requirement makes compression methods unattractive; the second leads to 'distance preserving' k-dimensional-to-1-dimensional mappings. Since the Hilbert curve has the best clustering properties among the known curves, we propose to store a VOLUME by sorting the voxels in Hilbert order and storing only the intensities, since their positions are implied. We have

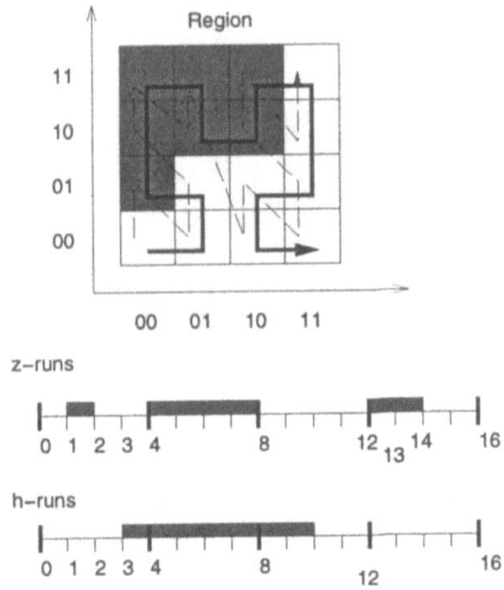

Fig. 4.2. Illustration of h- and z-runs in 2D for the shaded REGION.

implemented the Z ordering, too, but it gives inferior clustering (yielding about 27% more runs for each of the REGIONs we tried).

4.2 Representation of a REGION

Here we study the problem of storing REGIONs to efficiently support spatial operations such as intersections (e.g., '*find the voxels that belong to the intersection of the hippocampus and the 32-63 intensity band*') and 'extractions' (e.g., '*find the intensities in the hippocampus of Sue's last PET study*'). We discuss alternative representations methods.

Given the above operations, we have chosen a volumetric representation of the REGIONs. Surface models cannot support these spatial operations efficiently; Constructive Solid Geometry is not applicable since arbitrary REGIONs of interest do not necessarily have simple analytical descriptions. With a volumetric representation, we can tap the vast literature on quadtrees/octrees [11] [25] with a wealth of algorithms for indexing and spatial operations (e.g., the spatial join [20]). We use surface models only on atlas structures (in addition to the volumetric one) because they support faster, better quality rendering.

Using a volumetric representation, a REGION is typically encoded as a list of the z-values of its (oblong) octants. We propose two improvements:

- Use 'runs' instead of (oblong) octants because they generally merge more voxels together. Note that every (oblong) octant is either a run or a part thereof, and every run consists of one or more (oblong) octants; therefore, the number of runs never exceeds the number of octants. Also note that most algorithms that efficiently process octants have close analogs that efficiently process runs, including the 'spatial join' algorithm for computing

intersections [20]. These algorithms operate by linearly scanning the runs or octants of two REGIONs in parallel (analogous to a merge of two sorted lists), optionally with some optimizations.
- Use Hilbert order, as opposed to Z order (i.e., h-runs instead of z-runs) because the Hilbert curve offers better spatial clustering and yields fewer runs.

In the current implementation, each run is stored with 8 bytes, using 4 bytes for each end-point of the run. Analysis of several compression methods is given in [1], among which the most promising one seems to be a scheme that encodes the lengths of gaps and runs, using a compression scheme proposed by Elias [7].

4.3 Conclusions

From this section, we come to the following conclusions:

- We will store VOLUMEs as a list of intensity values, sorted on Hilbert order.
- We will store REGIONs as a list of Hilbert runs.
- We observe that the ratio of the number of h-runs to z-runs is approximately 1:1.27 in this application for various query regions. This translates to roughly 27% savings in disk accesses.

5. System Issues

5.1 Starburst Extensions

Our prototype makes use of several extensibility features in Starburst [26] [17], most notably long fields and user-defined functions.
Long-fields: We store each large object, such as a REGION or VOLUME, in a separate long field. The Long Field Manager (LFM) stores long fields directly in an operating system disk device (not a file system) using a buddy allocation scheme to promote contiguity, thereby exploiting the clustering properties of the Hilbert curve. The LFM supports fast random I/O to arbitrary pieces of long fields directly to and from client memory without internal buffering. The long field is a Structured Query Language (SQL) data type in Starburst that SQL functions may accept and return. We rely heavily on these low-level features to reduce disk traffic and response time in our prototype. (Although the Starburst SQL query compiler sees our REGIONs and VOLUMEs as instances of the same long-field type, we 'encapsulate' these 'types' by using SQL functions to operate on them.)
User-defined SQL Functions: We implemented the operators of Section 3.2 in Starburst as user-defined SQL functions. Starburst embeds these operators (like all other SQL functions) within query execution plans at compile

time and invokes them in the run-time environment. We can therefore use the complex predicate construction and query block nesting features of the SQL language to express and execute a wide variety of spatial queries, even over multiple studies.

5.2 System Architecture

User interface: IBM Data Explorer/6000 (DX), a scientific visualization package [13], provides the foundation for the end-user interface in our prototype. We wrote a DX 'visual program' which accepts the user's query specifications through entry fields and renders the result in a variety of ways in 3D. Figure 5.1 shows the workstation screen during a sample session. The user can specify a study, some anatomical structures, and intensity values of interest (e.g., *the data from Jane's last PET study with intensity above 200 in the right brain hemisphere*). DX renders the selected information in a variety of ways: just the anatomical data, just the intensity data, both together, or a solid-textured mapping of the intensity data onto the surfaces of the structures (see Figure 5.2). The user can interact with the rendered picture to change the viewpoint and zoom factor, or further manipulate the selected data, by adding a cutting plane, computing a gradient field, or generating an animation, for example. Because of the caching mechanism built into DX, the user can quickly review and manipulate the results of several recently issued queries without necessitating a database reaccess.
Division of labor: Figure 5.3 depicts the overall architecture of the system. Its components perform the following functions:

- DX is responsible for all visualization tasks. It consists of a user-interface process for interacting with visual programs and an executive process for performing most of the computations. We added a new module called ImportVolume to the DX executive; it accepts the user's query and converts the spatially restricted data from the database into a DX object.
- Starburst manages the medical data and performs the query processing, including the operations designed to spatially restrict the answer set.
- MedicalServer translates high-level query specifications it receives from DX into SQL (consider the example of Section 3.4), sends the query strings to Starburst, and then returns the results to DX. MedicalServer accesses Starburst through a shared-library application programming interface (API) and runs in the same process.
- The DX executive and Starburst/MedicalServer processes communicate with each other using Remote Procedure Calls (RPCs) and can thus run on separate machines (even with different low-level data formats).

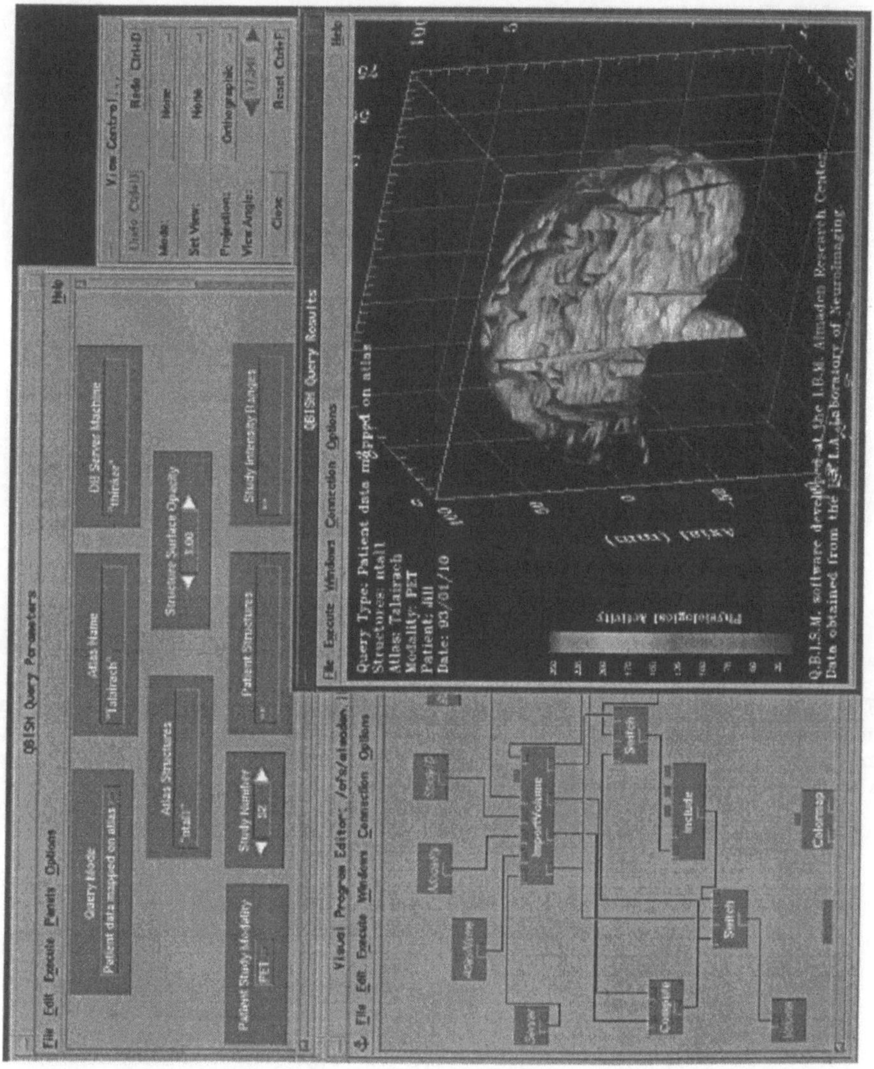

Fig. 5.1. A sample QBISM session. After entering a query in the upper-left window, the user can see the results in the lower-right (and change the viewpoint with the controls in the upper-right corner). The partially-visible window on the lower-left shows a portion of the DX visual program, which is typically hidden from the user.

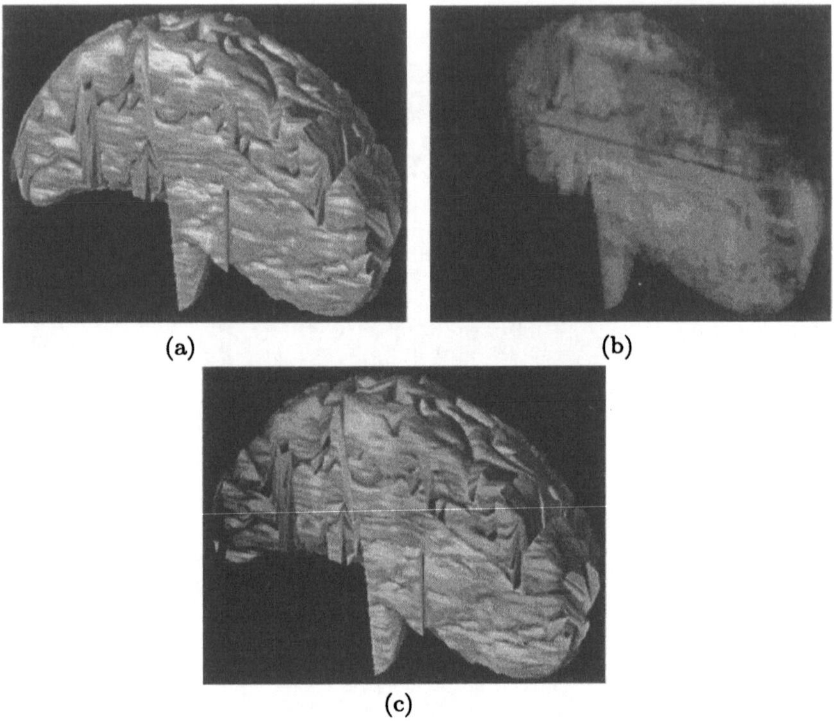

Fig. 5.2. Sample query results. (a) One brain hemisphere from the atlas. (b) The intensity data from a PET study inside the hemisphere. (c) The same PET data mapped onto the surface of the hemisphere. Note the difference in shading between a and c, which is more prominent in color.

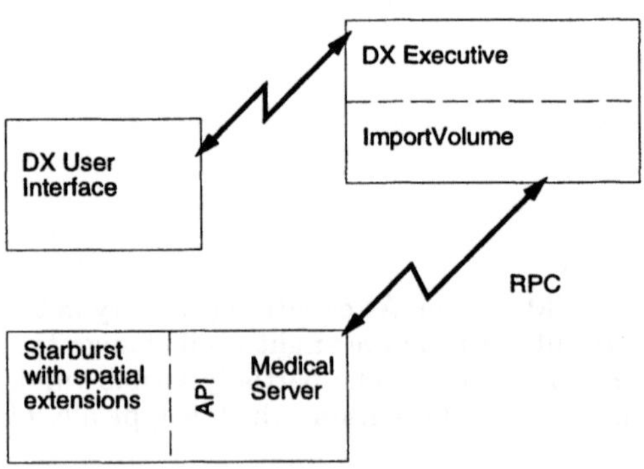

Fig. 5.3. System architecture. Each box represents a process. The arrows represent the network.

6. Performance Experiments

We conducted some experiments to see how our prototype performs, to identify bottlenecks, and to gather information that permits extrapolation of the results to other hardware, larger databases, and different methods. We describe the system configuration, the experiments on single studies and finally, experiments on multiple studies.

6.1 Experimental Environment

Our system consisted of two IBM Risc System/6000 Model 530 workstations running AIX 3.2 (see Figure 6.1).

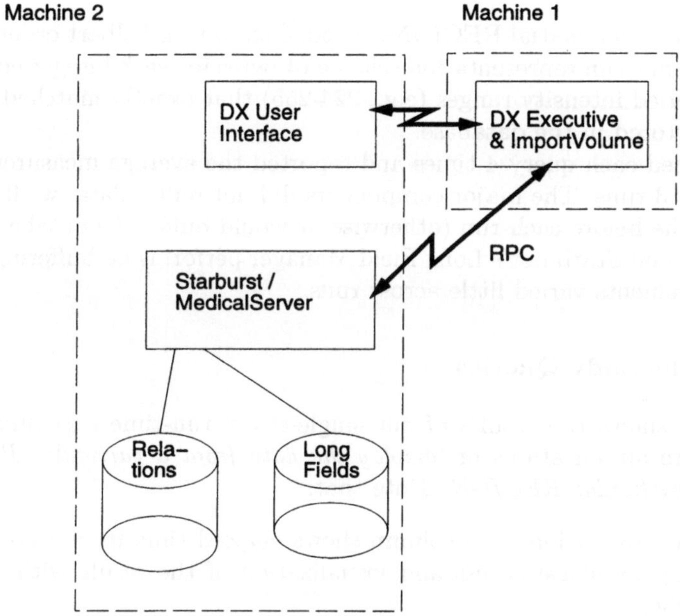

Fig. 6.1. System configuration illustrating the assignment of storage and processes to machines.

- On machine 1, with 64MB of memory, we ran the Starburst/MedicalServer process and the DX user-interface process; this machine did not utilize any special graphics rendering hardware. It held the relational data in a local AIX file system and the long field data in an AIX logical volume.
- On machine 2, with 48MB of memory, we ran the DX executive process. Running the Starburst/MedicalServer and DX executive processes on the same machine may improve performance. However, we believe that

a real world system may benefit from separate dedicated visualization and database server machines and chose to conduct our experiments with a similar configuration. Note that the DX user interface process does not perform much processing, so we ran it on the database server machine rather than on a third workstation.
- Machine 1, on a 16Mbps Token Ring, communicated through a router with the second, on a 10Mbps Ethernet (ping reported a 4ms round-trip packet travel time).

We used the same data as in Section 4. and warped and banded it in advance to produce the schema shown in Figure 3.1. Since the atlas space had dimensions 128x128x128, each warped VOLUME consisted of 2 million, single-byte intensity values. We did not create indexes on any of the relation columns. Finally, for each query, unless otherwise mentioned:

- We used exact spatial REGIONs encoded as runs in Hilbert order with the 8 bytes-per-run representation scheme (4 bytes for each integer end-point).
- We queried intensity ranges (e.g., 224-255) that exactly matched intensity bands stored in the database.
- We issued each query 4 times and reported the average measurements for the last 3 runs. The major components did not buffer data: we flushed the DX cache before each run (otherwise, it would buffer the database's query result), and Starburst's Long Field Manager performs no buffering anyway. Measurements varied little across runs.

6.2 Single-study Queries

Table 6.1 shows the results of our single-study run-time experiments. The queries are all variations of '*display the data from a particular PET study inside a particular REGION*'. Note that:

- The total execution time column shows elapsed time from start to finish, including database access and visualization of the result with an empty DX cache.
- The Starburst/MedicalServer column covers all database activity. The spatial extensions to Starburst (e.g., INTERSECTION() and EXTRACT_DATA()) and the LFM account for most of the CPU time. LFM I/O wait time accounts for the difference between the real and CPU times.
- The network column measures traffic between the MedicalServer and DX executive. It shows the number of network messages sent and their total real time cost, including both software time (e.g., RPC overhead) and 'wire' time.
- The DX column covers all visualization activity. The 'rendering+' time represents all processing in DX after ImportVolume is finished, primarily

related to computing the 3D image. It includes some network communication between the DX user interface and executive processes, such as the transmission of the final image.

– The 'other' column shows any other time the remaining columns do not measure. It consists mainly of time to run an atlas query that retrieves coordinate space information, time to compile the SQL queries, and some round-off error.

	h-runs	voxels	Starburst			Network		DX			Other	Total
	(1)	(2)	(3)	(4)	(5)	(6)	(7)	(8)	(9)	(10)	(11)	(12)
Q1: entire study	1	2097152	513	0.18	**3.4**	2103	**24.8**	10.44	**10.7**	**27**	**3.1**	**69**
Q2: 71x71x71 rectangular solid	5252	357911	450	0.45	**3.5**	372	**4.4**	3.19	**3.2**	**13**	**3.9**	**28**
Q3: ntal	1088	16016	29	0.14	**0.6**	22	**0.5**	0.15	**0.2**	**10**	**3.7**	**15**
Q4: ntal1	14364	162628	265	0.35	**2.5**	195	**2.3**	1.44	**1.5**	**14**	**3.7**	**24**
Q5: band 224-255	508	2383	32	0.13	**0.7**	7	**0.4**	0.10	**0.1**	**12**	**3.8**	**17**
Q6: band 224-255 in ntal1	150	683	72	0.32	**1.0**	4	**0.4**	0.06	**0.1**	**10**	**4.5**	**16**

Table 6.1. Full-system run-time measurements for single-study queries. All times are in seconds. The numbers in bold are independent real time components of the totals in the last column. (1): number of h-runs; (2): number of voxels; (3): LFM Disk I/Os (4K pages); (4): CPU time in Starburst; (5): real time in Starburst; (6): number of IPC messages; (7): network answer time; (8): CPU time for ImportVolume; (9): real time for ImportVolume; (10): rendering+ time; (11): Other time; (12): Total execution time.

Our single-study queries fall into the following classes:

- A 'simple' query (Q1), '*show a full PET study*', which provides a reference point for comparing more selective queries. A 'flat file' system that ships the whole VOLUME to the visualization module would have similar disk I/O and network measures as this full-study query.
- Spatial queries (Q2-Q4), such as '*show the data from a PET study inside a rectangular-solid with corners (30,30,30) and (100,100,100)*', which demonstrate I/O and time savings throughout the system for brain structures (e.g., ntal and ntal1) or simple geometric objects compared to the times for the full-study query.
- Attribute queries (Q5), such as '*show the data from a PET study within the intensity range 224-255*', which demonstrate similar savings for more complicated REGIONs.
- Mixed queries (Q6), such as '*show the data from a PET study inside ntal1 within the intensity range 224-255*, which demonstrate the ability to filter data even more finely through spatial intersection computations while yielding further time savings. Notice that query Q6, which computes the intersection of queries Q4 and Q5, requires much fewer I/Os than Q4 and Q5 combined, and less overall execution time than either Q4 or Q5.

6.3 Multi-study Queries

Table 6.2 shows the Starburst activity from our multi-study run-time experiments. These queries are all variations of '*compute the REGION in which each study's intensity values are consistently in a particular intensity band*'. Such queries require the database to compute an n-way spatial intersection. We used different REGION encoding methods, to measure their relative performance. Specifically, we used z-runs, h-runs and octants. We found h-runs to be superior, as expected.

Encoding method	LFM Disk IOs (4K pages)	Execution Time	
		CPU	real
h-runs	446	1.02	5.7
z-runs	593	1.26	7.3
octants (z order)	664	1.49	8.1

Table 6.2. Run-time measurements for Starburst multiple-study queries. All times are in seconds. Query: *compute the REGION in which all 5 PET studies consistently have intensities in the range 128-159.*

6.4 Results from the Performance Experiments

From these measurements we draw the following conclusions:

- The database component of the system is I/O bound since the real times far exceed the CPU times. This implies that the computational cost of managing REGIONs and performing spatial operations on them is low.
- By comparing the full-study query Q1 to the others, we can see that it is crucial to reduce the data traffic: bytes read from the disk, shipped through the network and imported for visualization. Without spatial processing support, the response time would always be comparable to the full-study time (69 seconds for Q1, versus 15-28 seconds for the others). In short, early filtering pays off.
- The early filtering will be even more beneficial in multiple-study queries, such as '*display the voxel-wise average intensity inside ntal for these 1,000 PET studies*'. In such queries, the database need only read the relevant disk pages of each study, compute the averages, and return the average values to DX. The reduction in data traffic will be linear in the number of studies involved.

7. Conclusions and Future Work

We have described the design and implementation of QBISM, a prototype system for querying and visualizing 3D medical images. We believe that such a system should be built on top of an extensible DBMS engine, appropriately extended to handle spatial data types, and combined with a high-quality visualization tool as the user interface. The challenges in the project were to define and implement operators and types that enable medical researchers to ask ad-hoc queries over numerous 3D patient studies, and to provide fast responses despite the large space requirements of even a single study.

The primary contributions of this work are:

- The articulation and identification of the database requirements for supporting medical research into functional and structural brain mapping.
- The development of a logical database design, including the introduction of data types VOLUME and REGION and the implementation of operations on them within an extensible DBMS.
- The study of physical database design alternatives, including the analysis of representation methods for the REGION data type and the proposal to use runs along the Hilbert curve.
- The performance results from our prototype, which show that the database component of the system is I/O bound and that reducing data traffic through compact representations and early filtering significantly improves performance.

Future directions for this work include:

- Spatial indexing and query optimization techniques for efficiently locating spatial objects in large populations of studies [22].
- The integration of data mining [3] and hypothesis testing techniques to support investigative queries like '*find PET study intensity patterns that are associated with any neurological condition in any subpopulation.*
- The determination of image feature vectors and the study of multi-dimensional indexing methods [5] [15] [16] for them, to enable similarity searching in queries [10], like '*find all the PET studies of 40-year old females with intensities inside the cerebellum similar to Ms. Smith's latest PET study*'.

We should note that creating a practically useful brain mapping environment also requires the integration of facilities for measurement, statistical analysis and general image processing of the data. Finally, we want to mention that we have recently re-implemented our prototype using the ObjectStore OODBMS from Object Design in place of Starburst.

Acknowledgments

We'd like to thank Walid Aref and Brian Scassellati for helping with the implementation and design; Felipe Cabrera, George Lapis, Toby Lehman, Bruce Lindsay, Guy Lohman, and Hamid Pirahesh for guiding us to use Starburst effectively; the UCLA LONI Lab staff for providing and helping to interpret the human brain data; and Peter Schwarz for providing a formatting template for this paper. Furthermore, Christos Faloutsos, who contributed to this work at the IBM Almaden Research Center while on sabbatical from the University of Maryland at College Park, would like to thank SRC and the National Science Foundation (IRI-8958546, EEC-94-02384, IRI-9205273) for their support as well as Empress Software Inc. and Thinking Machines Inc. for matching funds.

References

[1] Manish Arya, William Cody, Christos Faloutsos, Joel Richardson, and Arthur Toga. Qbism: Extending a dbms to support 3d medical images. *Tenth Int. Conf. on Data Engineering (ICDE)*, pages 314–325, February 1994.

[2] Rakesh Agrawal, Tomasz Imielinski, and Arun Swami. Mining association rules between sets of items in large databases. *Proc. ACM SIGMOD*, pages 207–216, May 1993.

[3] Rakesh Agrawal and Ramakrishnan Srikant. Fast algorithms for mining association rules in large databases. *Proc. of VLDB Conf.*, pages 487–499, September 1994.

[4] T. Bially. Space-filling curves: Their generation and their application to bandwidth reduction. *IEEE Trans. on Information Theory*, IT-15(6):658–664, November 1969.

[5] N. Beckmann, H.-P. Kriegel, R. Schneider, and B. Seeger. The r*-tree: an efficient and robust access method for points and rectangles. *ACM SIGMOD*, pages 322–331, May 1990.

[6] Thomas A. DeFanti, Maxine D. Brown, and Bruce H. McCormick. Visualization: Expanding scientific and engineering research opportunities. *IEEE Computer*, 22(8):12–25, August 1989.

[7] P. Elias. Universal codeword sets and representations of integers. *IEEE Trans. on Information Theory*, IT-21:194–203, 1975.

[8] Henry Fuchs, Marc Levoy, and Stephen M. Pizer. Interactive visualization of 3d medical data. *IEEE Computer*, 22(8):46–51, August 1989.

[9] C. Faloutsos and S. Roseman. Fractals for secondary key retrieval. *Eighth ACM SIGACT-SIGMOD-SIGART Symposium on Principles of Database Systems (PODS)*, pages 247–252, March 1989. also available as UMIACS-TR-89-47 and CS-TR-2242.

[10] Christos Faloutsos, M. Ranganathan, and Yannis Manolopoulos. Fast subsequence matching in time-series databases. *Proc. ACM SIGMOD*, pages 419–429, May 1994. 'Best Paper' award; also available as CS-TR-3190, UMIACS-TR-93-131, ISR TR-93-86.

[11] I. Gargantini. An effective way to represent quadtrees. *Comm. of ACM (CACM)*, 25(12):905–910, December 1982.

[12] James Helman and Lambertus Hesselink. Representation and display of vector field topology in fluid flow data sets. *IEEE Computer*, 22(8):27–36, August 1989.

[13] IBM. IBM AIX visualization data explorer/6000 user's guide,, 1992. Second Edition, Publication No. SC38-0496-1.

[14] H.V. Jagadish. Linear clustering of objects with multiple attributes. *ACM SIGMOD Conf.*, pages 332–342, May 1990.

[15] H.V. Jagadish. A retrieval technique for similar shapes. *Proc. ACM SIGMOD Conf.*, pages 208–217, May 1991.

[16] Ibrahim Kamel and Christos Faloutsos. Hilbert r-tree: an improved r-tree using fractals. In *Proc. of VLDB Conference,*, pages 500–509, Santiago, Chile, September 1994.

[17] T.J. Lehman and B. Lindsay. The starburst long field manager. *VLDB Conf. Proc.*, pages 375–383, August 1989.

[18] Wayne Niblack, Ron Barber, Will Equitz, Myron Flickner, Eduardo Glasman, Dragutin Petkovic, Peter Yanker, Christos Faloutsos, and Gabriel Taubin. The qbic project: Querying images by content using color, texture and shape. *SPIE 1993 Intl. Symposium on Electronic Imaging: Science and Technology, Conf. 1908, Storage and Retrieval for Image and Video Databases*, February 1993. Also available as IBM Research Report RJ 9203 (81511), Feb. 1, 1993, Computer Science.

[19] A. Desai Narasimhalu and Stavros Christodoulakis. Multimedia information systems: the unfolding of a reality. *IEEE Computer*, 24(10):6–8, October 1991.

[20] J.A. Orenstein and F.A. Manola. Probe spatial data modeling and query processing in an image database application. *IEEE Trans. on Software Engineering*, 14(5):611–629, May 1988.

[21] J. Orenstein. Spatial query processing in an object-oriented database system. *Proc. ACM SIGMOD*, pages 326–336, May 1986.

[22] J.A. Orenstein. Redundancy in spatial databases. *Proc. of ACM SIGMOD Conf.*, May 1989.

[23] C.A. Pelizzari, G.T.Y. Chen, D.R. Spelbring, R.R. Weichselbaum, and C.T. Chen. Accurate three-dimensional registration of ct, pet and/or mr images of the brain. *J. Comput. Assisted Tomogr.*, 13:20–26, 1989.

[24] Paul Reilly. Data visualization in archeology. *IBM Systems Journal*, 28(4):569–579, 1989.

[25] H. Samet. *Applications of Spatial Data Structures Computer Graphics, Image Processing and GIS.* Addison-Wesley, 1990.

[26] P. Schwarz, W. Chang, J.C. Freytag, G. Lohman, J. McPherson, C. Mohan, and H. Pirahesh. Extensibility in the starburst database system. *Proc. 1986 Int'l Workshop on Object-Oriented Database Systems*, pages 85–92, September 1986.

[27] A.W. Toga, P. Banerjee, and B.A. Payne. Brain warping and averaging. *Int. Symp. on Cereb. Blood Flow and Metab.*, 1991.

[28] A.W. Toga, P.K. Banerjee, and E.M. Santori. Warping 3d models for interbrain comparisons. *Neurosc. Abs.*, 16:247, 1990.

[29] Arthur W. Toga. A digital three-dimensional atlas of structure/function relationships. *J. Chem. Neuroanat.*, 4(5):313–318, 1991.

[30] J. Talairach and P. Tournoux. Co-planar stereotactic atlas of the human brain, 1988.

[31] Albert W.K. Wong, Ricky K. Taira, and H.K. Huang. Digital archive center: Implementation for a radiology department. *AJR*, 159:1101–1105, November 1992.

Retrieval of Pictures Using Approximate Matching

A. Prasad Sistla and Clement Yu

Department of Electrical Engineering and Computer Science
University of Illinois at Chicago, Chicago, Illinois 60680

Summary. In this paper, we describe a general-purpose picture retrieval system based on approximate matching. This system accommodates pictorial databases for a broad *class* of applications. It consists of tools for handling the following aspects— user interfaces, reasoning about spatial relationships, computing degrees of similarity between queries and pictures. We briefly describe the model that is used for representing pictures/queries, the user interface, the system for reasoning about spatial relationships, and the methods employed for computation of similarities of pictures with respect to queries.

1. Introduction

We are currently witnessing an explosion of interest in multimedia technology. Consequently, pictorial and video databases will become central components of many future applications. Access to such databases will be facilitated by a query processing mechanism that retrieves pictures relevant to user queries. Existing pictorial database management systems have been mostly application dependent (for example see [2], [7], [9], [4]). Some preliminary work towards a unified framework for content based retrieval of images can be found in [6], [5]. In this paper, we describe a general-purpose pictorial retrieval system based on approximate matching. This system accommodates pictorial databases for a broad *class* of applications. It consists of tools for handling the following aspects— user interfaces, reasoning about spatial relationships, computing degrees of similarity between queries and pictures. In this paper, we briefly describe the model that is used for representing pictures/queries, the user interface, the system for reasoning about spatial relationships, and the methods employed for computation of similarities of pictures with respect to queries.

We assume that there is a database containing the pictures. We also assume that there is some meta-data associated with each picture which describes the contents of the picture. This meta-data contains information about the objects in the picture, their properties and the relationships among them. For example, consider a picture containing a man shaking hands with a woman and is to the left of the woman. The meta-data about this picture identifies two objects, man and woman, and the spatial relationship *left-of* and the non-spatial relationship hand-shaking. We assume that this meta-data is generated a priori (possibly, by image processing algorithms, or manually, or by a combination of both), and is stored in a separate database. This meta-data will be used by the query processing mechanism in determining the pictures that need to be retrieved in response to a query. The meta-data facilitates efficient query processing, i.e. it avoids the invocation of the expensive image processing algorithms each time a query is processed.

Similarity based retrieval of pictures consists of retrieving those pictures that closely match with user's query. Such retrievals are needed when the user cannot provide a precise specification of what he/she wants. Even if the user can precisely specify the his/her requirements, there may not be any pictures in the database that exactly match with the user's query, and in this case the user may want the closest matches.

We consider three aspects in matching the query against the pictures in the database. These are matching of the objects in the query against the ones in the pictures, and satisfaction of non-spatial and spatial relationships. Approximate matching is achieved by computing similarity values for each picture that denotes how closely the picture matches with the query, and retrieving pictures with highest similarity values.

This paper is organized as follows. In section 2, we describe the E-R model for representing contents of pictures. Section 3 contains the description of the user interface component. Section 4 describes the computation of similarity of values of pictures relative to queries. This section describes the computation of similarity values corresponding to the matching of objects, matching of the non-spatial relationships and the satisfaction of the spatial relationships.

2. Picture Representation

We make use of E-R diagrams to represent contents of pictures (This can also be conceptualized as object oriented modeling). The contents of a picture is a collection of objects related by some associations. Thus, a picture can be represented by an E-R diagram [3] as follows.

entities: objects identifiable in a picture.
attributes: properties (color, size etc) that qualify or characterize objects.
relationships: associations among the identified objects.

An E-R diagram can thus be used to represent the contents of a picture. However, the entities and relationships used in this paper are different from those of the standard E-R diagram. In a standard E-R diagram, each rectangular box, denoting an entity set, represents an object type, a set of objects having the same types of properties. In the representation of a picture, a rectangular box represents a particular object and each box in the shape of a diamond represents a single association of the related objects instead of a relationship set.

The example picture, given in the introduction, contains a man standing to the left of a woman, and is shaking hands with the woman. The entities in the picture are the man and the woman. Attributes are the properties or qualities that describe the entities. In this example, "state of motion" is an attribute and the value of this attribute for the man is "standing".

Analysis of relationships found in different pictures indicates that the relationships can be grouped into two types: *action* and *spatial.*

1. Action: Relationships which describe an action are classified under this group. In the above example "shaking hands" is an action relationship.
2. Spatial: The type of relationships that state the relative positions of two entities are grouped under type *spatial.* Examples are *above*, *in_front_of*, *below*, etc. In the above example *left_of* is a spatial relationship.

Another example is the X-ray image of the lungs of a patient. The image indicates a large tumor inside the left lung. The entities in this picture are the two lungs and the tumor. The "size" attribute value of the tumor is "large". The spatial relationship is *inside.*

3. User Interface

The user interface has to be made as simple as possible for the casual user to interact easily with the picture retrieval system. We have developed an iconic interface that guides the user step by step in specifying the contents of the picture that the user has in mind. The interface has features to identify the objects (entities), their characteristics (attribute values), and the associations (relationships) among the objects.

The user interface is organized into several distinct parts, which take the form of separate windows or frames. The first frame is the *picture representation area*,(or *canvas*) which displays the description-in-progress. The picture representation area shows a symbolic version of the picture, using icons and text labels. The second major frame is the *icon palette*, which contains icons representing objects to be inserted into the picture.

Upon startup, the interface displays the picture representation area and the icon palette. The palette contains icons which represent several classes of entities, which have been chosen based on the range of object types which may occur in real pictures. Examples of these are *man, woman, boy, girl, baby, building, thing* (generic entity), *plant,* and *animal.* The palette can be changed to suit the needs of application domain. The user is prompted to choose one or more icons with the pointing device and drag them into the picture representation area. After moving a new icon into the picture representation area, the user is immediately prompted to specify the values of a set of attributes such as name,age,etc. This consists of first selecting a set of attributes. Whenever an attribute is selected, a dialog box for the attribute is displayed. The user either chooses a value among a given set of values or input a value from the keyboard. Some attribute values are automatically selected. For example, the value of *position-within-picture* is indicated simply by dragging an icon to an appropriate position in the picture (currently, the picture representation area is divided into a 3 by 3 grid, and the position of an object is given by one or more grid positions). This provides immediate feedback, relating the current description to the picture the user wants to retrieve.

When the user has finished populating the picture with icons, he may immediately attempt retrieval by choosing a button labeled *Retrieve*, or he may choose a button labeled *Define Relationships.* To specify relationships among objects, the novice user is guided through a sequence of input frames which elicit the relationship description, one piece of information at a time. The goal in using this method is to gain both ease of use and lack of ambiguity in the final description. For experienced users, the sequence of frames can be bypassed via a menu option which displays a single frame containing all input fields. The design objective in using both schemes is to allow maximum efficiency while assuring ease of use for all levels of familiarity with the interface.

The first pair of frames in the relationship contain texts to briefly describe the types of relationships, and then prompt the user to classify the relationship as either *action* or *spatial*, and as either *directional* or *mutual.* The difference between action and spatial relationships is indicated with examples such as *handshake* (which is an action relationship), versus *to-left-of* (a spatial relationship). Mutual action, for example "man *shakes hands* with woman" is distinguished from directional action, for example "boy *chases* dog". In the case of action relationship, the user is prompted for a name describing the action, such as *holding* or *chasing.* In the case of a spatial relationship, the user is given a fixed list of names from which to choose, and there is no need for the user to specify whether it is a mutual or a directional relationship.

The final step is to specify the entity or entities that are involved in the relationship. In the case of a directional relationship, message boxes instruct the user to select in turn each member of the *subject* entity set and the *object* entity set with the pointing device. Simultaneously, a text phrase is built up from the information given by the user, and displayed in a corner of the picture area. For example, if the relationship name is *watching*, the relationship description initially appears simply as *Group_1 watching Group_2.* Now, if the user specifies *Group_1* to be the singleton set {*man*}, the phrase will be changed to *man watching Group_2.* Now, if the user specifies *Group_2* to be the set {*cat, dog*}, then the phrase appears as *man watching* {*cat, dog*}. Thus, the system provides constant feedback, contributing to ease of use and a more accurate description.

It is to be noted that the positions of objects in the query picture may imply certain spatial relationships among these objects. However, in cases, when two objects have the same grid position, their spatial relationships need to be explicitly specified. Furthermore, spatial relationships in the third dimension (i.e. the depth dimension) require user specification even if the objects have different grid positions.

4. Computation of Similarity Values

As indicated in the previous sections, each user query is represented conceptually by an E-R diagram. The picture retrieval system contains a database that is (again conceptually) a collection of the E-R diagrams of pictures. Currently, the meta-data representing the contents of the pictures using the E-R diagrams are created manually. We expect that computer vision and pattern recognition techniques will help in identifying some of the objects and the relationships automatically.

Processing a query involves finding E-R diagrams in the database which are very similar to the E-R diagram corresponding to the user's query. Either the user is asked to specify a number, say u, of pictures to be retrieved for examination, or a default value, which usually is the number of thumbnails that can fit into one screen, is used. The u pictures which are closest in similarity values to the user's description are retrieved.

4.1 Similarity Functions

Given a query Q, we compute a similarity value for each picture P in the database that reflects how closely the picture matches the query Q. We assume that this similarity value is given by a function f that takes Q and P as arguments and gives a real number; the higher the value of $f(Q, P)$, the more similar the picture is to the query. In order to determine how closely the P matches with Q, we need to first match the objects in Q to the appropriate objects in P and determine which of the various relationships among objects in Q are satisfied by the corresponding matched objects in P. In general, an object in Q can be matched against more than one object in P. If there are multiple objects in Q, then there are many combinations of such matchings. Consider the following example. The query Q has two objects, a man and a woman, and the picture P has three men and two women. The man and the woman in Q can be matched against any of the three men and any of the two women in P, respectively. Thus, there are six possible combinations of matchings. With each such possible combination of matchings, we compute a similarity value and take the maximum of such similarity values.

For the above reasons, we define $f(Q, P) = \max_\rho \{g(Q, P, \rho)\}$, where ρ and g are as given below, and $\max_\rho$ is the maximum over all possible ρs; here ρ is any partial one-one function, called *matching*, that maps each object in Q to a distinct object, if it exists, in P; g is a similarity function that gives a real number denoting how closely Q is to P under the matching of objects given by ρ.

The value $g(Q, P, \rho)$ is the sum of three real numbers. The first number is purely based on the matching of the objects in the query Q against the objects in P; this number is itself the sum of the similarity values, over all objects A in the query Q, denoting how closely the object A matches with the object $\rho(A)$ in P (this similarity value for object A is zero if $\rho(A)$ is undefined). The computation of the similarity value between two objects/entities is given in subsection 4.2. The second number is based on the matching of the non-spatial relationships, and is the sum of the similarity values, over all non-spatial relationships r in Q, denoting how the relationship r is satisfied by P and ρ. Subsection 4.3 describes the computation of this value. The third number is based on matching of the spatial relationships. Subsection 4.4 describes the computation of this similarity value.

Consider the previous example. We extend it as follows. The query Q has two objects, a man and a woman, with attribute values denoting that the man is young and the woman is beautiful; furthermore, Q specifies that the man is to the left of the woman. Now consider the picture P that has three men who are very young, young and middle aged respectively, and two women one of whom is beautiful and the other is moderately so; furthermore, only the young man is to the left of the beautiful woman. It is easy to see that the only relevant values of ρs are those in which the man and the woman in Q are mapped to one of the three men and to one of the two women in P respectively. Clearly, there are six such mappings and all these need to be considered for computing $f(Q, P)$. Let a_i (for $i = 1, 2, 3$) denote the similarity value of matching the man in Q with the ith man in P based on age; similarly, let b_j (for $j = 1, 2$) be the similarity value of matching the woman in Q with the jth woman in P based on beauty; also, let c_{ij} be the similarity value for satisfaction of the $left\_of$ spatial relationship between the ith man and the jth woman. Then $f(Q, P) = max_{i=1,2,3;j=1,2}\{a_i + b_j + c_{ij}\}$.

In a general case, the number of matchings (i.e. ρs) to be considered, for the computation of $f(Q, P)$, can be exponential in the number of objects present in Q and P. It can be shown that the problem of computing $f(Q, P)$ is NP-hard.

4.2 Object Similarities

Two entities are similar if

(i) the types of the entities are the same, or they are related by some IS-A relationship, and
(ii) the attribute values of the two entities are the same or are close as specified at the end of this subsection.

Let e be a user specified entity and E be an entity stored in the database. Let n and N be the types of entities e and E respectively and a_i and A_i be the ith attribute values of the corresponding entities. The similarity of entities e and E can be defined as

$$Sim(e,E) = \begin{cases} Sim(n,N) + \sum_{i=1}^{k} Sim(a_i,A_i) & \text{if Sim(n,N)} > 0 \\ 0 & \text{if Sim(n,N)=0} \end{cases}$$

where $Sim(n, N)$ is the similarity of the two entity types and $Sim(a_i, A_i)$ is the similarity of two attributes. $Sim(n, N)$ is computed according to the following cases.

1. The two types are the same. In this case, $Sim(n, N) = w$, where w is given by the inverse document frequency method of [10], which assigns higher weights to entity types occurring in fewer pictures.
2. The two types are in a IS-A hierarchy. When the partial match is a result of an IS-A relationship, the degree of similarity is an inverse function of the number of edges between two nodes representing the entities where each edge represents a distinct IS-A relationship.
3. If neither of the above conditions holds, then $Sim(n, N) = 0$.

Now we describe the computation of the similarity of two attribute values of entities of the same type. We say that an attribute is *neighborly* if there is a *closeness* predicate that determines, for any two given values of the attribute, whether the two values are close or not. For example, the age attribute is neighborly; it can take one of the values— "very young","young","middle-age","old" and "very old"; two values are considered close if they occur next to each other in the above list.

Now, we define similarity of two values a and A of a neighborly attribute as follows.

$$Sim(a,A) = \begin{cases} w & \text{if a = A} \\ cw & \text{if a or A are close} \\ -\infty & \text{if a and A are not close} \end{cases}$$

It is to be noted that , by giving a similarity value of $-\infty$ when the attribute values are not close, we make sure that the entity in the query is not matched with the entity in the picture.

If the attribute is not neighborly, the similarity of two values a and A are given as follows.

$$Sim(a,A) = \begin{cases} w & \text{if a = A} \\ 0 & \text{otherwise} \end{cases}$$

In the above definitions, w is determined using the inverse document frequency method and c is a positive constant less than 1.

4.3 Similarities of Non-spatial Relationships

Now, we consider the computation of the similarity between a relationship, r, of some entities which are specified in the user's description and another relationship, R, of some entities which are given in a picture stored in the system.

Informally, the relationships r and R are the same or similar if (i) the names of the relationships are the same or synonyms and (ii) the entities of r and those of R can be placed in 1-1 correspondence such that each entity in r is similar to the corresponding entity in R. The following example illustrates the need to relax this second condition: Consider a picture where a family of four people plays basketball. The relationship can be specified as play from the subject entities {father, mother, child 1, child 2} to the object entity "basketball". Alternatively, it can be specified as "play basketball" among the entities {father, mother, child 1, child 2}. Thus, in the process of computing similarity, we relax the 1-1 correspondence requirement between the entities in one relationship and the entities in another relationship. As long as the entities in one relationship are a subset/superset of the entities in another, and the common subset contains at least two entities, then matching is assumed, although the degree of matching is higher for an exact match than that for a partial match.

4.4 Spatial Similarity Functions

In this subsection we discuss some of the properties that need to be satisfied by spatial similarity functions. Recall that spatial similarity functions define the component of the similarity value contributed by the spatial relationships. Now, we introduce some definitions needed in the remainder of this section.

4.4.1 Deduction and Reduction of Spatial Relationships. Let F be a finite set of spatial relationships. We say that a relationship r is *implied by F*, if every picture that satisfies all the relationships in F, also satisfies the relationship r. For example, the set of relationships $\{A\ left\_of\ B\ ,\ B\ left\_of\ C\}$ implies $A\ left\_of\ C$.

In [11], we presented various rules for deducing new spatial relationships from a given set of relationships. Each rule is written as $r\ ::\ r_1, r_2, ..., r_k$. In this rule r is called the head of the rule and the list $r_1, ..., r_k$ is called the body of the rule. For example, the rule $A\ left\_of\ C\ ::\ \{A\ left\_of\ B\ ,\ B\ left\_of\ C\}$ denotes the transitivity of the *left_of* relationship. We say that a relationship r is *deducible in one step* from a set of relationships F using a rule, if r is the head of the rule, and each relationship in the body of the rule is contained in F. Let R be a set of rules and F be a set of relationships. We say that a relationship r is *deducible* from F using the rules in R, if r is in F, or there exists a finite sequence of relationships $r_1, ..., r_k$ ending with r, i.e. $r_k = r$, such that r_1 is deducible in one step from F using one of the rules in R, and for each $i = 2, ..., k$, r_i is deducible in one step from $F \cup \{r_1, ..., r_{i-1}\}$ using one of the rules in R. The set of rules given in [11] is shown to be *sound* and *complete* for 3-dimensional pictures. The soundness and completeness of this set of rules states that the set of relationships deducible from F is identical to the set of relationships implied by F.

For any set F of relationships, let $ded(F)$ denote the set of relationships deducible from F. Furthermore, let $red(F)$ (called the *reduction* of F) be the minimal subset of F such that every relationship in F is deducible from $red(F)$. It has been shown [12] that $red(F)$ is unique if the following conditions are satisfied: (i) we identify *dual overlaps* relationships, i.e. identify A *overlaps* B and B *overlaps* A; (ii) we cannot deduce both A *inside* B and B *inside* A from F for any two distinct objects A and B. We call the relationships in $red(F)$ as *fundamental* relationships in F, and those in $ded(F) - red(F)$ as *non-fundamental* relationships in F.

4.4.2 Properties of Spatial Similarity Functions. Let Q be a given user query. We say that a spatial similarity function h satisfies the *monotonicity* property if for any two pictures P_1 and P_2 and matchings ρ_1 and ρ_2 the following condition holds— if the set of spatial relationships satisfied by P_1 (with respect to the matchings ρ_1) is contained in the set satisfied by P_2 (with respect to ρ_2), then $h(Q, P_1, \rho_1) \leq h(Q, P_2, \rho_2)$. The following similarity function satisfies the monotonicity property. It assigns a weight to each spatial relationship specified in the query or is deducible from the query, and computes the similarity value of a picture to be the sum of weights of the spatial relationships satisfied by it.

Now, consider the query Q specified in the following example (called example X). The query Q specifies that object A is to the left of B, B is to the left of C , A is to the left of C, and D is above E. Suppose that there are two pictures. In the first picture, the first three *left_of* relationships are satisfied, but the above relationship is not satisfied. In the second picture, the first and the third *left_of* relationships, and the *above* relationship are satisfied but not the second *left_of* relationship. Both pictures satisfy 3 out of the 4 user specified relationships. If we use the above similarity function and assign equal weights to all the spatial relationships, then both the pictures in this example will have equal similarity values. However, it can be argued that the second picture should have higher similarity value. This anomaly occurs because we did not distinguish non-fundamental relationships from fundamental relationships. The first and the second *left_of* relationships and the *above* relationship are the fundamental relationships in the query (i.e. they are in the minimal reduction of the query). The first picture satisfies two out of the three fundamental relationships, while the second picture satisfies a fundamental *left_of* relationship , a fundamental *above* relationship, and a non-fundamental *left_of* relationship whose satisfaction does not come as a consequence of the satisfaction of the two fundamental relationships. In this sense, the second picture should have a higher similarity with respect to the query than the first picture.

We now construct a class of similarity functions, called *discriminating* similarity functions, that avoid the above anomaly and also satisfy the monotonicity property. The class of discriminating similarity functions work as follows.

- Assign weights to the relationships in $ded(Q)$; recall that Q is the user query.
- For any picture P, compute its similarity value to be the sum of the weights of all relationships in the set $red(sat(Q, P, \rho))$, where $sat(Q, P, \rho)$ is the set of spatial relationships in $ded(Q)$ that are satisfied by P with respect to the matching ρ.

Note that discriminating similarity functions ignore all the relationships satisfied by P that are outside the reduction, because such relationships are directly implied by those in the reduction. It is easy to see that in example X, if we give equal positive weights to all the relationships and use the above method, then the second picture will have a higher similarity value than the first picture.

To ensure monotonicity, when using discriminating similarity functions, we need to choose the weights of the relationships carefully. Consider the user query Q defined as follows. In this query, all the "A" objects (i.e. $A_1, ..., A_n$) are to the left of B, and all the "C" objects (i.e. $C_1, ..., C_m$) are to the right of B. Now, consider two pictures P_1 and P_2 as given below. P_1 is identical to the query. P_2 has all the A, C objects but not B and all A objects are to the left of all the C objects in P_2. It should be easy to see that $red(sat(Q, P_1, \rho_1))$ contains exactly $m + n$ relationships which are of the form $A_i\ left\_of\ B$ or $B\ left\_of\ C_j$, while $red(sat(Q, P_2, \rho_2))$ contains mn relationships of the form $A_i\ left\_of\ C_j$. Here ρ_1 matches each object in Q to a corresponding object of the same type and of same index in P_1; ρ_2 is similar except that the "B" objects in Q are not matched. Clearly, assignment of equal weights to all the relationships does not ensure monotonicity.

Now, we give a simple sufficient condition on weight assignments that ensures monotonicity when using the discriminating similarity functions. We say that a set C of relationships is *minimal* if $red(C) = C$, i.e. none of the relationships in C is deducible from the others in C.

LEMMA 5.2: A discriminating similarity function satisfies monotonicity if for every pair of minimal sets C_1 and C_2 the following condition is satisfied: If every relationship in C_2 is deducible from those in C_1, then the sum of the weights of relationships in C_1 should be greater than equal to the sum of weights of the relationships in C_2.

For example, let r_1, r_2, r_3 be the relationships *A left_of B*, *B left_of C* and *A left_of C* respectively. If we take C_1 to be $\{r_1, r_2\}$ and C_2 to be $\{r_1, r_3\}$, then to satisfy the condition of the lemma, the weight of r_3 should be less than or equal to the weight of r_2. Similarly, if we take C_1 to be $\{r_1, r_2\}$ and C_2 to be $\{r_2, r_3\}$, then to satisfy the condition of the lemma, the weight of r_3 should be less than or equal to the weight of r_1. Thus, to ensure monotonicity of a discriminating similarity function, it is sufficient to choose the weight of r_3 to be less than or equal to the minimum of the weights of r_1 and r_2.

The following method gives a way of assigning weights so that the condition of the lemma is satisfied. Let Q be a user query. We define a directed graph $H = (V_H, E_H)$. The set of vertices V_H is exactly the set of relationships in *ded(Q)* (here, for any pair of *overlaps* relationships of the form *A overlaps B* and *B overlaps A*, we have a single vertex in the graph). There exists an edge from the relationship r_i to r_j if there is a one step deduction of r_j that employs r_i. It can be shown that the graph H is acyclic. All the source nodes in the graph (i.e. nodes with no incoming edges) denote elements in *red(Q)*. Each vertex is assigned a level number as follows. The level number of any vertex r is the length of the longest path from any source node to v. The level number of a source node is zero, and the level number of any other node r is 1+ max{level number of s : (s, r) is an edge in H}. The level numbers can be computed by a topological sort of H. We can assign arbitrary weights to all the source vertices, i.e. all the relationships in *red(Q)*. For example, each such relationship can be assigned a weight inversely proportional to the logarithm of its frequency of occurrences in the collection of pictures [10]. Thus, if a relationship is satisfied by very few pictures then it will be assigned a high weight. For all other vertices we assign weights inductively based on their level numbers. All the vertices having the same level number are assigned equal weights. Assume that there are k_i vertices at level i. For each level i node, assign a weight which is less than or equal to (the minimum weight of any vertex at level $(i-1)/(1+k_i)$).

LEMMA 5.3: Any discriminating similarity function using weight assignments based on level numbers as given above satisfies the monotonicity property.

When the database of pictures is large then it is not feasible to compute the similarity of each picture individually with respect to the given query. In [12] we describe two different methods for computing similarities, that consider only those pictures that have some commonality with the query, are presented. These methods make use of indices to facilitate efficient retrieval. They also make use methods for deduction (see [11]) and reduction of spatial relationships.

5. Conclusion

In this paper we have described an ongoing project on picture retrieval based on approximate matching. This project uses similarity based retrieval fir retrieving picture from a database. We assume that the user query is specified by the properties of different objects, and the relationships between the objects. The relationships have been divided into non-spatial and spatial relationships. In a companion paper, we have described how to employ indices together with deduction and reduction of spatial relationships for computing spatial similarity values. We have built a prototype system based on concepts described above. Preliminary experimental results are encouraging [1], [12].

References

[1] A. Aslandogan, C. Thier, C. T. Yu, et al "Implementation and Evaluation of SCORE(A System for COntent based REtrieval of Pictures)", IEEE Data Engineering Conference, March 1995.

[2] Amdor, F.G. et al., *Electronic How Things Work Articles: Two Early Prototypes*, IEEE TKDE, 5(4), Aug. 1993, pp611-618.

[3] Chen P. P. : "The Entity-Relationship Model Toward a Unified View of Data", ACM Transactions on Database Systems 1(1), March 1976, pp 9-36.

[4] S.K. Chang, T.Y. Hou, and A. Hsu, *Smart Image Design for Large Image Databases*, Large image Databases, 1993.

[5] Venkat N. Gudivada, Vijay V. Raghavan, and Kanonkluk Vanapipat *A Unified Approach to Data Modeling for a Class of Image Database Applications* Tech. Report 1994

[6] Gupta, A., Weymouth, T., and Jain, R. *Semantic Queries with Pictures: The VIMSYS Model* International Conference on Very Large Data Bases, Barcelona, Spain, pp.69-79 1991

[7] Lee Eric, Whalen T.: "Computer Image Retrieval by Features: Suspect Identification", INTERCHI '93, pp.494-499.

[8] Niblack W. et. al. : "The QBIC-project: Query images by content matching color, texture and shape", IBM Technical Report February 1993.

[9] Rabitti, F and P Savino, *An Information Retrieval Approach for Image Database*, VLDB, Canada, August 1992, pp 574-584.

[10] Salton G. : "Automatic Text Processing", Addison Wesley, Mass., 1989.

[11] Sistla P., Yu C., Haddad R. : "Reasoning About Spatial Relationships in Picture Retrieval Systems", VLDB '94.

[12] Sistla A.P., Yu C., et al: "Similarity Based Retrieval of Pictures Using Indices on Spatial Relationships", Technical Report, Dept. of EECS, University of Illinois at Chicago 1994.

Ink as a First-Class Datatype in Multimedia Databases

Walid G. Aref, Daniel Barbarà, and Daniel Lopresti

Matsushita Information Technology Laboratory
Panasonic Technologies, Inc., Two Research Way, Princeton, NJ 08540

1. Introduction

In this chapter, we turn out attention to databases that contain ink. The methods and techniques covered in this chapter can be used to deal effectively with the NOTES database of the Medical Scenario described in the Introduction of the book. With these techniques, doctors would be able to retrieve the handwritten notes about their patients, by using the pen as an input device for their queries.

The pen is a familiar and highly precise input device that is used by two new classes of machines: full-fledged pen computers (*i.e.*, notebook- or desktop-sized units with pen input, and, in some cases, a keyboard), and smaller, more-portable personal digital assistants (PDA's). In certain domains, pen-based computers have significant advantages over traditional keyboard-based machines, including the following:

1. As notepad computers continue to shrink and battery and screen technology improves, the keyboard becomes the limiting factor for miniaturization. Using a pen instead overcomes this difficulty.
2. The pen is language-independent – equally accessible to users of Kanji, Cyrillic, or Latin alphabets.
3. A large fraction of the adult population grew up without learning how to type and have no intentions of learning; this will continue to be the case for many years to come. However, everyone is familiar with the pen.
4. Keyboards are optimized for text entry. Pens naturally support the entry of text, drawings, figures, equations, etc. – in other words, a much richer domain of possible inputs.

In Section 2. of this chapter, we consider a somewhat radical viewpoint: that the immediate recognition of handwritten data is inappropriate in many situations. Computers that maintain ink *as ink* will be able to provide many novel and useful functions. However, they must also provide new features, including the ability to search through large amounts of ink effectively and efficiently. This functionality requires a database whose elements are samples of ink.

In Sections 3. and 4., we describe pattern-matching techniques that can be used to search linearly through a sequence of ink samples. We give data concerning the accuracy and efficiency of these operations. Under certain circumstances, when the size of the database is limited, these solutions are sufficient in themselves. As the size of the database grows, however, faster methods must be used. Section 5. describes database techniques that can be applied to yield sublinear search times.

2. Ink as First-Class Data

For the most part, today's pen computers operate in a mode which might be described as "eager recognition." Using handwriting recognition (HWX) software, pen-strokes are translated into ASCII[1] as soon as they are entered; the user corrects the output of the recognizer; and processing proceeds as if the characters had been typed on a keyboard.

It can be argued, however, that pen computers should not be simply keyboard-based machines with a pen in place of the keyboard. Rather than take a very expressive medium, ink, and immediately map it into a small, pre-defined set of alphanumeric symbols, pen computers could be used to support a concept we call *Computing in the Ink Domain*, as shown in Figure 2.1. Ink is a natural representation for data on pen computers in the same way that ASCII is a natural representation for data on keyboard-based machines. An ink-based system, which defers or eliminates HWX whenever possible, has the following advantages:

1. Many of a user's day-to-day tasks can be handled entirely in the ink domain using techniques more accurate and less intrusive than HWX.
2. No existing character set captures the full range of graphical representations a human can create using a pen (*e.g.*, pictures, maps, diagrams, equations, doodles). By not constraining pen-strokes to represent "valid" symbols, a much richer input language is made available to the user.
3. If recognition should become necessary at a later time, additional context for performing the translation may be available to improve the speed and accuracy of HWX.

The second point – ink is a richer representation language – deserves further discussion. An important advantage of computing in the ink domain is the fact that people often write and draw patterns that have no obvious ASCII representation. With only a fixed character set available, the user is sometimes forced to tedious extremes to convey a point graphically. Figure 2.2 shows an Internet newsgroup posting that demonstrates this awkward mode of communication. Contrast this with Figure 2.1, which illustrates the philosophy of treating all ink patterns as meaningful semantic entities that can be processed as first-class data.

[1] For concreteness, we assume HWX returns ASCII strings, but the reader may substitute whichever fixed character set is appropriate.

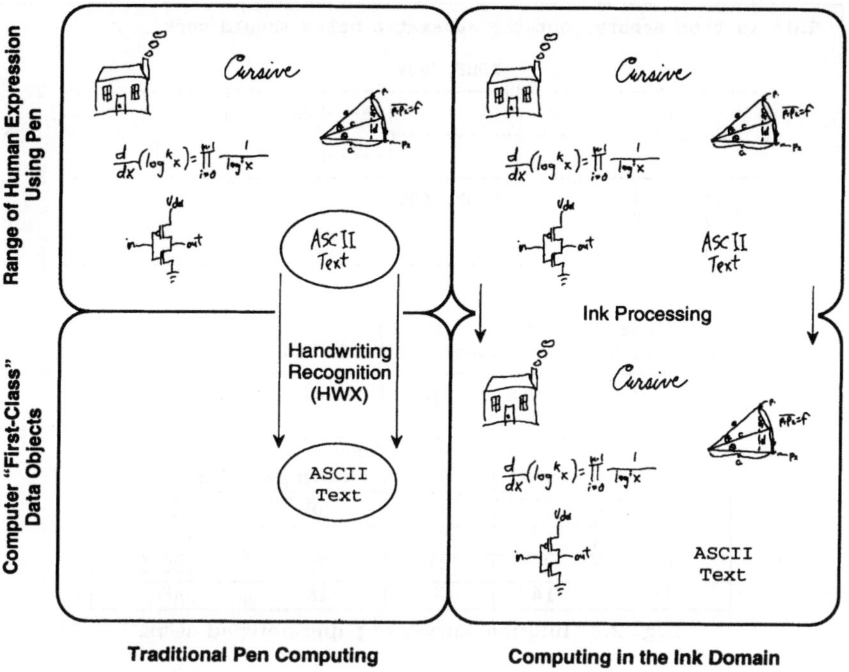

Fig. 2.1. Traditional pen computing versus computing in the ink domain.

2.1 Expressiveness of Ink

Our intuition tells us that ink is more expressive than ASCII. To test this assertion, we conducted an informal survey of the notebooks of a small number of university students. We asked each to provide examples of their handwritten notes, and broke the pages into three distinct categories:

1. ASCII-representable. This includes straight text, as well as text employing simple "typesetting" conventions such as underlining, etc.
2. Special character set. This includes symbols not found in standard ASCII, but sometimes present in extended character sets, such as mathematical symbols ($\int, \sum, \prod, \ldots$), unusual typographic symbols (Å,§,↗,♮,⏞), etc.
3. Drawings. This includes all ink not falling into one of the first two categories.

The results of our survey, shown in Figure 2.3, suggest that an electronic "notepad" dependent on converting all input to ASCII would be limiting for these users.

```
This is from memory, but the schematic below should work...

                            10uF, 63V
    --------o-------------||-----------------------o--------------- 2
    |       |                           |-----22K-----|
   |O      2K2       ----------------o                                 X
    |       |        |                  |-----22K-----|
    -----o--|---o----o----||-----------------------o--------------- 3  L
        +|  |   |+          10uF, 63V
         Z  |   C                                                      R
         |  |   |
     ----o--o---o-------------------------------------------------- 1

   Z: Zener diode (I used 15V I think)
   C: 10uF tantalum 25V, bypassed with 10nF plastic film
```

Fig. 2.2. An example of ASCII "graphics."

Data Set	Number of Pages ASCII	Special	Drawings	Percent Non-ASCII
A	54	0	58	52%
B	10	9	12	68%
C	0	33	78	100%
D	14	3	18	60%

Fig. 2.3. Informal survey of paper notepad users.

2.2 Approximate Ink Matching

Ink has the advantage of being a rich, natural representation for humans. However, ASCII text has the advantage of being a natural representation for computers; it can be stored efficiently, searched quickly, etc. If ink is to be made a "first-class datatype" for pen computers, it must be:

- **Transportable.** The ASCII character set made a specific (and somewhat arbitrary) set of 128 characters essentially universal. Standards like JOT [23] are now being developed to make ink data usable across a wide variety of platforms.
- **Editable.** Years of research and development have led to text-oriented word processors that are both powerful and easy-to-use. We need similar editors for ink data. It should be as easy to edit ink (*e.g.* copy, paste, delete, insert) as it is to edit ASCII text.
- **Searchable.** Computers excel at storing and searching textual data – the same must hold for ink. In particular, it should be possible for the user to locate previously saved pen-stroke data by specifying a query and having the computer return the closest matches it can find.

While these three properties are all of fundamental importance, the last, searchability, is a primary topic of this chapter. Since no one writes the same word exactly the same way twice, we cannot depend on exact matches in the case of ink. Instead, search is performed using an *approximate ink matching* (or AIM) procedure. AIM takes two sequences of pen strokes, an *ink pattern* and an *ink database*, and returns a pointer to the location in the ink database that matches the ink pattern as closely as possible.

Such a procedure is a surprisingly general tool for ink-based computing. We now give several examples to show how AIM can be used to provide a wide range of functionality to the user:

- Andrew writes a short note to Bill. Using AIM, Bill's address is located in a database of past addresses to which Andrew has sent mail. The message itself is compressed and sent to Bill to be read as ink – full HWX of the message body is never performed. Indeed, Bill will do a far better job of reading the message than current HWX algorithms, especially if it contains cursive script, diagrams, or other non-ASCII symbols. Figure 2.4 illustrates this. Figure 2.2, on the other hand, is an example of a message that would have been more simply and effectively communicated via digital ink.
- Martha runs an application on her pen computer and names all of her documents using pen strokes. In many cases, she finds her documents by browsing through the names – HWX is not necessary. In other cases, she enters a query for which the system searches using AIM. This particular AIM problem is made simpler by the fact that the query must only be matched against the current database of filenames instead of a larger, more general database.
- Joe has an on-line discussion with Martha about a mathematical idea they have been considering. Later, he wishes to retrieve the document. He enters one of the equations he recalls from the conversation. The system searches through his pen-stroke data and finds a similar-looking sequence of strokes, returning the page in question.

Thus, AIM is central to computing in the ink domain. Of course, we can think of approximate ink matching as exactly the problem of searching a database in which the keys are pen-strokes. Thus, we expect ink to become an important new form of multimedia data.

3. Pictographic Naming

We now consider an application in which AIM can be applied to provide necessary functionality, allowing a traditionally text-based operation to be performed entirely using ink. The domain is that of file names. Traditionally, a name is a short string of alphanumeric characters with the property that it can be easily stored, recognized, and remembered. However, the current approach to specifying names using a pen has received widespread criticism: the user writes the name letter-by-letter into a comb or grid and the computer performs HWX on each character. Error rates are high enough that the user must often pause to redraw an incorrectly recognized letter. Other options

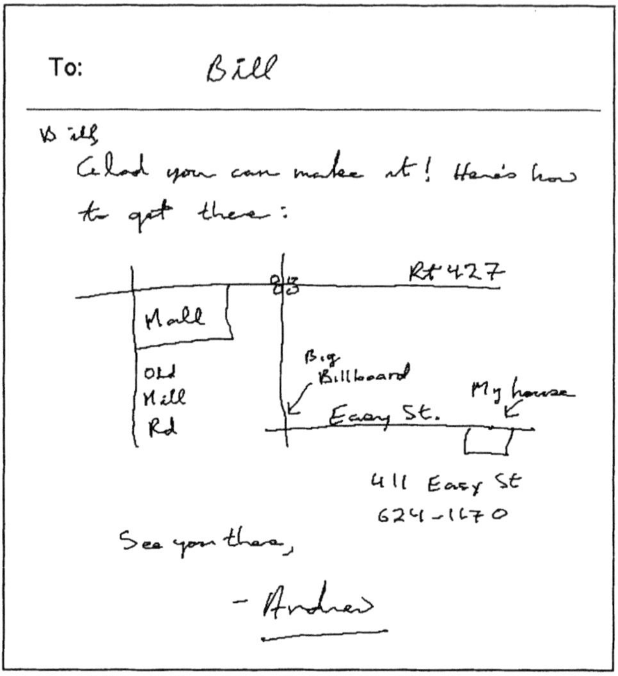

Fig. 2.4. A sample ink e-mail message.

seem even less appealing: the user could follow a path through a menu system to specify a letter uniquely, or tap a pen on a simulated keyboard provided by the system. None of these methods feels like a natural way to specify a name, though.

Consider instead extending the space of acceptable names to include arbitrary hand-drawn pictures of a certain size, which we call *pictographic names*, or simply *pictograms* [17], [16]. The precise semantics of the pictograms are left entirely to the user. Intuitively, the major advantages of the pictogram approach are ease of specification and a much larger name-space. A disadvantage is that people cannot be expected to re-create perfectly a previously drawn pictogram; hence, looking up a document by name requires AIM. In this section we study techniques for performing ink search in this limited domain, and present some experimental results.

3.1 Motivation

Broadly speaking, a computer user can specify the name of an existing file or document in either of two ways: *Direct manipulation*, selecting the desired name from a list of possible options in a scrollable graphical browser; and *Reproduction*, duplicating the original name by retyping or redrawing it, and then letting the computer search for a match.

The motivation behind pictographic naming is the following: since users of graphical interfaces often specify files through direct manipulation rather than reproduction, HWX of a name may never be necessary and should be deferred whenever possible. A natural way to defer HWX is to leave the name as ink, in the form of a pictogram, which the user can browse later. This leaves the user free to choose complex and varied pictographic names, but forces the operating system to search for reproduced names approximately rather than exactly, a more difficult problem.

As a concrete example, suppose the user has produced the note shown in Figure 3.1. Perhaps it is part of a paper he/she is working on, a slide for a presentation, or something drawn to communicate an idea to a friend. The user wants to store the document, and to be able to access it later on. A natural idea is to write a small pictogram describing its contents – for example, Figure 3.2. When the user wants to retrieve the set of equations, he/she can easily browse through the list of pictograms to find the appropriate one, without resorting to the use of a keyboard, and without a complicated and inaccurate translation to a computer representation of characters.

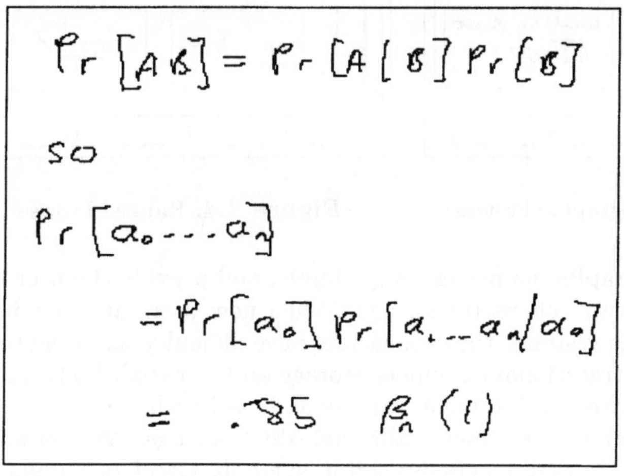

Figure 3.1. An example document

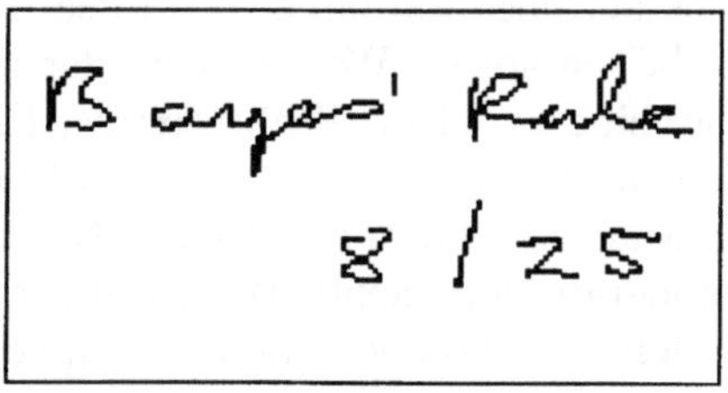

Figure 3.2. Its pictographic name

3.2 A Pictographic Browser

To implement a file naming paradigm such as this, consider providing the user with a document browser, much like the browsers used in traditional mouse-based graphical user interfaces. However, rather than select a text string, the user selects an appropriate pictographic name. Such a browser is shown in Figure 3.3.

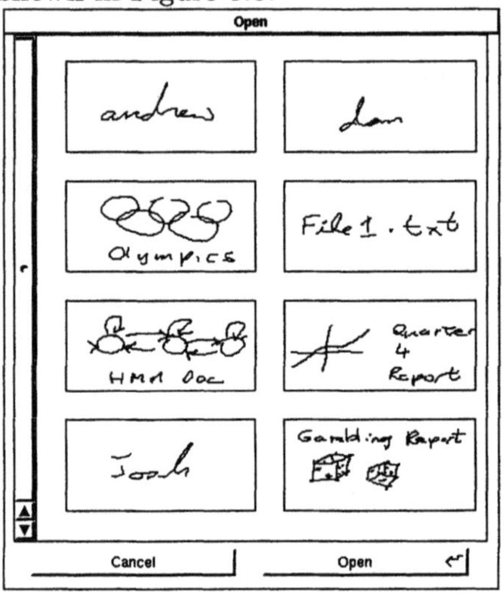

Figure 3.3. Pictographic browser

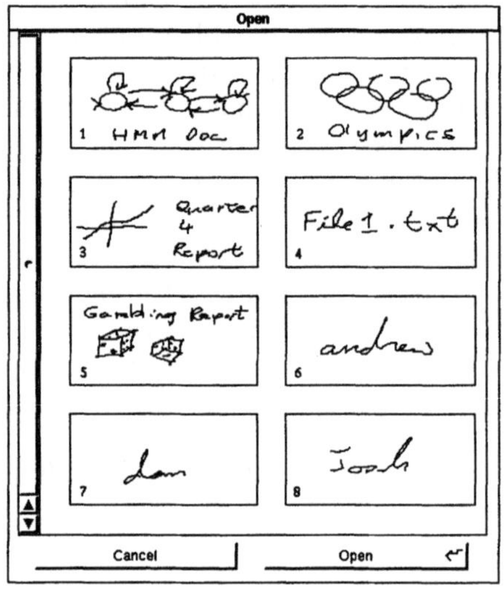

Figure 3.4. Ranked browser

Note that pictographic names are very simple, and provide the user with far more flexibility than character strings. When new users are first introduced to standard file systems, they sometimes have difficulty adapting to the rigid conventions of traditional document storage and retrieval. Pictographic names allow the user to specify names rapidly and easily, while making available a much larger name space than traditional ASCII strings. Written words, sketches, non-ASCII characters, cursive script, symbols, Greek or Cyrillic letters, Kanji or other Eastern characters, or any combination of these are all valid names, as long as the user can recognize what he/she drew at a later time.

When the number of names becomes too large to browse manually, automatic search methods must be employed. We now consider an algorithm for solving this pictogram matching problem. While simple, this approach can produce results better than those obtained using nominally more powerful techniques such as Hidden Markov Models and Neural Nets. This seems appropriate for domains of moderate complexity (*e.g.*, the browser of Figure 3.3). As the complexity increases, however, more advanced tools may be necessary; in later sections, we examine a number of these more difficult tasks.

3.3 The Window Algorithm

If we knew that the same pictogram drawn twice by the same individual would tend to line up point-for-point, we could measure similarity between pictograms by summing the distances between corresponding points. Unfortunately, for real-world samples the points are not likely to correspond so closely. A two-step approach allows us to overcome this difficulty. First we compress the curves down to a small number of points. Then we allow the two curves to "slide" along one another. Given two pen-stroke sequences p and q, each re-sampled to contain N points, and an integer Δ representing the maximum "slide" we are willing to allow, define the distance D to be

$$D(p,q) \equiv \sum_{i=1}^{N} \left(\sum_{\delta=-\Delta}^{\Delta} w_\delta \, d(p_i, q_{i+\delta}) \right) \tag{3.1}$$

We assume that the point-wise distance function d returns 0 for boundary conditions where $i+\delta \notin [1..N]$. The values for w_δ are a parameter – we typically use $w_\delta = 1/(|\delta|+1)$.

This procedure is similar to the dynamic programming "template matching" algorithms used in character recognition. However, it is computationally more efficient, and it allows us to make use of the fact that given two similar sequences p and q, we expect some similarity between p_i and all of $\{q_{i-1}, q_i, q_{i+1}\}$.

Experimental results for the Window algorithm are given in Figure 3.5. Each of four subjects created a database of 60 names. The first was in Japanese, the remainder in English. Each subject then re-drew each of the 60 names three times to create a 180-word test set. For each element of the test set, we used the Window algorithm to select and rank the eight most similar-looking words in the database. On average, this operation took 1/3 of a second to complete for each element of the test set, running on a 40MHz NeXT workstation. The table shows how often the correct element of the database was ranked first ("Ranked First"), and how often it was ranked in the top eight choices ("Ranked In Top 8").

Success Criterion	Data Set A	B	C	D	Ave.
Ranked First	97%	83%	94%	88%	90%
Ranked In Top 8	100%	95%	99%	98%	98%

Fig. 3.5. Experimental evaluation of the Window algorithm.

3.4 Hidden Markov Models

In this section, we present an overview of Hidden Markov Models in the context of handwritten pictogram matching. The reader is referred to [20] for a tutorial. We assume that each of the pictograms is modeled by a Hidden Markov Model (HMM) as done in [14], [15]. The HMM of a pictogram is stored along with the document to allow subsequent matching with the input.

Formally, an HMM is a doubly stochastic process that contains a non-observable underlying stochastic process (hidden) that can be uncovered by a set of stochastic processes that produce the sequence of observed symbols. Mathematically, an HMM is a tuple $< \Sigma, Q, a, b >$, where

- Σ is a (finite) alphabet of output symbols.
- Q is a set of states, $Q = \{0, ..., N-1\}$ for an N-state model.
- a is a probability distribution that governs the transitions between states. The probability of going from state i to j is denoted by a_{ij}. The transition probabilities a_{ij} are real numbers between 0 and 1, such that
  for all $i \in Q$: $\sum_{j=0}^{N-1} a_{ij} = 1$
  The distribution includes the initial distribution of states, that is the probability a_i of the first state being i.
- b is an output probability distribution $b_i(s)$ that govern the distribution of output symbols for each state. That is, $b_i(s)$ is the probability of producing the symbol $s \in \Sigma$ while being in state i. These probabilities follow the rules:
  for all $i \in Q$ and $s \in \Sigma : 0 \leq b_i(s) \leq 1$
  for all $i \in Q$, $\sum_{s \in \Sigma} b_i(s) = 1$

A variety of HMMs have been used to model handwriting. Also, a variety of features have been selected to describe the output symbols. In [15], the authors divide the hand-drawn figure in points and extract four features per point: direction, velocity, change of direction and change of velocity. Each feature is drawn from a set of four possible values, hence the feature vector for a point is represented using eight bits. Each vector value is one of the output symbols in Σ.

Usually the transition probabilities (a) and the state set (Q) are computed by best-fitting the model to a series of samples. This is known as training the model. Algorithms for training models using samples of handwriting are described in [3]. These algorithms are fast and require no intervention from the writer. Each sample used for the training consists of a sequence of output symbols (points), with which the parameters of the model can be adjusted. However, in applications like the one we are describing, the model has to be described using a single sample (a sequence of output symbols for the document that is to be filed). Quite commonly, then, the structure of the model is fixed to accommodate for the lack of samples with which to train it. A choice used in [13] is that of a left-to-right HMM, i.e. a model in which it is only possible to remain in the current state or to jump to the next one in sequence. These models are sufficiently powerful to capture pictograms, as we have found out in practice. The rest of the adjustable parameters (branching probabilities, number of states, and output probabilities) provide a broad spectrum of choices to accomodate for pictogram differences. An example of such model is given in Figure 3.6. This model contains 5 states numbered from 0 to 4, and the probability to jump from state i to $i+1$ is 0.5, while the probability of staying in the same state is 0.5. For the last state, the probability of staying in it is 1.0.

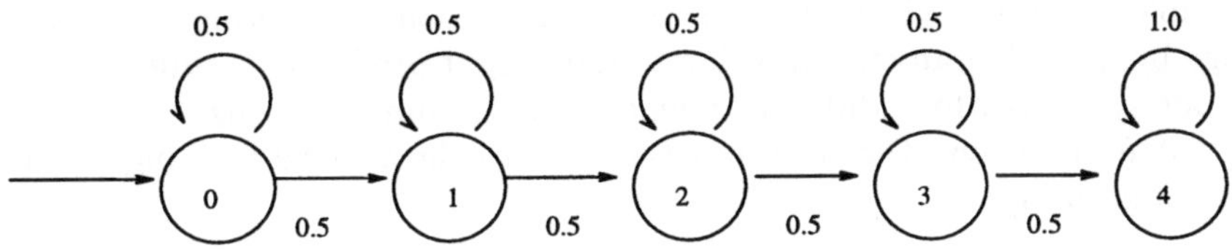

Fig. 3.6. A left-to-right HMM.

Several authors have used HMMs to model handwriting and hand-written documents (e.g., [14], [15], [5], [26]).

We assume that each pictogram in the database is modeled by a left-to - right HMM, i.e., a model in which it is only possible to remain in the current state or to jump to the next one in sequence. An example of such model is given in Figure 3.7. The HMM of a pictogram is stored along with the pictogram to allow subsequent matching with the input.

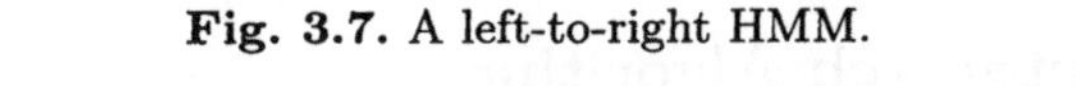

Fig. 3.7. A left-to-right HMM.

This model contains 4 states numbered from 0 to 3, and the probability to jump from state i to $i+1$ is $\frac{N}{N+T}$, while the probability of staying in the same state is $\frac{T}{N+T}$. For the last state, the probability of staying in it is 1.0. Notice that we adjust the transition probabilities so that the HMM is *encouraged* to remain in the same state until it consumes the symbols in the input pattern that correspond to this state. More concretely, consider an HMM with N states and an input pattern with T symbols. Assume that each of the N states is responsible for consuming $\frac{T}{N}$ symbols. Therefore, we can adjust the transition probability matrix a in the following way:

$$a_{ii} = \frac{\frac{T}{N}}{\frac{T}{N}+1} = \frac{T}{N+T} \text{ for } i = 0, ..., N-1 \tag{3.2}$$

$$a_{i,i+1} = \frac{1}{\frac{T}{N}+1} = \frac{N}{N+T} \text{ for } i = 0, ..., N-1 \tag{3.3}$$

This way, it is expected that the HMM consumes the symbols intended for a given state before moving to the next state. The model is then trained using multiple sample inputs (see [3] for a detailed discussion about training using multiple patterns). Smoothing is performed upon completing the training stage by assigning an epsilon value to the output probability value for all the output symbols which did not appear in the training patterns.

Table 3.1 shows the results obtained with the various training methods presented in [3].

Row	Training Method	Rank					Tot.Rnk
		1st	2nd	3rd	5th	10th	
0	No Training	42.25%	55.00	63.75	74.75	87.50	1685
1	Levinson's [12]	85.25%	91.25	94.25	96.25	98.50	252
2	Plain average	85.50%	90.75	93.75	97.00	98.25	240
3	Biased average (normalized)	80.25%	90.00	92.75	96.25	98.25	285
4	Biased average (unnormalized)	85.00%	91.00	94.25	97.00	98.75	220
5	Binary merge (normalized)	81.00%	90.00	93.00	96.25	98.25	283
6	Binary merge (unnormalized)	81.75%	90.25	94.00	96.50	98.75	239

Table 3.1. A comparison of various training methods.

4. The ScriptSearch Algorithm

We now turn our attention to a more difficult problem, that of searching through a continuous ink text. In the domain of pictographic naming, we are essentially solving a dictionary look-up problem: given a dictionary of words and a search key, we wish to locate the key in the dictionary. We know that the key will never span multiple entries, and that it will always match the intended entry from beginning to end.

Now, however, imagine a pen computer on which a user has written many pages of notes. If the user wishes to re-enter and search for a particular phrase, the system must be able to locate the phrase even though it crosses an unknown number of word boundaries. The problem is made all the more difficult when one considers that word segmentation algorithms sometimes make mistakes, breaking one word into two or merging two into one. We next describe an algorithm that requires no *a priori* segmentation of the database – it is searched as though it were a continuous stream of text [18]. We begin with some definitions.

4.1 Definitions

Ink is a sequence of time-stamped points in the plane:[2]

$$ink = (x_1, y_1, t_1), (x_2, y_2, t_2), \ldots, (x_k, y_k, t_k) \quad (4.1)$$

Given two ink sequences T and P (the *text* and the *pattern*), the ink search problem consists of determining all locations in T where P occurs. This differs significantly from the exact string matching problem in that we cannot expect perfect matches between the symbols of P and T. No one writes a word precisely the same way twice. Ambiguity exists at all levels of abstraction: points can be drawn at slightly different locations; pen-strokes can be deleted, added, merged, or split; characters can be written using any of a number of different "allographs," etc. Hence, approximate string matching is the appropriate paradigm for ink search.

A standard model for approximate string matching is provided by *edit distance*, also known as the "k-differences problem" in the literature. In the traditional case [29], the following three operations are permitted:

1. delete a symbol,[3]
2. insert a symbol,
3. substitute one symbol for another.

Each of these is assigned a cost, c_{del}, c_{ins}, and c_{sub}, and the edit distance, $d(P,T)$, is defined as the minimum cost of any sequence of basic operations that transforms P into T. This optimization problem can be solved using a well-known dynamic programming algorithm. Let $P = p_1 p_2 \ldots p_m$, $T = t_1 t_2 \ldots t_n$, and define $d_{i,j}$ to be the distance between the first i symbols of P and the first j symbols of T. Note that $d(P,T) = d_{m,n}$. The initial conditions are

$$\begin{aligned} d_{0,0} &= 0 & & \\ d_{i,0} &= d_{i-1,0} + c_{del}(p_i) & 1 \le i \le m & \quad (4.2) \\ d_{0,j} &= d_{0,j-1} + c_{ins}(t_j) & 1 \le j \le n & \end{aligned}$$

and the main dynamic programming recurrence is

[2] Pen-tip pressure is another parameter that is sometimes available, but we do not make use of it in this chapter.

[3] The term "symbol" is often taken to mean a text character. Here we use it much more generally – a symbol could be a pen-stroke, for example.

$$d_{i,j} = \min \begin{cases} d_{i-1,j} & + \; c_{del}(p_i) \\ d_{i,j-1} & + \; c_{ins}(t_j) \\ d_{i-1,j-1} & + \; c_{sub}(p_i, t_j) \end{cases} \qquad 1 \le i \le m, \; 1 \le j \le n \tag{4.3}$$

When Equation 4.3 is used as the inner-loop step in an implementation, the time required is $O(mn)$ where m and n are the lengths of the two strings.

This formulation requires the two strings to be aligned in their entirety. The variation we use for ink search is modified so that a short pattern can be matched against a longer text. We make the initial edit distance 0 along the entire length of the text (allowing a match to start anywhere), and search the final row of the edit distance table for the smallest value (allowing a match to end anywhere). The initial conditions become

$$\begin{aligned} d_{0,0} &= 0 \\ d_{i,0} &= d_{i-1,0} + c_{del}(p_i) \qquad 1 \le i \le m \\ d_{0,j} &= 0 \end{aligned} \tag{4.4}$$

The inner-loop recurrence (*i.e.*, Equation 4.3) remains the same. Finally, we must define our evaluation criteria. It seems inevitable that any ink search algorithm will miss true occurrences of P in T, and report false "hits" at locations where P does not really occur. Quantifying the success of an algorithm under these circumstances is not straightforward. The field of information retrieval concerns itself with a similar problem in a different domain, however, and has converged on the following two measures [24]:

Recall The percentage of the time P is found.
Precision The percentage of reported matches that are in fact true.

Obviously it is desirable to have both of these measures as close to 1 as possible. There is, however, a fundamental trade-off between the two. By insisting on an exact match, the precision can be made 1, but the recall will undoubtedly suffer. On the other hand, if we allow arbitrary edits between the pattern and the matched portion of the text, the recall will approach 1, but the precision will fall to 0. For ink to be searchable, there must exist a point on this trade-off curve where both the recall and the precision are sufficiently high.

4.2 Approaches to Searching Ink

Ink can be represented at a number of levels of abstraction, as indicated in Figure 4.1. At the lowest level, ink is a sequence of points; at the highest, ink is ASCII text. It is natural to assume that ink search could take place at any given level, with attendant advantages and disadvantages.

As can be seen from the figure, at each stage ink is represented as a collection of higher-level objects. Some of the earlier information is lost, and a new representation is created that (hopefully) captures the relevant information

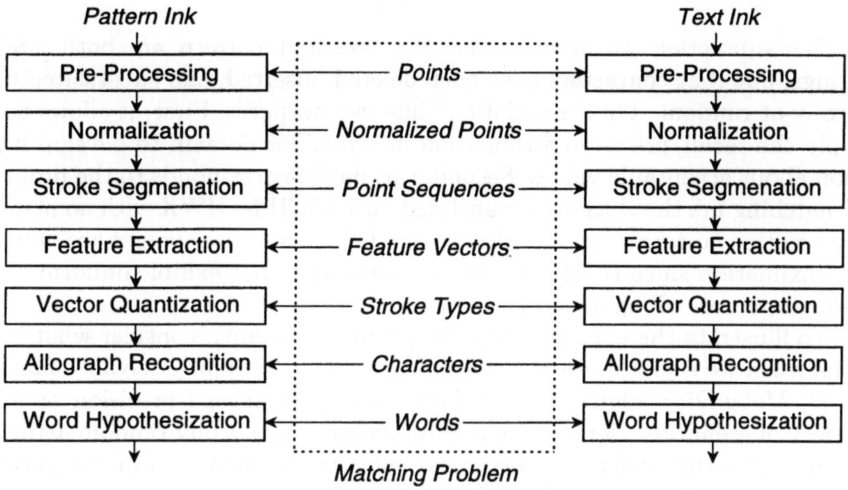

Fig. 4.1. Handwriting recognition stages and potential matching problems.

from the previous level in a more concise form. So, for instance, it may be impossible to know from the final word which allographs were used, or to know from the feature vectors exactly what the ink looked like, etc. Each stage in the process can be viewed as a recognition task (*e.g.*, strokes from points, words from allographs), and introduces the possibility of new errors.

An ink search algorithm could perform approximate matching at any level of representation. At one end of the spectrum, an algorithm like the Window algorithm of Section 3. could be used to match individual points in the pattern to points in the text. At the other extreme, we could perform full HWX on both the pattern and the text, and then apply "fuzzy" matching on the resulting ASCII strings (to account for recognition errors).

In the next subsection, we consider the latter option by examining how randomly introduced "noise" affects recall and precision for text searching. The point here is to gain some intuition about the performance of ink search algorithms built on top of traditional handwriting recognition.

Section 4.4 presents an in-depth examination of an algorithm we call *ScriptSearch* that performs matching at the level of pen-strokes. This approach has the advantage of allowing us to do quite well against a broad range of handwriting, including some so bad that a human might find it illegible. ScriptSearch also allows the possibility of matching strings with no obvious ASCII representation, such as equations, drawings, doodles, etc.

4.3 Searching for Patterns in Noisy Text

In this subsection we assume that the text and pattern are both ASCII strings, but that characters have been deleted, inserted, and substituted uniformly at random. This "simulation" has two purposes. First, it allows us to apply the recall/precision formulation in a familiar domain to develop intuition about acceptable values. Second, this model corresponds to the problem of matching ink that has been translated into ASCII by HWX with no manual intervention to correct recognition errors. Of course, these values are only an approximation since HWX processes in general do not exhibit uniform error behavior across all characters.

To illustrate the effects of noise on pattern matching, consider what happens when we search for a number of keywords in Herman Melville's famous novel, *Moby-Dick*. Figure 4.2 tabulates average recall and precision under a variety of scenarios. Here *garble rate* represents a uniformly random artificial noise source that deletes, inserts, and substitutes characters in the pattern and the text. Note that when there is some "fuzziness," the precision can drop off rapidly if we require perfect recall. At some point, the text is no longer searchable as too many false hits are returned to the user. This is what we mean when we ask the question: Is ink searchable?

Edit Distance Threshold	Garble Rate 0%		10%		20%	
	Recall	Precision	Recall	Precision	Recall	Precision
0	1.000	1.000	0.274	0.995	0.003	0.996
1	1.000	0.875	0.643	0.901	0.280	0.944
2	1.000	0.610	0.910	0.581	0.664	0.700
3	1.000	0.329	0.986	0.326	0.886	0.424
4	1.000	0.121	1.000	0.097	0.981	0.154
5	1.000	0.021	1.000	0.015	0.999	0.048
6	1.000	0.010	1.000	0.010	1.000	0.013

Fig. 4.2. Searching for keywords in *Moby-Dick* (as a function of threshold).

Another view of the data is to consider the precision realizable for a given recall rate. This is shown in Figure 4.3. An intuitive interpretation of this figure is that setting a threshold is unnecessary if a ranked list of matches is returned to the user. In this case, for example, at a 10% garble rate, the user will experience a precision of 0.928 in viewing 50% of the true hits for the pattern.

Of course, real text (without noise) is searchable using routines like Unix `grep`, etc. However, handwriting is inherently "noisy" – it is not possible to say *a priori* that a given handwriting sample is just as searchable as its textual counterpart. That is the purpose of studies such as this.

	Garble Rate		
	0%	10%	20%
Recall	Precision	Precision	Precision
0.1	1.000	0.950	0.901
0.2	1.000	0.950	0.901
0.3	1.000	0.950	0.896
0.4	1.000	0.950	0.771
0.5	1.000	0.928	0.678
0.6	1.000	0.909	0.616
0.7	1.000	0.814	0.564
0.8	1.000	0.744	0.408
0.9	1.000	0.604	0.289
1.0	1.000	0.102	0.018

Fig. 4.3. Searching for keywords in *Moby-Dick* (as a function of recall rate).

4.4 The ScriptSearch Algorithm

As we noted above, representations for ink exist at various different levels of abstraction. In this subsection we examine an algorithm for writer-dependent ink search at the pen-stroke level. The algorithm applies dynamic programming with a recurrence similar to that used for string edit distance, but with a different set of operations and costs. The top-level organization of the ScriptSearch algorithm is shown in Figure 4.4.

As can be seen from the figure, there are four phases to the algorithm. First, the incoming ink points are grouped into strokes. Next, the strokes are converted into vectors of descriptive features. Third, the feature vectors are classified according to writer-specific information. Finally, the resulting sequence of classified strokes is matched against the text using approximate string matching over an alphabet of "stroke classes." We now describe the four phases in more detail.

4.4.1 Stroke Segmentation. There are several common stroke segmentation algorithms used in handwriting recognition. For our experiments, we break strokes at local minima of the y values. Figure 4.5 shows a sample line of stroke-segmented text.

4.4.2 Feature Extraction. As with segmentation algorithms, there are many different feature sets employed by handwriting researchers today. We have taken a set created by Dean Rubine in the context of gesture recognition [21]. This particular feature set, which converts each stroke into a real-valued 13-dimensional vector, seems to do well at discriminating single strokes, and can be efficiently updated as new points arrive. The feature set includes the length of the stroke, total angle traversed, angle and length of the bounding box diagonal, etc.

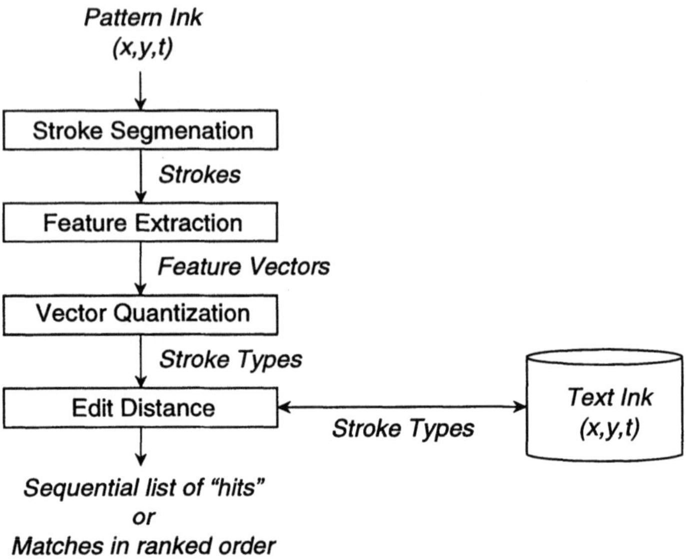

Fig. 4.4. Overview of the ScriptSearch algorithm.

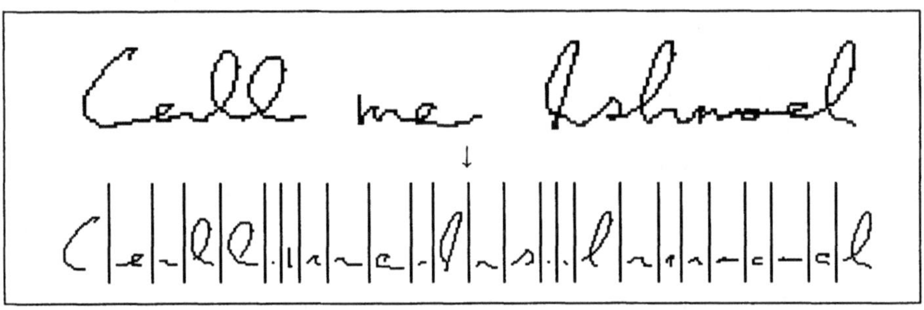

Fig. 4.5. Example of pen-stroke segmentation.

4.4.3 Vector Quantization. In the vector quantization stage, the complex 13-dimensional feature space is segmented or "quantized" into 64 clusters. From then on, instead of representing a feature vector by 13 real values, we represent it by the index of the cluster to which it belongs. Thus, rather than maintain 13 real numbers, we maintain 6 bits. This technique is common in speech recognition and many other pattern recognition domains [11]. The quantization makes the remaining processing much more efficient, and seeks to choose clusters so that useful semantic information about the strokes is retained by the 6 bits of the index. We now describe how to build and use the clusters. First, we must describe how distances are calculated in the feature space.

We collect a small sample of handwriting from each writer in advance. This is segmented into strokes, each of which is converted into a feature vector $\mathbf{v} =< v_1, v_2, \ldots, v_{13} >^T$. We use the sample to calculate the average of the ith feature, μ_i, and use these averages to compute the covariance matrix Σ defined by

$$\Sigma_{ij} \equiv E\left[(v_i - \mu_i)(v_j - \mu_j)\right] \tag{4.5}$$

Hence, for instance, the diagonal of Σ contains the variances of the features.

Instead of standard Euclidean distance, we employ *Mahalanobis distance* [22]. This is defined on the space of feature vectors as follows:

$$\|\mathbf{v}\|_M^2 \equiv \mathbf{v}^T \Sigma^{-1} \mathbf{v} \tag{4.6}$$

$$d(\mathbf{v}, \mathbf{w}) \equiv \|(\mathbf{v} - \mathbf{w})\|_M \tag{4.7}$$

With a suitable distance measure for our feature space, we can now proceed to describe a vector quantization scheme. We cluster the feature vectors of the ink sample into 64 groups using a clustering algorithm from the literature known as the k-means algorithm [19]. The feature vectors of the sample are processed sequentially. Each vector in turn is placed into a cluster, which is then updated to reflect the new member. Each cluster is represented by its centroid, the element-wise average of all vectors in the cluster.

The rule for classifying new feature vectors uses the centroids that define each cluster: a new vector belongs to the cluster with the nearest centroid, using Mahalanobis distance as the measure. The 64 final clusters can be thought of as "stroke-types," and the feature extraction and VQ phases can be thought of as classifying strokes into stroke-types.

After these phases of processing have been performed, the text and pattern are represented as sequences of quantized stroke-types:

$$< \textit{stroke-type 7} >< \textit{stroke-type 42} >< \textit{stroke-type 20} > \ldots \tag{4.8}$$

Recall that $P = p_1 p_2 \ldots p_m$ and $T = t_1 t_2 \ldots t_n$. From now on, we shall assume that the p_i's and t_j's are vector-quantized stroke-types.

The operations described above can be computed without significant overhead from the Mahalanobis distance metric. First, note that the inverse covariance matrix is positive definite (in fact, any matrix defining a valid distance must be positive definite). So we perform a Cholesky decomposition to write:

$$\Sigma^{-1} = A^T A \tag{4.9}$$

This being the case, we note that the new distance simply represents a coordinate transformation of the space:

$$\mathbf{v}^T \Sigma^{-1} \mathbf{v} = \mathbf{v}^T (A^T A) \mathbf{v} = (\mathbf{v}^T A^T) \cdot (A\mathbf{v}) = \mathbf{w}^T \mathbf{w} \tag{4.10}$$

where $\mathbf{w} = A\mathbf{v}$. Thus, once all the points have been transformed, we can perform future calculations in standard Euclidean space.

4.4.4 Edit Distance. Finally, we compute the similarity between the sequence of stroke-types associated with the pattern ink, and the pre-computed sequence for the text ink. We use dynamic programming to determine the edit distance between the sequences. The cost of a deletion or an insertion is a function of the "size" of the ink being deleted or inserted, where size is defined to be the length of the stroke-type representing the ink, again using Mahalanobis distance. The cost of a substitution is the distance between the stroke-types. We also allow two additional operations: two-to-one *merges* and one-to-two *splits*. These account for imperfections in the stroke segmentation algorithm. We build a merge/split table that contains information of the form "an average stroke of type 1 merged with an average stroke of type 4 results in a stroke of type 11." The cost of a particular merge involving strokes α and β and resulting in stroke γ is, for instance, a function of the distance between $merge(\alpha, \beta)$ and γ. We compute the edit distance using these operations and their associated costs to find the best match in the text ink.

Again, recall that $d_{i,j}$ represents the cost of the best match of the first i symbols of P and some substring of T ending at symbol j. The recurrence, modified to account for our new types of substitution (1:2 and 2:1), is as follows:

$$d_{i,j} = \min \begin{cases} d_{i-1,j} & + \quad c_{del}(p_i) \\ d_{i,j-1} & + \quad c_{ins}(t_j) \\ d_{i-1,j-1} & + \quad c_{sub1:1}(p_i, t_j) \\ d_{i-1,j-2} & + \quad c_{sub1:2}(p_i, t_{j-1}t_j) \\ d_{i-2,j-1} & + \quad c_{sub2:1}(p_{i-1}p_i, t_j) \end{cases} \qquad 1 \leq i \leq m,\ 1 \leq j \leq n \tag{4.11}$$

4.5 Evaluation of ScriptSearch

In this section, we describe the procedure we used when evaluating the ScriptSearch algorithm. We asked two individuals to hand-write a reasonably large amount of text taken from the beginning of *Moby-Dick*. Throughout the remainder of this discussion, we shall refer to these two primary datasets as "Writer A" and "Writer B." Figure 4.6 summarizes some basic statistics concerning the test data.

Text	Strokes	Characters	Words	Lines	Style
Writer A	34,560	23,262	4,045	625	Cursive
Writer B	19,324	12,269	2,194	363	Printed

Fig. 4.6. Statistics for the test data used to evaluate ScriptSearch.

We then asked each writer to write a sequence of 30 short words and 30 longer phrases (two-to-three words each), also taken from the same passages of *Moby-Dick*. These were the search strings, which we sometimes refer to as "patterns" or "queries." In ASCII form, the short patterns ranged in length from 5 to 11 characters, with an average length of 8 characters. The long patterns ranged from 12 to 24 characters, with an average length of 16. Since ScriptSearch is meant to be writer-dependent, we were primarily interested in the results of searching the text produced by a particular writer for patterns produced by the same writer.

As indicated earlier, the task of the algorithm is to find all the lines of the text that contain the pattern. For each writer (A and B), we augmented by hand the ASCII source text with the locations of the line breaks. Thus, the ASCII text corresponded line-for-line to the ink text. Using exact matching techniques, we found all occurrences of the ASCII patterns in the ASCII text, and noted the lines on which they occurred. For an ink search to be successful, the ink patterns must be found on the corresponding lines of the ink text.

We then segmented the ink texts into lines using simple pattern recognition techniques, and associated each stroke of the ink text with a line number. Figure 4.7 shows an example of a page of ink with the center-points of the lines determined by the algorithm, and also serves to illustrate the quality of the handwriting in the test data.

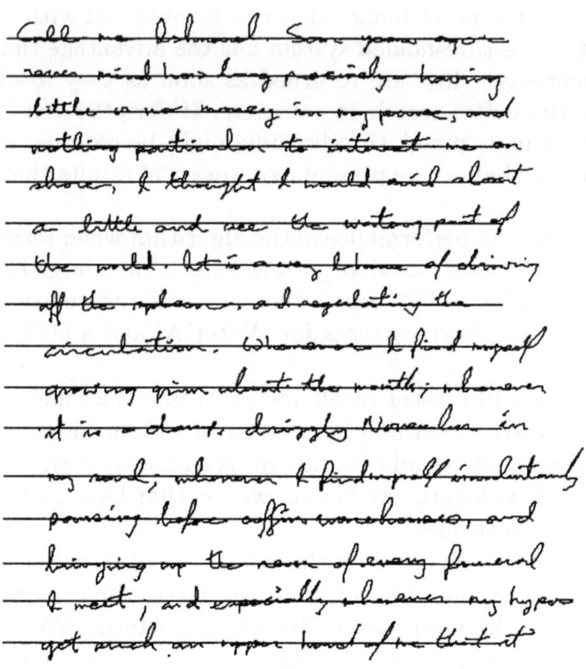

Fig. 4.7. Estimation of line center-points (ScriptSearch line segmentation).

Using ScriptSearch, we found all matches for the ink pattern in the ink text. When combined with the line segmentation information, this determined the lines of the ink text upon which matches occurred. Since the ASCII text had been placed in line-for-line correspondence to the ink text, we could quickly determine which matches were valid, which were "false hits," and which were missed by the algorithm. From this information, we computed the recall and precision of the ScriptSearch procedure.

4.6 Experimental Results

As mentioned previously, there are two ways of viewing the output of a pattern matching algorithm like ScriptSearch. If hits are returned in a ranked order, precision can be calculated by considering the number of spurious elements in the ranking above a certain recall value. If all hits exceeding a fixed threshold are returned, recall and precision can be calculated by determining the total number of hits returned and the number of valid hits returned for a particular threshold.

There is a common thread relating these two points of view. If it were possible to choose an optimal threshold for each search, then a system that returns all hits above that threshold will have the same recall (*i.e.*, 1) and precision as a ranked system. Thus, a ranked system represents, in some sense, an upper-bound on the performance that can be obtained with a thresholded system. In contrast, a thresholded system has the advantage that ink can be processed sequentially – hits are returned as soon as they are found, without waiting for the entire search to complete. If ScriptSearch is used as an intermediate stage in a "pipe," thresholding might be required in certain applications. Hence, as before, we present experimental results that reflect both viewpoints.

Figure 4.8 shows the performance of the algorithm when returning ranked hits. These results demonstrate that pattern length has a large impact on performance. For example, at 100% recall, there is a 47% difference in the average precision for long and short patterns for Writer A, and a 50% difference for Writer B.

Figures 4.9 and 4.10 present recall and precision as a function of edit distance threshold for Writers A and B, respectively. From these results, we can conclude that thresholds should be chosen dynamically based on properties of the pattern such as length. As before, we see that long patterns are more "searchable" than short ones.

In order to explore our intuition that this form of stroke-based matching is not appropriate for multiple authors, we asked three more writers (C, D, and E) to write the entire set of 60 search patterns. We then matched these patterns against the text of Writer A. The results for this test are shown in Figure 4.11 for the ranked case. As expected, the performance of the algorithm degrades dramatically. This implies that ink search at the stroke

	Writer A			Writer B		
Recall	Short Patterns	Long Patterns	All Patterns	Short Patterns	Long Patterns	All Patterns
0.1	0.506	1.000	0.753	0.522	0.826	0.674
0.2	0.494	0.983	0.738	0.493	0.826	0.659
0.3	0.452	0.983	0.718	0.452	0.814	0.634
0.4	0.431	0.973	0.702	0.440	0.814	0.627
0.5	0.403	0.968	0.686	0.416	0.814	0.615
0.6	0.349	0.917	0.633	0.272	0.721	0.496
0.7	0.271	0.873	0.572	0.226	0.678	0.452
0.8	0.268	0.873	0.571	0.217	0.681	0.449
0.9	0.227	0.687	0.457	0.179	0.681	0.430
1.0	0.215	0.684	0.450	0.179	0.681	0.430

Fig. 4.8. Ranked precision values for Writers A and B.

	Writer A					
	Short Patterns		Long Patterns		All Patterns	
Threshold	Rec	Prec	Rec	Prec	Rec	Prec
10	0.023	0.916	0.000	1.000	0.011	0.958
20	0.357	0.652	0.000	1.000	0.178	0.826
30	0.632	0.299	0.011	1.000	0.321	0.649
40	0.955	0.071	0.119	0.988	0.537	0.529
50	1.000	0.010	0.322	0.910	0.661	0.460
60	1.000	0.010	0.572	0.643	0.786	0.326
70	1.000	0.010	0.783	0.431	0.891	0.220
80	1.000	0.010	0.909	0.268	0.954	0.139
90	1.000	0.010	0.961	0.115	0.980	0.062
100	1.000	0.010	0.991	0.075	0.995	0.042
110	1.000	0.010	1.000	0.024	1.000	0.017
120	1.000	0.010	1.000	0.011	1.000	0.010

Fig. 4.9. Recall and precision as a function of edit distance threshold for Writer A.

	Writer B					
	Short Patterns		Long Patterns		All Patterns	
Threshold	Rec	Prec	Rec	Prec	Rec	Prec
10	0.041	0.973	0.000	1.000	0.020	0.986
20	0.215	0.677	0.000	1.000	0.107	0.834
30	0.539	0.383	0.017	1.000	0.278	0.691
40	0.757	0.094	0.075	1.000	0.416	0.547
50	0.946	0.041	0.195	0.948	0.570	0.494
60	1.000	0.010	0.500	0.679	0.750	0.344
70	1.000	0.010	0.626	0.398	0.813	0.204
80	1.000	0.010	0.914	0.304	0.957	0.157
90	1.000	0.010	0.931	0.103	0.965	0.062
100	1.000	0.010	1.000	0.039	1.000	0.024
110	1.000	0.010	1.000	0.006	1.000	0.008
120	1.000	0.010	1.000	0.005	1.000	0.007

Fig. 4.10. Recall and precision as a function of edit distance threshold for Writer B.

level should probably be restricted to patterns and text written by the same author, unless a more complex notion of stroke distance can be developed.

	Writer C			Writer D			Writer E		
Rec	Short	Long	All	Short	Long	All	Short	Long	All
0.1	0.024	0.027	0.025	0.033	0.070	0.052	0.048	0.099	0.073
0.2	0.022	0.014	0.018	0.032	0.041	0.037	0.032	0.028	0.030
0.3	0.013	0.014	0.013	0.031	0.042	0.036	0.032	0.024	0.028
0.4	0.013	0.015	0.014	0.029	0.023	0.026	0.033	0.021	0.027
0.5	0.013	0.015	0.014	0.030	0.022	0.026	0.034	0.021	0.028
0.6	0.010	0.013	0.011	0.018	0.016	0.017	0.018	0.018	0.018
0.7	0.010	0.013	0.011	0.017	0.015	0.016	0.018	0.018	0.018
0.8	0.010	0.013	0.011	0.017	0.014	0.016	0.016	0.017	0.017
0.9	0.010	0.012	0.011	0.017	0.013	0.015	0.015	0.017	0.016
1.0	0.010	0.012	0.011	0.017	0.013	0.015	0.015	0.016	0.016

Fig. 4.11. Cross-writer precision (text by Writer A).

4.7 Discussion

In this section, we have discussed techniques for searching through an ink text for all occurrences of a pattern. We presented data that suggests using HWX and then performing fuzzy matching at the character level is one viable option. We also described ScriptSearch, a pen-stroke matching algorithm that performs quite well for same-author searching, both in thresholded and ranked systems. The latter approach has a paradigmatic advantage as it treats ink as a first-class datatype.

In the future, it would be interesting to evaluate approaches that represent ink at different levels of abstraction (recall Figure 4.1), for example as allographs, perhaps performing dynamic programming on the associated adjacency graph to locate matches. Another intriguing extension of the work we have just described concerns searching non-textual ink, and languages other than English. We observe that if the VQ classes are trained using a more general set of strokes, it should be possible to run ScriptSearch as-is on drawings, figures, equations, other alphabets, etc. It would be instructive to examine its effectiveness in these domains, especially since traditional HWX-based methods do not apply.

It is also clearly important to address the issue of writer-independence with regard to ink matching. We now briefly sketch an approach that appears to have some potential. Recall that since the VQ codebooks for two authors may be different, there is no natural stroke-to-stroke mapping. Let us assume that by some means it is possible to put text from two authors A and B into a rough correspondence, and then to determine for each of A's strokes a distribution of similarities to B's strokes. We can represent these distributions as a *Stroke Similarity Matrix*, S. The ith row of such a matrix describes how A's i^{th} stroke corresponds to all of B's strokes. Assume that the $(i, j)^{th}$ entry of matrix $D_{B \to B}$ gives the Mahalanobis distance from B's stroke i to stroke j. We wish to compute $D_{A \to B}$, the matrix giving distances from each of A's strokes to each of B's strokes. We can do so as follows:

$$D_{A \to B} = S \cdot D_{B \to B} \tag{4.12}$$

That is, to compute the distance between the ith stroke of A and the jth stroke of B, we view the ith stroke of A as corresponding to various strokes of B with the weights given in the ith row of S. We extract the distance from each of these strokes to B's j^{th} stroke, and take the weighted sum of these values. This is the inner product of the ith row of S with the jth column of $D_{B \to B}$, as indicated in Equation 4.12. This approach should yield a reasonable "cross-writer" distance measure that we can substitute for Mahalanobis distance. The ScriptSearch algorithm could then be used without further changes.

Finally, since the amount of ink to be searched will undoubtedly grow as pen computers proliferate, it is important to consider sub-linear techniques that employ more complex pre-processing of the ink text. Some of these are treated in the next section.

5. Searching Large Databases

Now that we have discussed some of the issues regarding ink as a first class datatype, we consider the issues of large ink databases. Using sequential searching techniques (like the ones explained previously), the running time grows linearly with the database size. This is clearly unacceptable for large databases. Thus, more sofisticated methods should be used to do the searching. In this section we show some techniques to index pictograms and speed up the searches for large databases.

As pointed out in Section 4.2, ink can be represented at a number of levels of abstraction. Different types of indices can be built for each one of these *granules* of representation. For instance, we can choose to model entire pictograms with HMMs and build indices that use the HMM characteristics to guide the search. We call such an index the *HMM-tree* [1]. Alternatively, we can choose to deal with alphabet symbols (or strokes) for granularity and represent the symbol classes by using HMMs. We call the resulting index the Handwritten Trie.

In the next subsections, we describe each one of these two approaches.

5.1 The HMM-Tree

Assume that we have M pictograms in our database and that each document has been modeled by an HMM (and hence we have M HMMs in the database).

Each one of the HMMs has the same transition distribution (a), number of states (N), output alphabet (Σ), and a fixed-length sequence of output symbols (points) (T) (i.e., that each input pattern is sampled by T sample points, each of which can assume one of the possible symbols of the output alphabet). Let the size of the output alphabet be n (i.e., $|\Sigma| = n$). The output distribution is particular to each HMM (and hence to each document). For each document D_m in the database, with $0 \leq m \leq M$, we call H_m the HMM associated with the document.

As suggested in [14], we use the following two measures of "goodness" of a matching method:

- a method is good if it selects the right picture first for reasonable size databases, because this way the user can simply confirm the highlighted selection.
- a method is good if it often ranks the right picture on the first k items (so that those can fit in the first page of a browser [14]) for reasonable size databases, because this way the user can easily select the picture.

In order to recognize a given input pattern I, we execute each HMM in the database and find which k models generate I with the highest probabilities. This approach is extremely slow in practice, as shown in Figure 5.1.

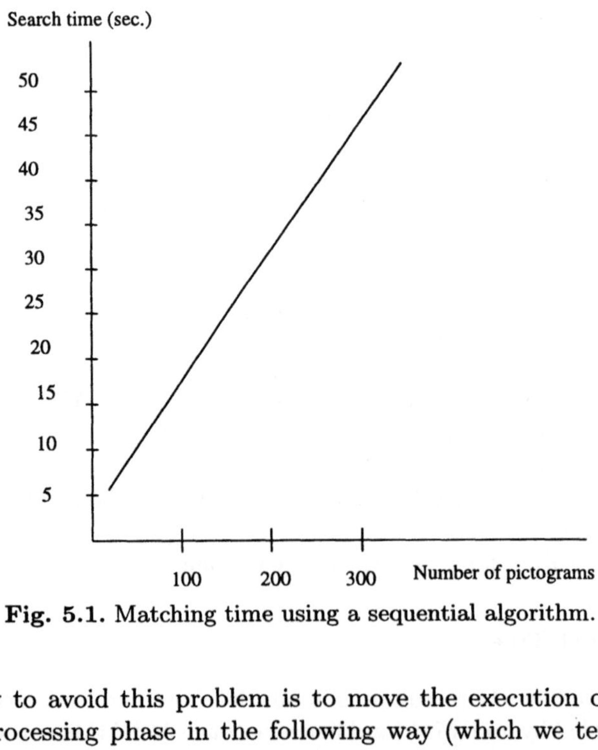

Fig. 5.1. Matching time using a sequential algorithm.

One way to avoid this problem is to move the execution of the HMMs to the preprocessing phase in the following way (which we term the *naive* approach). At the preprocessing phase we enumerate all the possible output sequences of length T. Since each output symbol can assume one of n values, we have n^T possible output sequences. For each sequence, we execute all the HMMs in the database and select the top k HMMs that generate the sequence with highest probability. We repeat this process for all the sequences. The output is a table of size kn^T where for each possible sequence the identifiers of the best k HMMs for this sequence are stored. At run time, for a given input pattern, we access this table at the appropriate entry and retrieve the identifiers of the corresponding HMMs. In order to insert a new document D_m (modeled by the HMM H_m) into the database, we need to execute H_m for every possible sequence (out of the n^T sequences) and for each output sequence S compare the probability, say p_m, that results from executing $H_m(S)$, with the other k probabilities associated with S. If $H_m(S)$ is higher than any of the other k probabilities, the list of identifiers associated with S is updated to include m. If the list of probabilities is kept sorted, then $\log k$ operations are needed to insert i and p_i in the proper location.

The complexity of the naive approach can be summarized as follows:

- **Preprocessing time**: $Mn^T C_H(\log k + \lceil \frac{k}{2} \rceil)$, where C_H is the average time to execute an HMM, given an input sequence, and $\log k + \lceil \frac{k}{2} \rceil$ is the time to maintain the indexes for the k HMMs with best probability values.
- **Space**: $(T + 2k)n^T$, i.e., is exponential in the number of sample points in the input pattern T. The factor (T+2k) is the size of each entry in the table; T is the number of symbols per sequence, and $2k$ is due to storing the HMM identifiers along with the probability that each of them generates the pattern. The latter is used when inserting a new document to test whether the new model generates the corresponding pattern with better probability than any of the given k HMMs.
- **Searching** (at runtime): $\log_2 n^T = T \log n$.
- **Insertion**: $n^T C_H(\log k + \lceil \frac{k}{2} \rceil)$.

In order to organize the above table, we use a tree structure. One possible tree (which we term the *HMM1-tree*) is a balanced tree of depth T and fanout n. Each internal node has a fixed capacity of n elements where an element corresponds to one of the symbols of the alphabet. Figure 5.2 shows an example of the HMM1-tree. The HMM1-tree is a variation of the *Pyramid* data structure [25], where in the case of the HMM1-tree, the fanout is not restricted to a power of 2 as in the case of a pyramid. In addition, the pyramid is used to index space while the HMM1-tree is used to index HMMs. However, the structure of both the HMM1-tree and the pyramid is similar. In the example of Figure 5.2, the alphabet has two symbols (and hence the nodes have two entries each), and the length of the sequence is 3 (3 output symbols must be entered to search documents). We see how nodes in the last level of the tree point to linked lists of documents. The dotted path in the tree shows the path taken by the traverse algorithm when the input contains the symbols $0, 1, 0$. This particular search retrieves documents D_3 and D_4.

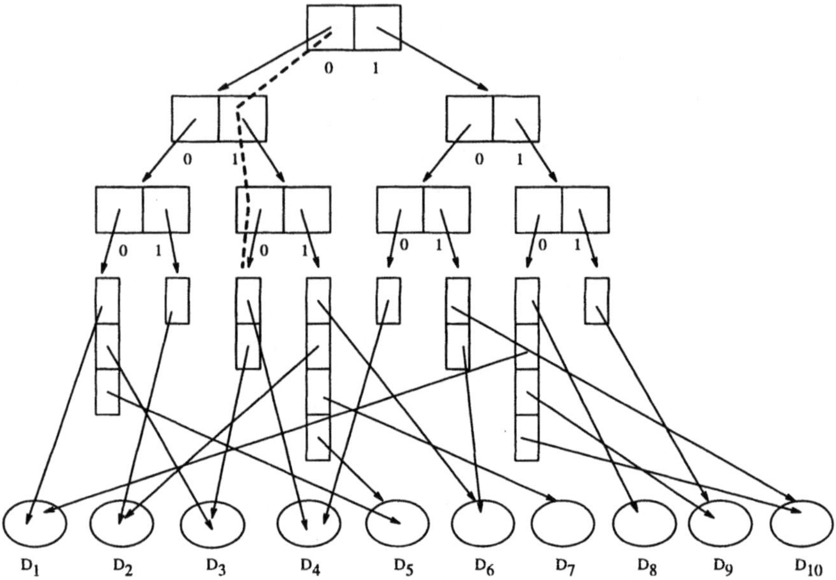

Fig. 5.2. An example of an HMM1-tree.

More formally, the HMM1-tree is constructed as follows.

- The HMM1-tree has $T + 1$ levels (the number of steps or length of the output sequence in the HMMs associated with the documents in the repository). The root of the tree is the node at level 0 and is denoted by r.
- Each internal node (including the root) in the tree is an n-tuple, where each entry in the n-tuple corresponds to a symbol of the output alphabet Σ and has a pointer to a subtree[4]. We denote by $v[k]$ the kth entry on the node v.
- Each internal node in the Tth level points to a leaf node that contains a linked list. The linked lists store pointers to the files that contain the documents in the repository.

The preprocessing time for the HMM1-tree is still $Mn^T C_H$, since we need to traverse each node at the leaf level and for each node find the best HMMs (by executing all M of them and selecting the ones with highest probabilities) that generate the output sequence that corresponds to this node.

To insert a document, we traverse all the nodes at the leaf level without having to descend the tree starting from the root. For each leaf node, we follow the same approach as the table approach described above and hence the complexity of insertion is the same, i.e., $\log kn^T C_H$.

[4] A pyramid can be implemented as a heap array where the address of any internal or leaf node can be computed and directly accessed if the symbols that lead from the root to that node are known [2], [27]. As a result, we can avoid storing explicit pointers and compute the address of each node instead.

To select a set of documents that are similar to an input D, we extract a set of T output symbols $O = \{O[i], 0 \leq i \leq T \textit{ and } 0 \leq O[i] \leq n-1\}$ from D and run the following algorithm.

Procedure traverse(O)
begin
    $v = r$
    for ($0 \leq \textit{level} \leq T$)
        $v = v[O[l]]$
    return every element in the list pointed by v
end

An alternative approach to traversing the tree which avoids storing pointers is based on the observation that since the HMM1-tree is a complete tree, i.e., none of the internal nodes is missing, then the addresses of the nodes can be easily computed and there is no need to store pointers to subtrees explicitly in the tree (this is similar to the technique used in the pyramid data structure [2], [27]).

The storage complexity of the HMM1-tree can be computed as follows. The number of non-leaf (internal) nodes is $\frac{n^T-1}{n-1}$ where each node is of size n (notice that since we assume that the addresses of the nodes can be easily computed we do not store pointers to subtrees explicitly as described above), while the number of leaf nodes is n^T where each node is of size $2k$ (to store the k HMM identifiers along with their corresponding probabilities). Therefore, the total space complexity is:

$$n\frac{n^T-1}{n-1} + 2kn^T$$

which is still exponential in the number of sample points in the input pattern T, although is less than the storage complexity of the naive approach (since $T > \frac{n}{n-1}$). The saving is due to the fact that for any two sequences that share the same prefix, this prefix is stored in the tree approach only once while is being repeatedly stored with each sequence in the naive approach.

The complexity of the HMM1-tree approach is summarized as follows.

- **Preprocessing time**: $Mn^T C_H(\log k + \lceil \frac{k}{2} \rceil)$, since at the leaf level we still have to store the k HMMs.
- **Space**: $n\frac{n^T-1}{n-1} + 2kn^T$ (still exponential).
- **Insertion**: $n^T C_H(\log k + \lceil \frac{k}{2} \rceil)$.
- **Searching** (at runtime): $O(T)$ since computing the address of the node depends on the path length to reach that node (or the length of the sequence that leads to the node)

5.1.1 Reducing the Preprocessing and Insertion Times. In this section, we show how to reduce the times for preprocessing and insertion.

The HMM2-tree

We show how to reduce the preprocessing and insertion times of the HMM1-tree. This results in what we term the HMM2-tree. Recall that in the case of the HMM1-tree, both the preprocessing and insertion times are exponential in the number of symbols per sequence. The HMM2-tree has the following additional properties.

- Each level l $(0 \leq l \leq T)$ in the HMM2-tree is associated with a threshold value ϵ_l $(0 \leq \epsilon_l \leq 1)$.
- For each node q in the HMM2-tree, at level l, and each symbol o in the output alphabet, let $O_q = O[i_1]O[i_2] \cdots O[i_l]$ denotes the sequence of symbols in the path from the root of the HMM2-tree to the node q. Then, there is an associated pruning function $f^m(l, q, O_q, o)$ that is computable for every model in the database. The use of the pruning function is demonstrated below.

To insert a document D_m (modeled by the HMM H_m) into the HMM2-tree, we perform the following algorithm.

Procedure HMM2-Insert(D_m)
begin
    Let r be the root of the tree
    $level = 0$
    call **search**$(r, level)$
end

Procedure search(v, l)
begin
    for $0 \leq k \leq n-1$
        if $(f^m(l, v, O_v, k) \geq \epsilon_l)$
            if $(l \leq T-1)$
                call **search**$(v[k], l+1)$
            else
                include a pointer to D_m in the list pointed by $v[k]$
end

In other words, during the insertion procedure, when processing node v at level l and output symbol k, if the condition $(f^m(l, v, O_v, k) \geq \epsilon_l)$ is true the subtree $v[k]$ is investigated. Otherwise, the entire subtree is skipped by the insertion algorithm. This helps reduce the time to insert each document into the database.

The preprocessing stage is reduced to inserting each of the documents into the database by following the above insertion algorithm for each document. Therefore, the reduction in insertion time is also reflected into the preprocessing time.

To select a set of documents that are similar to an input D, we extract a set of T output symbols $O = \{O[i], 0 \leq i \leq T \textit{ and } 0 \leq O[i] \leq n-1\}$ from the input and we run procedure *traverse*, the one used for the HMM1-tree. Similar to the HMM1-tree, we can also compute the address of the leaf node from O and directly access the k HMMs associated with it.

At this point it is worth mentioning that the index described above will work provided that we supply the pruning function $f^m(l, q, O_q, o)$. The performance of the index will be affected by how effective the pruning function is. In the following Section, we describe several methods to compute such a function provided that some conditions are met by the underlying database of documents.

5.1.2 Pruning Functions. In this section, we present several methods for computing pruning functions.

In order to compute $f^m(l, q, O_q, o)$, we assume that the following conditions are met by the underlying database of documents.

- All the documents in the database are modeled by left-to-right HMMs with N states.
- The transition probabilities of these HMMs are the following:

$$a_{ij} = 0.5 \text{ for } i = 0, ..., N-2 \text{ and } j = i \text{ or } j = i+1 \tag{5.1}$$

$$a_{N-1N-1} = 1.0 \tag{5.2}$$

$$a_0 = 1, a_i = 0 \text{ for } i = 1, ..., N-1 \tag{5.3}$$

- For all the documents in the database, a sequence of output symbols of length T has been extracted. All inputs for which the index is going to be used have to be presented in the form of a T sequence of output symbols, taken from the alphabet (Σ) of the HMMs.

The Unconditional Method

Define $\phi^m_{i,j}$ to be the probability that the HMM H_m is in state j at step i of its execution ($0 \leq i \leq T-1$ and $0 \leq j \leq N-1$). Notice that $\phi^m_{i,j}$ is independent of the output sequence. Now, define $\Phi^m_i(o)$ to be the probability that the HMM H_m outputs the symbol o at step i of execution. We can compute $\Phi^m_i(o)$ using $\phi^m_{i,j}$ as follows:

$$\Phi^m_i(o) = \sum_{j=0}^{N-1} \phi^m_{i,j} b_j(o) \tag{5.4}$$

$\Phi^m_i(o)$ is used as the pruning function f_1, i.e.,

$$f^m_1(i, q, O_q, o) = \Phi^m_i(o) \tag{5.5}$$

It remains to show how we compute ϕ_{ij}^m. Based on the HMM structure of Figure 3.6, $\phi_{i,j}^m$ can be expressed recursively as follows:

$$\phi_{i,0}^m = 0.5^i, \text{ for } i = 0, ..., T-1 \tag{5.6}$$

$$\phi_{0,j}^m = 0, \text{ for } j = 1, ..., N-1 \tag{5.7}$$

and

$$\phi_{i,j}^m = 0.5(\phi_{i-1,j-1}^m + \phi_{i-1,j}^m) \text{ for } i = 1, ..., T-1 \text{ and } j = 1, ..., N-1 \tag{5.8}$$

Notice that $\phi_{0,0}^m = 1$ and $\phi_{i,i}^m = 0.5^i$ for $1 \leq i \leq N-1$. An additional optimization that is based on the structure of the HMM of Figure 3.6 is that at step i, H_m cannot be past state $j > i$ since at best, H_m advances to a new state at each step. In other words,

$$\phi_{i,j}^m = 0 \text{ for } 0 \leq i < j \leq N-1 \tag{5.9}$$

Therefore, the recurrence for $\phi_{i,j}^m$ reduces to

$$\phi_{i,j}^m = 0.5(\phi_{i-1,j-1}^m + \phi_{i-1,j}^m) \text{ for } 1 \leq j \leq i \leq N-1 \text{ and } i = 1, ..., T-1 \tag{5.10}$$

Figure 5.3 illustrates the recursion process for computing $\phi_{i,j}^m$.

The process of computing $\phi_{i,j}^m$ and $\Phi_i^m(o)$ is independent of which branch of the HMM2-tree we are processing. It is dependent only on the HMM model (H_m). As a result, when inserting an HMM model H_m into the HMM2-tree, we build a two-dimensional matrix Φ^m of size $T \times N$ such that $\Phi^m[i][j]$ corresponds to the probability that the jth output symbol appears at the ith step of executing the HMM H_m (i.e., $\Phi^m[i][j] = \Phi_i^m(o_j)$). This matrix is accessed while inserting the model H_m into the HMM2-tree to prune the number of paths descended by the algorithm (see procedure HMM2-Insert, given at the beginning of Section 5.1.1).

The Conditional Method

An alternative approach to computing pruning functions is to make use of the dependencies between the output symbols. Instead of computing the probability that an output symbol appears at step i of the execution of an HMM, we compute the probability that the sequence $O[0]O[1]\cdots O[i]$ appears after executing the first i steps of the HMM. This leads to the following new pruning function which depends on the path in the HMM2-tree where we are to insert a new HMM model into.

Our objective is to insert the index m of an HMM H_m into the linked list belonging to a leaf node q, when the probability that the sequence $O_q = O[0]O[1]\cdots O[T-1]$ (denoting the sequence of symbols in the path from the root of the HMM2-tree to the node q) is produced by H_m is high (or above a given threshold). This corresponds to the probability: $Prob[O[0]O[1]\cdots O[T-1]|H_m]$. In order to save on insertion and preprocessing times, we need to avoid computing this probability for every possible pattern (of length T) in

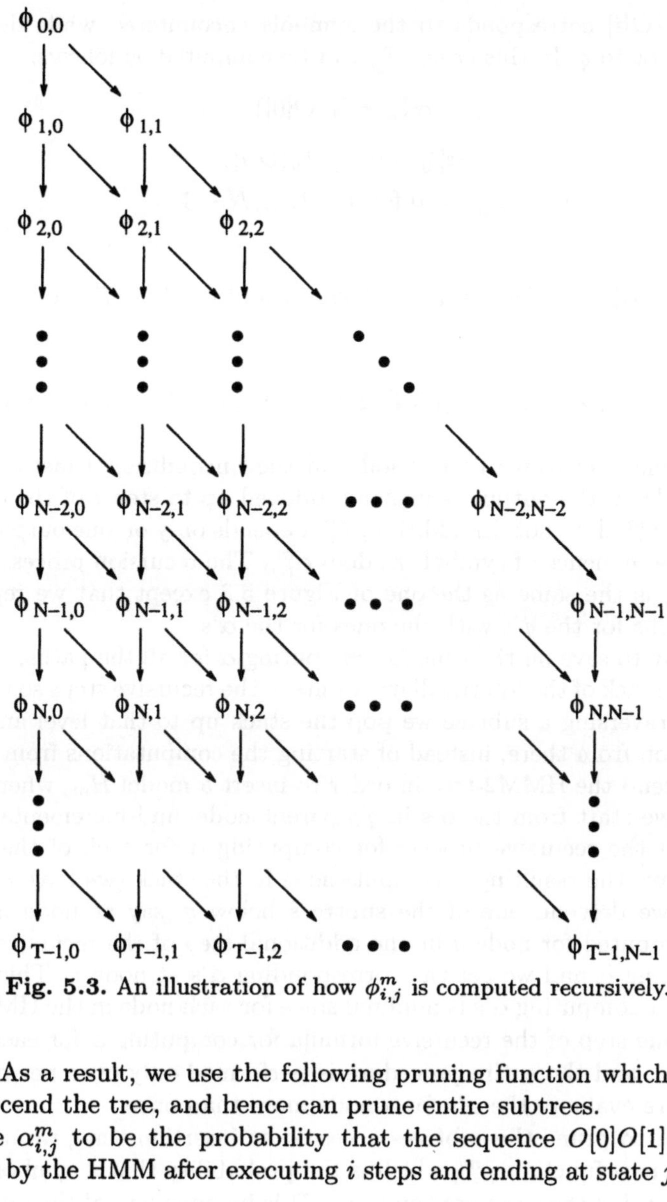

Fig. 5.3. An illustration of how $\phi^m_{i,j}$ is computed recursively.

the tree. As a result, we use the following pruning function which we apply as we descend the tree, and hence can prune entire subtrees.

Define $\alpha^m_{i,j}$ to be the probability that the sequence $O[0]O[1]\cdots O[i]$ is produced by the HMM after executing i steps and ending at state j. In other words,

$$\alpha^m_{i,j} = Prob[O[0]O[1]\cdots O[i] | \text{ the state at step } i \text{ is equal to } j] \qquad (5.11)$$

At the time an HMM model H_m is inserted into the HMM2-tree, $\alpha^m_{i,j}$ is computed dynamically as we descend the tree while constructing the sequence $O[0]O[1]\cdots O[i]$ on the fly. Assume that we descend the tree in a depth-first order, and we are in level j of the tree at node q. The sequence $O_q =$

$O[0]O[1]\cdots O[i]$ corresponds to the symbols encountered while descending from the root to q. In this case, $\alpha_{i,j}^m$ can be computed as follows:

$$\alpha_{0,0}^m = b_0(O[0]) \tag{5.12}$$

$$\alpha_{i,0}^m = \alpha_{i-1,0}^m b_0(O[i]) \tag{5.13}$$

$$\alpha_{0,j}^m = 0 \text{ for } j = 1, ..., N-1 \tag{5.14}$$

In general,

$$\alpha_{i,j}^m = 0 \text{ for } 0 \leq i < j \leq N-1 \text{ and } i = 1, ..., T-1 \tag{5.15}$$

and

$$\alpha_{i,j}^m = 0.5(\alpha_{i-1,j}^m + \alpha_{i-1,j-1}^m) b_j(O[i]) \text{ for } 1 \leq j \leq i \leq N-1 \text{ and } i = 1, ..., T-1 \tag{5.16}$$

The difference between this method and the unconditional method is that $\alpha_{i,j}^m$ depends on the output sequence produced up to step i of the computation, while $\phi_{i,j}^m$ does not. In addition, Φ_i^m depends only on one output symbol and not the sequence of symbols as does $\alpha_{i,j}^m$. The recursion process for computing $\alpha_{i,j}^m$ is the same as the one of Figure 5.3 except that we replace the computations for the ϕ's with the ones for the α's.

One way to save on the time for computing α for all the paths, is that we maintain a stack of the intermediate results of the recursive steps so that when we finish traversing a subtree we pop the stack up to that level and restart the recursion from there, instead of starting the computations from the $\alpha_{0,0}^m$. As we descend the HMM2-tree in order to insert a model H_m, when we visit a node q, we start from the α's in q's parent node, and incrementally apply one step of the recursive process for computing α for each of the symbols in q. We save the resulting n computations in the stack (we have n symbols in q). As we descend one of the subtrees below q, say at node u, we use the α's computed for node q in one additional step of the recursive formula for computing α and we get the corresponding α's at node u. This way the overhead for computing α's is minimal since for each node in the HMM2-tree, we apply one step of the recursive formula for computing α for each symbol in the node, and the entire procedure is performed only once per node, i.e., we do not re-evaluate the α's for a node more than once.

In order to prune the subtrees accessed at insertion time, we use $\alpha_{i,j}^m$ to compute a new function φ_i^m, which is the probability that a symbol $O[i]$ appears at step i of the computation (i.e., φ_i^m is independent of the information about the state of the HMM). This can be achieved by summing $\alpha_{i,j}^m$ over all possible states j. Then,

$$\varphi_i^m = Prob[O[0]O[1]\cdots O[i] | H_m \text{ is at step } i] \tag{5.17}$$

$$\varphi_i^m = \sum_{j=0}^{N-1} \alpha_{i,j}^m \tag{5.18}$$

φ_i^m is computed for each symbol in a node and is compared against a threshold value. The subtree corresponding to a symbol is accessed only if its corresponding value of φ_i^m exceeds the threshold. In other words, the pruning function for each node is set to be:

$$f^m(l, q, O_q, o) = \varphi_l^m \tag{5.19}$$

The Upper-Bounds Method

The Viterbi algorithm [7] is an efficient way to compute the probability that a sequence of outputs is explained by a particular model.

The upper-bounds method is an approximation of the pruning function φ_l^m. The computations for φ_l^m are exact and hence may be expensive to evaluate for each input pattern and each tree path that is accessed by the insertion algorithm. The upper-bounds method tries to overcome this problem by approximating φ_l^m so that it is dependent only on the level of a node q and not on the entire tree path that leads to q.

Define $p_k^m(s)$ to be the computed probability (or an estimate of it) that a model puts the output symbol s in the kth stage of executing the HMM H_m. Then, $p_0^m(s)$ is the probability of finding output symbol s in the first step. According to [4], $p_k^m(s)$ can be estimated as follows (the derivations can be found in [4]):

$$p_k^m(s) = \sum_{j=0}^{N-1} A_{T-k+1,j} \tag{5.20}$$

where $A_{T-k+1,j}$ is an upper bound of $\alpha_{i,j}$, and can be estimated as follows:

$$A_{T-k+1,j} = (0.5)^T(\binom{T-K+1}{j} b_0(O[k]) + \tag{5.21}$$

$$\binom{T-K+1}{j-1} R_1 b_1(O[k]) + \ldots + \tag{5.22}$$

$$\binom{T-K+1}{j-k+1} R_j b_j(O[k])) \text{ for } k \leq j \leq N-1 \tag{5.23}$$

where R_r is the number of paths that one can take to get to state r in $k-1$ steps and is evaluated as follows:

$$R_r = \binom{k-1}{r-1} \tag{5.24}$$

The values A and $p_k^m(s)$ can be computed by the following procedures [4]:

Procedure solve_recurrence(k, j)
begin
  $A_{T-k+1,j} = 0$
  for $i = j$ to 0

$$A_{T-k+1,j} = A_{T-k+1,j} + \binom{T-k+1}{i} R_i b_i(O[k])$$

$A_{T-k+1,j} = (0.5)^T A_{T-k+1,j}$
return($A_{T-k+1,j}$)
end

Function $p(k, m, s)$
begin
$p = 0$
for ($j = 0$ to $N - 1$)
$p = p+$ solve_recurrence(k, j)
return(p)
end

5.1.3 Reducing the Space Complexity - The HMM-Tree. The problem with the HMM2-tree is its exponential storage complexity. The typical values of the number of samples in a pattern (T) and the number of possible output symbols (n) are 50 and 256, respectively [14], [13]. As a result, the number of leaf nodes in the HMM2-tree is $256^{50} = 2^{400} \approx 10^{120}$, which is almost intractable. In this section, we describe a new data structure (termed the HMM-Tree) which is an enhancement over the HMM2-tree in terms of its storage complexity.

The basic idea of the HMM-tree is that we use the pruning function not only to prune the insertion time but also to prune the amount of space occupied by the tree. We use Figure 5.4 for illustration.

Assume that we want to insert model H_m into the HMM-tree. Given the pruning function (any of the ones given in Section 5.1.2), we compute the two-dimensional matrix P^m where each entry $P^m[i][o]$ corresponds to the probability that H_m produces symbol o at step i of its execution. Notice that P is of size $n \times T$. From $P^m[i][o]$, we generate a new vector L^m where each entry in L^m, say $L^m[i]$, contains only the high probable symbols that may be generated by H_m at step i of its execution. In other words, each entry of L^m is a list of output symbols such that:

$$L^m[i] = [o | P^m[i][o] > \epsilon_i \text{ for all } 0 \leq o < n] \tag{5.25}$$

For example, Figures 5.4a, 5.4b, and 5.4c give the vectors L^1, L^2, and L^3 which correspond to the HMMs H_1, H_2, and H_3. respectively. Initially the HMM-tree is empty (Figure 5.4d). Figure 5.4e shows the result of inserting H_1 into the HMM-tree. Notice that the fanout of each node in the tree is $\leq n$. The output symbols are added in the internal nodes only as necessary. Figures 5.4f and 5.4g show the the resulting HMM-tree after inserting H_2 and H_3, respectively. Notice how we expand the tree only as necessary and hence avoid wasting extra space.

The HMM-tree is advantageous since it has the nice features of both the HMM1-tree and the HMM2-tree while winning against both structures in

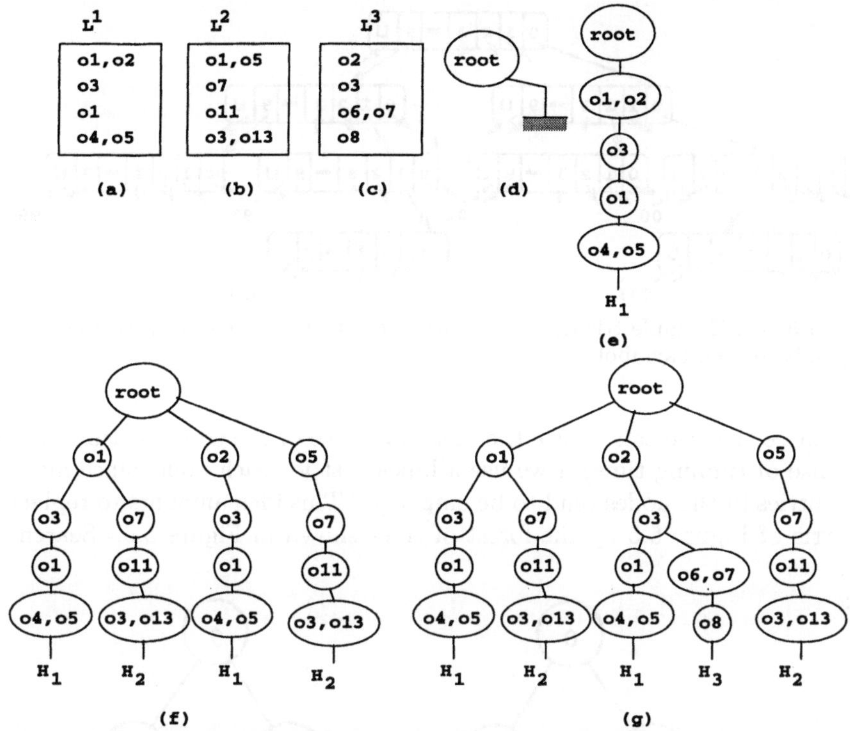

Fig. 5.4. An example illustrating the savings of space achieved by the new HMM-tree.

terms of the space complexity. The HMM-tree has a searching time of $O(T)$ similar to the HMM1-tree, and uses the same pruning strategies for insertion as the HMM2-tree and hence reducing the insertion time.

5.2 The Handwritten Trie

The Trie structure [8] is an M-ary tree, whose nodes have M entries each, and each entry corresponds to a digit or a character of the alphabet. An example trie is given in Figure 5.5 where the alphabet is the digits $0 \cdots 9$. Each node on level l of the trie represents the set of all keys that begin with a certain sequence of l characters; the node specifies an M-way branch, depending on the $(l+1)$st character. Notice that in each node an additional *null* entry is added to allow for storing two numbers a and b where a is a prefix of b. For example, the trie of Figure 5.5 can store the two words 91 and 911 by assigning 91 to the null entry of node A.

Searching for a word in the trie is simple. We start at the root and look up the first letter, and we follow the pointer next to the letter and look up the second letter in the word in the same way (see [10] for a detailed description).

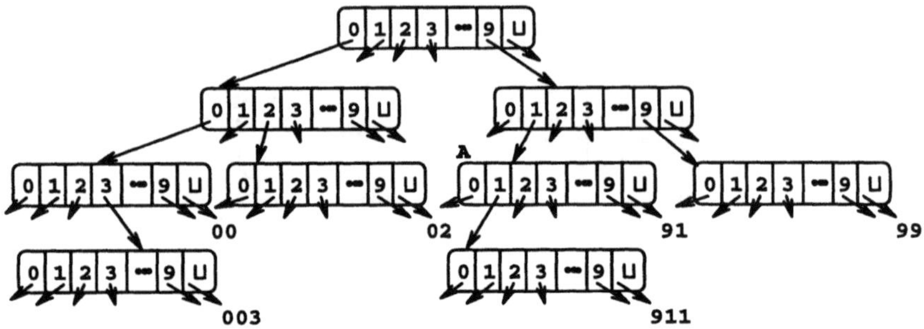

Fig. 5.5. An Example trie data structure. The right-most entry of each node corresponds to a null symbol.

Notice that we can reduce the memory space of the trie structure (at the expense of running time) if we use a linked list for each node, since most of the entries in the nodes tend to be empty [6]. This idea amounts to replacing the trie of Figure 5.5 by the forest of trees shown in Figure 5.6. Searching

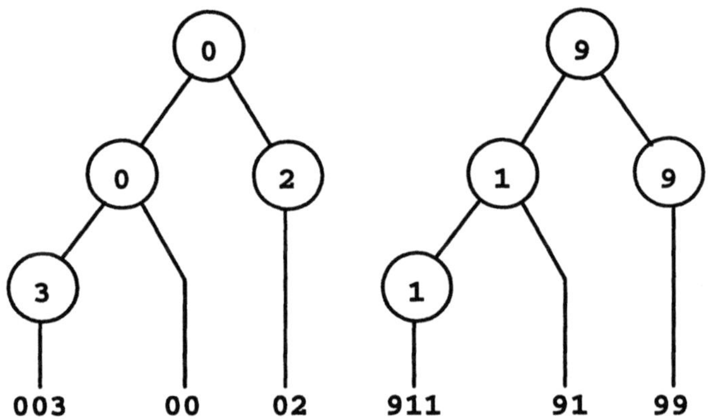

Fig. 5.6. A forest of trees representing the trie of Figure 5.5.

in such a forest proceeds by finding the root which matches the first letter in our input word, then finding the son node of that root that matches the second letter, etc. It can be shown (see [10]) that the average search time for N words stored in the trie is $\log_M N$ and that the "pure" trie requires a total of approximately N/lnM nodes to distinguish between N random words. Hence the total amount of space is MN/lnM.

Because of the high space complexity, the trie idea pays off only in the first few levels of the tree. It has been suggested in [9] that we can get better performance by mixing two strategies: using a trie for the first few characters of a word and then switching to some other technique, e.g., when we reach part of the tree where only, say, six or less words are possible, then we can sequentially run through the short list of the remaining words. As reported in [10], this mixed strategy decreases the number of trie nodes by roughly a factor of six, without substantially changing the running time.

Consider a simple extension of the trie data structure where each letter is handwritten. Assume that we are given a handwritten cursive word w that is composed of a sequence of letters $l_1 l_2 \cdots l_L$, where L is the number of characters in w. In order to search for a handwritten word in the trie we need to match the letters of w with the letters in the trie. We start at the root and descend the tree so that the path that we follow depends on the best match between the letter l_i of w and the letters at level i of the tree. One problem with this approach is the difficulty in matching the individual letters in w with the letters in the trie. The reason is that it is difficult to handwrite a word twice in exactly the same way. As a result, a more elaborate matching method is needed.

Each handwritten letter in our alphabet is modeled by an HMM. The HMM is constructed so that it accepts the specific letter with high probability (relative to the other letters in the alphabet). As a result, in order to match and recognize a given input letter, we execute each of our alphabet HMMs and select the one that accepts the input letter with the highest probability. An example handwritten trie is given in Figure 5.7.

Fig. 5.7. An example of a handwritten trie.

Several advantages emerge from using a trie:

1. Using the trie serves as a way of pruning the search space since the search is limited only to those branches that exist in the trie.
2. Using the trie also helps add some semantic knowledge of the possible words to look for, versus considering all possible letter combinations as in the level-building algorithm.

In order for the handwritten trie to function properly, two challenging issues have to be addressed:

1. **Cursive character segmentation**: since the input handwritten word is cursive, characters in the word has to be segmented so that each character can be used to match the corresponding character in one of the trie nodes.

2. **Inter-character strokes**: the extra strokes that are used to connect the letters in cursive writing have to be treated in such a way that they do not interfere with the matching process.

In the following sections, we propose techniques to deal with each of these issues.

5.2.1 Cursive Character Segmentation. Given a cursive handwritten word w, our goal is to partition w into the point sequences $s_1 s_2 \cdots s_n$ so that each sequence can be used separately in the matching process while descending the handwritten trie. In this section, we provide several techniques that achieve this goal and hence has the same effect as character segmentation.

Using Counts of Minima and Maxima

One way to determine the point where one letter ends and another letter starts in a handwritten word is by counting the number of local minima and local maxima (in the values of the y coordinate - the vertical direction) and the number of inflection points that are associated with each letter. For example (refer to Figure 5.8), the stroke information of the letter a contains three local minima and three local maxima and one inflection point. As a result, we store the number of local minima and maxima and inflection points with each letter in a given node of the trie. More specifically, (we use Fig-

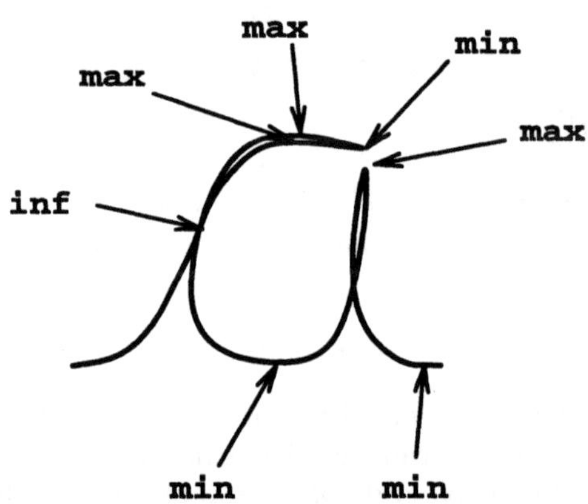

Fig. 5.8. The handwritten letter "a" marked with the locations of the local maximum, local minimum, and inflection points.

ure 5.9 for illustration) a node n in the handwritten trie h contains f entries $e_1, e_2, \cdots, e_f$, where each entry e_i corresponds to a letter l_i and contains the following five fields: a pointer p_h to the HMM that corresponds to l_i, three values v_{min}, v_{max}, and v_{inf} that correspond to the number of local minima, local maxima, and inflection points in l_i, respectively, and a pointer p_c to a child node. The matching algorithm proceeds as follows:

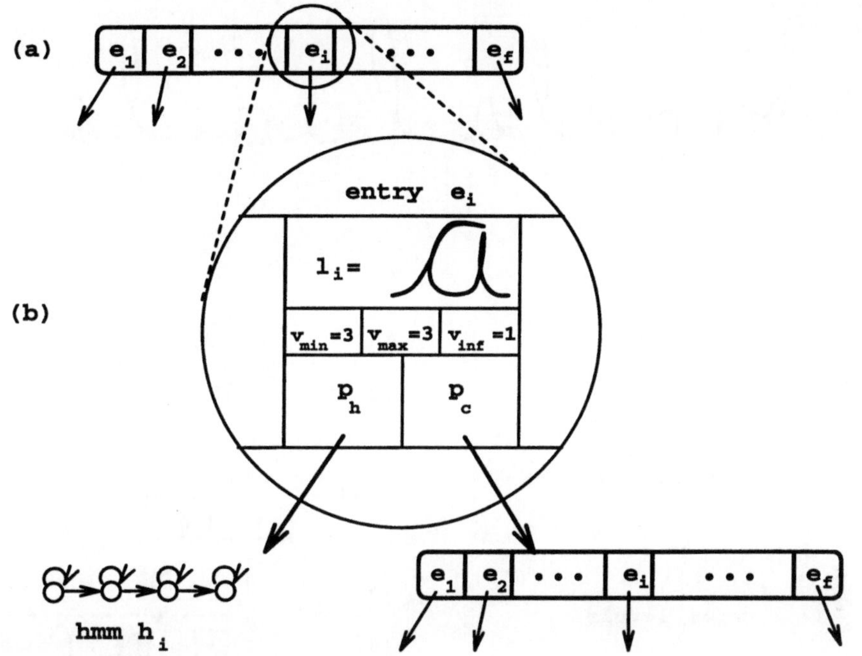

Fig. 5.9. (a) A node of the handwritten trie (b) an example showing the fields in one entry of a node in the trie.

1. given the input handwritten word w, start at the root node r,
2. for each entry e_i in r,
   a) scan w and retrieve into s the prefix of w that contains the same number of local minima and maxima and inflection points as in $e_i.v_{min}$, $e_i.v_{max}$, and $e_i.v_{inf}$.
   b) retrieve the HMM H pointed at by $e_i.p_h$.
   c) compute the probability$(s|H)$ and maintain the maximum.
3. Let e_k be the entry that corresponds to the maximum probability for all e_i in r.
4. assign to r the child node pointed at by $e_k.p_c$, i.e., $r \leftarrow e_k.p_c$.
5. discard the prefix s from w.
6. repeat the above process till all of w is consumed or a leaf node node is reached.
7. the letters that correspond to the path that is descended from the root node till the last visited node compose the resulting recognized word.

Figure 5.10 illustrates this procedure. Figure 5.10a shows an input word (the word "bagels") where it is segmented in Figure 5.10b into letters using the number of local minima, local maxima, and inflection points. Figures 5.10c and 5.10d shows how the trie is traversed where each level consumes a portion of the input word.

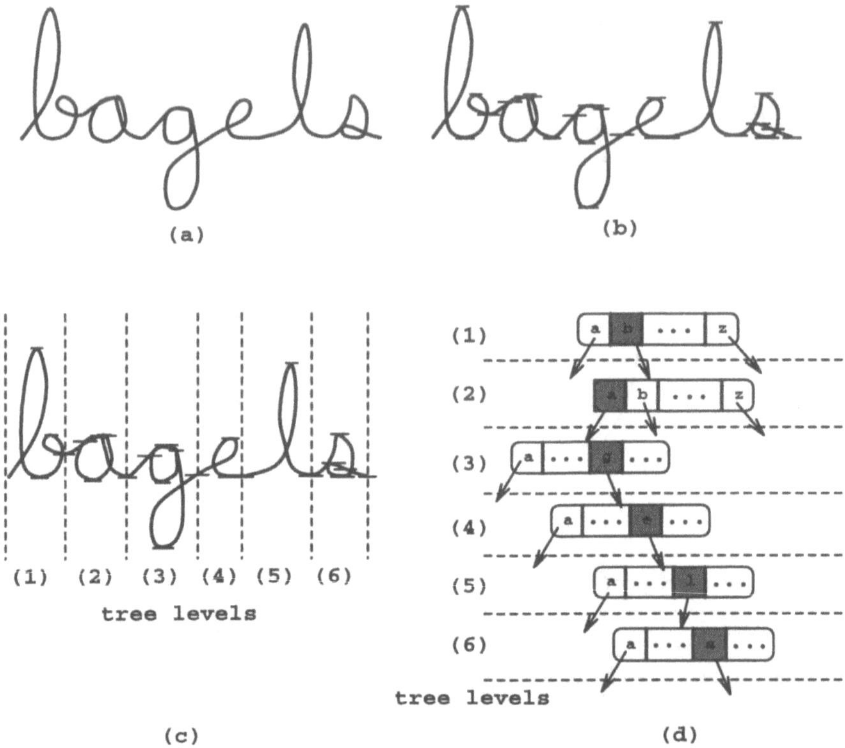

Fig. 5.10. Example illustrating the execution of the algorithm. (a) an input word, (b) its segmentation, (c) the portions of the input word that are consumed by each level of the trie, and (d) the path from the root of the trie to the leaf during the recognition of the word "bagels".

Utilizing the Most-likely HMM States

This method uses a modified version of the Viterbi algorithm [28] to segment the characters in a cursive handwritten word. The modified Viterbi algorithm is used as a guide to partition the input pattern into character segments.

The main obstacle facing the Handwritten trie, is that we are not able to know the number of sample points T that we should consume by each HMM at any level in the tree. The main idea behind the new algorithm that we describe here is that we start at the root of the trie, and consider all possible pairs of letters that exist in the trie (refer to Figure 5.11 for illustration). For example, we combine the HMM of each letter in the root node with the HMM of each letter in the children nodes (as in Figure 5.12). For example, in Figure 5.11, we combine the HMMs of the root node r with the HMMs of the children nodes c_1, c_2, and c_4. This will result in the pairs:

$$(H_{1a}, H_{2a}), (H_{1a}, H_{2b}), \cdots, (H_{1a}, H_{2z})$$

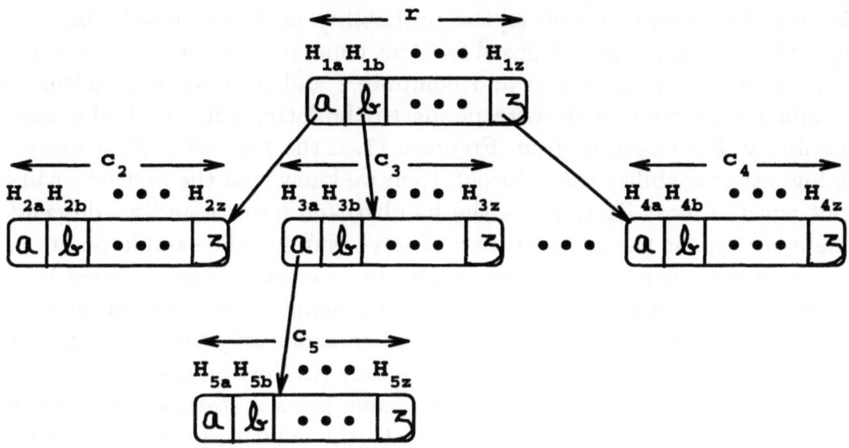

Fig. 5.11. An example illustrating the new recognition procedure using the handwritten-trie and the modified-Viterbi algorithm.

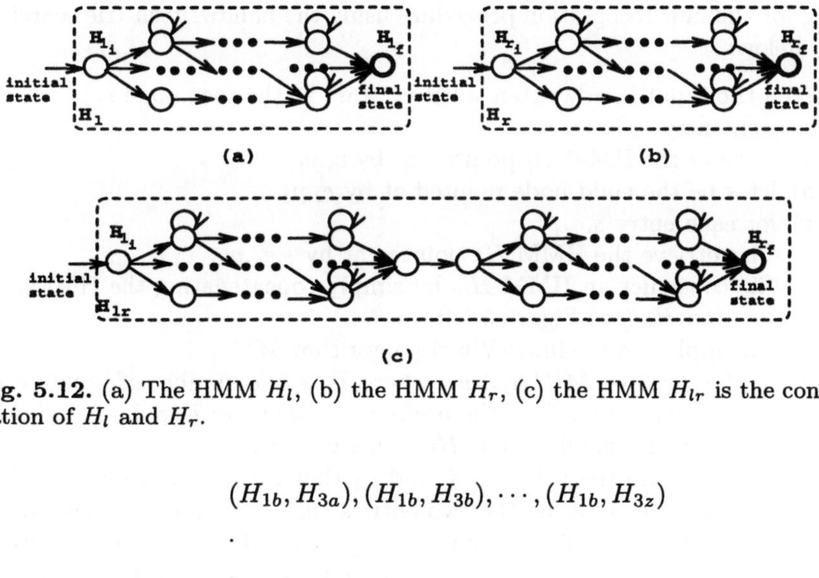

Fig. 5.12. (a) The HMM H_l, (b) the HMM H_r, (c) the HMM H_{lr} is the concatenation of H_l and H_r.

$$(H_{1b}, H_{3a}), (H_{1b}, H_{3b}), \cdots, (H_{1b}, H_{3z})$$

$$\vdots$$

$$(H_{1z}, H_{4a}), (H_{1z}, H_{4b}), \cdots, (H_{1z}, H_{4z})$$

Let H_l and H_r be two such pairs and H_{lr} be their combined version. We apply a variant of the Viterbi algorithm on H_{lr}, with w as input, in order to find out the two consecutive input points p_i and p_{i+1} of the input pattern w such that p_i is most likely to be the last point processed by the final state of H_l and p_{i+1} is most likely to be processed by the initial state of H_r.

We save the index i as well as the probability *prob* associated with it. We apply this technique for all possible letter combinations in the root and the child nodes (as given above) and compute i and *prob* for each letter-pair. We follow that path that corresponds to the letter pairs with the highest probability. For example, from Figure 5.11, if the pair (H_{1b}, H_{3a}) results in the highest probability value (*prob*), then we know that the first letter in the input word is most likely to be the handwritten letter b and we descend to node c_3 to repeat the same process after consuming the sample points in w that represent the letter b. These points are detected by the Modified Viterbi Algorithm (described in Section 5.2.3) and is maintained by the variable T_k in the procedure given below. In this case, we consume only the first T_k points of w, i.e., the ones that are generated by H_l only (in the example of Figure 5.11, H_l corresponds to H_{1b}). We repeat the same process starting with the child node that contains H_r, i.e., we descend to the child node that contains the second HMM in the HMM-pair that corresponds to the maximum *prob*. In the example of Figure 5.11, the algorithm proceeds to the child node c_3 that contains H_{3a} since the pair (H_{1b}, H_{3a}) corresponds to the maximum *prob*. The listing for the new recognition procedure using the handwritten-trie search is given below.

1. given the input handwritten word w, start at the root node r,
2. for each entry e_i in r,
   a) retrieve the HMM H_l pointed at by $e_i.p_h$
   b) let s be the child node pointed at by $e_i.p_c$
   c) for each entry $s.e_j$,
      i. retrieve the HMM H_r pointed at by $s.e_j.p_h$
      ii. construct an HMM H_{lr} by simply concatenating the HMMs H_l and H_r (see Figure 5.12).
      iii. apply the modified-Viterbi algorithm MV
      $T_1, prob \leftarrow MV(H_{lr}, w)$, where T_1 is the number of points consumed from w (i.e., the prefix w_p of w of size T_1 points) and *prob* is the probability that H_{lr} generates w_p.
      iv. maintain the values s, j, and T_1 that correspond to max *prob*.
3. Let $r.e_k$ and $r.e_k.p_c.e_l$ be the two entries that corresponds to the maximum probability for all $r.e_i$ and all $r.e_i.p_c.e_j$, and let w_k be the prefix of w of length T_k that corresponds to the points consumed from w in this case.
4. assign to r the child node pointed at by $e_k.p_c$, i.e., $r \leftarrow e_k.p_c$.
5. discard the prefix w_k from w.
6. repeat the above process till all of w is consumed or a leaf node node is reached.
7. the letters that correspond to the path that is descended from the root node till the last visited node compose the resulting recognized word.

The modified-Viterbi algorithm remains to be explained. Before presenting the new modified-Viterbi algorithm, we start by a brief overview of the Viterbi algorithm.

5.2.2 The Viterbi Algorithm. The Viterbi algorithm [28] is used to find the single best (or most likely) state sequence $q = (q_1 q_2 \cdots q_T)$, for the given observation sequence $O = (o_1 o_2 \cdots o_T)$. Define the quantity $\delta_t(i)$ to be the highest probability along a single path at time t which accounts for the first t observations and ends in state i, i.e.,

$$\delta_t(i) = \max_{q_1, q_2, \cdots, q_{t-1}} Prob(q_1 q_2 \cdots q_{t-1}, q_t = i, o_1 o_2 \cdots o_t) \tag{5.26}$$

This can be expressed recursively as:

$$\delta_t(j) = \max_{1 \le i \le N} [\delta_{t-1}(i) a_{ij}] b_j(o_t), \; 1 \le j \le N, \; 2 \le t \le T \tag{5.27}$$

$$\delta_1(i) = \pi_i b_i(o_1), \; 1 \le i \le N \tag{5.28}$$

To actually retrieve the state sequence, we use the array $\psi_t(j)$ to keep track of the state that maximizes Equation 5.27, Therefore,

$$\psi_t(j) = \arg \max_{1 \le i \le N} [\delta_{t-1}(i) a_{ij}], \; 1 \le j \le N, \; 2 \le t \le T \tag{5.29}$$

Now, in order to find the best state sequence, we first find the state with highest probability at the final stage, and then backtrack in the following way.

$$p^* = \max_{1 \le i \le N} [\delta_T(i)] \tag{5.30}$$

$$q_t^* = \arg \max_{1 \le i \le N} [\delta_T(i)] \tag{5.31}$$

$$q_t^* = \psi_{t+1}(q_{t+1}^*), \; t = T-1, T-2, \cdots, 1. \tag{5.32}$$

Figure 5.13 illustrates one application of the Viterbi algorithm for an HMM with four states and an input sequence of size 15 points. The dotted lines give the best state sequence at the intermediate stages, while the bold line gives the state sequence with the highest probability that is identified by the Viterbi algorithm.

5.2.3 The Modified-Viterbi Algorithm - Estimating *T*. Our goal is the following: We are given an HMM H_{lr}, which is a composition of the two HMMs H_l and H_r, and an input pattern w of length T points. H_l is assumed to be best at recognizing a prefix of w. The problem is that we do not know the length T_k of the prefix w_p For example, (refer to Figure 5.14), assume that we are given the input word "bagels" (Figure 5.14a), and a left-to-right HMM (Figure 5.14b) for recognizing the letter b (Figure 5.14c). Because the final state of the HMM (the right most state in the HMM of Figure 5.14b) contains a cyclic transition probability of value 1, all the input points past the letter b in the word "bagels" can be consumed in this state. The modified-

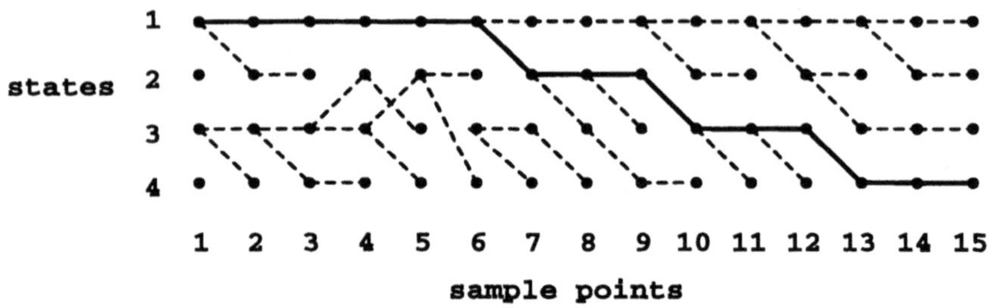

Fig. 5.13. An example illustrating the execution of the Viterbi Algorithm. The dotted lines indicate the best state sequence at the intermediate stages, while the bold line indicates the overall best state sequence for the given input pattern.

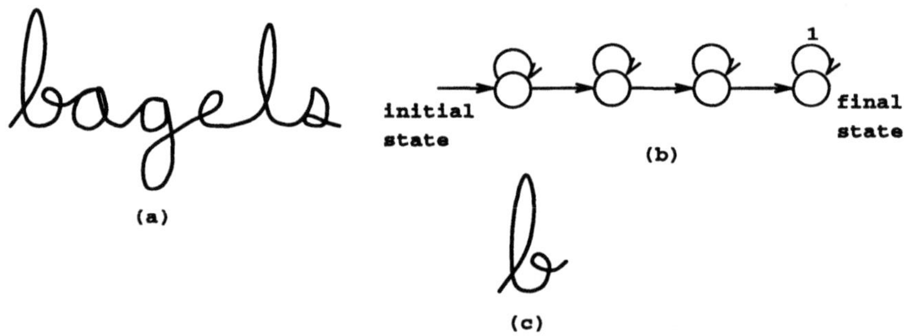

Fig. 5.14. (a) An input word, (b) an HMM for recognizing the letter *b* given in (c).

Viterbi algorithm that we present in this section addresses this problem. In other words, it identifies the point of the input word at which we stop, and hence isolating the letter *b* from the rest of the input word. It achieves this by appending another HMM (H_r) at the end of H_l (resulting in the HMM H_{lr}) and detect the point in time when it is best (according to the highest probability values generated) that a state transition (in H_{lr}) from the final state in H_l to the initial state in H_r takes place. This point is registered (T_k) and is returned by the algorithm. The procedure is applied repeatedly for the rest of the letters in the word, as explained in Section 5.2.1.

We make use of the following observations regarding the Viterbi algorithm.

1. the forward part of the Viterbi algorithm does not involve any backtracking, i.e., once a point t is processed and the best states were assigned to it, we do not backtrack at any point in computation to recompute or change these best-state assignments.
2. once we encounter the last input symbol of the tree, e.g., o_{T_k}, the way to figure out the best state sequence is to find the state with maximum probability and trace back the state sequences using the array ψ, as shown in Section 5.2.2.

Here, we show how we make use of these two properties of the Viterbi algorithm. Assume that we are given two HMMs H_l and H_r, where each HMM has one initial and one final states and that we concatenate the two HMMs to produce a new HMM H_{lr} (see Figure 5.12) by adding a transition from the final state of H_l to the initial state of H_r. Notice that some probability value has to be assigned to the newly added transition. For example, in left-to-right models, this can be achieved by changing the transition probability of the final state of the left HMM (H_l), as given in Figure 5.15. Let the final state of H_l be H_{l_f} and the initial state of H_r be H_{r_i}.

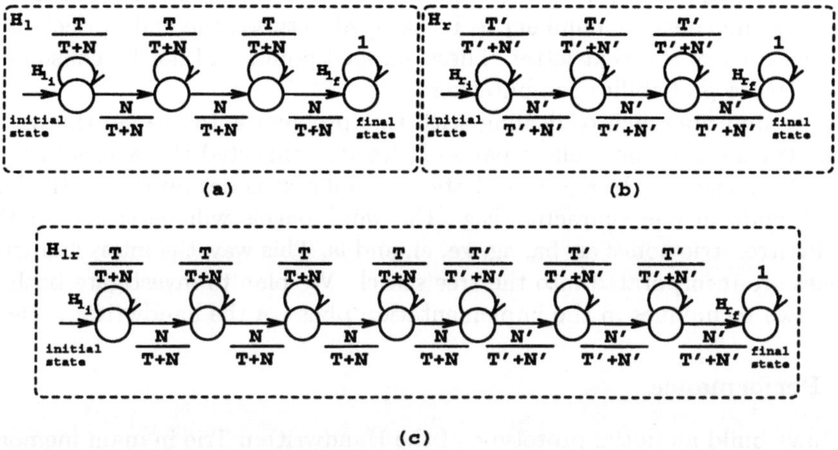

Fig. 5.15. (a) The left-to-right HMM H_l, (b) the left-to-right HMM H_r, (c) the HMM H_{lr} is the concatenation of H_l and H_r.

In order to find the value of T_k, we apply the Modified Viterbi algorithm, which is the same as the Viterbi algorithm except that for each iteration that involves one of the T input symbols, we monitor the probability values of the two states H_{l_f} and H_{r_i} until for some $t = T_k, 2 \leq T_k l T$, the following conditions are satisfied (in the given order):

1.

$$H_{l_f} = \arg \max_{1 \leq i \leq N} [\delta_{T_k - 1}(i) a_{ij}],\ 1 \leq j \leq N \tag{5.33}$$

2. for $t = T_k + 1$ (i.e., the next input point),

$$H_{r_i} = \arg \max_{1 \leq i \leq N} [\delta_{T_k}(i) a_{ij}],\ 1 \leq j \leq N \tag{5.34}$$

Once these two conditions are satisfied for some $t = T_k$, then we stop the algorithm and return the value T_k which indicates that the input points $o_1, o_2, \cdots, o_{T_k}$ are the prefix of w that are supposed to be recognized by the HMM H_l.

We plan to investigate the performance of the two techniques for character segmentation, presented in this paper, in the implementation phase of the handwritten-trie.

5.3 Inter-character Strokes

In cursive writing, some additional strokes are introduced to interconnect the handwritten characters. The shape of these strokes depends on the letters that are to be connected, i.e., the letters to the left and to the left of the connecting stroke. We discuss briefly how we can deal with them in the handwritten trie.

One way of dealing with inter-character strokes is to allow for some input points (some constant number) to be skipped between the end of one letter and the start of the next letter. These skipped points will not be considered in the HMM probability computation.

A second approach to dealing with this problem is to change the nodes of the trie so that they reflect pairs of already connected characters instead of single characters. In addition, letters in children nodes overlap with their parent node in one character. E.g., the word bagels will be stored in the handwritten-trie nodes as: ba, ag, ge, el, and ls. This way, the inter-character strokes are incorporated into the tree search. We plan to investigate both of these two techniques in the implementation phase of the handwritten trie.

5.4 Performance

We have build an initial prototype of the Handwritten Trie in main memory. Initial results show that we can accommodate up to 18,000 pictograms in less than one million bytes of memory (including the space taking by the index and the HMM representations), using an alphabet of 26 symbols (roman characters). The matching rate of the index is better than 90%.

Figure 5.16 compares the matching time when using our indexing technique versus using a sequential matching algorithm. As expected, the search time of the sequential matching algorithm grows linearly with the size of the database. On the other hand, the search time of our indexing technique tends to grow logarithmically (slow growth) in the size of the database.

6. Conclusions

We have presented several techniques of indexing large repositories of pictograms. Preliminary results show that the index helps drastically in reducing the search time, when compared to sequential searches. The results show search times on the order of 2 seconds for database sizes up to 150,000 words (running on a 40MHz NeXT workstation).

We are currently experimenting with these techniques to implement both main memory and disk-based implementations of ink databases. In doing so,

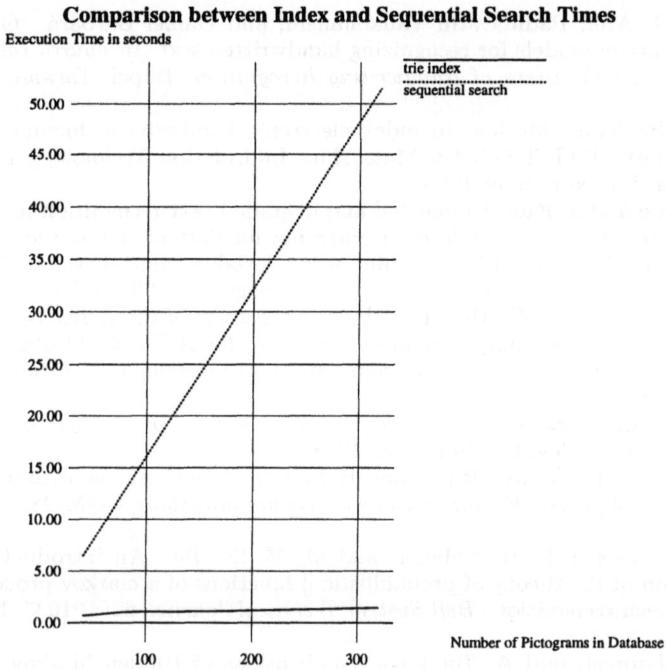

Fig. 5.16. A comparison between the matching time using our indexing technique versus using a sequential algorithm. The x-axis corresponds to various database sizes.

we hope to obtain a better understanding of the issues involved in handling large volumes of pictograms.

Acknowledgments

The *Moby-Dick* text we used in our experiments was obtained from the Gutenberg Project at the University of Illinois, as prepared by Professor E. F. Irey from the Hendricks House edition.

References

[1] Walid Aref and Daniel Barbará. The Hidden Markov Model Tree Index: A Practical Approach to Fast Recognition of Handwritten Documents in Large Databases. Technical Report MITL-TR-84-93, MITL, January 1994.

[2] W. G. Aref and H. Samet. Efficient processing of window queries in the pyramid data structure. In *Proceedings of the 9th. ACM SIGACT-SIGMOD-SIGART Symposium on Principles of Database Systems (PODS)*, pages 265–272, Nashville, TN, April 1990. (also in Proceedings of the Fifth Brazilian Symposium on Databases, Rio de Janeiro, Brazil, April 1990, 15–26).

[3] Walid G. Aref, Padmavathi Vallabhaneni, and Daniel Barbará. On training hidden markov models for recognizing handwritten text. In *Fourth International Workshop on Frontiers of Handwriting Recognition*, Taipei, Taiwan, December 1994.

[4] Daniel Barbará. Method to index electronic handwritten documents. Technical Report MITL-TR-77-93, Matsushita Information Technology Laboratory, Princeton, NJ, November 1993.

[5] C.B. Bose and S. Kuo. Connected and degraded text recognition using Hidden Markov Models. In *International Conference on Pattern Recognition*, 1992.

[6] Rene de la Briandais. File searching using variable length keys. In *Proceedings of the Western Joint Computer Conference*, pages 295–298, 1959.

[7] G. D. Forney. The Viterbi Algorithm. *Proceedings of the IEEE*, 61, 1973.

[8] E. Fredkin. Trie memory. *Communications of the ACM*, 3:490–500, 1960.

[9] E. H. Sussenguth, Jr. Use of tree structures for processing files. *Communications of the ACM*, 6:272–279, 1963.

[10] D. E. Knuth. *The Art of Computer Programming, Vol. 3: Sorting and Searching*. Addison-Wesley, Reading, MA, 1978.

[11] Yoseph Linde, Andres Buzo, and Robert M. Gray. An algorithm for vector quantizer design. *IEEE Transactions on Communications*, COM-28, No 1:84–95, 1980.

[12] S. E. Levinson, L. R. Rabiner, and M. M. Sondhi. An introduction to the application of the theory of probabilistic [] functions of a markov proces to automatic speech recognition. *Bell System Technical Journal*, 62(4):1035–1074, April 1983.

[13] D. P. Lopresti and A. Tomkins. Applications of Hidden Markov Models to Pen-Based Computing. Technical Report MITL-TR-32-92, M.I.T.L, November 1992.

[14] D. P. Lopresti and A. Tomkins. Pictographic Naming. Technical Report MITL-TR-21-92, M.I.T.L, August 1992.

[15] D. P. Lopresti and A. Tomkins. Approximate Matching of Hand-Drawn Pictograms. In *Proceedings of the Third International Workshop on Frontiers in Handwriting Recognition*, May 1993.

[16] Daniel Lopresti and Andrew Tomkins. Approximate matching of hand-drawn pictograms. In *Proceedings of the Third International Workshop on Frontiers in Handwriting Recognition*, pages 102–111, Buffalo, NY, May 1993.

[17] Daniel Lopresti and Andrew Tomkins. Pictographic naming. In *Adjunct Proceedings of the 1993 Conference on Human Factors in Computing Systems (INTERCHI'93)*, pages 77–78, Amsterdam, the Netherlands, April 1993.

[18] Daniel P. Lopresti and Andrew Tomkins. On the searchability of electronic ink. In *Proceedings of the Fourth International Workshop on Frontiers in Handwriting Recognition (to appear)*, Taipei, Taiwan, December 1994.

[19] J. MacQueen. Some methods for classification and analysis of multivariate observations. *Proceedings of the Fifth Berkeley Symposium on Mathematics, Statistics and Probability*, 1:281–296, 1967.

[20] L. R. Rabiner. A tutorial on hidden markov models and selected applications in speech recognition. *Proceeding of the IEEE*, 77(2):257–285, February 1989.

[21] Dean Rubine. *The Automatic Recognition of Gestures*. PhD thesis, School of Computer Science, Carnegie Mellon University, 1991.

[22] Robert Schalkoff. *Pattern Recognition. Statistical, Structural and Neural Approaches*. John Wiley & Sons, Inc, 1992.

[23] Slate Corporation, Scottsdale, AZ. *JOT: A Specification for an Ink Storage and Interchange Format (ver. 1.0)*, 1993.

[24] Gerard Salton and Michael J. McGill. *Introduction to Modern Information Retrieval.* McGraw-Hill, Inc., 1983.

[25] S. Tanimoto and T. Pavlidis. A hierarchical data structure for picture processing. *Computer Graphics and Image Processing*, 4(2):104–119, June 1975.

[26] C. Tappert, C. Y. Suen, and T. Wakahara. The state of the art in on-line handwriting recognition. *IEEE Transactions on Pattern Analysis and Machine Intelligence*, 12(8), August 1990.

[27] L. Tucker. *Computer Vision Using Quadtree Refinement.* PhD thesis, Polytechnic Institute of New York, Brooklyn, May 1984.

[28] A. J. Viterbi. Error bounds for convolutional codes and an asymptotically optimum decoding algorithm. *IEEE Transactions on Information Theory*, IT-13:260–269, 1967.

[29] Robert A. Wagner and Michael J. Fischer. The string-to-string correction problem. *Journal of the Association for Computing Machinery*, 21(1):168–173, 1974.

Indexing for Retrieval by Similarity

H.V. Jagadish

AT&T Bell Labs, Murray Hill, NJ 07974

Summary. In multimedia databases, it is often the case that objects to be retrieved only approximately meet the conditions specified in the query. Notions of similarity are diverse and application dependent. Nevertheless, the need for indexing is still present. The standard technique for this purpose is to map the query and each object to a point is some multi-dimesional "feature space" such that two similar objects are guaranteed not to be too far apart in this space. Then multidimensional point index structures can be used, with the query region appropriately expanded around the specified query point.

In this chapter we illustrate the use of this technique with experimental results from two domains: the first a set of machine-generated rectiliner shapes; and the second a set of English words from an online dictionary.

1. Introduction

Given a large set of objects (or records), selecting a (small) subset that meets certain specified criteria is a central problem in databases. For records with alphanumeric fields, index structures such as B-trees are well-understood and widely used in commercial products today. Recently, there has been much excellent work in devising novel index structures to retrieve geometric objects that intersect a specified spatial extent [13], [16], [4], [14], [5]. These structures are useful to locate objects in a spatial database that lie within (or intersect) a specified coordinate range, but are not directly applicable to most multimedia search queries.

In the case of multimedia objects, not only do we want to retrieve objects that match the specified query criteria exactly, but often also those that match it approximately. The question then is what is similarity? One can conceive of many different dimensions along which one can measure similarity. (See [11] for an eloquent treatment of this subject).

From the perspective of the database, one can represent similarity in terms of a *transformation function* with an associated transformation cost. The choice of language used to describe these transformation functions determines the notion of similarity in a particular application. This transformation language applies to a *pattern description language* in which the multimedia objects themselves are described, and can in turn be embedded in a general *query language* such as relational algebra. See [8] for details on this framework.

Given all of this conceptual machinery, the question we wish to address in this chapter is how to construct an index structure that can enable efficient retrievals by "similarity".

Our solution technique is, based upon the (application-specific) notion of similarity, to obtain an appropriate "feature vector" for each object. In other words, we map each multimedia object to a point in an attribute space. This mapping is carefully selected so that no two "similar" objects, (with a low cost of transformation from one to the other), can be mapped to distant points. (However, it is acceptable for two dissimilar objects to be mapped close, as long as this does not happen "too often").

Now, given a query point, it can be expanded into a query region of appropriate size, depending on the approximation tolerance desired. A multi-dimensional index structure can be used to retrieve objects corresponding to data points from this query region. The retrieved objects may include some that do not satisfy the query, but many times can be guaranteed to include all that will satisfy the query. A more sophisticated matching algorithm, or a human, can then sort through these hits.

While the basic idea, as described above, is very simple, each specific application has its own idiosyncracies. To help the reader understand how index structures of the type just described can be constructed, and to give a sense of the sort of performance that can be expected, we now describe two specific and very dissimilar applications. The first application deals with rectilinear shapes and uses area-difference as the measure of similarity. The second application uses words from an English dictionary with edit-distance as the measure of similarity.

2. Shape Matching

We restrict ourselves to rectilinear shapes in two dimensions, that is, to polygons, not necessarily convex, all of whose angles are right angles so that all edges are horizontal or vertical. Since any general shape can be approximated by a fine enough rectilinear "staircase", and since digitization produces this effect in any case, we believe that this restriction to rectilinear shapes is not too limiting. We study the two-dimensional case for its ease of exposition, and because it is by far the most important case in practice. Extensions to higher dimensions are conceptually straightforward.

Shape matching is an important image processing operation. Considerable work has been done on this problem, with different techniques being used to identify shapes, usually in terms of boundary information or other local features (*cf.* [17], [1]). Most techniques for shape matching in the pattern recognition literature are *model-driven*, in that given a shape to be matched, it has to be compared individually against each shape in the database, or at least against a large number of clusters of features.

Our goal is to devise a *data-driven* technique. In other words, we wish to construct an index structure on the data such that given a template shape, similar shapes can be retrieved in time that is less than linear in the size of the database, that is, by means of an indexed look-up.

One measure of similarity that is clearly of value is "area difference". That is, two shapes are similar if the error area (where the two do not match) is small when one shape is placed "on top of" the other. In a digital domain, we obtain a pixel-wise exclusive OR of the two shapes, and pronounce the two shapes similar if the number of pixels ON in the result is small. We use this area-difference notion of similarity (and also some extensions of it) in this section.

2.1 Rectangular Shape Covers

Rectangular covers for two-dimensional (rectilinear) shapes have been studied extensively (*cf.* [2], [3]). In this paper, we shall primarily be concerned with two types of rectangular covers. *Additive* rectangular covers are what we think of naturally: the given rectilinear shape is obtained as the union of several rectangles. *General* rectangular covers permit both addition and subtraction of rectangles, with subtraction treated as a pixel-wise set difference.

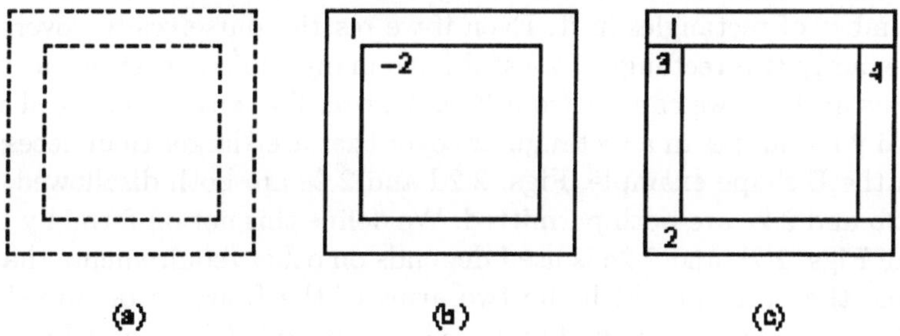

Fig. 2.1. (a) An annular shape, (b) A general rectangular cover for it, and (c) An additive rectangular cover for it

The benefit of a general rectangular cover is the possibility of considerably more succinct descriptions, as can be seen in Fig. 2.1. The drawback is that the process of obtaining good descriptions becomes more complex, as we shall see below.

Let C_i, with integer $i >= 0$, be the *current* (partial) cover after i rectangles have been included in the (prospective) cover. C_0 is the empty set (of pixels or points in the plane). In an additive rectangular cover, $C_{j+1} = C_j \cup R_{j+1}$, where R_j is the $jsupth$ rectangle added. In a general rectangular cover, either $C_{j+1} = C_j \cup R_{j+1}$ or $C_{j+1} = C_j - R_{j+1}$, depending on whether the new rectangle is added or subtracted.

Call the shape to be covered S. For every finite rectilinear shape there exists an integer K such that we can find a $C_K = S$. No further rectangles need be added to C_K, so we define $C_j = C_K$ for $j >= K$.

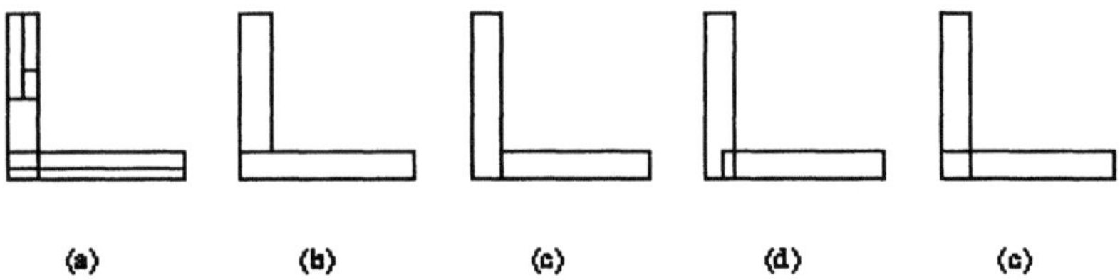

Fig. 2.2. Some potential additive rectangular covers for an L shape

Neither the additive rectangular cover nor the general rectangular cover for a given shape is unique. Fig. 2.2 shows some different ways that an L shaped object could be covered additively. Clearly, we prefer the covers shown in Figs. 2.2b–e to the cover shown in Fig. 2.2a: the latter has an unnecessarily large number of rectangles in it. Even if we restrict ourselves to covers comprising exactly two rectangles, we still have many choices, even for as simple a shape as an L, as we can see from Figs. 2.2b–e. By convention, we shall not permit any rectangles in a rectangular cover that are "larger than necessary". Thus in the L-shape example, Figs. 2.2d and 2.2e are both disallowed, while Figs. 2.2b and 2.2c are both permitted. We define this notion formally below. Which of Figs. 2.2b and 2.2c is used depends on other requirements that may determine the order in which the two arms of the L are to be added, with Fig. 2.2b being selected if the horizontal arm is added first, and Fig. 2.2c if the vertical arm is.

When a rectangle R is added to the current additive rectangular cover C_i, there must not exist a rectangle R' contained in R ($R' \subseteq R$) such that $R \subset R' \cup C_i$ (that is, such that $R' \cup C_i = R \cup C_i$). Note that thus preventing rectangles from being larger than necessary is not the same thing as saying there should be no overlap. In particular, an additive rectangular cover for a "cross" is simply two rectangles that overlap in middle of the cross.

The same "not larger than necessary" rule applies to general rectangular covers as well. When a rectangle R is added to the current general rectangular cover C_i, there must not exist a rectangle R' that is contained in R ($R' \subseteq R$) such that $R' \subset R \cup S \cup Csubi$. When a rectangle R is subtracted from the current cover C_i, there must not exist a rectangle R' that is contained in R ($R' \subseteq R$) such that $(R - R') \cap C_i = \emptyset$.

In [6] it has been suggested that it may be possible to describe the features of an object "sequentially" so that the most important features are described first, and any truncation of the sequence is a "good" approximation of the shape. A description thus comprises a sequence of "units" of description, where each unit iteratively refines the information provided thus far. A "Cumulative Error Criterion" has been defined to identify the best possible sequential description. According to this criterion, the error after the first unit of description, after two units of description, and so on, is accumulated, until the complete description is obtained. Thus, the error in the last stages is counted many times, while the error in the first stages is counted only a few times, and there is an incentive to minimize the error early. A general technique has been provided to find the best sequential description of a given shape.

This idea of sequential description applies in particular to rectangular covers. Our notion is to obtain such a sequential description of an image and then truncate it to obtain an approximate description. The claim is that this approximation leaves out the less essential features of the image, and is likely to have a small error given the criterion used to obtain the sequential description in the first place. Moreover, the truncation is likely to get rid of high frequency noise, such as specks of dirt, and other low area artifacts.

The specific algorithm used to obtain a good sequential description is immaterial as long as one has been agreed upon. As far as we are concerned, each shape in our database comprises an (ordered) set of rectangles (along with a positive or negative sign, if we use general rather than additive rectangular covers). The shape is described by means of the relative positions of these rectangles. In the next section we describe a storage structure for such shapes, and show how an index structure may be constructed for matching shapes.

2.2 Storage Structure

For each rectangle one can identify a lower-left and an upper-right corner, which we shall call the L and U corner respectively. Each corner can be represented by a pair of X,Y coordinates in an appropriate coordinate system, such as position on the digitizing camera or screen pixels. Thus a set of K rectangles can be represented by a set of $4K$ coordinates (K rectangles times 2 corners each times 2 coordinates per corner).

To aid in the retrievals that we intend to perform, rather than store these coordinates directly, we apply a few transformations to them. First, rather than store the L and U corner points directly for each rectangle, we obtain distinct position and size values. The position of the rectangle is given in terms of the mean of the L and U corner points, i.e., the point $(x_L + x_U/2, y_L + y_U/2)$. Here x_L is the X coordinate of the L corner point, and so forth. The size of the rectangle is obtained as the difference between the L and U corner points, i.e., as the pair $(x_U - x_L,\ y_U - y_L)$. Thus, we still have four values, or two pairs of numbers, to store for each rectangle. However, after this transformation they represent the position and size of the rectangle rather than the locations of the corner points.

Second, the position of the first rectangle is used to normalize the positions of the other rectangles. That is, the center of the first rectangle is placed at the origin, and all coordinates are taken with respect to this origin. This transformation is represented by a shift, which is a pair of constants that has to be subtracted from all the X coordinates and all the Y coordinates respectively of the position values for each of the rectangles. Their size values remain unaffected. Since the center position of the first rectangle is 0,0 after the shift, we do not store it. Instead, we store the amount of the shift, which is given by the coordinates of this center point before the shift.

Third, the size of the first rectangle is used to normalize the positions and sizes of the other rectangles. For this, the X and Y size parameters of the first rectangle are used to divide the X and Y (both size and position) parameters respectively of all the other rectangles. (Note that the X and Y size parameters of the first rectangle are both strictly positive, and therefore can safely be used as divisors for this normalization). Further, we take the (natural) logarithms of the normalized size values, thus making them "additive" like the position values. (No logs are required for the position values). After the normalization, the size of the first rectangle is 1,1 (and its logarithm is 0,0). Rather than store this value, we store the original size parameters of this rectangle, obtained after the first transformation, which were used as the constants for this third transformation. This pair of constants are scale factors in the X and Y dimensions for the other rectangles.

Finally, we make one additional change. Rather than retain two global scale factors, one for each dimension, we retain their product as "the scale factor" (this is the square of a linear scale factor, and is an area scale factor), and their ratio (the Y scale factor divided by the X scale factor) as a "distortion factor".

Thus, a shape, described by a set of K rectangles, can be stored as a pair of shift factors for the X and Y, a scale factor, and a distortion factor, all of which are stored as "part of" the first rectangle, and a pair of X and Y coordinates for the center point and a pair of X and Y size values for each of the remaining $K-1$ rectangles, after shifting and scaling.

The value of K, the number of rectangles required to describe a shape, could be very large for some shapes. It may not be practical to construct index structures for attribute spaces with such high dimensionality. However, we are guaranteed that "most" of the interesting shape information will be in the first few rectangles. Moreover, the basic requirement on indexing in a database is that it provide sufficient discrimination to prevent the retrieval of a large fraction of the database, and not that it produce only the exact match. This is especially true when dealing with a similarity match rather than an exact match. So it suffices to index on a small number, k, of rectangles. Our experience, in trying out various synthetic shapes, appears to indicate that a value of k, the number of rectangles indexed, of 2 to 5 suffices to provide only a few hits in a large database, even if K is an order of magnitude larger for many shapes in the database.

The shape description has, by this means, been converted into a set of coordinates for a point in $4k$-dimensional space. We can now use any multi-dimensional point indexing method that we desire, such as grid-files [12], k-D-B trees [14], buddy trees [15], holey-brick trees [10], z-curves [13], etc. The only concern is that many of these techniques may have been designed for a small number of dimensions, and may perform poorly if k is large.

Our mapping from objects to multidimensinal space has the additional virtue that the more important attributes occur first and are distinguished from the elss important attributes. In consequence, it is possible to use a multi-dimensional indexing structure specifically designed for large numbers of dimensions: in particular, the TV-tree, for this purpose.

Ideally, we would like that (some measure of) distance between two objects in feature space be a lower bound on their dissimilarity. In other words, we would like a guarantee that two similar objects can never be mapped to two distance points in feature space. Unfortunately, distance in feature space, in this case does not provide a lower bound. We explicitly address this situation in subsection 2.4.2 below.

2.3 Queries

We consider four different types of queries on a database structured as described above. These are:

- Full match
- Match with Shift
- Match with Uniform Scaling
- Match with Independent Scaling

We describe each of these below in turn. Observe that the last three are really "similarity" queries, where a match in some feature value is taken out of consideration when comparing two shapes.

2.3.1 Full Match. A full match for a given query shape is a database shape that has the correct shape in the correct position. This is the sort of thing humans do very well when riffling through the pages of a book for a particular page that we "remember". Such a match would be used, for example, if there is a large set of images, one of which has been reproduced and we now have to determine which.

To perform a full match, the query shape is transformed in the same way as each data shape has been, described in Section 3.1 above. We thus obtain a query point, and this point can be used as a key in an index search, which locates data points that are in the vicinity.

2.3.2 Match with Shift. Usually, when we think of what a shape locks like, we do not care about the position of the shape in any coordinate system. As such, we would like to retrieve similar shapes from the database irrespective of their positions in the coordinate system used to describe them. We can achieve this result as follows: transform the given query shape into a point as discussed above. Then "throw away" the two shift factor coordinates of the point, and make the query region an infinite rectangle around the point, permitting any value whatsoever for the shift factor. The relative position coordinates of the centers of all rectangles other than the first are invariant to any shifting of the entire rectilinear shape as a whole. Similarly, the scale and distortion factors are independent of any shifting. The query region obtained as above is can then be used as a key in an index search, which retrieves data points that match in all dimensions except for the two shift factors. (Since the key in the search leaves these unspecified, all values of shift factors will be retrieved).

2.3.3 Match with Uniform Scaling. Often, besides not caring about the position of the shape, we may not care about the size either. For example, the size may depend on how far the shape was from the camera, or what scale factor is used for the representation. In such a case, we can throw out the scale factor in addition to the two shift factors, and perform a retrieval as described above.

2.3.4 Match with Independent Scaling. Occasionally we may wish to permit independent scaling along the X and Y axes, rather than the uniform scaling that we normally expect. Such scaling may occur, for example, if a picture is taken at an angle to the shape. Retrieval with such a match can be performed by transforming the query shape into a point as in all the previous cases, and then using infinite ranges rather than fixed coordinate values for not just the shift factors and the scale factor, but for the distortion factor as well.

2.4 Approximate Match

In the previous subsection, we described the basic data structure and technique to retrieve shapes that match a given query shape in any one of several ways. The retrievals described there would each perform an exact match on the relative position and sizes of the first k rectangles in the object description (and also the distortion factor, scale factor, and shift factors, unless these have explicitly been ignored in the query). In this section we discuss the issues involved in permitting an approximate match: permitting the retrieval of shapes that are similar, though not necessarily identical, to the query shape.

2.4.1 Approximation Parameters. The obvious way to obtain objects of similar shape is to retrieve all objects whose shape descriptions have rectangles with similar, even if not identical, position and size as the query shape

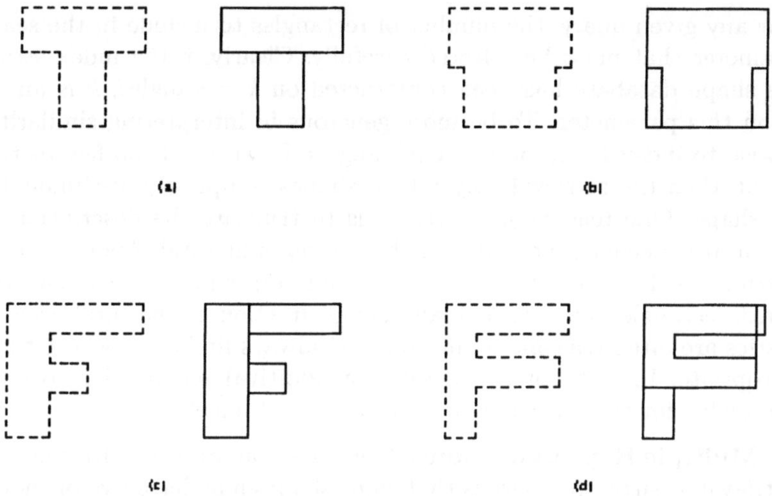

Fig. 2.3. Similar shapes may have very different optimal (general rectangular cover) descriptions

description. The way to do this is to "blur" the query point, by specifying a range along each attribute axis, corresponding to some flexibility with regard to the exact values for the position and size of each rectangle. The extent of this blurring can be determined independently for each attribute axis, by means of appropriate parameters. The larger the amount of blurring permitted, the weaker the search criterion, and the larger the set of objects selected as being "similar" to the given query shape. In most applications, rather than specify independent parameters for the blur permitted in the position and size of each rectangle, global parameters can be specified. These global parameters can, for example, define the blur permitted to be an affine function of the value. Thus larger position or size values will have proportionately larger error margins allowed, but with some error margin allowed even for small values.

Given that the shape descriptions being used are sequential rather than arbitrary, a more subtle way to obtain approximation is not to use all the rectangles in the description of the query shape. Since most of the key features of the shape are expected to have been defined in the first few rectangles, similar, but not identical shapes can be expected to differ only in the last few rectangles of their descriptions. Thus by controlling the number of rectangles of description used, one can choose how strongly a shape must be similar to a given query shape for it to be retrieved. In the extreme case, for example, one could use only the first rectangle, so that a match with uniform scaling, say, would retrieve all shapes the largest part of whose mass was proportioned (height to width) in roughly the same ratio as the query shape.

For any given query, the number of rectangles to include in the search is a parameter that must be selected carefully. Clearly, if the index structure in the shape database has been constructed on k rectangles, k is an upper limit on this parameter. To be more generous in interpreting similarity, we may wish to index based on fewer rectangles. However, if too few rectangles are used, then the retrieval may return shapes completely dissimilar to the query shape. One reasonable heuristic is to truncate the description when the error area becomes a small enough fraction of he total. Another heuristic is to truncate the description when the size of error fixed by (or the size of) the next rectangle becomes a small enough fraction of the total area. Such heuristics are often reasonable, but one can always find cases where they are inappropriate. In fact, for a general (not additive) rectangular cover, it is even possible for the error not to decrease monotonically!

2.4.2 Multiple Representations. One potential problem with the similarity retrieval as suggested here is that some shapes may have two or more dissimilar sequential descriptions that are almost equally good, or equivalently that two fairly similar shapes may have very different sequential descriptions.

In Fig. 2.3, the optimal (sequential general rectangular cover) descriptions are presented for two familiar shapes (T and F). Observe how the optimal description changes as the relative sizes of the parts is changed. In both cases, there is some threshold where the switch-over occurs from one description to the other. Where a mathematical criterion would place a sharp dividing line, humans may have a fuzzy transition. Two shapes close to, but on opposite sides of, this dividing line may appear quite similar to a human eye, even though their optimal sequential descriptions are completely different. For example, a human may consider the "F" in Fig. 2.3c quite similar to the one in Fig. 2.3d. However, their descriptions are completely different.

This problem occurs not just for general rectangular covers, but for additive rectangular covers as well. Recall the additive rectangular covers for an "L" shape shown in Fig. 2.2. The cover of Fig. 2.2b is preferred if the horizontal arm of the shape has greater area, and Fig. 2.2c if the vertical arm has greater area.

Even worse, consider an "H" shape. In any properly balanced rendering of this letter, the left and right vertical strokes are both approximately as long and approximately as thick. Which gets selected to be the first rectangle in a sequential description is a matter of chance. The error criterion is likely to be almost identical either way. This sort of problem with multiple equally good descriptions almost always arises for symmetric shapes. The same (or almost the same) shape with two different choices of sequential description will map to two completely different points in the attribute space over which we index.

One way to resolve this problem if two or more sequential descriptions are almost as good is to keep all of them. Thus, unless the "T" shape is really skinny and definitely a "T", its sequential description may be stored both ways. Similarly, for an "H" shape, two sequential descriptions may be stored, with one having the left vertical stroke as the first rectangle and the right vertical stroke as the second, and the other having the two in reversed order. While this approach does solve the problem, it has the disadvantage of multiplying the size of the database. In the worst case, the number of different "reasonable" sequential descriptions could be exponential in the length of the description.

A better solution is to obtain multiple "good" sequential descriptions of the given query shape and then to perform a query on each of them, taking the union of the results obtained. This way, a little more effort is required at query time, but the database and index structure do not have to expand. Moreover, the number of different sequential descriptions that have to be tried is exponential in the length of the query description which is likely to be considerably shorter than the length of the full sequential description for the query shape (and for objects in the database). In practice, this number is typically smaller than this already acceptable worst case.

2.4.3 Dimension Mismatch. In general, the length of the sequential description of an object need not match the number of dimensions in the index. If an object in the database has a longer sequential description, only the first part of it is used in the index structure. This will usually be the case.

Consider, however, the case where there is an object in the database with a very short description. For example, there may even be a pure rectangular shape, which requires exactly one rectangle to describe it. For such shapes with a K (the number of rectangles in the sequential description) smaller than k (the number of rectangles over which an index structure is to be constructed) we have a problem because some of the rectangles over which the index structure is to be constructed do not exist.

This problem is solved by adding to such a description $k - K$ dummy "rectangles", all with one size parameter zero, but with the other size parameter and the position parameters (in the X and Y) that represent a range from $-\inf$ to $\inf$ instead of a single value. Thus, these objects become hyper-rectangles in attribute space rather than simple points. Most multi-dimensional index structures can handle such hyper-rectangles, in addition to points. Since there are two size parameters, there are two choices for each rectangle and 2^{k-K} choices for the sequence of $k - K$ dummy rectangles. Thus, 2^{k-K} entries, one corresponding to each possible choice, are required for such an object.

In the case of an exact match, this scheme works in a straightforward way. In the case of a similarity match, consider a query shape that has a few additional rectangles. If the query shape is similar to the object of concern in the database (with a short description), these additional rectangles must have a small area, and therefore for each additional rectangle at least one of the two size parameters must be small. Once "blurring" is introduced for similarity retrieval, the small size parameter of each additional rectangle maps to a range that includes zero. Irrespective of the position parameter and the other size parameter of these rectangles, they will intersect appropriate dummy rectangles in (at least one of the multiple representations of) the object of concern in the database.

Conversely, if a particularly simple query shape is supplied, the above procedure can be applied to extend the query shape description. However, we also have the alternative of simply ignoring the additional attribute axes, at the cost of potentially retrieving too many objects from the database.

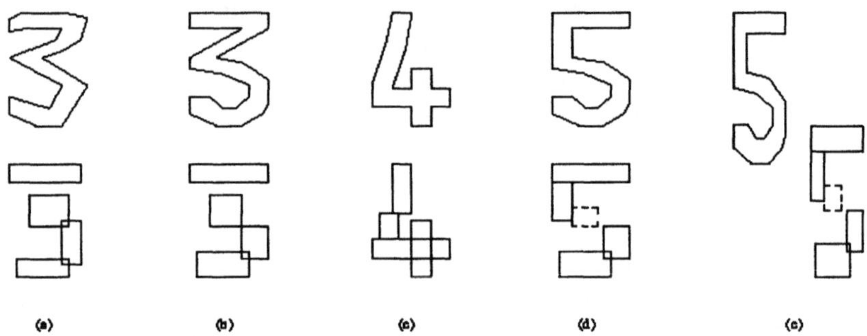

Fig. 2.4. Some numerals and the first few rectangles in their shape descriptions
(a) [0.25] (+0.05,-2.00,-0.60,+0.51) (-0.05,-5.00,-0.31,+0.00) (+0.36,-3.50,-1.31,+0.85)
(b) [0.25] (-0.08,-4.83,-0.40,+0.29) (-0.04,-2.00,-0.87,+0.51) (+0.33,-3.67,-1.11,+0.51)
(c) [0.25] (+0.13,+0.00,-1.39,+1.10) (-0.13,+3.17,-1.39,+0.98) (-0.29,+1.17,-1.39,+0.29)
(d) [0.25] (-0.08,-4.83,-0.40,+0.29) (+0.33,-3.67,-1.11,+0.51) (-0.38,-1.50,-1.39,+0.69) (-0.08,-2.33,-1.11,+0.00)
(e) [0.50] (-0.08,-4.83,-0.40,+0.29) (+0.33,-3.67,-1.11,+0.51) (-0.38,-1.50,-1.39,+0.69) (-0.08,-2.33,-1.11,+0.00)
Rectangular Cover Descriptions of the Shapes Above
(a') [0.25] (-0.05,-5.00,-0.31,+0.00) (+0.05,-2.00,-0.60,+0.51) (+0.36,-3.50,-1.31,+0.85)
(a") [0.25] (-0.05,-5.00,-0.31,+0.00) (+0.36,-3.50,-1.31,+0.85) (+0.05,-2.00,-0.60,+0.51)
Modified Rectangular Cover Descriptions of the Query Shape (a)

As mentioned above, each object with too short a description requires multiple entries in the database with the number of entries being exponential in $k - K$. This may be acceptable, if $k - K$ is small (say, 1), and there are only a few objects with such short descriptions, which is usually the case. Otherwise, the database can be redesigned as follows:

Rather than have independent size values in the X and Y dimensions, we could obtain a single size value for each rectangle as the product of the two values. This number gives the area of that rectangle relative to the first rectangle. We also obtain the ratio of the X and Y sizes, giving the distortion of each rectangle relative to the first. Now, an object with a short description need only have the single size parameter set to zero for the dummy "rectangles" in the description, and the distortion parameter set to an infinite range. Thus each objects requires a single entry in the database. The reason we have not selected this alternative is that after two ratios are taken, the value of the distortion parameter becomes sensitive to minor changes, and hence less useful as a metric for shape similarity. See Sec. 5.3 for a discussion of sensitivity issues.

2.5 An Example

Consider the shapes, representing Hindu numerals, shown in Fig. 2.4. For each shape, the first four rectangles in a general rectangle cover are shown below it. We have chosen to show the first four rectangles since the fifth rectangle onwards their sizes were considerably smaller than those shown. (The only exception is the '5', for which the fifth rectangle was not much smaller than the fourth, and hence is shown dashed). For all the cases, all first four rectangles were added (no subtraction until the fifth rectangle). Ignoring the global shift and scale parameters (which are roughly identical for all these shapes), the global distortion parameter and the attributes (two position values, two size values) of the second, third, and fourth rectangles are given for each shape.

Note that the numeral '3' in Fig. 2.4b and the numeral '5' in Fig. 2.4d are very similar, in fact being identical over the lower half and the top bar. As a consequence, three of the first four rectangles are identical for the rectangular cover descriptions of the two numerals.

Consider a small database comprising the three numerals in Figs. 2.4b–d. Suppose that the somewhat crooked numeral '3' of Fig. 2.4a is supplied as a query to this database. Let us see how well this query shape matches each of the three shapes in the database. Comparing the vector of values for (a) and (b) above, the distortion factors are identical, and the X positions of the second rectangles are close to zero (+0.05 and -0.08) in both cases. However, there is a large difference between the Y position of the second rectangle in (a) and in (b). Therefore we conclude that (b) is not a good match for (a). By a similar argument, we also conclude that neither (c) nor (d) is a good match for (a). However, let us recall Sec. 4.2 and try a few different representations for the given query shape. Since the areas of the biggest rectangles do not differ by very much, we could try reordering them. In this case (unlike for the 'L' shape example of Figs. 2.2b and 2.2c), the rectangles themselves are not altered when the order is permuted. (Not all permutations need be tried – only those in which the rectangles remain in roughly decreasing order of area. The more forgiving we are in calling some order "roughly decreasing", the more the matches we will find of similar shapes). Two of these permutations are shown below. (The other permutations produce no matches in this database).

Now we find that the shape described in (a') is an excellent match to (b) in terms of position (maximum absolute error in any of the position parameters is 0.17 normalized units) and a moderately good match in terms of size (maximum absolute error in any of the size parameters is 0.34). Thus, we may accept (b) as a shape similar to (a), provided our threshold is low enough for accepting differences in size, and for permuting the sequential order.

The shape described in (a") is a reasonable match for (d). If only the first three rectangles are considered, with the last rectangle in (a") ignored, then we have the same maximum absolute error values as above: 0.17 units for position and 0.34 units for size. However, with the fourth rectangle included, these error values increase to 0.5 for position, and 0.79 for size. These error values are large enough that a selective enough similarity query may not report (d) as a match for (a). In other words, in spite of the numerals '3' and '5' in Figs. 2.4b and d being so similar, our similarity retrieval technique is able to find the '3' of Fig. 2.4b as being more similar to the crooked '3' query shape of Fig. 2.4a. It also find the '4' shape less similar to the '3' shape than the '5' shape. Both these results are exactly what we would hope for, in terms of human intuition.

Finally, suppose that the shape of Fig. 2.4e is specified in the query. This shape is identical to that in Fig, 2.4d except that it is much taller and thinner. In fact, its sequential representation is the same as that of Fig. 2.4d except for the change in distortion factor. A retrieval of '5' as the matching shape poses no difficulty.

2.6 Experiment

To verify the practical utility of our proposed technique a database of 16,000 synthetic shapes was constructed. Each shape was created by the amalgamation of 10 randomly generated rectangles. Sequential descriptions using additive rectangular covers were obtained for each shape, and stored in the database. Various query shapes were tried. As expected, when a shape from the database was used as the query shape, the shape itself was always retrieved in response to the query. If the error margins were small, no other shapes were retrieved. Also, as expected, if a small perturbation on a database shape was used for the query, the original database shape was still retrieved, and no other shapes were retrieved, provided the error margins were small enough, and a long enough description was used to perform the query.

A more interesting query is shown in Fig. 2.5. Here, an arbitrary shape, shown in Fig. 2.5a, was used to query the database. Not surprisingly, the space of all possible two-dimensional shapes is amazingly large, and no shapes were retrieved when the error margins were small. However, as the error margins were relaxed, we began to retrieve "similar" shapes. Figs. 2.5b shows the "most" similar shape in the database, retrieved using an approximate match on ten parameters: size, distortion, and four parameters for each of

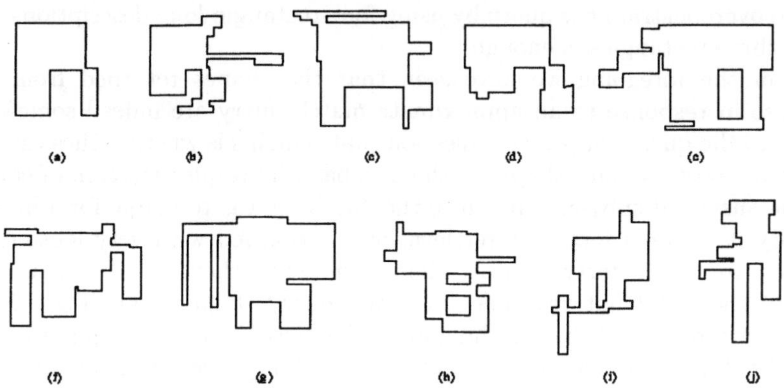

Fig. 2.5. (a) A query shape, (b-j) "similar" shapes in a database

two rectangles. If the size parameter is dropped, and the search based on nine parameters, then the shape of Fig. 2.5c is also retrieved. Observe that this shape is perhaps more like the query template than Fig. 2.5b, but it is certainly a lot bigger. Finally, if the distortion parameter is dropped, and the search based only on eight local parameters, then Figs. 2.5d and 5e are retrieved as well. Observe that both these shapes are too broad, and Fig. 2.5d is not tall enough, to match the template without distortion. However, appropriate scaling (independently) in the two dimensions, can achieve a good match, and these shapes have been retrieved since by dropping the distortion parameter we indicated that we were willing to permit such scaling.

All the above matches were performed using the first three rectangles of the description. We next varied the length of description used in the query to observe the effects. When the description used in the query was reduced to two rectangles, so that only 4 parameters were used, with the error margins the same as before, almost a hundred shapes were retrieved. Once the error margins were tightened enough, the only shape retrieved was the one in Fig. 2.5f. Here the two biggest rectangles in the additive cover match the template almost perfectly. However, the shape as a whole really does not look like the template. So, in this database, a query on less than three rectangles appears too weakly constrained.

Next we tried indexing on a longer description: four instead of just three rectangles. The problem now is that the shape in Fig. 2.5a has only three rectangles in its description. Following the discussion of Sec. 4.3, we tried two different queries: one with the fourth (dummy) rectangle having a height of zero, and another with a width of zero. With error margins comparable to those before, only Fig, 2.5e was ruled out in both cases. (Figs. 2.5b and 2.5c were both accepted in the zero height case, and Fig. 2.5d in the zero width case). Since most of the matching shapes returned were similar whether three or four rectangles were used in the query, we may conclude that there is no need to overconstrain the query by using four-rectangle-long descriptions: the use of three rectangles is enough.

From the foregoing we have seen that the shapes returned from the database in response to an approximate match query are indeed somewhat similar to the query shape. The question that remains is whether these are indeed the "most similar" shapes in the database. This question can, of course only be answered subjectively. Since the database was too large for a human to study it, a three rectangle retrieval was performed with very loose error margins, to obtain forty shapes. These forty were then visually examined. Most of them did not resemble the given query shape at all. Figs. 2.5b–e were indeed judged, by one human, to be closest to the template out of the forty. The argument then is that if our technique can find the four best matches out of the forty shapes that are somewhat like the template, and hence most likely to cause confusion, then our technique must also have done a good job in selecting these four out of the 16,000. Figs. 2.5g–j show four out of the forty shapes that were subjectively judged closest to the query shape, after the shapes in Fig. 2.5b–f (which were all also included in the forty). To the extent that you, the reader, agree that the shapes in Figs. 2.5g–j are less like the query shape than the ones in Figs. 2.5b–e, you are agreeing with the subjective evaluation described in this paragraph.

3. Word Matching

Words may sometimes be mis-spelled, due to errors in typing or in optical character recognition. Given a mis-spelled word, we may wish to find its correct spelling. Using "edit distance" (number of letters added or dropped[1]) as our measure of dissimilarity, we can ask a similarity query with a given mis-spelled word to find altenrative suggestions for its correct spelling.

How to map this notion of similarity into a feature space? We choose, for features, letter counts ignoring the 'case' of the letters. Thus, each word is mapped to a vector v with 27 dimensions, one for each letter in the English alphabet, and an extra one for the non-alphabetic characters. The L_1 (Manhattan) distance among two such vectors is a minimum bound on the editing distance.

We now have a mapping for each word in the English language into a 27-dimensional space. We now need an effective multi-dimensional index structure for a space with such a large dimensionality. If we could somehow order the dimensions in order of importance, as we were able to do in the case of shape description above, then we could use a TV-tree[9].

We accomplish this by applying the Hadamard Transform to these letter-count vectors, appropriately zero-padded. The Hadamard transform multiplies a row vector of dimension 2^k by the Hadamard matrix H_k, which is

[1] Modifications are treated as an add and a drop.

defined recursively as follows:

$$H_1 = \begin{pmatrix} 1 & 1 \\ 1 & -1 \end{pmatrix}, H_{k+1} = \begin{pmatrix} H_k & H_k \\ H_k & -H_k \end{pmatrix}$$

The Hadamard coefficients together carry all the information in the original vector, but the first few coefficients have "most" of the information, and thus may form a good basis for distinguishing objects (words represented as letter-count vectors)

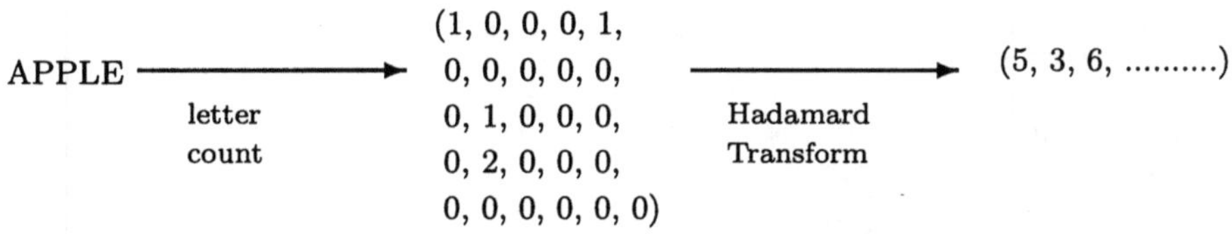

Fig. 3.1. Example of the Hadamard transform

Experiment

As a test database we used a collection of dictionary words from `/usr/dict/words`. Using an implementation of the TV-tree several experiments were run, and are described in [9]. Here we mention the highlights.

Experiments on 1,000 to 10,000 words are run, with words being randomly drawn from the dictionary. Error tolerance of 0-2 was considered.

We measured both the number of disk accesses (assuming that the root is in core), as well as the number of leaf accesses. The former measure corresponds to an environment with limited buffer space; the latter approximates an environment with so much buffer space that, except for the leaves, the rest of the tree fits in core.

The diagrams report the number of disk accesses per 1000 queries.

Diagrams (3.2)-(3.4) show the number of disk/leaf accesses as a function of the database size (number of records). The number of leaf access is the lower curve, in each set. For comparison, performance with an R^*-tree is also shown.

The main point to note is that a "decent" job of indexing was accomplished, in that the examination of a only a small fraction of the data set was required for a query trying to find matching words.

4. Discussion

In this chapter, we sought to give the reader an overview of the problem of similarity retrieval in a multimedia database. Reasoning about similarity is

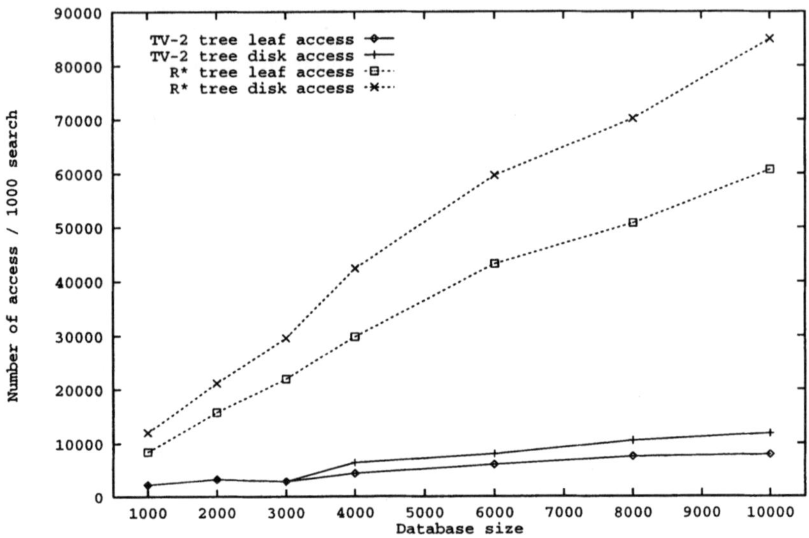

Fig. 3.2. Disk/leaf accesses vs. db size - exact match queries

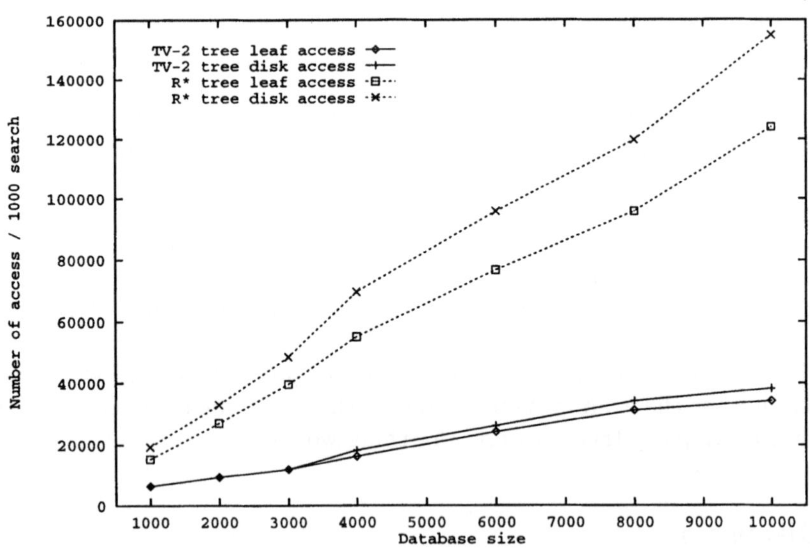

Fig. 3.3. Disk/leaf accesses vs. db size - range queries (tolerance=1)

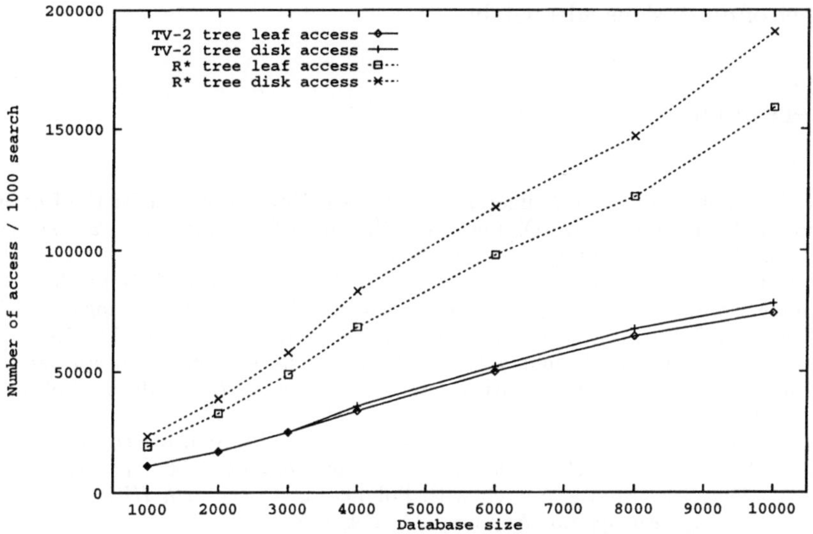

Fig. 3.4. Disk/leaf accesses vs. db size - range queries (tolerance=2)

hard. We use the notion of a transformation cost from one object to another, using allowed transformations, to provide a quantitative measure of similarity. This measure is specific to the set of transformations allowed, and is therefore application-dependent.

The core concept presented here is the technique of mapping an object into a point in an appropriate multi-dimensional feature space, and then using an appropriate index structure on this multi-dimensional space to aid rapid query response.

The hardest step in this process is the choice of an appropriate feature space. The mapping of objects into this space has to satisfy the requirement that no two similar objects be mapped into distance points in feature space. That is, given any two objects with a transformation cost of δ to go from one to another, there must exist an ϵ, monotonically non-decreasing function of δ, such that the two objects are guaranteed to map to points no more than a distance ϵ apart. Further, if the index is to have reasonable selectivity, too many dissimilar objects should also not be clustered close together.

By example, we illustrated how to choose a good feature space for two distinct domains. For each, we validated our choice through experimental results.

If the dimensionality of the feature space is high, many traditional multi-dimensional index structures may perform poorly, since they were originally designed for 2 and 3 dimensional spaces. However, more recent index structures, such as the TV-tree discussed here, are capable of handling a very large number of dimensions adequately.

References

[1] N. J. Ayache and O. D. Faugeras. HYPER - A New Approach for the Recognition and Position of Two-Dimensional Objects. *IEEE Trans. on Pattern Analysis and Machine Intelligence.* PAMI-8, 1986. 44-54.

[2] S-K. Chang, Y. Cheng, S. S. Iyengar, and R. L. Kashyap. A New Method of Image Compression Using Irreducible Covers of Maximal Rectangles. *IEEE Trans. on Software Engineering.* Vol. 14, no. 5, May 1988. pp. 651-658.

[3] D. S. Franzblau. Performance Guarantees on a Sweep-Line Heuristic for Covering Rectilinear Polygons with Rectangles. *SIAM J. Disc. Math..* Vol. 2, no. 3, 1989. pp. 307-321.

[4] A. Guttman. R Trees: A Dynamic Index Structure for Spatial Searching. *Proc. ACM SIGMOD Int'l Conf. on the Management of Data*, 1984. pp. 47-57.

[5] H. V. Jagadish. Spatial Search with Polyhedra. *Proc. Sixth IEEE Int'l Conf. on Data Engineering.* Los Angeles, CA, Feb 1990.

[6] H. V. Jagadish and A. M. Bruckstein. On Sequential Shape Descriptions. *Pattern Recognition.* Vol. 25, no. 2, 1992. pp. 165-172.

[7] H. V. Jagadish. A Retrieval Technique for Similar Shapes. *Proc. ACM-SIGMOD Int'l Conf. on the Management of Data.* Denver, CO, May 1991.

[8] H. V. Jagadish, A. Mendelzon, and T. Milo. Similarity-based Queries. *Proc. Int'l Conf. on the Principles of Database Systems.* San Jose, CA, May 1995.

[9] K-I. Lin, H. V. Jagadish, and C. Faloutsos. The TV-tree: An Index Structure for High-Dimensional Data. to appear in the *VLDB Journal*, 1994.

[10] D. B. Lomet and B. Salzberg. A Robust Multi-Attribute Search Structure. *Proc. Fifth IEEE Int'l Conf. on Data Engineering.* Los Angeles, CA, Feb. 1989. 296-304.

[11] D. Mumford The Problem of Robust Shape Descriptors. Center for Intelligent Control Systems Report CICS-P-40. Harvard University, Cambridge, Mass. , Dec. 1987.

[12] J. Nievergelt, H. Hinterberger, and K. C. Sevcik. The Grid file: An Adaptable Symmetric Multikey File Structure. *ACM Trans. on Database Systems.* Vol. 9, no. 1, 1984.

[13] J. A. Orenstein and F. A. Manola. PROBE Spatial Data Modeling and Query Processing in an Image Database Application. *IEEE Trans. Software Engg..* Vol. 14, no. 5, May 1988. pp. 611-629.

[14] J. T. Robinson. K-D-B-tree: A Search Structure for Large Multidimensional Dynamic Indices *Proc. ACM SIGMOD Conf. on the Management of Data*, 1981.

[15] B. Seeger and H. P. Kriegel. The Buddy Tree: An Efficient and Robust Access Method for Spatial Database Systems. *Proc. 16th Int'l Conf on Very Large Databases.* Brisbane, Australia, Aug. 1990. pp. 590-601.

[16] T. Sellis, N. Roussopoulos and C. Faloutsos. The R+ Tree: A Dynamic Index for Multidimensional Objects. *Proc. 13th Int'l Conf on Very Large Databases.* Brighton, U. K., Sep. 1987. pp. 507-518.

[17] T. P. Wallace and P. A. Wintz. An Efficient Three-Dimensional Aircraft Recognition Algorithm Using Normalized Fourier Descriptors. *Computer Graphics and Image Processing.* Vol. 13, 1980. pp. 99-126.

A Data Access Structure for Filtering Distance Queries in Image Retrieval

A. Belussi[1], E. Bertino[2], A. Biavasco[2], and S. Rizzo[2]

[1] Dipartimento di Elettronica e Informatica
Politecnico di Milano, P.zza da Vinci 32, 20133 Milano, Italy
[2] Dipartimento di Scienze dell'Informazione
Università degli Studi di Milano, Via Comelico 39/41, 20135 Milano, Italy

Summary. In this paper, we describe Snapshot, a data structure for supporting distance queries in image databases. This data structure is defined as combination of several techniques, namely regular grid with locational keys, corner stitching and clustering technique for spatial objects, extensible hashing. The paper discusses how distance predicates are supported. In particular, algorithms are presented for two types of distance predicate: the FAR predicate, retrieving all objects within a given distance from a given point, and the MIN predicate, retrieving all objects at the minimum distance from a given point.

1. Introduction

In last few years a part of database research has addressed the evolution of data models and operations for Data Base Management Systems (DBMSs). The goal has been to extend the application scope of the database technology to new areas dealing with huge non-traditional datasets. In particular, image information systems have become a topic of increasing interest, because of the recent advances in technologies for the storage, transmission and manipulation of images. This new technology has created many new application areas for image storage and retrieval. These applications cover different contexts and are characterized by different expectation and requirements.
The main application areas are:

- Geographical area: it includes all applications involving maps and in particular those cases where raster data are relevant. For example, when environmental or atmospheric phenomena are described through remotely sensed images, which cover a huge geographical area.
- Computer graphics and CAD area: it concerns images of three-dimensional objects in the space, which can represent parts of a machinery or sections of a building, or images which describe, for example, the evolution of some phenomenon acting on real objects.
- Computer vision area: storing and retrieving images is a critical aspect of robotics.
- Medical picture management: in this environment storing temporal series of images and the retrieval of images through some similarity evaluation predicates is a fundamental task.

Considering the general structure of an image information system, as it is proposed in [5], three stages can be identified in image processing:

- Image analysis and pattern recognition.
- Image structuring and image understanding.
- Spatial reasoning and image retrieval.

The first stage concerns the interpretation of the image content to recognize a set of objects from raw images. In the second stage some image knowledge structures are constructed, so that spatial reasoning and image retrieval can be supported. Such structures can be: knowledge-based structures, for example semantic networks, topological structures, for example directed graphs representing spatial relationships, or spatial indexes for the recognized image objects. The final stage represents the interaction between user applications and the image database system: some of these applications are oriented to spatial reasoning and some others to image retrieval.

The wide range of applications, that image databases are conquering, produces different requirements with respect to both data model and operations. For example, both these scenarios are common:

1. The image database consists of sets of images that describe objects embedded in some space. This scenario implies that spatial links between images and space, but also between images themselves, are to be represented in the model. Spatial reasoning might play an important role in querying such databases. This scenario is often the case in GIS (Geographical Information Systems) area or in some computer vision applications.
2. The image database consists of a set of images that describes different instances of the same object type; these instances could belong, for example, to temporal series or they describe a set of distinct physical objects. In this scenario image retrieval with similarity predicates will certainly be the most interesting task for applications. Medical picture management and, in general, pictures management (for example concerning person faces) are the most important examples of such situation.

Considering the two above scenarios, in scenario 1 the emphasis of queries is on image objects. Instead, in scenario 2 the image as a whole is the target of most queries, and sets of images could be the result of some queries. Considering some image query languages proposed in literature [14], [4], the most important predicates in image retrieval are:

- spatial predicates;
- similarity predicates.

Notice that, for the definition of both these types of predicates an important role is played by the spatial relationships. These relationships are based on topological and metric properties and can involve image objects of an image or image objects belonging to different images. In the first scenario such relationships are derived from the embedding of all images in the same reference space, in the second scenario similarity predicates can be based on spatial relationships between image objects contained in the same image. Thus two images are similar, if the same spatial relationships exist among their objects.

The relevance of the spatial relationships in image databases requires to design specialized data access structures. These structures (usually called Spatial Access Method, SAM) are used to optimize the selection of image objects or the selection of images in queries that involve spatial predicates. Extending the traditional access methods to spatial queries is not straightforward. The volume of data is much larger than in traditional databases, the query set is richer and at physical level there are raw, non-structured images. Many SAMs have been proposed in literature, but most of them only solve some kind of queries, such as point or range queries. We focus in particular on queries based on the metric relationships, that is on queries that involve some kind of distance concept between two image objects. Moreover, since systems able to manage in an integrated way image data, and attributive and textual data, are still in preliminary stage of research, we refer to an architecture that separates the management of images and image objects from the management of related traditional information, usually stored in a relational database. The basic components of this architecture are: the Relational Database Management System (RDBMS) and the Image Processor (IP), which are integrated together through a High-level Query Interpreter (HQI), as proposed in [29]. The binding between the two modules is achieved by maintaining some kind of linkage pointers between the two parts of information: structured alphanumeric information stored in relations, on one side, and images with image objects, on the other side.

In Section 2 we describe some ideas for the design of an image query processor. In the same section we also give a formal definition of spatial predicates involving a distance concept. In Section 3 we describe in detail the proposed SAM, Snapshot. Section 4 contains some algorithms for distance queries and finally in Section 5 we summarize some ideas for optimization of spatial queries.

2. Spatial Access Methods and Image Retrieval

2.1 Query Processor

Images are huge data objects and the access to secondary storage to retrieve such objects is more time-consuming than in traditional databases. This situation gives increasing relevance to the query processing and optimization tasks, that have become a crucial part of any image database.

In order to reduce the amount of data that has to be loaded in main memory to process an image, different levels of auxiliary data structures are constructed above it, so that in processing queries either the image access is avoided, or the number of images to be processed in main memory is reduced.

A set of image objects represents the lowest level of this hierarchical structure that describes the content of an image in the database. Image objects can be represented in different ways, such as through a single point representing their location in the image, through the vector representation of their boundary, or through their Minimum Bounding Rectangle (MBR). At a higher level, data structures that represent relationships among image objects are built and, in particular for spatial relationships, Spatial Access Methods are the candidate structures to be used.

When such auxiliary structure is built, most spatial queries can then be processed according to the following phases [19]:

- an initial filter phase: it uses a spatial access method to identify a set of candidates which could be contained in the query result;
- a successive refinement phase: it applies the algorithm of computational geometry, which implements the query predicate, to the set of candidates obtained from the previous phase, so that the final result set is calculated.

This approach in spatial query processing can be useful in two different ways in the context of image retrieval.

- When the emphasis is on image objects (scenario 1 of section 1.), it reduces the set of image objects that have to be loaded in main memory in order to process the query. Indeed, using the auxiliary structure, all objects, that certainly are not in the query result set, are discarded and not considered in the following phase. Moreover, if the query execution requires loading the whole image which contains the object, the images to be considered are only those that contain at least one candidate image object.
- When emphasis in on single images (scenario 2 of section 1.), it reduces the set of images that have to be loaded in main memory to process the query, because a selection of the candidate images can be performed on the basis of the auxiliary structures that describe the relationships between its image objects. Moreover, since implementation of spatial predicates, based on computational geometry, is more time-expensive than the equality and range predicates of traditional databases, reducing the number of images to be processed can reduce the total time in a non-negligible way.

In both cases performance increases, if the auxiliary structures referring to a single image or to the image objects of a set of images, can reside in main memory.

Since we focus on spatial relationships between image objects and in particular on distance relationships, in the following section we propose a general definition of image objects and define some metric predicates.

2.2 Image Objects and Spatial Predicates

Image query languages always contain a set of spatial predicates on image objects, since spatial reasoning is a relevant part of image retrieval. The properties of an image object are difficult to fix in a general definition, since the features of an image object can vary in accordance with the interpretation criteria of the pattern recognition task. However, an image object must have a shape and a location on an image somewhere, so the following definition is certainly general enough to be useful for all image objects. For simplicity we suppose to limit the address space to the Euclidean Plane E^2.

An image objects is any planar shape embedded in the Euclidean Plane E^2, which can be represented as a closed set of points [1]. The set of all image objects is called IO.

$$IO = \{g \mid g \subset E^2 \wedge g \text{ is closed}\}$$

Two geometric functions from IO to E^2 can be defined:

Boundary: $IO \rightarrow E^2$

$$\text{Boundary}(g) = \partial g \text{ where } \partial g \subseteq g$$

- It returns the portion of the input image object that can be considered as the frontier of the object itself. We do not define precisely what boundary is, since it is not necessary for our purpose. Any boundary definition can be used, provided it satisfies the above condition: $\partial g \subseteq g$.

□

In some image applications, the boundary of an image object could be, for example, a buffer region around the object itself.

Interior: $IO \rightarrow E^2$

$$\text{Interior}(g) = g^\circ \text{ where } g^\circ = g - \partial g$$

- It returns the portion of the input image object that is not the boundary of the object itself.

□

From the above definitions we have that:

$$\forall g \in IO : \partial g \cup g^\circ = g \quad \wedge \quad \partial g \cap g^\circ = \emptyset$$

The process of objects recognition inside an image is considered to be a task which depends on the application domain. Thus we suppose that each application can supply its own procedure to translate an image into a set of image objects [6]. This can be done either using image processing and pattern recognition techniques, or through manual annotations of the users.

---

[1] We suppose that the closure of a set of points is known to the reader: intuitively, a closed set of points contains its boundary

2.2.1 Spatial Relationships in the Euclidean Plane. Embedding image objects in the Euclidean Plane E^2 implies the existence of several relationships among them. These relationships can be classified into two groups:

- **Topological relationships:** these relationships are completely independent from any distance concept and they always involve close image objects, that is objects that have some interferences among them. An interesting classification of topological relationships is described in [8]. In this approach, the boundary, interior and complement of a spatial object are defined and a 3×3 matrix is used to represent all topological relationships between two image objects. The matrix contains the result of the intersection between the boundary, interior and complement of two spatial objects, considering all possible combinations.
- **Distance relationships:** these relationships derive from the introduction in the embedding space of a function called Distance. It represents how far two image objects are from each other. In the Euclidean Plane this function is called Euclidean distance and its definition for points is the following one:
  $E\_dist : E^2 \times E^2 \rightarrow R$

  $$E\_dist(p,q) = SQR((x_p - x_q)^2 + (y_p - y_q)^2)$$

  The extension of this function to a generic image object, which is represented as a set of points, is the following:
  $Dist : IO \times IO \rightarrow R$

  $$Dist(g,f) = min(\{d : (\exists x \in g)(\exists y \in f)(d = E\_dist(x,y)\})$$

  Of course, this is not the only definition of distance between two sets of points in the plane. Specific application contexts may require a more complex definition, referring for example to some predefined paths which were recognized on the image. The predicate that immediately follows from the *Dist* function is the range predicate:
  $FAR_{r,s} : IO \times IO \rightarrow \text{BOOLEAN} \quad (r, s \in R^2)$

  $$FAR_{r,s}(g,f) = true \Leftrightarrow r \leq Dist(g,f) \leq s$$

  Other predicates concerning distance can be defined. In [7] we find for example the min and max predicates, which define the search of the nearest neighbor and the search of the furthest neighbor respectively. Formally, they are defined as follows:
  $MIN_B : IO \times IO \rightarrow \text{BOOLEAN} \quad (B \in powerset(IO))$

  $$MIN_B(g,f) = true \Leftrightarrow \forall x \in B : Dist(g,f) \leq Dist(g,x)$$

  $MAX_B : IO \times IO \rightarrow \text{BOOLEAN}$

[2] R denotes the set of real numbers.

$$MAX_B(g, f) = true \Leftrightarrow \forall x \in B : Dist(g, f) \geq Dist(g, x)$$

In this paper we focus on spatial queries having distance relationships as predicates. These queries can produce as result *a set of image objects*, for example:

Q1: "Select the image objects representing the blocks in the town 'X', where people, who have Z syndrome, live"

Q2: "Select the image objects representing villages within 10 miles form a toxic waste dump D"

or, *a set of images*, for example:

Q3: "Select all the images representing a flooding where the water reached the main hospital of town 'X' "

or, *a set of alphanumeric data*, for example:

Q4: "Select names and addresses of all patients, who live within one mile from river 'Y' and had the 'Z' syndrome "

In the above queries, the selection condition contains also alphanumeric predicates. These predicates are processed by the RDBMS, which produces a set of candidate objects/images. The final result is obtained by the Image Processor considering the spatial part of the predicate.

3. Snapshot

The access data structure we propose is a combination of several techniques found in access structures defined for traditional databases and access structures specifically developed for spatial data. Those techniques are: the regular grid with locational key, clustering technique for spatial objects used in R^+-tree, extensible hashing.

The proposed access data structure, called Snapshot, has the same leaf-node of an R^+-tree, but it replaces the tree-based structure of the R^+-tree with a directory table. The entries of this table are associated with the cells of a regular grid superimposed onto the reference space. Moreover, using locational keys as names of the cells, a fast technique to navigate the directory is supplied.

Consider selection queries that involve distance predicates, such as the identification of the nearest (furthest) neighbor. The advantage of this new access structure compared to the R^+-tree is due to the use of a grid approach that clusters objects according to their position in the space (space-based partition). This permits to navigate through the space from one cell of the grid to its adjacent cells by applying some translation function to the locational keys, which represent the names of the cells. By contrast, the object-based partitioning adopted by the R^+-tree implies, for the nearest (furthest) neighbor queries, the scan of all the leafs of the tree structure, as no links between nodes and embedding space is provided. Moreover, the use of the space objects in Snapshot avoids the analysis of empty cells during the execution of the search algorithms.

For range queries ($FAR_{x,y}$), the performance is similar to that obtained using an R^+-tree. Indeed, consider a set of N rectangles which represents the leaf-nodes of an R^+-tree. The height of the tree structure is $\log_m(N)$. In the case of minimum utilization, m = 2. Therefore $\log_m(N)$ is also the complexity of a range query when an R^+-tree is used Consider the Snapshot structure, the complexity for a range query, see Section 4.1, is function of the cardinality of the query result, thus it depends on the distance that defines the search region. In particular, if the search region is completely contained in one cell of the grid, the disk page with the candidate objects can be obtained in $O(1)$ time. Using an R$^+$-tree the query cost does not change with the query result and is $\log_m(N)$ in any case.

In the remainder of this section we briefly illustrate each technique used to define Snapshot. Then, we present the overall organization of Snapshot and we show an illustrative example.

3.1 Regular Grid with Locational Keys

The method is based on a regular, recursive subdivision of the space. The plane is initially partitioned into four subquadrants called NW, NE, SW and SE. To each such subquadrants the keys 00, 01, 10 and 11 are assigned, respectively. The plane is then recursively partitioned until a desired detail level is reached. The subquadrants obtained as last step of the partitioning are called *cells*. At each partitioning step, the subquadrant keys are generated according to the following inductive step. Let K be the key of a given quadrant, denoted as *quad*(K). The decomposition of *quad*(K) into four subquadrants generates the following four subquadrant keys:

$$K \Longrightarrow \begin{cases} K \cdot 00 & \text{key of the NW subquadrant of } quad(K) \\ K \cdot 01 & \text{key of the NE subquadrant of } quad(K) \\ K \cdot 10 & \text{key of the SW subquadrant of } quad(K) \\ K \cdot 11 & \text{key of the SE subquadrant of } quad(K) \end{cases}$$

where $\cdot$ operator is the string concatenation. For example, consider the grid illustrated in Figure 3.1. The partitioning of *quad*(01) generates the following four keys for its sub- quadrants: 0100 (identifying subquadrant NW),

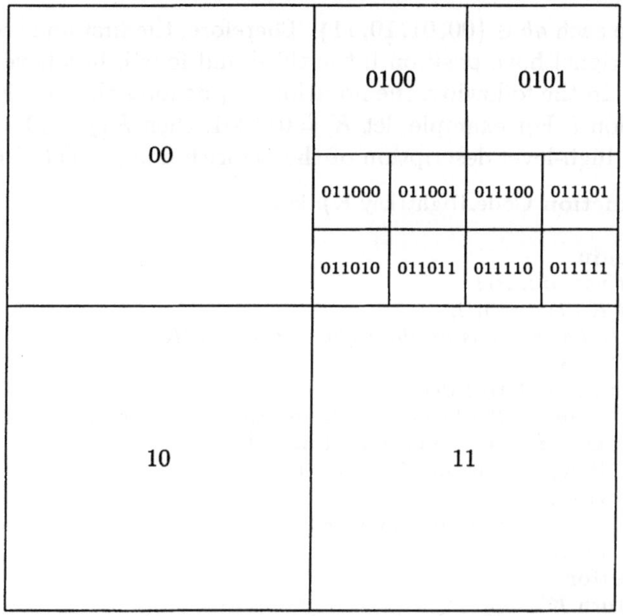

Fig. 3.1. Locational Keys structure

0101 (identifying subquadrant NE), 0110 (identifying subquadrant SW), 0111 (identifying subquadrant SE). Note that if l is the level of recursion that has been reached, $2 * l$ is the length of the key. Moreover, l is reached for all the keys, thus producing a regular grid.

An important reason for choosing this organization is that navigation among contiguous cells is very inexpensive. Indeed, given the key of a cell, the key of adjacent cells is simply obtained by an algorithmic transformation of this key.

In the following we present the algorithm that given K, key of a cell, determines the key of the cell on the *right* of the cell with key K.

The algorithm makes use of the following *conversion rule*:

$$00 \Longrightarrow 01$$

$$01 \Longrightarrow 00$$

$$10 \Longrightarrow 11$$

$$11 \Longrightarrow 10$$

Let K be input key. Each bit of the key is assigned a position, starting from rightmost bit, as follows:

$$K = \overbrace{ab}^{l} \ldots \cdot \overbrace{ab}^{4} \cdot \overbrace{ab}^{3} \cdot \overbrace{ab}^{2} \cdot \overbrace{ab}^{1}$$

where each $ab \in \{00, 01, 10, 11\}$. Therefore, the first and second bits (starting from right) have position 1, the third and fourth bits have position 2, and so forth. In the following, the notation $K_{\downarrow i}$ denotes the two bits of key K having position i. For example, let $K = 011001$, then $K_{\downarrow 2} = 10$.

A high-level description of the algorithm is presented below.

```
function Code_Right(key K): key

begin
let pos: integer;
let K': bistring(l);
if K has no cells on the right then return(K);
K' ← K;
for pos = 1 to l do
    "convert the two bits of K' having position equal to pos
    according to the conversion rule";
    if K↓pos = 00 or K↓pos = 10
    then
        "exit from the for-loop"
    endif
endfor
return K'
end
```

The algorithm basically converts each pair of bits of the given key, according to the above conversion rule. The algorithm terminates when either the last pairs of converted bits was ending by 0, before the conversion, or when all pairs of bits in the key have been converted.

Consider the example in Figure 3.1. Suppose that the key must be determined of the cell on the right of the cell with key $K = 011001$. According to the algorithm, the following transformation steps are performed on K:

$$011001 \longrightarrow 011000 \longrightarrow 011100$$

Notice that the conversion has stopped here (011100), since the pair of bits, before the conversion, was 10.

Therefore, the key of the cell on the right is 011100. By simply modifying the conversion rule, similar algorithms for the navigation of the grid are obtained, that is, *Code_Left, Code_Up* and *Code_Down*.

3.2 Clustering Technique

Given a set of image objects in the plane, many choices exist for organizing the data in order to provide an efficient query filter. We use an organization based on the notion of *bounding regions* (BRG, for short). A BRG is a rectangular region of the plane and has one of the following two types:

- Object
- Space

Every Object BRG contains some of the image objects of the given plane. On other hand, every image object is contained in at least one Object BRG. The number of the image objects contained in each Object BRG depends on the secondary storage page size. Indeed, a secondary storage page is allocated for each Object BRG. Therefore, an Object BRG has the purpose of clustering image objects. The definition and the construction technique for Object BRGs are the same of those used for the leaves of the R^+-tree data structure. Therefore, the extension of an Object BRG is the minimum bounding rectangle of the objects contained in the leaves of an R^+-tree.

Every Space BRG corresponds to empty portions of the plane, that is, regions containing no image objects. On the other hand, every empty portion of the plane not contained in any Object BRG, is contained in at least one Space BRG. The definition of Space BRGs is given according to the Corner Stitching technique. Such technique considers two types of objects: *space* and *solid*. *Solid* objects correspond to rectangles representing the image objects, that is, to the Object BRG of our organization. The space among the various Object BRG is represented by *space* objects. Therefore, the *space* objects are maximal horizontal stripes: they cannot be right or left adjacent to other *space* objects. A result is the following: let n be the number of *solid* objects in the plane, then the number of maximal stripes is at most $3n+1$. Therefore, if the number of Object BRGs for a given plane is n, the maximum number of Space BRGs will be $3n + 1$.

In order to reduce the level of recursion in the grid, that is the number of cells and the number of BRGs in each cell, the Minimum Bounding Rectangles (MBR) associated with each BRG is snapped in some cases to the grid cells. This means that the process of building a snapshot structure is composed of three phases. First the granularity of the grid must be fixed according to the required level of precision, then BRGs and their MBRs are built according to the Pack algorithm of the R^+-tree, stopped at the first level [32]. Finally, the space BRGs are built and, if a cell contains more than 4 BRGs, the boundaries of these BRGs are moved and snapped to the grid, in order to obtain at most 4 BRGs in each cell.

Figure 3.2 illustrates the main steps in constructing the BRGs. Figure 3.2(a) illustrates a plane containing some image objects. As first step, the various Object BRGs are generated, as illustrated in Figure 3.2(b). Then, as second step, the Space BRGs are determined. The final organization in terms of Object and Space BRGs is illustrated in Figure 3.2(c).

3.3 Extensible Hashing

The Extensible Hashing technique is a well known technique which was initially introduced to index alphanumeric data. Here we provide a short overview of this technique and we refer the reader to [10] for additional details.

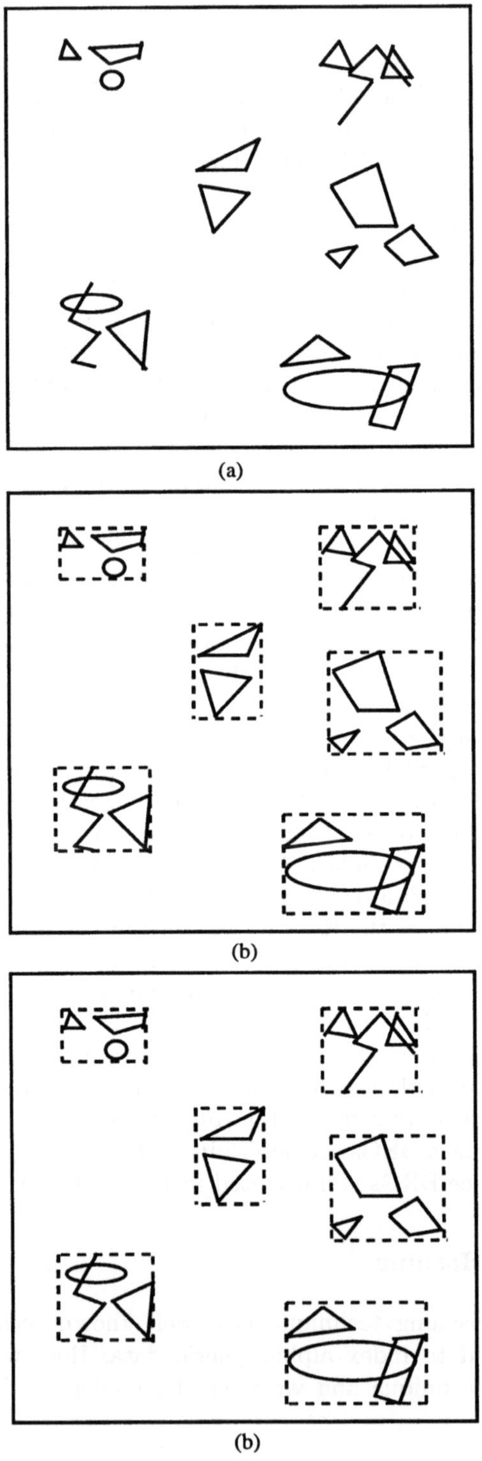

Fig. 3.2. Spatial entities clustering

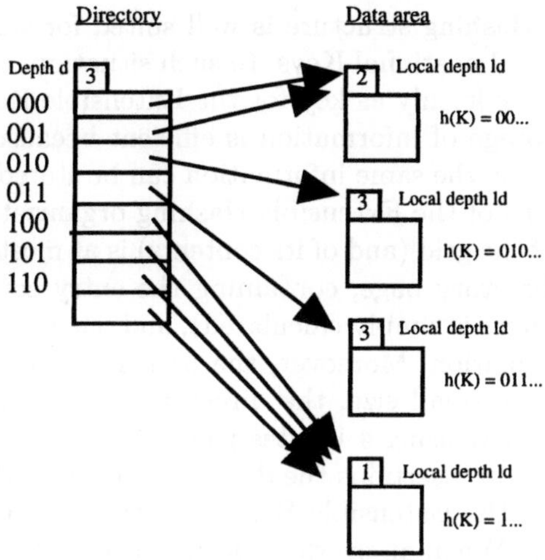

Fig. 3.3. Organization of Extendible Hashing

Suppose that the data to be stored have a record structure with a key to be used for indexing information. The extensible hashing organization makes use of a function h that given a value K for the key, returns a bitstring K', called pseudo-key value, that is, $h(K) = K'$.

The organization of extensible hashing is based on two levels: *directory* and *leaves*. The leaves contain pairs of the form $(K, I(K))$ where K is a value of the key and $I(K)$ is the associated information (record or pointer to record). The directory has an header, denoted as *deepth* (shortly, d), which denotes the number of bits of the pseudo-key, to be used for accessing the information, given a value for the key. Each entry in the directory is addressed by using the first d bits of the pseudo-key. The entry corresponding to a given value K' of the pseudo-key contains the reference to a leaf storing records whose first d bits of the pseudo-key are equal to K'. There is a total number of 2^d references from the directory to the leaves. Moreover, every leaf is characterized by a parameter called *localheader* (shortly, ld). For a given leaf, ld indicates that all records stored within this leaf have the first ld bits of the pseudo-key which are equal. Note that $ld \leq d$ and, moreover, that every leaf may have a different value for ld. Since the same leaf may be referenced by several entries, this means that the leaf may contain records whose first d bits pseudo-key may be different. However, all those records have the first ld bits pseudo-key which are equal (recall that $ld \leq d$).

Figure 3.3 presents an example of the Extensible Hashing organization. The directory has depth $d = 3$. Consider two objects having has key values K_0 and K_1, respectively, such that $h(K_0) = 000100\ldots$ and $h(K_1) = 001101\ldots$. These objects will be stored in the same leaf. Indeed, in the directory, the cells corresponding to 000 and 001 refer to the same leaf, and therefore to the same page of the disk.

The Extensible Hashing structure is well suited for storing a grid whose cells are addressed by Locational Keys. In such situation, the Locational Key of a cell can be used not only as key for the Extensible Hashing, but also as pseudo-key. The storage of information is efficient because cells of the same portion of space having the same information can be stored in the same page.

A main advantage of the Extensible Hashing organization is that the access cost for a cell of the grid (and of its contents) is at most two disk accesses: one to reach the directory page, containing the entry corresponding to the grid cell (whose address is simply calculated), and one to obtain the leaf-page containing the information. Moreover, the first access is often unnecessary. Indeed, because of its small size, the directory can be kept in main memory. Statistics show that using 4-Kbytes pages, 7-bits keys and 3-bytes page pointers, after a million insertions the directory occupies three pages only. A further advantage of the Extensible Hashing organization is in its efficiency in overflow handling. When an overflow occurs, it is sufficient, in most cases, to allocate an additional page and to re-distribute the records between the new page and the page originating the overflow.

3.4 Organization of Snapshot

The overall organization of Snapshot consists of:

- A set of Bounding Regions (BRGs), which are rectangles contained in the reference space. Those bounding regions can be either object or space regions.
- A grid covering the reference space of the database, which is represented as a portion of the Euclidean Space E^2. The grid is thus sumperimposed on the set of BRGs, into which the set of image objects have been clustered.

Figure 3.4(b) illustrates the cell decomposition of the NW quadrant of the space, illustrated in Figure 3.4(a).

Every cell of the grid is addressed via the Extensible Hashing structure using Locational Keys as pseudo-keys. Each cell of the grid corresponds, thus, to an entry in the directory. An entry contains information about the BRGs (at most four) intersected by the cell corresponding to the directory entry. Therefore, the set of information stored by the Snapshot access structure is organized on two levels:

1. *Directory level.*
   The entry with key K corresponds to the grid cell having locational key equal to K. The entry has the following format:
   $(nbrg, [ptr_1, id_1, (p_{1_1}, p_{1_2})], [ptr_2, id_2, (p_{2_1}, p_{2_2})], [ptr_3, id_3, (p_{3_1}, p_{3_2})],$
   $[ptr_4, id_4, (p_{4_1}, p_{4_2})])$
   where:
   - $nbrg$, $1 \leq brg \leq 4$, denotes the number of BRGs intersected by the grid cell;

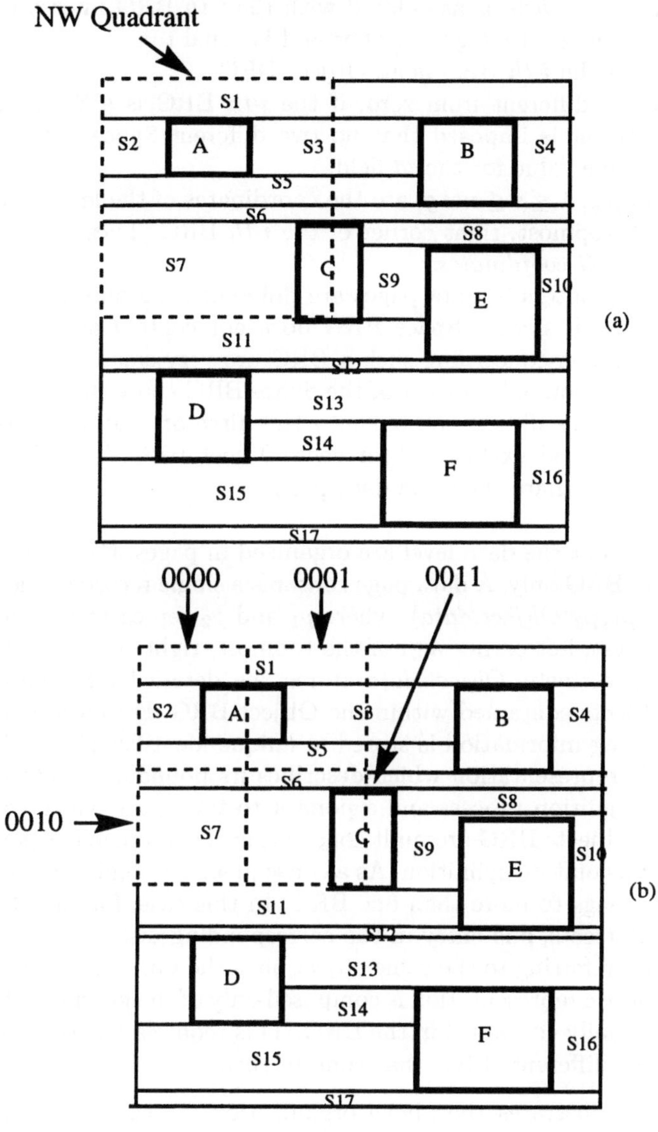

Fig. 3.4. An example of imposing a grid on a set of BRGs

- ptr_i, $1 \leq i \leq nbrg$, is associated with the *i-th* BRG intersected by the grid cell; it is a pointer and is equal to:
  - a null pointer, denoted as ptr_{NULL}, if the *i-th* BRG is a Space BRG;
  - the address of a data page, containing information about the *i-th* BRG, if the *i-th* BRG is an Object BRG;

- id_i, $1 \leq i \leq nbrg$, is associated with the *i-th* BRG intersected by the grid cell; it is an integer number and is equal to:
  - zero, if the *i-th* BRG is an Object BRG;
  - a value different from zero, if the *i-th* BRG is a Space BRG; the constraint is imposed that no two different Space BRGs can have the same value for the *id* field.
- p_{i_1} and p_{i_2}, $1 \leq i \leq nbrg$, are the coordinates of the lowest, left corner and the topmost, right corner of the *i-th* BRG. These two points are called *BRG coordinates.*

Note that pointers to data pages are different from null only for Object BRGs. Indeed, since a Space BRG does not contain any image object the information concerning such a BRG are very small in size: basically such information only consist of the Space BRG coordinates. Thus, these information are directly stored into the directory. By contrast, a data page is allocated exclusively for each Object BRG. Therefore, no two Object BRGs share the same data page.

2. *Data level.*

   Information at the data level are organized in pages. Pages are allocated to Object BRG only. A data page contains a single record of the following format: $(p_1, p_2, Object\_data)$, where p_1 and p_2 represent the coordinates of the lowest, left corner and of the topmost, right corner of the Object BRG, respectively. *Object_data* stores the detailed information of the image objects contained within the Object BRG. For each image object the following information is stored: a unique identifier of the object, the geometric representation which describes its boundary produced by the image recognition process and a pointer to the image which contains it. Since the objects BRG are built considering the approach of the R^+-tree, they are disjoint by definition. As a consequence, it might happen that an object belongs to more than one BRG. In this case, for each BRGs, the object intersects, one entry in the corresponding disk page is contained. All entries referring to the same object have the same identifier, however, the geometric representation is composed only of the portion of the object that is actually contained in the BRG. This requires splitting the objects among the different BRGs that contain them.

Figure 3.5 illustrates the above organization for the cells contained in the NW quadrant of the reference space illustrated in Figure 3.4(a). In the example, we have not included, for simplicity, the BRG coordinates in the directory entries. Note from the example in Figure 3.5 that the Object BRG A intersects two cells of grid, namely the cells with keys 0000 and 0001. Therefore, the entries in the directory corresponding to these keys have a pointer to the data page containing the information on the Object BRG A. Moreover, note that the grid cell with key 0010 only intersects two BRGs. Therefore, only the first two entries are significant.

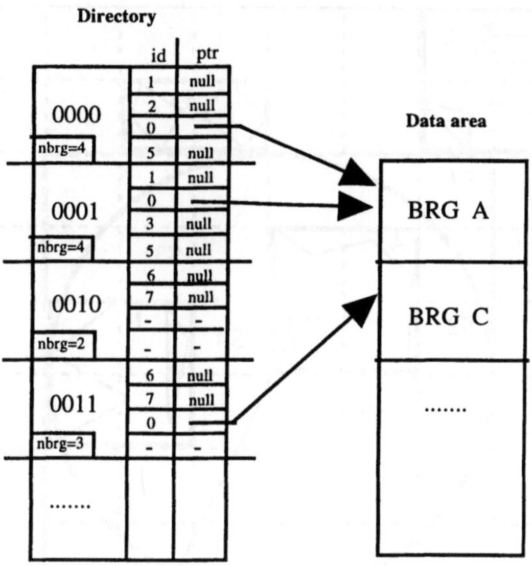

Fig. 3.5. An example of the Snapshot organization

The total number of data pages needed to store the information contained by the Snapshot organization is equal to $N_{OBRG} + N_{dir}$, where N_{OBRG} is the number of Object BRGs in the reference plane, and N_{dir} is the number of data pages needed to store the directory. Note that, in general, N_{dir} is quite small and thus the directory can reside in main memory.

4. Filtering Metric Queries with Snapshot

In this section, we discuss how Snapshot can be used for filtering distance queries based on distance relationships as reviewed in Section 2.3.1. Therefore, we are interested in filtering queries based on the $FAR_{r,s}$, MIN_B and MAX_B predicates. As an example, suppose we want to find all image objects that lie within three kilometers from a given point O. Such query could be expressed, in a SQL-like formalism, as:

select g
from *set_obj* g
where $FAR_{0,3}(O, g)$;

As an example of filtering such query with Snapshot, consider Figure 4.1 representing the above query. First, the circle having center in O is approximated with its bounding square, denoted by dashed lines. Then all Object BRGs must be determined which are contained in such square. We call such a square *query region*. Remember that in the filtering phase it is important to restrict as much as possible the set of objects that could participate in

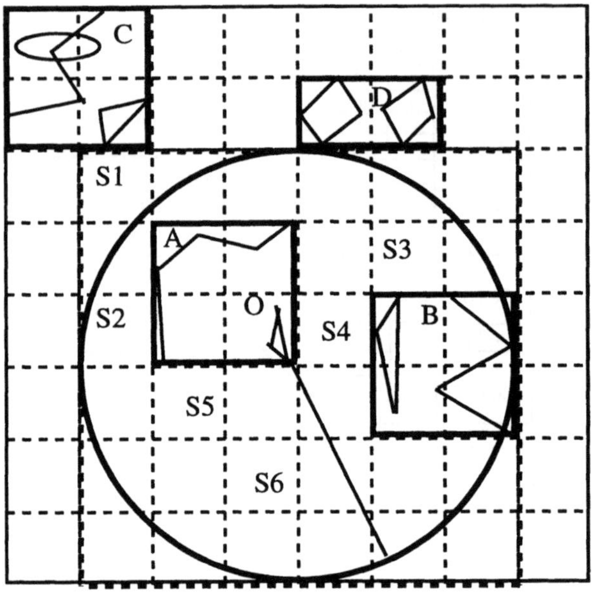

Fig. 4.1. A query example

the results of a query, thus discarding the majority of objects that cannot be involved in the result.

The example shows how rectangular "regions of interest" are often used as filtering criteria for spatial queries, especially for distance queries. In order to have fast response time in solving such queries, algorithms must be devised that, on a given data structure, retrieve objects that are intersected by rectangular "regions of interest".

In this section we present the Search algorithm for the Snapshot structure. Such algorithm determines all objects that are located within a certain distance from a given object. Then we present the algorithms for filtering queries involving MIN_B predicate. We refer the reader to an extended version of this paper for the algorithm concerning the MAX_B predicate [2].

4.1 Search Algorithm

The Search algorithm is based on a navigational technique of the subspace determined by the query region in which every retrieved (either space or object) BGR determines at most two more BGRs to retrieve at the following step.

The list of identifiers and coordinates of BRGs to be visited is stored in a main memory *priority queue*. We make the assumption that each BRG in the queue is identified by the pair *ptr*, *id*, where *ptr* is the pointer to the data page and *id* is the integer identifier. We recall that *ptr* is null for Space

BRGs and *id* is zero for Object BRGs. Thus, each pair (ptr, id) uniquely identifies each BRG, either space or object. Those pairs are recorded in the directory entry. Note that the information that are stored in the queue for each BRG are extracted from the directory component of Snapshot. Thus no access to the data level pages is needed during the search. An element of such queue has the highest priority if it lies nearer to the left-upper corner of the rectangular region of interest. Beside the ISEMPTY predicate, two operations are defined for the priority queue, namely DELETEMIN and INSERT. The former returns and then removes from the queue the object with the highest priority. The latter inserts an object in the queue. By implementing the queue as a balanced tree, the complexity of those operations is $O(logn)$ where n is the number of objects in the queue. In the remainder, we make the assumption that the region of interest to the search is identified by the key of two cells, namely the upper-left cell and the lower-right cell of the subgrid corresponding to the query region[3]. As an example, consider Figure 4.1. The query region is identified by the following keys: 001001 (key of the upper-left cell), 111110 (key of the lower-right cell). In the following, those two keys will be denoted by parameters ul-key and lr-key, respectively.

The search algorithm makes use of the following functions:

- upperR(brg,ul-key,lr-key)
  given the BRG identified by parameter *brg* and a query region identified by parameters ul-key and lr-key, this function finds (if exists) the upper-right BRG adjacent to the right side of *brg*, intersected by the query region. If such upper-right BRG does not exist, a null pointer is returned. For example, consider Figure 4.1, the function call upperR(A,001001,111110) will return the Space BRG S3.
- lowerL(brg,ul-key,lr-key)
  given the BRG identified by parameter *brg* and a query region identified by parameters ul-key and lr-key, this function finds (if exists) the lower-left BRG adjacent to the bottom side of *brg*, intersected by the query region. If such lower-left BRG does not exist, a null pointer is returned. For example, consider Figure 4.1, the function call lowerL(A,001001,111110) will return the Space BRG S5.
- first_obj(ul-key,lr-key)
  given a query region identified by parameters ul-key and lr-key, this retrieves the upper left BRG in such subgrid. For example, consider Figure 4.1, the function call first-obj(001001,111110) will return the Space BRG S1.

Functions upperR and lowerL are implemented in terms of the functions Code_Right, Code_Let, Code_Up, and Code_Down. In particular, from the geometric dimensions of the input BRG[4], it is possible to determine how

[3] Note that, when a query region is not coincident with a subgrid, we use the smallest subgrid which contains the query region.

[4] The geometric dimensions of a BRG are determined from its coordinates.

many cells are intersected by the BRG. Thus the adjacent upper-right BRG is determined by accessing the rightmost upmost cell intersected by the input BRG, whereas the adjacent lower-left BRG is determined by accessing the leftmost lowest cell intersected by the input BRG. Note that determining the keys of such cells only requires algorithmic transformation and no access to secondary storage.

A temporary auxiliary main memory structure is used. Such structure contains all BRGs which are or have been in the priority queue. Thus, each time a BRG is inserted into the priority queue, it is also added to this list. However, each time a BRG is extracted from the priority queue, such BRG is not removed from this temporary structure. This auxiliary structure is used to avoid inserting the same BRG more than once in the priority queue. Thus, we are sure that each BRG is examined only once. In discussing the algorithm, we will use a Boolean function called flag_isin. This function receives as argument a BRG and returns True if this BRG is in the temporary auxiliary structure; it returns False otherwise. We make the assumption that such structure is implemented as a list. A predicate and two operations are also used for the list. When the list is empty, the LISEMPTY predicate returns True; it returns False, otherwise. The two operations are LINSERT and LREMOVE, the former inserting a BRG in the list, the latter returning a BRG from the list and deleting it from the list itself.

```
procedure SEARCH(ul-key,lr-key)
var cand: BRG;
var Q: priority queue;
var T: list;        /* temporary auxiliary list */
begin
INSERT(first_obj (ul-key,lr-key), Q);
LINSERT(first_obj (ul-key,lr-key), T);
while ¬ ISEMPTY(Q) do
    cand ← DELETEMIN(Q);
    if ¬ flag_isin (upperR (cand,ul-key,lr-key))
then
        INSERT(upperR (cand,ul-key,lr-key),Q);
        LINSERT(upperR (cand,ul-key,lr-key),T);
    endif
    if ¬ flag_isin(lowerL (cand,
ul-key,lr-key)) then
        INSERT(lowerL (cand,ul-key,lr-key),Q);
        LINSERT(lowerL (cand,ul-key,lr-key),T);
    endif
endwhile
while ¬ LISEMPTY(T) do
    cand ← POP(T);
    deactivate isin in (cand);
    if type of cand: Object then
        output cand;
    endif
endwhile
end
```

Note that the Search algorithm only returns the addresses and coordinates of the Object BRG that have been selected by the Search filter. Then, the actual content of each BRG can be retrieved from the data pages component of Snapshot.

To illustrate the algorithm, we show how the query represented in Figure 4.1 is executed. For each step in the algorithm, we show the BRG which is currently examined (not for the initial step), the BRGs which are added to the priority queue, the resulting state of the queue, and the resulting state of temporary list T.

Step 0 : (initial step) Q ← S1; resulting state of Q = S1; resulting state of T = S1;

Step 1 : current BRG: S1; Q ← S2; resulting state of Q = S2; resulting state of T = S1, S2;
note that S1 does not have an adjacent upper-right region. Thus, only a single BRG is added to the priority queue at this step.

Step 2 : current BRG: S2; Q ← A, S5; resulting state of Q = A, S5; resulting state of T = S1, S2, A, S5;

Step 3 : current BRG: A; Q ← S3; resulting state of Q = S5, S3; resulting state of T = S1, S2, A, S5, S3;
note that BRG A has as adjacent regions S3 and S5. S5, however, is already present in Q, thus it is not inserted again.

Step 4 : current BRG: S5; Q ← B, S6; resulting state of Q = S3, B, S6; resulting state of T = S1, S2, A, S5, S3, B, S6;

Step 5 : current BRG: S3; Q ← S4; resulting state of Q = B, S6, S4; resulting state of T = S1, S2, A, S5, S3, B, S6, S4;

Step 6 : current BRG: B; resulting state of Q = S6, S4; resulting state of T = S1, S2, A, S5, S3, B, S6, S4;

Step 7 : current BRG: S6; resulting state of Q = S4; resulting state of T = S1, S2, A, S5, S3, B, S6, S4;

Step 8 : current BRG: S4; resulting state of Q is empty; resulting state of T = S1, S2, A, S5, S3, B, S6, S4;

Step 9 : (final step) output A, output B.

4.2 Min Algorithm

The Min algorithm determines, given a query object, the nearest image object. For simplicity reasons, we make the assumption that such query object to be a point P and we do not put any constraint about the class of the entities to be retrieved.

At the basis of the algorithm there are the following considerations:

1. Every image object accessed by the algorithm determines an upper bound U for the subgrid to be searched.

2. The management of empty space via the Corner Stitching technique ensures that an entity which lies *near* the query point P can be found in O(1) time. This follows from the property that no Space BRG is horizontally adjacent to another space BRG. Therefore, if P lies in a Object BRG we are sure to find a real object in it. If P lies in a Space BRG, we can find an Object BRG horizontally adjacent to it.
3. If the query point P lies in an Object BRG, we are **not** ensured that the nearest entity lies in the same BRG.

The idea of the algorithm is based on a refinement of the Search algorithm presented in the previous subsection. The query point P determines four subquadrants of the plane by simply considering a pair of orthogonal axis centered in P. For every subquadrant a search is executed which retrieves the nearest entity of each subquadrant and sets a global variable to the value of the distance of the nearest entity found from P. This value, namely U, is used by the searches executed in the remaining subquadrants as range value for scanning the subquadrant. Figure 4.2 illustrates an example of query requiring to find the closest entity to object O. The figure also shows the four subquadrants that are obtained by considering the orthogonal axis centered in O.

In the following algorithms, two global variables are used:

- MINOBJ denoting the entity *currently* being the nearest to the query point P.
- U denoting the distance between MINOBJ and P.

Beside such variables, we use the function flag_isin defined for the Search algorithm for determining the visited BRGs and the temporary list T used to list all the visited BRGs.

In practice, the algorithm starts by searching the BRG containing the point P and, if such BRG contains other entities, sets U to the value of the distance of the nearest entity to P (MINOBJ) in the BRG. In the recursive step, the algorithm checks if there exists a BRG which lies closer than MINOBJ from P in each subquadrant of the plane. If such BRG exists and contains an entity that lies closer than MINOBJ, MINOBJ and U are updated accordingly.

First we describe the *check_near* algorithm which, given a BRG, checks whether any entity in this BRG is nearer to P than the current nearest entity, referenced by variable MINOBJ. If such an entity is found, variables MINOBJ and U are updated accordingly.

```
procedure check_near(BRG)
var objmin: image object;
begin
    /* Updates the temporary structure*/
    LINSERT(BRG,T);
    /* Test if any entity in BRG is nearer to P than MINOBJ */
    objmin := the nearest entity to P in BRG;
```

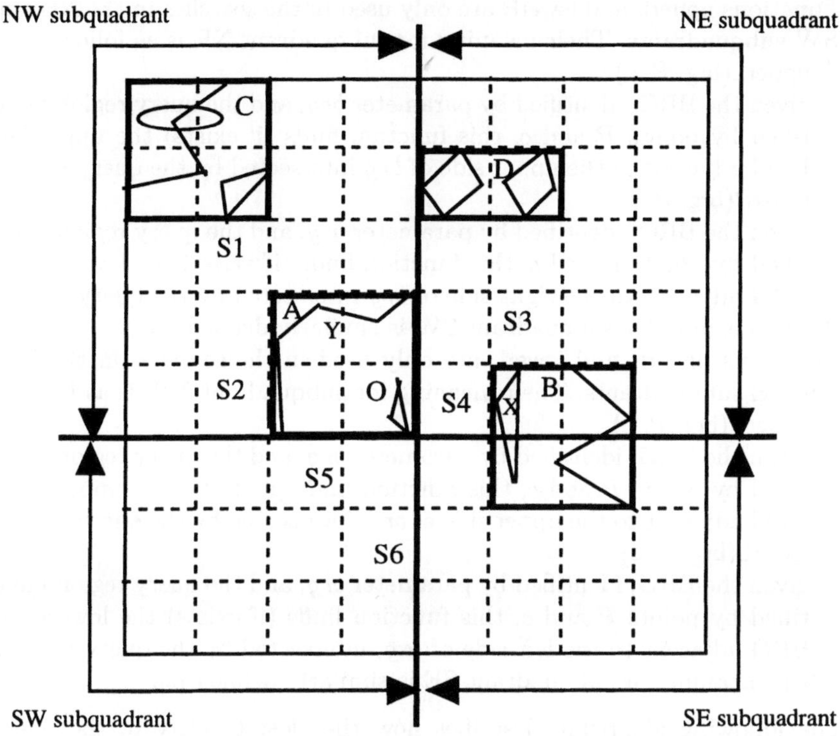

Fig. 4.2. An example of query with a min predicate

```
    if distance(objmin,P) < U then
        MINOBJ := objmin;
        U:= distance (objmin, P);
    endif
end
```

We now describe the checkNE_near algorithm which determines the nearest entity to P in the NE subquadrant. Algorithms checkNW_near, checkSE_near and checkSW_near for determining the nearest entity to P in the other subquadrants are similar to the checkNE_near algorithm and we do not describe them here.

The above four algorithms (namely, checkNE_near, checkNW_near, checkSE_near and checkSW_near) require the following functions, lowerR(brg, P, c), upperL(brg, P, c), lowerL(brg, P, c) and upperR(brg, P, c) whose meaning and implementation is analogue to lowerR, upperL defined for the Search algorithm. The only difference is that the query region is specified in terms of the query point P and of the point c which is a corner of the grid. We will indicate c_{ne} the north-east corner of the grid, c_{nw} the north-west corner and so on. In particular:

1. Functions upperL and lowerR are only used in the searches in the NE and SW subquadrants. Their meaning for subquadrant NE is as follows:
   - upperL(brg, P, c)
     given the BRG, identified by parameter *brg*, and the query region identified by points *P* and *c*, this function finds (if exists) the upper-left BRG adjacent to the upper side of *brg* intersected by the query region.
   - lowerR(brg, P, c)
     given the BRG, identified by parameter *brg*, and the query region identified by points *P* and *c*, this function finds (if exists) the lowest-right BRG adjacent to the right side of *brg* intersected by the query region.

   Their meaning for subquadrant SW is similarly defined [2].
2. Functions upperR and lowerL are only used in the searches in the NW and SE subquadrants. Their meaning for subquadrant NW is as follows:
   - upperR(brg, P, c)
     given the BRG, identified by parameter *brg*, and the query region identified by points *P* and *c*, this function finds (if exists) the upper-right BRG adjacent to the upper side of *brg*, intersected by the query region.
   - lowerL(brg, P, c)
     given the BRG, identified by parameter *brg*, and the query region identified by points *P* and *c*, this function finds (if exists) the lowest-left BRG adjacent to the left side of *brg*, intersected by the query region.

   Their meaning for subquadrant SE is similarly defined [2].

The following algorithm describes how the closest entity to the query point *P* is determined for the NE subquadrant.

```
procedure checkNE_near(brg)
begin
   if typeof(brg) = object and ¬flag_isin(brg) then
      check_near(brg);
   else if typeof(brg) = space and ¬flag_isin(brg)
then
      LINSERT(brg, T);
   endif
   /* If the lower-right BRG in the north east subquadrant */
   /* is nearer to P than MINOBJ, then recursively call checkNE */
   if distance(lowerR(brg, P,c_ne),P) < U then
      checkNE_near(lowerR(brg,P,c_ne));
   endif
   /* Check if the upper-left BRG in the north east subquadrant */
   /* is nearer to P than MINOBJ and call recursion */
   if distance(upperL(brg,P,c_ne),P) < U then
      checkNE_near(upperL(brg,P,c_ne));
   endif
end
```

The main algorithm for the Min predicate is the following:

```
Algorithm MIN(P)
var brg: BRG;
var MINOBJ: image object;
var U: Real;
var L: List;

begin
    /* Find the BRG in which P lies and set up global vars */
    Initialize_min(P,MINOBJ,U,brg);
    check_near(brg);
    checkNE_near(brg);
    checkNW_near(brg);
    checkSW_near(brg);
    checkSE_near(brg);
    return(MINOBJ, U);
end
```

Note that in the above algorithm, subquadrants are sequentially checked. This approach may be not efficient if the first subquadrant checked contains no objects. If this fact occurs, it means that the subquadrant contains only a few Space BRGs. Thus, no major performance penalties are incurred, since no data page accessed are performed. Indeed, all information about Space BRGs, needed for the search, are stored in the Snapshot directory. A possible solution, that improves performance in all cases, is to parallelize the Min algorithm, by executing checkNE_near, checkNW_near, checkSW_near and checkSE_near in parallel. The only constraint on the parallel execution of these four procedures is the proper synchronization on the global variables.

To illustrate the Min algorithm, we show how the nearest entity in the NE subquadrant is determined for the query illustrated in Figure 4.2. We assume that the entity denoted by X in the figure is the nearest to object O. Moreover, we assume that the the entity denoted by Y in the figure is the nearest to object O in the BRG A. In the example, we list for each step the current BRG which is examined, the set N of BRGs which are determined for future examination, and the resulting state of list T.

Step 0 : (initial step) current BRG: A; MINOBJ = Y; N = {S4}; resulting state of T = A, S4;

Step 1 : current BRG: S4; MINOBJ = Y; N= {S3, B}; resulting state of T = A, S4, S3, B;

Step 2 : current BRG: S3; MINOBJ = Y; N= {B}; resulting state of T = A, S4, S3, B;
note that S1 is not added to the set of BRGs to be examined, since its distance from O is greater than the distance of the current MINOBJ;

Step 3 : current BRG: B; MINOBJ = X; resulting state of N is empty; resulting state of T = A, S4, S3, B; since N is empty the search in the NW subquadrant ends and X is returned as the nearest object to O in this subquadrant.

5. Optimization of Spatial Queries

The data structure and the algorithms proposed in this paper are well suited for solving distance queries. Such structure, however, can be also used for solving other types of spatial queries by simple extensions to the proposed algorithms. In this section we briefly discuss preliminary ideas for such extensions. In the discussion, we use the classification of spatial queries proposed in [7].

Topological queries. The Snapshot data structure provides fast disk accesses when looking for clusters containing image objects. If the topological features are stored on the representation of the image objects via a topological model, for example, topological queries can then be performed in main memory, once the proper BRGs have been loaded, without requiring additional disk accesses. As an example consider the adjacency problem. We can store with each image object pointers to all its adjacent objects, without the need of modifying the Snapshot directory. When loading an Object BRG containing a given image object, we load all the objects that are spatially close to this object. Thus, topological information can be retrieved without additional disk access.

Set-theoretic queries. Given an image object stored in the database, we are interested in retrieving all image objects that intersect such entity. The same considerations, carried out about topological queries, apply.

Interference queries. When looking for the image objects intersected by some user-defined geometric entity, say g, (that does not exist in the database), we can use the Snapshot data structure in the following way:

- determine the minimal rectangular subgrid intersected by g;
- use the Search algorithm on such subgrid;
- test intersection between g and each BRG returned;
- determine the image objects intersected by g in the BRGs returned by the previous step.

Metric queries. The proposed algorithms solve such queries, as we have discussed in the previous section.

Complex queries. A complex query contains several predicates. Snapshot shows its strength when dealing with such queries because it supports a simultaneous evaluation of multiple predicates from the same query. Consider the following example: "find all the towns intersected by Tames that lie closer than 400kms from London". A conventional query processor would evaluate the selectivity of each of the two predicates, and would evaluate the one having the best selectivity, and then would evaluate the second predicate on the entities selected by the first predicate. Using Snapshot we can filter the entities by using both predicates together as follows:

- find the rectangular subgrid of interest for the first predicate;
- find the rectangular subgrid of interest for the second predicate;

- intersect the two subgrids determined by the previous steps and determine the rectangular common subgrid of interest;
- if the common subgrid of the preceding step is not empty, use the Search algorithm for retrieving the Object BRGs contained in such subgrid.

Other examples of queries, whose execution performance can be improved by Snapshot, are the following: "find the mountain that lies within 700kms from Paris and is the closest mountain to Rome", "find all roads in the region R that are intersected by the A7 highway and lie within 100kms from the point P", and so forth.

6. Conclusions and Future Work

In this paper we have presented an access data structure, tailored to supporting distance queries. Such type of queries have not been specifically addressed so far in the literature. We have also presented algorithms for evaluating two types of distance predicates. The first is the Far predicate, that determines all entities within a given distance from a give point specified in the query. The second is the Min predicate, that determines the entity which is closer to a given point specified in the query. Finally, we have discussed how the Snapshot data structure can be used to optimize other types of spatial predicates. An important aspect is the optimization of queries containing conjunctions of several predicates. We have briefly discussed how several predicates could be simultaneously evaluated by using the Snapshot data structure.

We are currently extending our work along several directions. First, a mathematical cost model is being developed to assess the performance of Snapshot and to compare it with other spatial data structures. The complexity of our algorithm is also being evaluated. Second, we are extending the previous Far and Min algorithms in order to consider as reference for the distance computation a general object instead of a simple point. Third, we are addressing issues concerning the simultaneous evaluation of multiple predicates, along the lines discussed in the previous section. Finally, we are also investigating implementation issues.

References

[1] N. Beckmann, H. Kriegel, R. Schneider and B. Seeger , "The R*-tree: an Efficient and Robust Access Method for Point and Rectangles", *Proc. ACM SIGMOD Conf.*, Atlantic City, NJ, 1990, pp. 322-331.

[2] A. Belussi, E. Bertino, A. Biavasco, S. Rizzo, "An Approach to Process Metric Queries in Geographical Database Systems", Technical Report, University of Milan, 1994.

[3] A. Belussi, E. Bertino, "A Uniform Representation of Geographical Queries", in preparation, 1994.
[4] S.K. Chang "Principles of Pictorial Information Systems Design", Englewood Cliffs, NJ, Prentice-Hall, 1990.
[5] S.K. Chang and A. Hsu "Image Information Systems: Where Do We Go From Here?", in *IEEE Transaction on Knowledge and Data Engineering*, Vol. 4, No. 5, Oct. 1992.
[6] C. C. Chang and S. Y. Lee "Retrieval of Similar Picture on Pictorial Databases", in *Pattern Recognition*, Vol. 24, No. 7, pp. 675-680, 1991.
[7] L. DeFloriani, P. Marzano, E. Puppo, "Spatial Queries and Data Models", in *Spatial Information Theory - A Theoretical Basis for GIS* (A.U. Frank, I. Congeni eds.) LNCS, Vol. 716, Springer Verlag, Sept. 1993.
[8] M. J. Egenhofer, "Reasoning about Binary Topological Relations" *Proc. 2nd Symposium on Spatial Databases*, 1991, p.143-160.
[9] C. Faloutsos and Y. Rong, "DOT: A Spatial Access Method Using Fractals", *Proc. 7th Data Engineering Conf.*, Kobe, Japan, 1991, pp. 152-159.
[10] M. J. Folk, B. Zoellick, *File Structures.* Second Edition, 1992, Addison-Wesley.
[11] A. U. Frank, "Properties of Geographic Data: Requirements for Spatial Access Methods", *Proc. Second Symposium Large Spatial Databases*, Zurich 1991, pp. 225-234.
[12] M. Freeston, "The BANG File: a New Kind of Grid File", *Proc. ACM SIGMOD Conf.*, 1987, pp. 260-269.
[13] O. Guenther, "Efficient Structures for Geometric Data Management", *Lecture Notes in Computer Science* No. 337, Springer Verlag, Berlin, 1988.
[14] A. Gupta, T. Weymouth and R. Jain, "Semantic queries with pictures: The VIMSYS model", in *Proc. VLDB '91*, Spain, 1991, pp. 69-79.
[15] A. Guttman, "R-tree: a Dynamic Index Structure for Spatial Searching", *Proc. ACM SIGMOD Conf.*, 1984, pp. 47-57.
[16] A. Henrich H.P. Siz and P. Widmayer, "The LSD Tree: Spatial Access to Multidimensional Point and Non Point Objects", *Proc. 15th VLDB Conf.*, 1989, pp. 45-53.
[17] H.V. Jagadish, "Spatial Search with Polyhedra", *Proc. Sixth IEEE International Conference on Data Engineering*, Feb. 1990.
[18] H. P. Kriegel, P. Heep, S. Heep, M. Schiwietz, R. Schneider, "An Access Method Based Query Processor for Spatial Database Systems", *Proc. Int. Workshop on DBMS's for geographical applications*, Capri, May 16-17, 1991.
[19] H. P. Kriegel, T. Brinkhoff and R. Schneider, "Efficient Spatial Query Processing in Geographic Database Systems", *Bulletin of the Technical Committee on Data Engineering*, Sept. 1993, Vol. 16 No. 3, p. 10-15.
[20] Hongjun Lu and Beng-Chin Ooi, "Spatial Indexing: Past and Future", *Bulletin of the Technical Committee on Data Engineering*, Sept., 1993 Vol.16, No. 3, pp.16-21.
[21] J. Nievergelt, H. Hinterberger, "The Grid File: An Adaptable, Symmetric Multikey File Structure", *ACM Transaction on Database Systems*, Vol. 9, No. 1, March 1984, pp. 38-71.
[22] J. Nievergelt, "7 +- 2 Criteria for Assessing and Comparing Spatial Data Structures", *Proc. First Symposium Large Spatial Databases*, Santa Barbara, California 1989, pp. 5-25.
[23] Y. Ohsawa and M. Sakauchi, "A New Tree Type Data Structure with Homogeneous Nodes Suitable for a Very Large Spatial Database", *Proc. 6th Data Engineering Conf.*, Los Angeles, California, 1990, pp. 296-303.

[24] P.J.M. Oosterom, "Reactive Data Structures for Geographic Information System", PhD thesis, Dept. of Computer Science at Leiden Univ., The Netherlands 1990.

[25] J. A. Orenstein, "Redundancy in Spatial Databases" in *Proc. 1989 ACM SIGMOD International Conference on Management of Data*, 294-305, Portland, Ohio, June 1989.

[26] J.A. Orenstein and T.H. Merrett, "A Class of Data Structures for Associative Searching", *Proc. 3rd ACM SIGACT- SIGMOD Symp. on Principles of Database Systems* 1984, pp. 181-190.

[27] H. Samet, "The Quad_tree and Related Data Structures", *ACM Computing Surveys*, Vol. 16, No. 2, 1984.

[28] H. Samet, *The Design and Analysis of Spatial Data Structures.* Addison-Wesley, 1990.

[29] H. Samet and W. Aref, "An Approach to Information Management in Geographical Applications", *Proc. 4th Spatial Data Handling* 1990, pp. 589-598.

[30] B. Seeger and H.P. Kriegel, "Techniques for Design and Implementation of Efficient Spatial Access Methods", *Proc. 14th VLDB Conf.*, Los Angeles, California 1988, pp. 360-371.

[31] B. Seeger and H. Kriegel, "The Buddy-tree: an Efficient and Robust Access Methods for Spatial Database Systems", *Proc. 16th VLDB Conf.*, Brisbane, Australia, 1990, pp. 590-601.

[32] T. Sellis, N. Roussopoulos and C. Faloutsos, "The R+-tree: a Dynamic Index for Multi-dimensional Objects", *Proc. 13th VLDB Conf.*, Brighton, U.K., 1987, pp. 507-518.

Stream-based Versus Structured Video Objects: Issues, Solutions, and Challenges

Shahram Ghandeharizadeh

Department of Computer Science, University of Southern California, Los Angeles, California 90089

Summary. An emerging area of database system research is to investigate techniques that ensure a continuous display of video objects. As compared to the traditional data types, e.g., text, a video object must be retrieved at a prespecified rate. If it is retrieved at a lower rate then its display may suffer from frequent disruptions and delays, termed *hiccups.* This paper describes two alternative approaches to representing video objects (stream-based and structured) and the issues involved in supporting their hiccup-free display. For each approach, we describe the existing solutions and the future research directions from a database systems perspective.

1. Introduction

Video in a variety of formats has been available since late 1800's: In the 1870's Eadweard Muybridge created a series of motion photographs to display a horse in motion. Thomas Edison patented a motion picture camera in 1887. In essence, video has enjoyed more than a century of research and development to evolve to its present format. During the 1980s, digital video started to become of interest to computer scientists. Repositories containing digital video clips started to emerge. The "National Information Infrastructure" initiative has added to this excitement by envisioning massive archives that contain digital video in addition to other types of information, e.g., textual, record-based data. Database management systems (DBMSs) supporting this data type are expected to play a major role in many applications including library information systems, entertainment industry, educational applications, etc.

In this study, we focus on video objects and its physical requirements from the perspectives of the storage manager of a database management system. A DBMS may employ two alternative approaches to represent a video clip:

1. **Stream-based**: A video clip consists of a sequence of pictures (commonly termed two dimensional frames) that are displayed at a pre-specified rate, e.g., 30 frames a second for TV shows, 24 frames a second for most movies shown in a theater due to the dim lighting. If an object is displayed at a rate lower than its prespecified bandwidth, its display will suffer from frequent disruptions and delays, termed *hiccups.*
2. **Structured**: A video clip consists of a sequence of scenes. Each scene consists of a collections of background objects, actors (e.g., 3 dimensional

representation of Mickey Mouse, dinosaurs, lions), light sources that define shading, and the audience's view point. Spatial constructs are used to place object that constitute a scene in a rendering space while temporal constructs describe how the objects and their relationship evolve as a function of time. The rendering of a structured presentation is hiccup-free when it satisfies the temporal constraints imposed on the display of each object. "Reboot" [1] is an animated Saturday morning children's show created using this approach.

Each approach has its own advantages and disadvantages. The stream-based approach benefits from more than a century of research and development on analog devices that generate high resolution frames. This is because the output of these devices is digitized to generate a stream-based video clip. However, it suffers from the following limitations. First, while humans are capable of reasoning about the contents of a stream-based presentation, it is difficult to design techniques to process the contents of a movie for query processing (e.g., select all scenes of a movie where one car chases another). Second, it is difficult to extract the contents of one stream-based presentation to be re-used in another. To illustrate, with animation, it is difficult to extract Mickey Mouse from one animated sequence to be incorporated in another; typically Mickey Mouse is re-drawn from scratch for the new animation. However, this is not to imply that this task is impossible. For example, the movie "Forrest Gump" incorporates Tom Hanks (the main actor) with different presidents (J. F. Kennedy, L. B. Johnson, and R. Nixon). This was a tedious, time consuming task that required the efforts of: 1) a creative director choosing from amongst the old news clips available on different presidents and selecting those that fit the movie's plot, 2) a skilled actor imagining the chosen scene and acting against a blue background[1], and 3) knowledgeable engineers who incorporated this footage with the old news clips on the different presidents.

A structured video clip eliminates the disadvantages of the stream-based approach because it provides adequate information to support query processing techniques, and re-usability of information. It enables the system to retrieve and manipulate the individual objects that constitute a scene. While structured video is directly usable in both animation and video games that employ animated characters, their use in video clips is limited. This is because there are no devices equivalent to a camcorder that can analyze a scene to compute either its individual objects or the temporal and spatial relationships that exist among these objects. Perhaps, another century of research and development is required before such devices become commercially available. However, it is important to note that once a repository of objects is constructed, the potential to re-use information to construct different scenarios and stories is almost limitless.

[1] A blue background is used because it can easily be eliminated once overlaid with the old news clip.

In this paper, we describe each of these two approaches in detail (Sections 2. and 3.). For each approach, we describe some of the existing solutions, and challenges that remain to be investigated. From a systems perspective, the structured approach has received little attention and requires further investigation. Brief conclusions are offered in Section 4..

2. Stream-based Presentation

Stream-based video clips exhibit two characteristics:

1. they require a continuous retrieval rate for a hiccup-free display: Stream-based objects should be retrieved at a pre-specified bandwidth. This bandwidth is defined by the object's media type. For example, the bandwidth required by NTSC[2] for "network-quality" video is approximately 45 megabits per second (Mbps) [14]. Recommendation 601 of the International Radio Consultative Committee (CCIR) calls for a 216 Mbps bandwidth for video objects [8]. A video object based on HDTV requires a bandwidth of approximately 800 Mbps.
2. they are large in size: A 30 minute uncompressed object based on NTSC is 10 gigabytes in size. With a compression technique that reduces the bandwidth requirement of this object to 1.5 Mbps, this object is 337 megabytes in size. A repository (e.g., corresponding to an encyclopedia) that contains hundreds of such clips is potentially terabytes in size.

One may employ a lossy compression techniques (e.g., MPEG [9]) in order to reduce both the size and the bandwidth requirement of an object. These techniques encode data into a form that consumes a relatively small amount of space; however, when the data is decoded, it yields a representation similar to the original (some loss of data).

Even with a lossy compression technique, the size of a stream-based video repository is typically very large. For example, the USC instructional TV program tapes approximately 1700 hours of video per semester. With MPEG-1 compression technique that reduces the bandwidth of each video object to 1.5 Mbps (unacceptably low resolution), this center produces approximately 1.1 terabytes of data per semester. The large size of these databases motivates the use of hierarchical storage structures primarily by dollars and sense: Storing terabytes of data using DRAM would be very expensive. Moreover, it would be wasteful because only a small fraction of the data is referenced at any given instant in time (i.e., some tapes corresponding to particular classes are more frequently accessed than the others, there exists locality of reference). A similar argument applies to other devices, i.e., magnetic disks. The most practical choice would be to employ a combination of fast and slow

[2] The US standard established by the National Television System Committee.

devices, where the system controls the placement of the data in order to hide the high latency of slow devices using fast devices.

Assume a hierarchical storage structure consisting of random access memory (DRAM), magnetic disk drives, and a tape library [5]. As the different strata of the hierarchy are traversed starting with memory, both the density of the medium (the amount of data it can store) and its latency increases, while its cost per megabyte of storage decreases. At the time of this writing, these costs vary from $40/megabyte of DRAM to $0.6/megabyte of disk storage to less than $0.05/megabyte of tape storage. An application referencing an object that is disk resident observes both the average latency time and the delivery rate of a magnetic disk drive (which is superior to that of the tape library). An application would observe the best performance when its working set becomes resident at the highest level of the hierarchy: memory. However, in our assumed environment, the magnetic disk drives are the more likely staging area for this working set due to the large size of objects. As described below, the memory is used to stage a small fraction of an object for immediate processing and display. We define the working set [6] of an application as a collection of objects that are repeatedly referenced. For example, in existing video stores, a few titles are expected to be accessed frequently and a store maintains several (sometimes many) copies of these titles to satisfy the expected demand. These movies constitute the working set of a database system whose application provides a video–on–demand service.

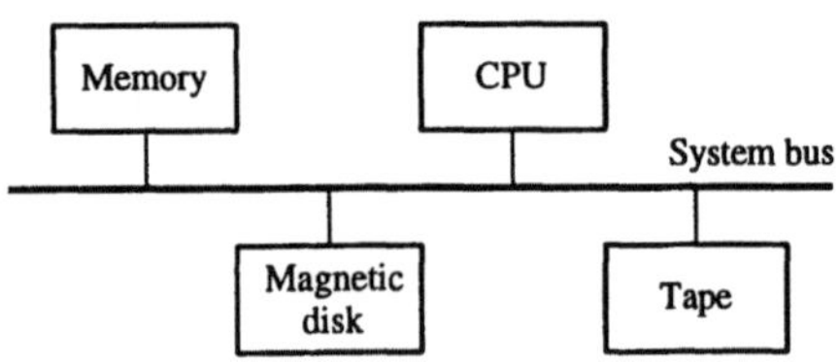

Fig. 2.1. Architecture.

To simplify the discussion, we assume the architecture of Figure 2.1 for the rest of this section. Using this platform, we describe: 1) a technique to support a hiccup-free display of stream-based objects, and 2) a pipelining mechanism to minimize the latency time of the system.

2.1 Continuous Display

In this paper, we make the following simplifying assumptions;

1. The disk drive has a fixed transfer rate (R_D) and provides a large storage capacity (more than one gigabyte). An example disk drive from the commercial arena is Seagate Barracuda 2-2HP that provides a 2 Gigabyte storage capacity and a minimum transfer rate of 68.6 Megabits per second (Mbps) [20].

2. A single media type with a fixed display bandwidth (R_C); $R_D > R_C$.
3. A multi-user environment requiring simultaneous display of objects to different users. Each display should be hiccup-free.

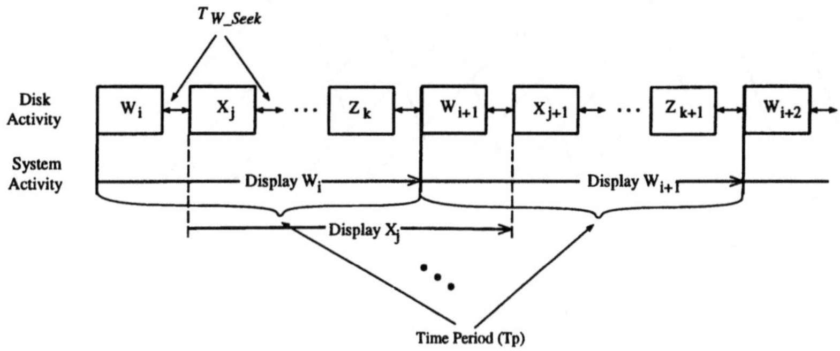

Fig. 2.2. Time period

To support continuous display of an object X, it is partitioned into n equi-sized blocks: X_0, X_1, ..., X_{n-1}, where n is a function of the block size ($\mathcal{B}$) and the size of X. A *time period* (T_p) is defined as the time required to display a block:

$$T_p = \frac{\mathcal{B}}{R_C} \tag{2.1}$$

When an object X is referenced, the system stages X_0 in memory and initiates its display. Prior to completion of a time period, it initiates the retrieval of X_1 into memory in order to ensure a continuous display. This process is repeated until all blocks of an object have been displayed.

To support simultaneous display of several objects, a time period is partitioned into fixed-size slots, with each slot corresponding to the retrieval time of a block from the disk drive. The number of slots in a time period defines the number of simultaneous displays that can be supported by the system. For example, a block size of 750 kilobytes corresponding to a MPEG-1 compressed movie ($R_C = 1.5$ Mbps) has a 4 second display time ($T_p = 4$). Assuming a magnetic disk with a transfer rate of 24 Mbps ($R_D = 24$ Mbps) and maximum seek time of 35 milliseconds, 14 such blocks can be retrieved in 4 seconds. Hence, a single disk supports 14 simultaneous displays. Figure 2.2 demonstrates the concept of a time period and a time slot. Each box represents a time slot. Assuming that each block is stored contiguously on the surface of the disk, the disk incurs a seek every time it switches from one block of an object to another. We denote this as T_{W_Seek} and assume that it includes the maximum rotational latency time of the disk drive. We will not discuss rotational latency further because it is a constant added to every seek time.

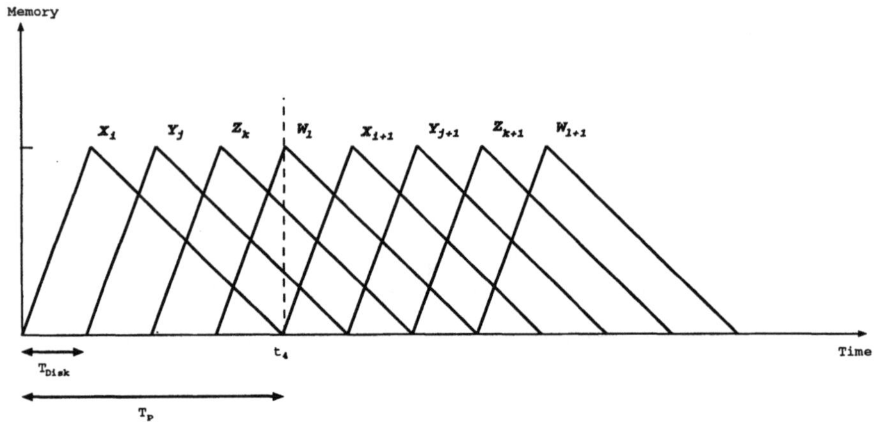

Fig. 2.3. Memory requirement for four streams

To display $\mathcal{N}$ simultaneous blocks per time period, the system should provide sufficient memory for staging the blocks. As described in [17], the system requires $\frac{\mathcal{N}\mathcal{B}}{2}$ memory to support $\mathcal{N}$ simultaneous displays (with identical R_C). To observe this, Figure 2.3 shows the memory requirements of each display as a function of time for a system that supports four simultaneous displays. A time period is partitioned into 4 slots. The duration of each slot is denoted T_{Disk}. During each T_{Disk} for a given object (e.g., X), the disk is producing data while the display is consuming it. Thus, the amount of data staged in memory during this period is lower than $\mathcal{B}$ (it is $T_{Disk} \times R_D - T_{Disk} \times R_C$). Consider the memory requirement of each display for one instant in time, say t_4: X requires no memory, Y requires $\frac{\mathcal{B}}{3}$ memory, Z requires $\frac{2\times\mathcal{B}}{3}$ memory, and W requires at most $\mathcal{B}$ memory. Hence the total memory requirement for these four displays is $2\mathcal{B}$ (i.e., $\frac{\mathcal{N}\mathcal{B}}{2}$); we refer the interested reader to [17] for the complete proof. Hence, if Mem denotes the amount of configured memory for a system, then the following constraint must be satisfied:

$$\frac{\mathcal{N} \times \mathcal{B}}{2} \leq Mem \tag{2.2}$$

To compute the size of a block, from Figure 2.2, it is trivial that:

$$\mathcal{B} = (\frac{T_p}{\mathcal{N}} - T_{W\_Seek}) \times R_D \tag{2.3}$$

By substituting $\mathcal{B}$ from Equation 2.3 into Equation 2.1 we obtain:

$$T_p = \mathcal{N} \times T_{W\_Seek} \times \frac{R_D}{R_D - (\mathcal{N} \times R_C)} \tag{2.4}$$

The duration of a time period (T_p) defines the maximum latency incurred when the number of active displays is fewer than $\mathcal{N}$. To illustrate the maximum latency, consider the following example. Assume a system that supports three simultaneous displays ($\mathcal{N} = 3$). Two displays are active (Y and Z) and a new request referencing object X arrives, see Figure 2.4. This request arrives a little too late to consume the idle slot[3]. Thus, the display of X is delayed by one time period before it can be activated. Note that this maximum latency is applicable when the number of active displays is less than the total number of displays supported by the system ($\mathcal{N}$). Otherwise, the maximum latency should be computed based on appropriate queuing models.

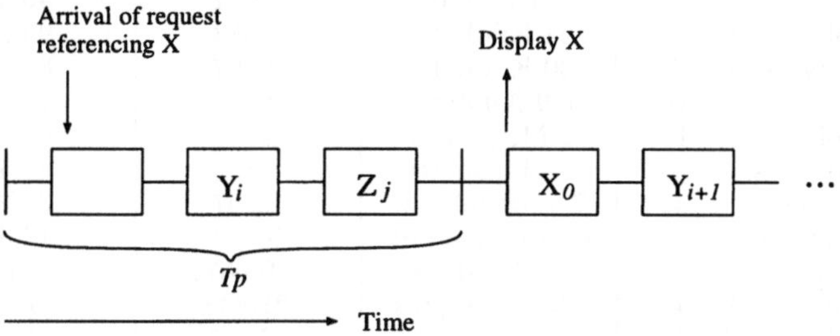

Fig. 2.4. Maximum latency for a request referencing object X

Observe from Figure 2.2 that the disk incurs a T_{W_Seek} between the retrieval of each block. The disk performs wasteful work when it seeks (and useful work when it transfers data). T_{W_Seek} reduces the bandwidth of the disk drive. The effective bandwidth of the disk drive is a function of $\mathcal{B}$ and T_{W_Seek}; it is defined as:

$$B_{Disk} = R_D \times \frac{\mathcal{B}}{\mathcal{B} + (T_{W\_Seek} \times R_D)} \tag{2.5}$$

The percentage of wasted disk bandwidth is quantified as:

$$\frac{R_D - B_{Disk}}{R_D} \times 100 \tag{2.6}$$

Equations 2.2 to 2.6 establish the relationship between: 1) maximum throughput and latency time of a system, and 2) the available memory and disk bandwidth of a system. To illustrate, assume a system with a fixed amount of memory and a single disk drive. Given a desired throughput, one may compute the worst latency time using Equation 2.4. The theoretical upper bound on the throughput is determined by the transfer rate of the disk drive (R_D) and is defined as $\lfloor \frac{R_D}{R_C} \rfloor$ (the lower bound on this value is 0). Using Equation 2.3, the size of a block can be determined. The system can be configured with such a block size to support the desired throughput only if it is configured with sufficient amount of memory, i.e., the constraint imposed

[3] Its display cannot start because it would interfere with the display of object Y, see Figure 2.4.

by Equation 2.2 is satisfied. Otherwise, the desired throughput should be reduced. This minimizes the amount of required memory, however, it results in a smaller block size that wastes a higher percentage of the disk bandwidth (Equations 2.5 and 2.6).

Block Size	No Users	Memory Required	Max Latency Seconds (Tp)	Wasted Disk Bandwidth (%)
8 Kilobytes	1	8 Kilobytes	0.042	96.526
16 Kilobytes	3	24 Kilobytes	0.083	93.285
32 Kilobytes	5	80 Kilobytes	0.167	87.416
64 Kilobytes	10	320 Kilobytes	0.333	77.645
128 Kilobytes	16	1 Megabytes	0.667	63.459
256 Kilobytes	24	3 Megabytes	1.333	46.476
512 Kilobytes	31	7.5 Megabytes	2.667	30.273
1 Megabytes	37	18.5 Megabytes	5.333	17.836
2 Megabytes	41	41 Megabytes	10.667	9.791
4 Megabytes	43	86 Megabytes	21.333	5.148
8 Megabytes	44	176 Megabytes	42.667	2.642

Table 2.1. An example

To illustrate these concepts, consider a database that consists of MPEG-1 objects with a bandwidth requirement of 1.5 megabits per second. Assume a disk drive with a maximum seek time of 17 milliseconds, rotational latency of 8.33 milliseconds, and a transfer rate of 68.6 megabits per second. (T_{W_Seek} = 25.33 milliseconds.) Table 2.1 presents the number of users that can be supported as a function of the blocksize. A small block size (8 kilobytes) has a small transfer rate and wastes a significant fraction of disk bandwidth. As one increases the block size, the percentage of wasted disk bandwidth drops. This enables the disk drive to support a higher number of users. However, note that this increases the maximum latency time that a user may observe and requires a larger amount of memory from the system.

Seek is a wasteful operation that minimizes the number of simultaneous displays supported by the system. (The disk performs useful work when it transfers data.) Moreover, the seek time is a function of the distance traveled by the disk arm [4], [13], [19]. REBECA [11] is a mechanism that minimizes the time attributed to a seek operation by minimizing the distance that the disk head travels when multiplexed among several requests. This is achieved as follows. First, REBECA partitions the disk space into $\mathcal{R}$ regions. Next, successive blocks of an object X are assigned to the regions in a zigzag manner as shown in Figure 2.5. The zigzag assignments of blocks to regions follows the efficient movement of disk head as in the elevator algorithm [21]. To retrieve the blocks of an object, the disk head moves *inward* until it reaches the center of the disk and then it moves *outward*. This procedure repeats itself once the head reaches the out-most track on the disk. This minimizes

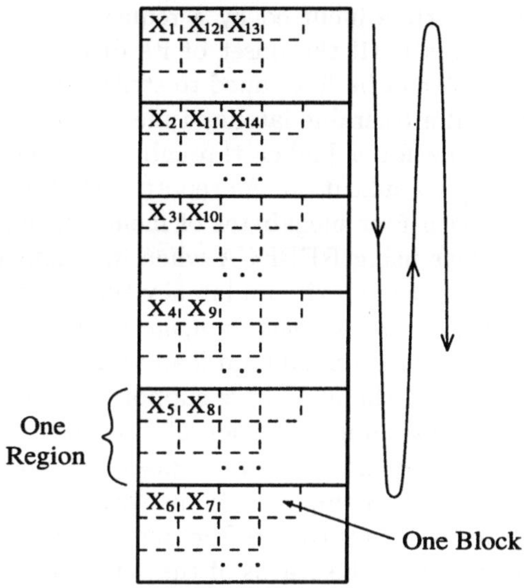

Fig. 2.5. REBECA

the movement of the disk head required to simultaneously retrieve $\mathcal{N}$ objects. To achieve this minimized movement, the display of the objects should follow the following rules:

1. The disk head moves in one direction (either *inward* or *outward*) at a time.
2. During a time period, the disk services requests corresponding to a single region (termed *active region*, R_{active}). In the subsequent time period, the disk services requests corresponding to either $R_{active} + 1$ (*inward* direction) or $R_{active} - 1$ (*outward* direction). The only exception is when R_{active} is either the first or the last region. In these two cases, R_{active} is either incremented or decremented after two time periods because the consecutive blocks of an object reside in the same region. For example, in Figure 2.5, X_6 and X_7 are both allocated to the last region and R_{active} changes its value after two time periods. This scheduling paradigm does not waste disk space (an alternative assignment/schedule that enables R_{active} to change its value after every time period would waste 50% of the space managed by the first and the last region).
3. Upon the arrival of a request referencing object X, it is assigned to the region containing X_1 (say R_X). The display of X does not start until the active region reaches R_X ($R_{active} = R_X$) **and** its direction corresponds to that required by X. For example, X requires an *inward* direction if X_2 is assigned to $R_X + 1$ and *outward* X_2 is assigned to $R_X - 1$.

REBECA results in a higher utilization of the disk bandwidth, providing for a higher number of simultaneous displays (i.e., throughput). However, it increases the latency time incurred by a request (i.e., time elapsed from when the request arrives until the onset of its display). The configuration parameters of REBECA can be fine tuned to strike a compromise between a desired throughput and a tolerable latency time.

Trading latency time for a higher throughput is dependent on the requirements of the target application. As reported in [11], the throughput of a single disk server (with four megabytes of memory) may vary from 23 to 30 simultaneous displays using REBECA when its number of regions varies from 1 to 21. This causes the maximum latency time to increase from a fraction of a second to 30 seconds. A *video-on-demand* server may expect to have 30 simultaneous displays as its maximum load with each display lasting two hours. Without REBECA, the disk drive supports a maximum of 23 simultaneous displays, each observing a fraction of a second latency. During peak system loads (30 active requests), several requests may wait in a queue until one of the active requests completes its display. These requests observe a latency time significantly longer than a fraction of second (potentially in the range of hours depending on the status of the active displays and the queue of pending requests). In this scenario, it might be reasonable to force each request to observe the potential worst case latency of 30 seconds in order to support 30 simultaneous displays.

Alternatively, with an application that provides a *news_on_demand* service with a typical news clip lasting approximately four minutes, a 30 second latency time might not be a reasonable tradeoff for a higher number of simultaneous displays. In this case, the system designer might decide to introduce additional resources (e.g., memory) into the environment to enable the system to support a higher number of simultaneous displays with each request incurring a fraction of a second latency time. [11] describes a configuration planner to compute a value for the configuration parameters of a system in order to satisfy the performance objectives of an application. Hence, a service provider can configure its server based on both its expected number of active customers as well as their waiting tolerance.

2.2 Pipelining to Minimize Latency Time

With a hierarchical storage organization, when a request references an object that is not disk resident, the system may service the request using the bandwidth of the tertiary storage device as long as: 1) the tertiary storage device is free, and 2) the bandwidth required to support a hiccup-free display of the referenced object ($\mathcal{R}_C$) is lower than the bandwidth of the tertiary storage device ($\mathcal{R}_T$). Indeed, one may envision multiplexing a tertiary storage device that provides a high transfer rate (e.g., Ampex DST [15] with a 116 Mbps sustained transfer rate) among several active devices using the paradigm of Section 2.1. However, this might be wasteful due to the significant seek time of these devices (in the order of seconds).

If $\mathcal{R}_C$ is higher than $\mathcal{R}_T$ (i.e., the tertiary cannot support a hiccup-free display of the referenced object) then the object must first be staged on the disk drive prior to its display. One approach might materialize the object on the disk drives in its entirety before initiating its display. In this case, the latency time of the system is determined by the bandwidth of the tertiary storage device and the size of the referenced object. Stream-based video objects require a sequential retrieval to support their display, hence, a better alternative is to use a pipelining mechanism that overlaps the display of an object with its materialization, in order to minimize the latency time.

With pipelining, a portion of the time required to materialize X can be overlapped with its display. This is achieved by grouping the subobjects of X into s logical slices ($S_{X,1}$, $S_{X,2}$, $S_{X,3}$, ..., $S_{X,s}$), such that the display time of $S_{X,1}$, $T_{Display}(S_{X,1})$, overlaps the time required to materialize $S_{X,2}$; $T_{Display}(S_{X,2})$ overlaps $T_{Materialize}(S_{X,3})$, etc. Thus:

$$T_{Display}(S_{X,i}) \geq T_{Materialize}(S_{X,i+1}) \; for \; 1 \leq i < s \qquad (2.7)$$

Upon the retrieval of a tertiary resident object X, the pipelining mechanism is as follows:

1: Materialize the subobject(s) that constitute $S_{X,1}$ on the disk drive.
2: For $i = 2$ to s do
   a. Initiate the materialization of $S_{X,i}$ from tertiary onto the disk.
   b. Initiate the display of $S_{X,i-1}$.
3: Display the last slice ($S_{X,s}$).

The duration of Step 1 determines the latency time of the system. Its duration is equivalent to $T_{Materialize}(X) - T_{Display}(X) +$ (one Time Period). Step 3 displays the last slice materialized on the disk drive. In order to minimize the latency time[4], $S_{X,s}$ should consist of a single subobject. To illustrate this, consider Figure 2.6. If the last slice consists of more than one subobject then the duration of the overlap is minimized, elongating duration of Step 1.

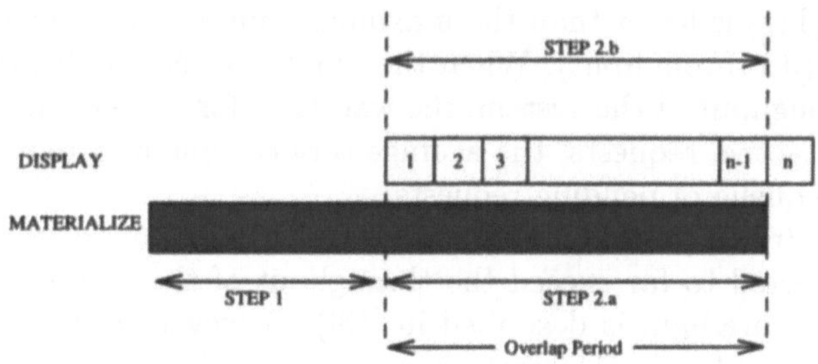

Fig. 2.6. The pipelining mechanism

[4] Maximize the length of the pipeline.

2.3 High Bandwidth Objects and Scalable Servers

There are applications that cannot tolerate the use of a lossy compression technique (e.g., video signals collected from space by NASA [7]). Clearly, a technique that can support the display of an object for both application types is desirable. Assuming a multi-disk architecture, staggered striping [2] is one such a technique. It is flexible enough to support those objects whose bandwidth requires either the aggregate bandwidth of multiple disks or fraction of the bandwidth of a single disk. Using the declustering technique of [12], it employs the aggregate bandwidth of multiple disk drives to support a hiccup-free display of those objects whose bandwidth exceeds the bandwidth of a single disk drive. Hence, it provides effective support for a database that consists of a mix of media types, each with a different bandwidth requirement. Moreover, its design enables the system to scale to thousands of disk drives because its overhead does not increase prohibitively as a function of additional resources.

In [10], the authors describe extensions of the pipelining mechanism to a scalable server that employs the bandwidth of multiple disk drives. In [3], the authors describe alternative techniques to support a hiccup-free display in the presence of disk failures.

2.4 Challenges

A server may process requests using either a *demand driven* or a *data driven* paradigm. With the demand driven paradigm, the system waits for the arrival of a request to reference an object prior to retrieving it. With the data driven paradigm, the system retrieves and displays data items periodically (similar to how a broadcasting company such as HBO transmits movies at a certain time). The clients referencing an object wait for the onset of a display, at which point, the system transmits the referenced stream to all waiting clients. Each paradigm has its own tradeoffs. With the demand driven paradigm, each request observes a relatively low latency time as long as the number of active displays is lower than the maximum number of displays supported by a system (its throughput). When the number of active displays is larger than the throughput of the system, the wait time for a queue depends on the status of the active requests, the average service time of a request, and the length of the queue of pending requests.

The data driven paradigm is appropriate when the number of active requests is expected to far exceed the throughput of the system (a technique based on this paradigm is described in [18]). However, with this paradigm, the system must decide: 1) what objects it should broadcast? 2) how frequently should each object be broadcast? 3) when is an object broadcast? and 4) what is the interval of time between two broadcasts of a single object? The answer to these questions are based on expectations. In the worst case, a stream might be broadcast with no client expressing interest in its display.

A limitation of this paradigm is starvation: requests referencing unpopular video clips might wait for a long time before the referenced clip is broadcast. Moreover, with this paradigm, multiple clients that share a stream of data may fall out of synchronization with each other every time a user invokes a pause or fast-forward functionality. The system might either disallow such functionalities (as is done with the current broadcasting companies) or implement sophisticated techniques based on resource reservation to accommodate such operations.

A challenging task is to design a system that can switch between these two alternative paradigms (or support both simultaneously) depending on the number of requests requiring service, the throughput of the system, the pattern of reference to the objects, and the quality of service desired by the clients. The precise definition of quality of service is application dependent. For video servers, it may refer to either the functionality provided to a client (e.g., fast-forward, pause) or the resolution of the display[5].

3. Structured Presentation

As an alternative to a stream-based presentation, a video object can be represented as a collection of objects, spatial and temporal constructs, and rendering features (termed structured presentation). The spatial and temporal constructs define where in the rendering space and when in the temporal space the component objects are displayed. The rendering features define how the objects are displayed.

A *Rendering Space* is a coordinate system defined by n orthogonal vectors, where n is the number of dimensions (i.e., $n = 3$ for 3D, $n = 2$ for 2D). A spatial construct specifies the placement of a component in the rendering space. Analogously, different components are rendered within a time interval, termed *Temporal Space*. For example, if a movie has 30 scenes of 3 minutes each then the temporal space of the movie is $[0, 90]$. Moreover there is a temporal construct specifying the subinterval within the temporal space that should render each scene. For example, a temporal construct for the first scene will specify the subinterval $[0, 3]$.

To illustrate the use of both constructs simultaneously, consider the motion of a rolling ball. The motion is captured by a sequence of snapshots, represented by a sequence of triplets: (the object (i.e., the ball), its positioning, subinterval). Each triplet specifies a spatial and a temporal constraint. In this section, we partition the information associated with a structured video into three layers:

[5] The resolution of a display dictates the bandwidth required to support that display. A system may maintain multiple copies of a video object based on different resolutions and service the different clients using a different copy based on how much they pay.

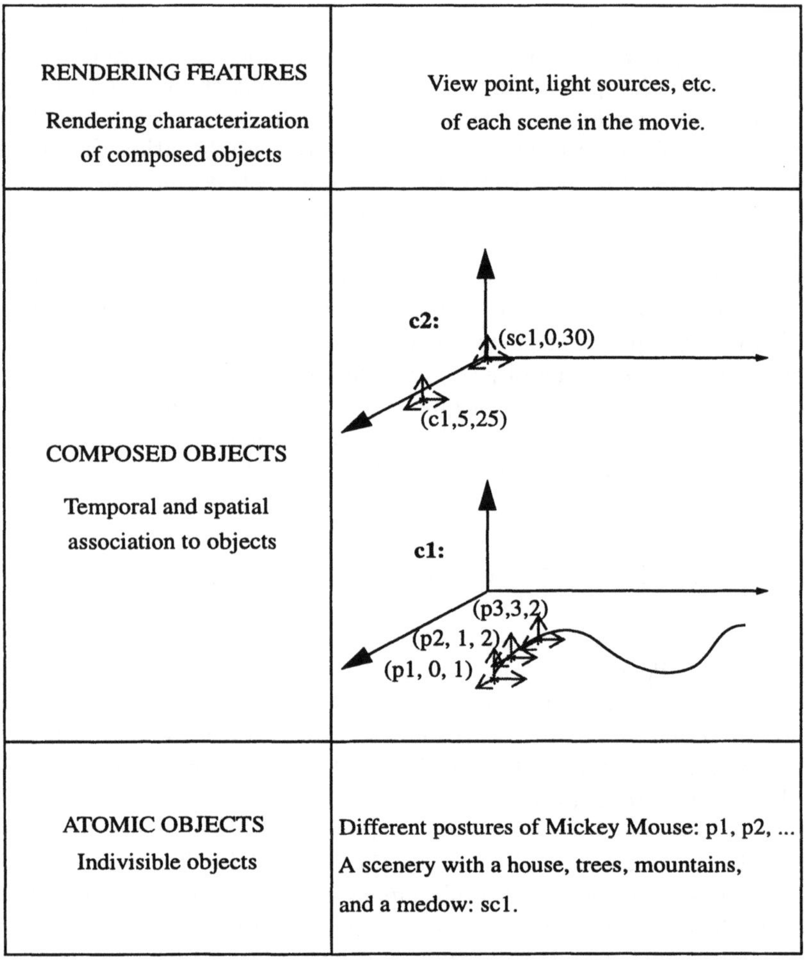

(a) (b)

Fig. 3.1. Three levels of abstraction

1. *Atomic* objects that define indivisible entities (e.g., the 3D representation of a ball).
2. *Composed objects* that consist of objects constrained using temporal and spatial constructs, e.g., a triplet: (the ball, a position, a subinterval).
3. The rendering features (e.g., viewpoint, light sources, etc.).

Figure 3.1 shows the different levels of abstraction of a media object and an example of the representation of a scene. Assume that the objective is to describe a character (e.g., Mickey Mouse) walking along a path in the scene. The atomic object layer contains the 3D representations of different postures of Mickey Mouse, denoted by p1, p2, etc. For example, his posture when he starts to walk, his posture one second later, etc. These postures might have been originals composed by an artist or generated using interpolation. We also include the 3D representation of the background (denoted by sc1) in the atomic object layer.

To represent the walking motion, the author specifies spatial and temporal constructs among the different postures of Mickey Mouse. The result is a composed object. The curve labeled **c1** specifies the path followed by Mickey Mouse (i.e., the different positions reached). Each of the coordinate systems describe the direction of a posture of the character. For each posture, a temporal construct specifies the time when the object appears in the temporal space. For example, the point labeled by (p1, 0, 1) indicates that posture p1 appears at time 0 and lasts for 1 second.

To associate the motion of Mickey Mouse to the background, we have the spatial and temporal constructs in the composed objects layer represented by **c2**. The spatial constructs define where in the rendering space the motion and the background are placed. The temporal constructs define the timing of the appearances of the background and the motion. In this example, the background sc1 appears at the beginning of the scene while Mickey Mouse starts to walk (c1) at the 5th second.

Finally, the rendering features are assigned by specifying the view point, the light sources, etc., for the time interval at which the scene is rendered. In the following two sections, we describe each of the atomic and composed objects layers in more detail.

3.1 Atomic Object Layer

This layer contains objects that are considered indivisible (i.e., they are rendered in their entirety). The exact representation of an atomic object is application dependent. In animation, as described in [22], the alternative representations include:

1. *wire-frame representation*: An object is represented by a set of segment lines.
2. *surface representation*: An object is represented by a set of primitive surfaces, typically: triangles, polygons, equations of algebraic surfaces or patches.
3. *solid representation*: An object is a set of primitive volumes.

From a conceptual perspective, these physical representations are considered as an unstructured unit, termed a BLOB. These objects can also be described as either:

1. A procedure that consumes a number of parameters to compute a BLOB that represents an object. For example, a geometric object can be represented by its dimensions (i.e., the radius, the length of a side of a square,

etc.), a value for these dimensions, and a procedure that consumes these values to compute a bitmap representation of the object. This type of representation is termed *Parametric*.

2. An interpolation of two other atomic objects. For example in animation, the motion of a character can be represented as postures at selected times and the postures in between can be obtained by interpolation. In animation, this representation is termed *In-Between*.
3. A transformation applied to another atomic object. For example the representation of a posture of Mickey Mouse can be obtained by applying some transformation to a master representation. This representation is termed *Transform*.

Figure 3.2 presents the schema of the type atomic that describes these alternative representations. The conventions employed in this schema representation as well as others presented in this paper are as follows: The names of built-in types (i.e., strings, integers, etc.) are all in capital letters as opposed to defined types that use lower case letters. ANYTYPE refers to strings, integers, characters and complex data structures. A type is represented by its name surrounded by an oval. The attributes of a type are denoted by arrows with single line tails. The name of the attribute labels the arrow and the type is given at the head of the arrow. Multivalued attributes are denoted by arrows with two heads and single value attributes by arrows with a single head. For multivalued attributes, an S overlapping the arrow is used to

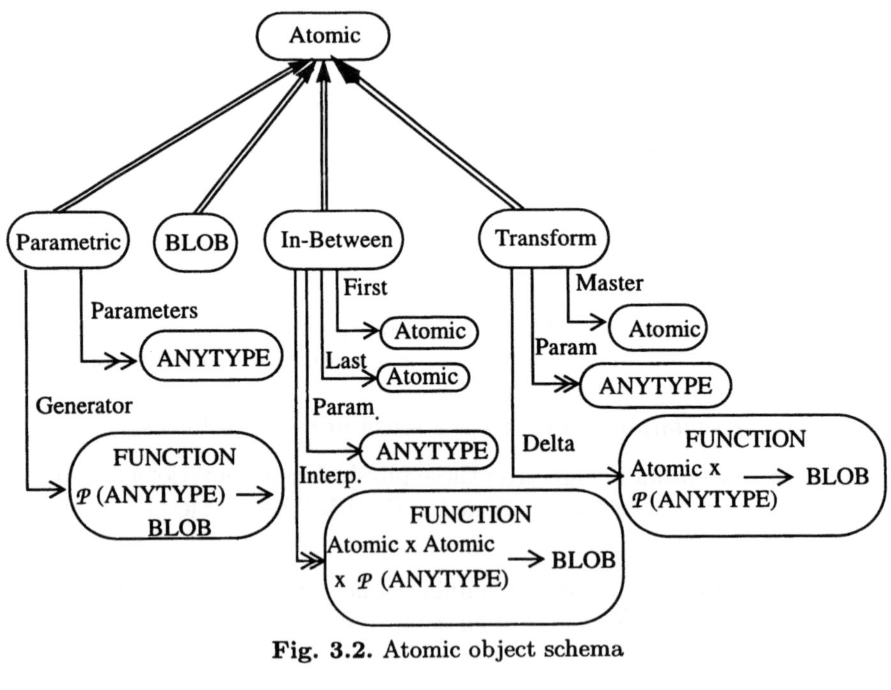

Fig. 3.2. Atomic object schema

denote a sequence instead of a set. The type/subtype relationship is denoted by arrows with double line tail. The type at the tail is the subtype and the type at the head is the supertype.

For example, in Figure 3.2 Parametric is a subtype of Atomic, and it has two attributes: Parameters and Generator. Parameters is a set of elements of any type and Generator is a function that maps a set of elements of any type (i.e., Parameters) into a BLOB.

3.2 Composed Object Layer

This layer contains the representation of temporal and spatial constructs. In addition to specifying positioning and timing of objects, these constructs define objects as composed by other objects. The composition might be recursive (i.e., a composed object may consist of a collection of other composed objects). For example, Mickey Mouse might be represented as a composed object consisting of 3D representation of: a head, two ears, a tail, two legs, etc. The spatial relationship between these atomic objects would define Mickey Mouse.

Spatial constructs place objects in the rendering space and implicitly define spatial relationships between objects. The placement of an object defines its position and direction in the rendering space. For example, consider a path from a house to a pond. The placement of a character on the path must include, in addition to its position, the direction of the character (e.g., heading towards the pond or heading towards the house).

A coordinate system defined by n orthogonal vectors defines unambiguously the position and direction of an object in the rendering space. For example, consider a 3D representation of a die. Figure 3.4 (a) shows three

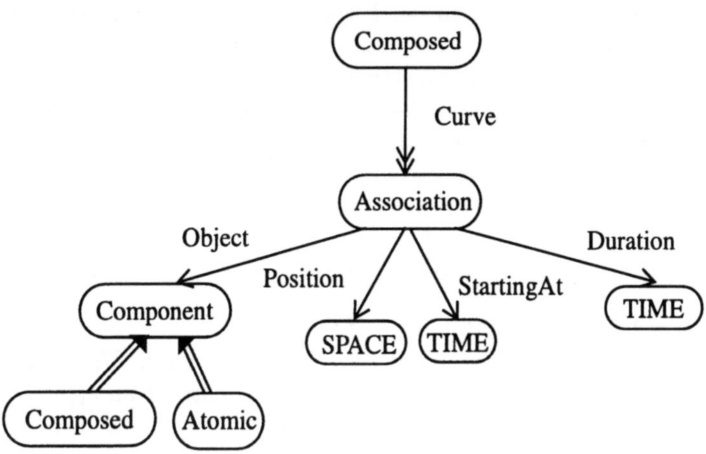

Fig. 3.3. Composed object schema

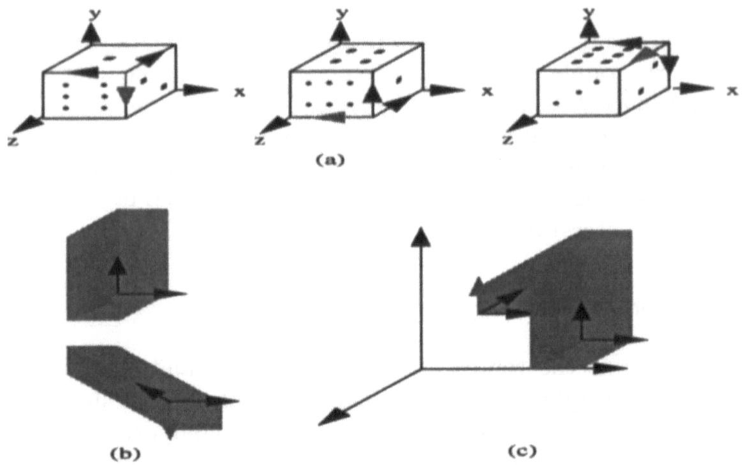

Fig. 3.4. (a) Three different directions for a die, (b) Two atomic objects, (c) A composed object constructed using spatial constructs and the atomic objects in (b).

different placements of the die in the rendering space defined by the x-y-z axis. Notice that the position of the die in each placement is the same. But the direction of the die varies (e.g., the face at the top is different for each placement). However, the coordinate systems defined by the red, green and blue axis specifies unambiguously the position and the direction of the die.

Formally, a *Spatial Construct* of a component object o is a bijection that maps n orthogonal vectors in o into n orthogonal vectors in the rendering space, where n is the number of dimensions. Let *o's coordinate system* and *the mapped coordinate system* be defined by the n orthogonal vectors in o and the mapped vectors, respectively. The *placement* of a component object o in the rendering space is the translation of o from its coordinate system to the mapped coordinate system, such that its relative position with respect to both coordinate systems does not change. Note that there is a unique placement for a given spatial construct.

Temporal constructs define the rendering time of objects and implicitly establish temporal relationships among the objects. They are always defined with respect to a temporal space. Given a temporal space $[0, t]$, a *Temporal Construct* of a component o of duration d, maps o to a subinterval $[i, j]$ such that $0 \leq i \leq j \leq t$ and $j - i = d$.

A *composed object* C is represented by the set:

$\{(e_i, p_i, s_i, d_i) \mid$ e_i is a component of C,
p_i is the mapped coordinate system in C's rendering space defined by the spatial construct on e_i, and
$[s_i, d_i]$ is the subinterval defined by a temporal construct on $e_i\}$

A composed object may have more than one occurrence of the same component. For example, a character may appear and disappear in a scene. Then, the description of the scene includes one 4-tuple for each appearance of the character. Each tuple specifies the character's position in the scene and a subinterval when the character appears.

The definition of composed objects establishes a hierarchy among the different components of an object. This hierarchy can be represented as a tree. Each node in the tree represents an object with spatial and temporal constructs (i.e., the 4-tuple in the composed object representation: *(component, position, starting time, duration))*, and each arch represents the relation *component of.*

3.3 Challenges

The presented data model is not necessarily complete and may need additional constructs. A target application (e.g., animation) and its users can evaluate a final data model and refine (or tailor) it to obtain the desired functionality. Assuming that a data model is defined, the following research topics require further investigation. First, a final system requires authoring packages to populate the database and tools to display the captured data. These tools should be as effective and friendly as their currently available stream-based siblings. An analogy is the archive of stream-based collections maintained by most owners of a camcorder. The camcorder is a friendly, and yet effective tool to capture the desired data. The VCR is another effective tool to display the captured data. A VCR can also record broadcast stream-based video objects.

Tools to author 3-D objects are starting to emerge from disciplines such as CAD/CAM, scientific visualization, and geometrical modeling (see [16] for a list of available commercial packages). There are packages that can generate a 3-D object as a list of triangles. For example, one can draw 2-D objects using either AutoCAD or MacDraw. Subsequently, a user can interact with these tools to convert a 2-D object into a 3-D one. Finally, this 3-D object is saved in a file as a list of triangles. At the time of this writing, there are two other approaches to author 3-D objects. If the actual object is available, then it can be scanned using a Cyberware scanner that outputs a triangle list. The second method employs volume based point sample techniques to extract triangle lists. With this method, a point sample indicates whether the point is inside or outside of a surface or object (like a CT or MRI might).

Tools to display structured video are grouped into two categories: compilers, and interpreters. A *compiler* consumes a structured video clip to produce its corresponding stream-based video to be stored in the database and displayed at a later time. An *interpreter*, on the other hand, renders a structured video either statically or interactively. A static interpreterdisplays a structure without accepting input. An interactive interpreter accepts input, allowing a user to navigate the environment described by a structured object (e.g., video games, virtual reality applications that either visualize a data set for a scientist or train an individual on a specific task). A challenging task when designing an interpreter is to ensure a hiccup-free display of the referenced scene. This task is guided by the structure of the complex object that describes a scenario.

For static interpreters, this structure dictates a schedule for what objects should be retrieved at what time. An intelligent scheduler should take advantage of this information to minimize the amount of resources required to support a display. At times, adequate resources (memory and disk bandwidth) may not be available to support a hiccup-free display. In this case, the interpreter might pursue two alternative paths. First, it may compute a *hybrid* representation by compiling the temporal constructs that exists among different objects to compute streams for these object. In essence, it would compute an intermediate representation of a structured video clip that consists of a collection of: 1) streams that must be displayed simultaneously, and 2) certain objects that should be interpreted and displayed with the streams. We speculate that this would minimize the number of constraints imposed on the display, simplifying the scheduling task. As an alternative, the interpreter may elect to prefetch certain objects (those with a high frequency of access) into memory in order to simplify the scheduling task.

Unlike the interpreter, the compiler is not required to support a continuous display. However, this is not to imply a lack of research topics in this area. Below, we list several of them. First, the compiler must compress the final output in order to reduce both its size and the bandwidth requirements. Traditional compression techniques that manipulate a stream-based presentation (e.g., MPEG) cannot take advantage of the contents of the video clip because none is available. With a structured presentation, the compiler should employ new algorithms that take advantage of the available content information during compression. We speculate that a content-based compression technique can outperform the traditional heuristic based technique (e.g., MPEG) by providing a higher resolution, a lower size, and a lower average bandwidth to support a hiccup-free display. Second, the compiler should minimize the amount of time required to produce a stream-based video object. It may create the frames in a non-sequential manner in order to achieve this objective (by computing the different postures of an object only once and reusing it in all the frames that reference it).

If the term "object-oriented" was the buzz word of the 1980s, "content-based retrieval" is almost certainly emerging as the catch phrase of the 1990s. A structured video clip has the ability to support content-based queries. Its temporal and spatial primitives can be used to author more complex relationships that exists among objects (e.g., hugging, chasing, hitting). This raises a host of research topics: What are the specifications of a query language that interrogates these relationships? What techniques would be employed by a system that executes queries? What indexing techniques can be designed to speedup the retrieval time of a query? How is the data presented at a physical level? How should the system represent temporal and spatial constructs to enable a user to author more complex relationships? Each of these topics deserves further investigation. Hopefully, in contrast to "object-oriented", a host of agreed upon concepts will emerge from this activity.

Finally, the system will almost certainly be required to support multiple users. This is because its data (e.g., 3 dimensional postures of characters, structured scenes) is valuable and, similar to software engineering, several users might want to share and re-use each other's objects in different scenes. Minimizing the amount of resources required to support the above functionality in the presence of multiple users is an important topic. A challenging task is to support interpreted display of different objects to several users simultaneously. This is due to the hiccup-free requirement of an interpreted structured video.

4. Conclusion

Video is a new communication medium shaping the frontiers of the computer technology (both hardware and software). In this paper, we described two alternative approaches to represent this data type: stream-based and structured. For each approach, we described some of its solutions and challenges. We believe that in the near future, the structured approach will gain increased popularity because it provides for an effective user interaction with a repository. Its representation can support virtual worlds where a user becomes an active participants (instead of a passive recipient of information). It will almost certainly have a tremendous impact on educational, scientific, and entertainment applications. Virtual reality environments currently employ this approach for their target application. However, their primary focus has been on graphics (i.e., rendering aspects) and tools to interact with a user. In order for this paradigm to become useful on a day-to-day basis, a significant amount of research and development is required on: 1) its storage and retrieval of data to support user queries and a hiccup-free display, and 2) tools to populate and query a database.

Acknowledgments

I want to thank Martha Escobar-Molano, Seon Ho Kim, Cyrus Shahabi, and Roger Zimmermann for contributing to the presented material. This research was supported in part by the National Science Foundation under grants IRI-9222926, IRI-9203389, IRI-9258362 (NYI award), and CDA-9216321, and a Hewlett-Packard unrestricted cash/equipment gift.

References

[1] S. Bernstein. Techno-Artists 'Tooning Up. *Los Angeles Times, Section F*, November 10 1994.

[2] S. Berson, S. Ghandeharizadeh, R. Muntz, and X. Ju. Staggered Striping in Multimedia Information Systems. In *Proceedings of ACM SIGMOD*, pages 79–89, 1994.

[3] S. Berson, L. Golubchik, and R. R. Muntz. A Fault Tolerant Design of a Multimedia Server. In *Proceedings of ACM SIGMOD*, 1995.

[4] D. Bitton and J. Gray. Disk shadowing. In *Proceedings of Very Large Databases*, pages 331–338, September 1988.

[5] M. Carey, L. Haas, and M. Livny. Tapes hold data, too: Challenges of tuples on tertiary storage. In *Proceedings of ACM SIGMOD*, pages 413–417, 1993.

[6] P. J. Denning. The Working Set Model for Program Behavior. *Communications of the ACM*, 11(5):323–333, 1968.

[7] J. Dozier. Access to data in NASA's Earth observing system (Keynote Address). In *Proceedings of ACM SIGMOD*, pages 1–1, June 1992.

[8] E. A. Fox. Advances in Interactive Digital Multimedia Sytems. *IEEE Computer*, pages 9–21, October 1991.

[9] D. Le Gall. MPEG: a video compression standard for multimedia applications. *Communications of the ACM*, April 1991.

[10] S. Ghandeharizadeh, A. Dashti, and C. Shahabi. A Pipelining mechanism to minimize the latency time in hierarchical multimedia storage managers. Technical report, University of Southern California, 1994.

[11] S. Ghandeharizadeh, S. H. Kim, and C. Shahabi. On Configuring a Single Disk Continuous Media Server. In *Proceedings of the ACM Sigmetrics Conference*, May 1995.

[12] S. Ghandeharizadeh and L. Ramos. Continuous Retrieval of Multimedia Data Using Parallelism. *IEEE Transactions on Knowledge and Data Engineering*, 5(4):658–669, August 1993.

[13] J. Gray, B. Host, and M. Walker. Parity striping of disc arrays: Low-cost reliable storage with acceptable throughput. In *Proceedings of Very Large Databases*, pages 148–162, August 1990.

[14] B. Haskell. International standards activities in image data compression. In *Proceedings of Scientific Data Compression Workshop*, pages 439–449, 1989. NASA conference Pub 3025, NASA Office of Management, Scientific and technical information division.

[15] C. Johnson. Architectural Constructs of AMPEX DST. *Third NASA GSFC Conference on Mass Storage Systems and Technologies*, pages 153–162, 1993.

[16] K. Kornbluh. Active data analysis: Advanced software for the '90s. *IEEE Spectrum*, 31(11):57–83, November 1994.

[17] R. Ng and J. Yang. Maximizing Buffer and Disk Utilization for News On-Demand. In *Proceedings of Very Large Databases*, 1994.

[18] B. Ozden, A. Biliris, R. Rastogi, and A. Silberschatz. A Low-Cost Storage Server for Movie on Demand Databases. In *Proceedings of Very Large Databases*, 1994.

[19] C. Ruemmler and J. Wilkes. An Introduction to Disk Drive Modeling. *IEEE Computer*, pages 17–28, March 1994.

[20] Seagate. Barracuda family. *The Data Technology Company Product Overview*, pages 1–25, March 1994.

[21] T.J. Teory. Properties of Disk Scheduling Policies in Multiprogrammed Computer Systems. In *Proc. AFIPS Fall Joint Computer Conf.*, pages 1–11, 1972.

[22] Nadia Magnenat Thalmann and Daniel Thalmann, editors. *Computer Animation Theory and Practice.* Springer-Verlag, 1990.

The Storage and Retrieval of Continuous Media Data

Banu Özden, Rajeev Rastogi, and Avi Silberschatz

AT&T Bell Laboratories, 600 Mountain Avenue, Murray Hill, NJ 07974

Summary. Continuous media applications, which require a guaranteed transfer rate of the data, are becoming an integral part of daily computational life. However, conventional file systems do not provide rate guarantees, and are therefore unsuitable for the storage and retrieval of continuous media data. To meet the demands of these new applications, *continuous media file systems*, which provide rate guarantees by managing critical storage resources such as memory and disks must be designed.

In this paper, we highlight the issues in the storage and retrieval of continuous media data. We first present a simple scheme for concurrently retrieving multiple continuous media streams from disks. We then introduce a clever allocation technique for storing continuous media data that eliminates disk latency and thus, drastically reduces RAM requirements. We present, for video data, schemes for implementing the operations fast-forward, rewind and pause. Finally, we conclude by outlining directions for future research in the storage and retrieval of continuous media data.

1. Introduction

The recent advances in compression techniques and broadband networking enable the use of continuous media applications such as multimedia electronic-mail, interactive TV, encyclopedia software, games, news, movies, on-demand tutorials, lectures, audio, video and hypermedia documents. These applications deliver to users continuous media data like video that is stored in digital form on secondary storage devices. Furthermore, continuous media-on-demand systems enable viewers to playback the media at any time and control the presentation by VCR like commands.

An important characteristic of continuous media that distinguishes it from non-continuous media (e.g., text) is that continuous media has certain timing characteristics associated with it. For example, video data is typically stored in units that are frames and must be delivered to viewers at a certain rate (which is typically 30 frames/sec). Another feature is that most continuous media types consume a large storage space and bandwidth. For example, a 100 minute movie, which is compressed using the MPEG-I compression algorithm, requires about 1.25 gigabyte (GB) of storage space. At a cost of 40 dollars per megabyte (MB), storing that movie in RAM would cost about 45,000 dollars. In comparison, the cost of storing data on disks is less than a dollar per megabyte and on tapes and CD-ROMs, it is of the order of a few cents per megabyte. Thus, it is more cost-effective to store video data on secondary storage devices like disks.

Given the limited amount of resources such as memory and disk bandwidth, it is a challenging problem to design a file system that can concurrently service a large number of both conventional and continuous media applications while providing low response times. Conventional file systems provide no rate guarantees for data retrieved and are thus unsuitable for the storage and retrieval of continuous media data. *Continuous media file systems*, on the other hand, guarantee that once a continuous media *stream* (that is, a request for the retrieval of a continuous media clip) is accepted, data for that stream is retrieved at the required rate.

The fact that secondary storage devices have relatively high latencies and low transfer rates makes the problem more interesting. For example, besides the fact that disk bandwidths are relatively low, the disk latency imposes high buffering requirements in order to achieve a cumulative transfer rate for streams that is close to the disk bandwidth. As a matter of fact, in order to support multiple streams, the closer the cumulative transfer rate gets to the disk bandwidth, the higher the buffering requirements become. Thus, since the available buffer space is limited, there is a limit on the number of requests that can be serviced concurrently.

In order to increase performance, schemes for reducing the impact of disk latency, as well as solutions for increasing bandwidth must be devised. Clever storage allocation schemes [8], [11], [15] as well as novel disk scheduling schemes [9], [12], [4], [13], [6] must be devised to reduce or totally eliminate latency so that buffering requirements can be reduced while bandwidth is utilized effectively. Storage techniques based on multiple disks such as replication and striping must be employed to increase the bandwidth.

In this paper, we first present a simple scheme for concurrently retrieving multiple continuous media streams from disks. We then show, how by employing novel striping techniques for storing continuous media data, we can completely eliminate disk latency and thus, drastically reduce RAM requirements. We present, for video data, schemes for implementing the basic VCR operations – fast-forward, rewind, and pause. We show how the schemes can be extended to benefit from the varying transfer rates of disks. We conclude by outlining directions for future research in the storage and retrieval of continuous media data.

2. Retrieving Continuous Media Data

In this section, we briefly review characteristics of disks (additional details can be found in [14]), and present our architecture for retrieving continuous media streams from disks. We then outline a simple scheme for retrieving multiple concurrent continuous media streams from disks, and compute the buffer requirements of this scheme.

Data on disks is stored in a series of concentric circles, or *tracks*, and accessed using a disk head. A disk rotates on a central spindle and the speed of rotation denotes the transfer rate of the disk. Data on a particular track is accessed by positioning the head on (also referred to as *seeking* to) the track containing the data, and then waiting until the disk rotates enough so that the head is positioned directly above the data. Seeks typically consist of a coast during which the head moves at a constant speed and a settle, when the head position is adjusted to the desired track. Thus, the latency for accessing data on disk is the sum of seek and rotational latency. Another feature of disks is that tracks are longer at the outside than at the inside. A consequence of this is that outer tracks may have higher transfer rates than inner tracks. Figure 2.1 illustrates the notation we use for disk characteristics and the characteristics of the Seagate Barracuda 2 disk (we choose the disk transfer rate to be the transfer rate of the innermost track.)

inner track transfer rate	r_{disk}	68 Mb/sec
Settle time	t_{settle}	0.6 msec
Seek time (worst case)	t_{seek}	17 msec
Rotational latency (worst case)	t_{rot}	8.34 msec

Fig. 2.1. The characteristics of Seagate Barracuda 2 disk.

In our architecture, we assume that continuous media clips are stored on disks and must be delivered at a rate r_{med}. The continuous media system is responsible for retrieving data for continuous media streams from disk into RAM at rate r_{med}. The data is then transmitted over a network to clients where they are delivered at the required rate. In this paper, we restrict ourselves to the problem at the server end – that is, the task of retrieving multiple continuous media streams from disk to RAM concurrently.

The maximum number of concurrent streams, denoted by p, that can be retrieved from disk is given by

$$p = \lfloor \frac{r_{disk}}{r_{med}} \rfloor \tag{2.1}$$

A simple scheme for retrieving data for m continuous media streams concurrently is as follows. Continuous media clips are stored contiguously on disk and a buffer of size d is maintained in RAM for each of the m streams. Continuous media data is retrieved into each of the buffers at a rate r_{disk} in a round robin fashion, the number of bits retrieved into a buffer during each round being d. In order to ensure that data for the m streams can be continually retrieved from disk at a rate r_{med}, in the time that the d bits from m buffers are consumed at a rate r_{med}, the d bits following the d bits consumed must be retrieved into the buffers for every one of the m streams. Since each retrieval involves positioning the disk head at the desired location and then transferring the d bits from the disk to the buffer, we have the following equation.

$$\frac{d}{r_{med}} \geq m \cdot (\frac{d}{r_{disk}} + t_{seek} + t_{rot})$$

In the above equation, $\frac{d}{r_{disk}}$ is the time it takes to transfer d bits from disk, and $t_{seek} + t_{rot}$ is the worst case disk latency. Hence, the size d of the buffer per stream can be calculated as

$$d \geq \frac{(t_{seek} + t_{rot}) \cdot r_{med} \cdot r_{disk}}{(\frac{r_{disk}}{m} - r_{med})} \tag{2.2}$$

Thus, the buffer size per stream increases both with latency of the disk and the number of concurrent streams. In the following example, we compute for a commercially available disk, the buffer requirements in order to support the maximum number of concurrent streams.

Example 2.1. Consider MPEG-I compressed video data stored on a Seagate Baracuda 2 disk. The video data needs to be retrieved at a rate of r_{med} =1.5 Mb/sec. Thus, the maximum number of streams that can be retrieved from the disk is 45. Since the worst-case rotational latency of 8.34 msec and worst case seek latency of 17 msec, the worst-case latency for the disk is 25.34 msec. From Equation 2.2, it follows that the minimum buffer size required in order to support 45 streams is 233 Mb. Since there is a buffer of size d for every stream, the total buffer requirements are 10 Gb. □

In the case of video streams, the VCR operations pause, fast-forward, and rewind can be implemented as follows. Pause is implemented by simply halting the consumption of bits from the buffer for the stream. Furthermore, the number of bits, d_1, read into the buffer during a round satisfies the following equality.

$$d_1 + d_2 = d$$

where d_2 is the number of unconsumed bits already contained in the buffer before data is read into it. Thus, it is possible that when a stream is paused, no data is read into the buffer for the stream until it is resumed again. Fast-forward is implemented by simply skipping a certain number of bits in the continuous media clip between the d bits retrieved during each successive round into the buffer for the stream. Similarly, rewind is implemented by retrieving preceding bits during each successive round, and skipping a certain number of bits between the d bits retrieved during successive rounds.

3. Matrix-Based Allocation

The scheme we proposed in Section 2. for retrieving data for multiple continuous media streams had high buffer requirements due to high disk latencies.

In this section, we present a clever storage allocation scheme for video clips that completely eliminates disk latency and thus, keeps buffer requirements low. However, the scheme results in an increase in the worst-case response time between the time a request for a continuous media clip is made and the time the data for the stream can actually be consumed.

3.1 Storage Allocation

In order to keep the amount of buffer required low, we propose a new storage allocation scheme for continuous media clips on disk, which we call the *matrix-based* allocation scheme. This scheme is referred to as phase-constrained allocation in [8] when it is used to store a single clip. The matrix-based allocation scheme eliminates seeks to random locations, and thereby enables the concurrent retrieval of maximum number of streams p, while maintaining the buffer requirements as a constant independent of the number of streams and disk latencies. Since continuous media data is retrieved sequentially from disk, the response time for the initiation of a continuous media stream is high.

Consider a *super-clip* in which the various continuous media clips are arranged linearly one after another. Let l denote the length of the super-clip in seconds. Thus, the storage required for the super-clip is $l \cdot r_{med}$ bits. Suppose that continuous media data is read from disks in portions of size d. To simplify the presentation, in this section, we shall assume that $l \cdot r_{med}$ is a multiple of $p \cdot d$. In Section 4., we will relax this assumption. Our goal is to be able to support p concurrent continuous media streams. In order to accomplish this, we divide the super-clip into p contiguous partitions. Thus, the super-clip can be visualized as a $(p \times 1)$ vector, the concatenation of whose rows is the super-clip itself and each row contains $t_c \cdot r_{med}$ bits of continuous media data, where

$$t_c = \frac{l}{p}$$

Note that the first bit in any two adjacent rows are t_c seconds apart in the super-clip. Also, a continuous media clip in the super-clip may span multiple rows. Since super-clip data in each row is retrieved in portions of size d, a row can be further viewed as consisting of n portions of size d, where

$$n = \frac{t_c \cdot r_{med}}{d}$$

Thus, the super-clip can be represented as a $(p \times n)$ matrix of portions as shown in Figure 3.1. Each portion in the matrix can be uniquely identified by the row and column to which it belongs. Suppose we now store the super-clip matrix on disk sequentially in column-major form. Thus, as shown in Figure 3.2, Column 1 is stored first, followed by Column 2, and finally Column n.

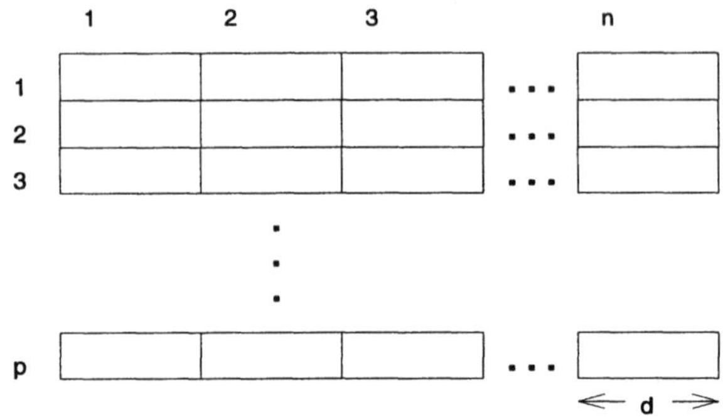

Fig. 3.1. The super-clip viewed as a matrix.

We now show that by sequentially reading from disk, the super-clip data in each row can be retrieved concurrently at a rate r_{med}. From Equation 2.1, it follows that:

$$\frac{p \cdot d}{r_{disk}} \leq \frac{d}{r_{med}} \tag{3.1}$$

Therefore, in the time required to consume d bits of continuous media data at a rate r_{med}, an entire column can be retrieved from disk. As a result, while a portion is being consumed at a rate r_{med}, the next portion can be retrieved.

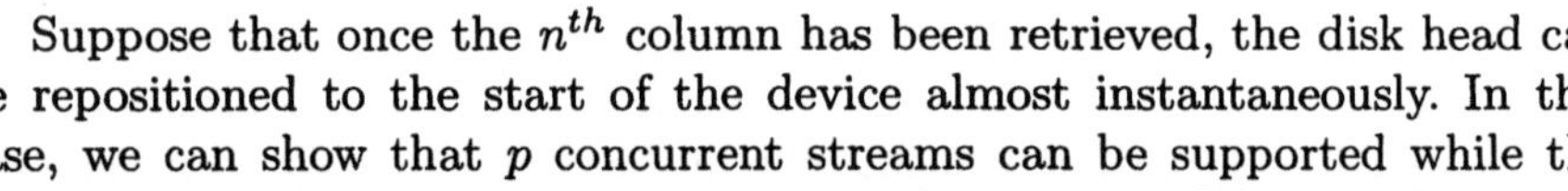

Fig. 3.2. Placement of n columns of the super-clip matrix.

Suppose that once the nth column has been retrieved, the disk head can be repositioned to the start of the device almost instantaneously. In this case, we can show that p concurrent streams can be supported while the worst case response time for the initiation of a stream will be t_c. The reason for this is that every t_c seconds, the disk head can be repositioned to the start. Thus, the same portion of a continuous media clip is retrieved every t_c seconds. Furthermore, for every other concurrent stream, the last portion retrieved just before the disk head is repositioned, belongs to Column n. Since we assume that repositioning time is negligible, Column 1 can be retrieved immediately after Column n. Thus, since the portion following portion (i, n) in Column n, is portion $(i+1, 1)$ in Column 1, data for concurrent streams can be retrieved from disk at a rate r_{med}. In Section 3.3, we present schemes that take into account repositioning time when retrieving data for p concurrent streams.

3.2 Buffering

We now compute the buffering requirements for our storage scheme. Unlike the scheme presented in Section 2 in which we associated a buffer with every stream, in the matrix-based scheme, with every row of the super-clip matrix, we associate a *row buffer*, into which consecutive portions in the row are retrieved. Each of the row buffers is implemented as a *circular* buffer; that is, while writing into the buffer, if the end is reached, then further bits are written at the beginning of the row buffer (similarly, while reading, if the end is reached, then subsequent bits are read from the beginning of the buffer).

With the above circular storage scheme, every $\frac{t_c}{n}$ seconds, consecutive columns of the super-clip data are retrieved from disk into row buffers. The size of each buffer is $2 \cdot d$, one half of which is used to read in a portion of the super-clip from disk, while d bits of the super-clip are consumed from the other half. Also, the number of row buffers is p. The row buffers store the p different portions of the super-clip contained in a single column – the first portion in a column is read into the first row buffer, the second portion into the second row buffer and so on. Thus, in the scheme, initially, the p portions of the super-clip in the first column are read into the first d bits of each of the corresponding row buffers. Following this, the next p portions in the second column are read into the latter d bits of each of the corresponding row buffers. Concurrently, the first d bits from each of the row buffers can be consumed for the p concurrent streams. Once the portions from the second column have been retrieved, the portions from the third column are retrieved into the first d bits of the row buffers and so on. Since consecutive portions of a super-clip are retrieved every $\frac{t_c}{n}$ seconds, consecutive portions of continuous media clips in the super-clip are retrieved into the buffer at a rate of r_{med}. Thus, in the first row buffer, the first n portions of the super-clip (from the first row) are output at a rate of r_{med}, while in the second, the next n portions (from the second row) are output and so on. As a result, a request for a continuous media stream can be initiated once the first portion of the continuous media clip is read into a row buffer. Furthermore, in the case that a continuous media clip spans multiple rows, data for the stream can be retrieved by sequentially accessing the contents of consecutive row buffers.

3.3 Repositioning

The storage technique we have presented thus far enables data to be retrieved continuously at a rate of r_{med} under the assumption that once the nth column of the super-clip is retrieved from disk, the disk head can be repositioned at the start almost instantaneously. However, in practice, this assumption does not hold. Below, we present techniques for retrieving data for p concurrent streams of the super-clip if we were to relax this assumption. The basic problem is to retrieve data from the device at a rate of r_{med} in light of the fact that no data can be transferred while the head is being repositioned at the start. If $\frac{d}{r_{med}} \geq \frac{p \cdot d}{r_{disk}} + t_{rot} + t_{seek}$ holds, then there is enough time to position the disk head after retrieving the last column. In this case, nothing special needs to be done. Otherwise, a simple solution to this problem is to maintain another disk which stores the super-clip exactly as stored by the first disk and which takes over the function of the disk while its head is being repositioned.

An alternate scheme, which does not require the entire super-clip to be duplicated on both disks, can be employed if t_c is at least twice the repositioning time. The super-clip data matrix is divided into two submatrices so that one submatrix contains the first $\lceil \frac{n}{2} \rceil$ columns and the other submatrix, the remaining $\lfloor \frac{n}{2} \rfloor$ columns of the original matrix, and each submatrix is stored in column-major form on two disks with bandwidth r_{disk}. The first submatrix is retrieved from the first disk, and then the second submatrix is read from the other disk while the first disk is repositioned. When the end of the data on the second disk is reached, the data is read from the first disk and the second disk is repositioned.

If the time it takes to reposition the disk head to the start is low, in comparison to the time it takes to read the entire super-clip, as is the case for disks, then almost at any given instant one of the disks would be idle. To remedy this deficiency, in the following, we present a scheme that is more suitable for disks. In the scheme, we eliminate the additional disk by storing some of the last columns of the column-major form representation of the super-clip in RAM. Let m be the smallest integer for which $m \cdot \frac{d}{r_{med}} \geq t_{rot} + t_{seek}$ holds, that is, $m = \lceil \frac{(t_{rot}+t_{seek}) \cdot r_{med}}{d} \rceil$. The scheme stores the last $m-1$ columns entirely and the last $p \cdot d - (m \cdot \frac{d}{r_{med}} - t_{seek} - t_{rot}) \cdot r_{disk}$ bits of the $(n-m+1)^{th}$ column in RAM, so that while the last $(m-1)$ columns and last portion of the $(n-m+1)^{th}$ column are consumed from RAM, the disk head is positioned. Thus, the total RAM required is $\min\{0, md(p - \frac{r_{disk}}{r_{med}}) - (t_{seek} + t_{rot})r_{disk}\} + 2dp$.

3.4 Implementation of VCR Operations

We now describe how the VCR operations begin, pause, fast-forward, rewind and resume can be implemented with the matrix-based storage architecture. As we described earlier, contiguous portions of the super-clip are retrieved into p row buffers at a rate r_{med}. The first n portions are retrieved into the first row buffer, the next n into the second row buffer, and so on.

- **begin:** The consumption of bits for a continuous media stream is initiated once a row buffer contains the first portion of the continuous media clip. Portions of size d are consumed at a rate r_{med} from the row buffer (wrapping around if necessary). After the $i \cdot n^{th}$ portion of the super-clip is consumed by a stream, consumption of data by the stream is resumed from the $i+1^{th}$ row buffer. We refer to the row buffer that outputs the continuous media data currently being consumed by a stream as the *current* row buffer. Since in the worst case, $n \cdot d$ bits may need to be transmitted before a row buffer contains the first portion of the requested continuous media clip, the delay involved in the initiation of a stream when a begin command is issued, in the worst case, is t_c.

- **pause:** Consumption of continuous media data by the stream from the current row buffer is stopped (note however, that data is still retrieved into the row buffer as before).
- **fast-forward:** A certain number of bits are consumed from each successive row buffer following the current row buffer. Thus, during fast-forward, the number of bits skipped between consecutive bits consumed is approximately $n \cdot d$ (note that this scheme is inapplicable if successive row buffers do not contain data belonging to the same continuous media clip).
- **rewind:** This operation is implemented in a similar fashion to the fast-forward operation except that instead of jumping ahead to the following row buffer, jumps during consumption are made to the preceding row buffer. Thus, a certain number of bits are consumed from each previous row buffer preceding the current row buffer.
- **resume:** In case the previously issued command was either fast-forward or rewind, bits are continued to be consumed normally from the current row buffer. If, however, the previous command was pause, then once the current row buffer contains the bit following the last bit consumed, normal consumption of data from the row buffer is resumed beginning with the bit. Thus, in the worst case, similar to the case of the begin operation, a delay of t_c seconds may result before consumption of data for a stream can be resumed after a pause operation.

For the disk in Example 2.1, t_c for a 100 minute super-clip is approximately 133 seconds. Thus, the worst case delay is 133 seconds when beginning or resuming a continuous media stream. Furthermore, the number of frames skipped when fast-forwarding and rewinding is 3990 (133 seconds of video at 30 frames/s). By reducing t_c, we could reduce the worst-case response time when initiating a stream.

We now show how multiple disks can be employed to reduce t_c. Returning to Example 2.1, suppose that instead of using a single disk, we were to use an array of 5 disks. In this case, the bandwidth of the disk array increases from 68 Mb/sec to 340 Mb/sec. The number of streams, p, increases from 45 to 226, and, therefore, t_c reduces from 133 seconds to approximately 26 seconds. In this system, the worst case delay is 26 seconds and the number of frames skipped is 780 (26 seconds of video at 30 frames/sec).

4. Variable Disk Transfer Rates

In Section 3., we have presented the matrix-based allocation scheme which enables retrieving the maximum number of streams from a disk. In that section, we assumed that each disk has a single transfer rate. This implies that if disks with varying transfer rates are used, the matrix-based allocation scheme uses the minimum transfer rate of the disk, denoted by $r_{disk_{min}}$, to determine the number of streams p that can be supported.

Commonly used SCSI disks do not provide a uniform transfer rate. If the storage capacity of a track is proportional to its length, then so is its transfer rate. Since an inner track is shorter than an outer track, the transfer rate of the inner track may be less than the outer one. Most disks utilize a technique called *zoning* which groups the cylinders in a number of zones such that each track within a zone has the same number of sectors [1]. The matrix-based allocation scheme uses the minimum transfer rate, namely, the transfer rate of the innermost zone. Thus, the number of streams p supported by matrix-based storage allocation where $p = \lfloor \frac{r_{disk_{min}}}{r_{med}} \rfloor$, is pessimistic. In the following two sections, we extend the matrix-based allocation scheme so that it can utilize a more accurate value of the transfer rate in order to support a larger number of streams.

Instead of selecting p with respect to the minimum transfer rate, p can be selected to be arbitrarily large at the cost of additional buffer space. In the case of the matrix-based allocation scheme, if p is selected to be greater than $\lfloor \frac{r_{disk_{min}}}{r_{med}} \rfloor$, then only $\frac{d}{r_{med}} \cdot r_{disk_{min}}$ bits of each column can be retrieved from disk within the time a column is consumed by p streams. Thus, $p \cdot d - \frac{d}{r_{med}} \cdot r_{disk_{min}}$ bits of each column need to be stored in RAM. In this case, the total buffer requirement becomes $\frac{d}{r_{med}} \cdot r_{disk_{min}} + n \cdot (p \cdot d - \frac{d}{r_{med}} \cdot r_{disk_{min}})$. However, by exploiting the varying transfer rates of disks, the total buffer requirement can be reduced despite selecting p larger than $\lfloor \frac{r_{disk_{min}}}{r_{med}} \rfloor$.

We are particularly interested in the values of p that satisfy

$$\frac{r_{disk_{min}}}{r_{med}} \leq p \leq \frac{r_{disk_{max}}}{r_{med}} \tag{4.1}$$

where $r_{disk_{max}}$ is the maximum transfer rate of the disk. Let r_{disk_j} be the transfer rate of the jth zone. We enumerate the zones in the decreasing order of their transfer rates. Thus, if there are z zones, for any j^{th} zone, $1 \leq j < z$, $r_{disk_j} \geq r_{disk_{j+1}}$ holds.

We present two schemes in the following two sections that exploit the varying transfer rates of disks. In the previous section, in order to simplify the presentation, we presented the matrix-based allocation scheme based on the assumption that the size of the super-clip data $l \cdot r_{med}$ is a multiple of $p \cdot d$. Both schemes we present next do not constrain the size of the super-clip data. Both schemes rely on the following matrix structure to represent the super-clip data. Furthermore, it can be easily shown that the matrix-based allocation scheme can also be based on this data structure in order to relax the assumption about the size of the super-clip data.

For a given p, the super-clip data can be divided into consecutive rows each of which contains $\lceil \frac{l \cdot r_{med}}{p} \rceil$ consecutive bits except the last row which contains the remaining bits of the super-clip data. We refer to a row which contains $\lceil \frac{l \cdot r_{med}}{p} \rceil$ bits as a full row. The number of rows $\lceil \frac{l \cdot r_{med}}{\lceil \frac{l \cdot r_{med}}{p} \rceil} \rceil$ will be p if p is sufficiently larger than the size of the super-clip, namely $l \cdot r_{med}$. For example, if $l \cdot r_{med} \geq p^2$ holds, then the number of rows will be p. [1] In order to simplify the presentation, we assume that the size of the super-clip, $l \cdot r_{med}$, is at least p^2 bits, and therefore, the super-clip matrix has p rows.

Furthermore, given d, each row can be divided into portions each of which contains consecutive d bits except the last portion which contains the remaining bits of the row. That is, the size of the last portion, denoted by d', of each full row is $d' = d$ if $\lceil \frac{l \cdot r_{med}}{p} \rceil \bmod d = 0$ holds, and it is $d' = \lceil \frac{l \cdot r_{med}}{p} \rceil \bmod d$ bits otherwise. The size of the last portion, denoted by d'', of the last row is $d'' = d'$ if $(l \cdot r_{med} \bmod \lceil \frac{l \cdot r_{med}}{p} \rceil = 0)$ holds; it is $d'' = (l \cdot r_{med} \bmod \lceil \frac{l \cdot r_{med}}{p} \rceil) \bmod d$ otherwise.

The number of columns denoted by n can be calculated as

$$n = \lceil \frac{l \cdot r_{med}}{p \cdot d} \rceil \tag{4.2}$$

Now, one can view super-clip data again as a $(p \times n)$ matrix where each element except the following ones is a portion of size d (see Figure 4.1). The elements of last column may contain portions of size d' which are less than d. The final elements of the last row may be empty and the last non-empty element of the last row may contain less than d bits. We assume the size of each column c is stored in variable col_size[c].

Modern disk drives allow various ways for managing the defective disk blocks to be specified[1]. We assume the following model for defect management. A number of spare sectors are reserved on each track. If the number of defective sectors on a track exceeds the number of spare sectors, the track is not used and slipping [14] is used to reorder logical addresses (i.e., the logical blocks that would map to the bad track and ones after it are "slipped" by one track). This defect management model yields a fixed transfer rate per zone even if there are defective disk segments.

5. Horizontal Partitioning

We present a scheme that partitions the super-clip matrix horizontally among zones in the sense that a group of zones stores a number of logically consecutive bits of the super-clip data. That is, a partition consists of as many

[1] Let x and y be two positive integers. If $x \geq y^2$, then $\lceil \frac{x}{\lceil \frac{x}{y} \rceil} \rceil$ is equal to y. To prove this claim, let us select x as $y^2 + k$, $k \geq 0$. Since $\lceil \frac{x}{\lceil \frac{x}{y} \rceil} \rceil \geq \lceil \frac{x}{\frac{x}{y}+1} \rceil$ holds, it is sufficient to show that $\frac{x}{\frac{x}{y}+1}$ is greater than $y - 1$. Suppose that x is equal to $y^2 + k$, however $\frac{x}{\frac{x}{y}+1} \leq y - 1$. That is, $\frac{y^2+k}{y+\frac{k}{y}+1} \leq y - 1$. This implies that $0 \leq -\frac{k}{y} - 1$ holds. Since k and y cannot be negative, this is a contradiction. Thus, if $x \geq y^2$, then $\lceil \frac{x}{\lceil \frac{x}{y} \rceil} \rceil = y$.

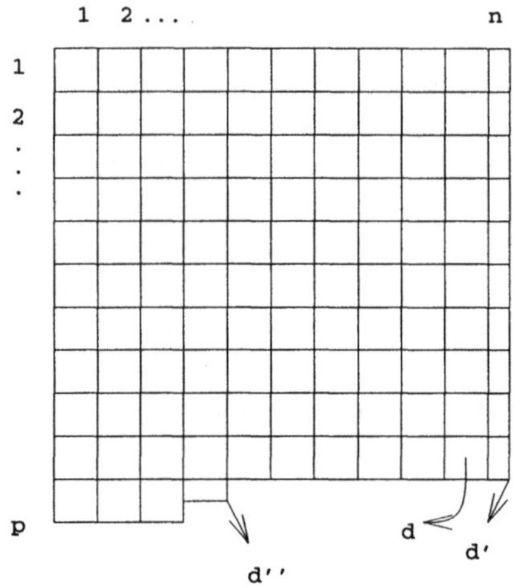

Fig. 4.1. A super-clip matrix where the non-empty elements of the nth column contains d' bits, $d' < d$ and the last non-empty element of the pth row contains d'' bits, $d'' < d$.

consecutive bits of the super-clip data as the storage capacity of one or more consecutive zones. The scheme stores each partition on the disk with the matrix-based storage allocation scheme in accordance with the $(p \times n)$ super-clip matrix. That is, if a partition contains portions of several consecutive columns of the $(p \times n)$ super-clip matrix, then the portion belonging to the column with the smallest index is stored first, the portion belonging to the column with the second smallest index is stored next, and so on. Let C_j denote the storage capacity of the jth zone. Suppose that each partition corresponds to one zone. In this case, the initial C_1 consecutive bits of the super-clip data are stored in the first zone, the next C_2 consecutive bits in the second zone and so on (see Figure 5.1).

5.1 Storage Allocation

Since a column is partitioned among groups of zones, retrieving each column will require disk head to be moved from one group of zones to another to retrieve the entire column. The sum of seek times from one group of zones to another during retrieval of a column will be less than $2 \cdot t_{seek}$. Furthermore, the overhead of rotational delay during retrieval of a column will be less than $k \cdot t_{rot}$ where k is the number of partitions. A simple partitioning method is to make each zone a partition. However, this may not be effective on disks of which number of zones is high. A more effective method is to select the number of partitions based on the value of $\frac{d}{r_{med}}$ such that $2 \cdot t_{seek} + k \cdot t_{rot} \leq \frac{d}{r_{med}}$.

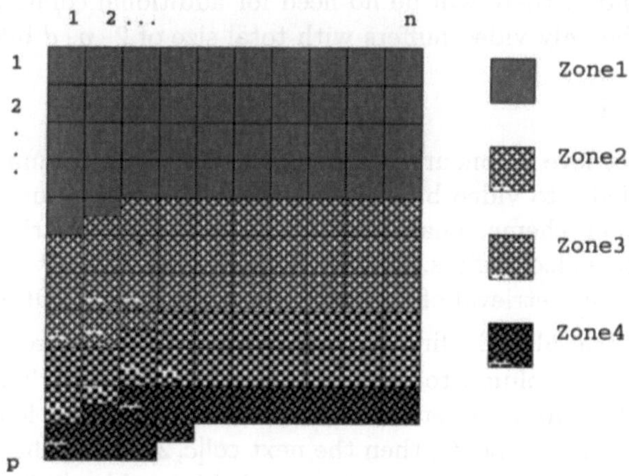

Fig. 5.1. Horizontal partitioning of a super-clip matrix.

Given a partitioning, let $\mathsf{col}[c, j]$ denote the portion of the cth column stored within j^{th} zone and z denote the number of zones. The portion of each column c except the nth column that can be stored on disk, denoted by $\sum_{j=1}^{z} \mathsf{col}[c, j]$, must satisfy the following condition such that the next consecutive d bits for all of the p streams can be loaded into the video buffers within the time d bits are consumed by a stream:

$$\sum_{j=1}^{z} \frac{\mathsf{col}[c, j]}{r_{disk_j}} + 2 \cdot t_{seek} + k \cdot t_{rot} \leq \frac{d}{r_{med}} \tag{5.1}$$

The portion of the nth column that can be stored on disk must satisfy

$$\sum_{j=1}^{z} \frac{\mathsf{col}[n, j]}{r_{disk_j}} + 2 \cdot t_{seek} + k \cdot t_{rot} \leq \frac{d'}{r_{med}} \tag{5.2}$$

For arbitrarily large values of p and d, it is possible that $\sum_{j=1}^{z} \mathsf{col}[c, j]$ is less than the size of the column (i.e., less than $\mathsf{col\_size}[c]$). In this case, the remaining portion of the cth column needs to be stored in buffer. If a portion of the cth column is stored in buffer, we refer to the buffer space that stores the final portion of the column as the *column buffer* of the cth column denoted by $\mathsf{col\_buf}_c$. The size of each column buffer denoted by $|\mathsf{col\_buf}_c|$ is equal to $\mathsf{col\_size}[c] - \sum_{j=1}^{z} \mathsf{col}[c, j]$.

Once the super-clip data is partitioned, the portion of each column that could have been stored in each zone if the disk bandwidth was infinite is determined and this information is stored in $\mathsf{col}[id, zone]$. Then, for each column c, Conditions 5.1 and 5.2 can be used to determine the amount of the column that must be stored on disk and $\mathsf{col\_buf}_c$ in buffer space. For some values of p and d, there will be no need for additional column buffers. That is there will be only video buffers with total size of $2 \cdot p \cdot d$ bits.

5.2 Retrieval

In order to retrieve p concurrent streams, consecutive columns of super-clip data are loaded into video buffers similar to the retrieval under the matrix-based allocation scheme. That is, let t be time when the retrieval of a column is started into video buffers. If this column is not the nth column, then at time $t + \frac{d}{r_{med}}$ the retrieval of the next column is started. Otherwise, at time $t + \frac{d'}{r_{med}}$ the retrieval of the first column is started. The difference is as follows. Let c be the next column to be loaded into video buffers. The next $\mathsf{col}[c, 1]$ bits of the cth column are retrieved from the first zone and loaded into video buffers. If $\mathsf{col}[c, 2] > 0$ holds, then the next $\mathsf{col}[c, 2]$ bits of the cth column are retrieved from the second zone and appended into video buffers and so on. If $|\mathsf{col\_buf}|_c > 0$ holds, then the last consecutive bits of the column are copied from the column buffer and appended into video buffers. The proof of the claim that it is possible to retrieve p concurrent streams for any value of p and d directly follows from the fact that the portion of each column that is stored on disk is selected such that its retrieval time is less than $\frac{d}{r_{med}}$. Furthermore, we need to show that none of the streams will starve while the first column is retrieved. Since Conditions 5.1 and 5.2 are satisfied, the retrieval of the $(n-1)^{th}$ column takes at most $\frac{d}{r_{med}}$ units of time and the retrieval of the nth column takes at most $\frac{d'}{r_{med}}$ units of time. Thus, at the time when the retrieval of the nth column is finished, there will be at least $d - \frac{d'}{r_{med}} \cdot r_{med} + d' = d$ bits. Therefore, none of the streams will starve during the retrieval of the first column.

Example 5.1. Consider a Seagate ST12550ND Baracuda 2 (2 GB) disk with the following characteristics: 19 surfaces, 2707 cylinders, $r_{disk_{max}} = 56.5$ Mbps, $r_{disk_{min}} = 34.3$ Mbps, $t_{seek} = 19$ ms, $t_{settle} = 1$ ms and $t_{rot} = 8.3$ ms. Let the size of super-clip be equal to the disk capacity. The buffer requirement for different values of p, k and d are gathered by running a program which calculates the total buffer requirement over values of d between 50 Kb and 3.5Mb in multiples of 50 Kb, values of k between 1 and 10 and values p between 22 to 29. Table 5.1 illustrates the minimum buffer requirement for each p over different runs. □

6. Vertical Partitioning

The previous scheme partitioned the super-clip matrix horizontally among the zones in order to exploit the varying transfer rates of different zones. We

Table 5.1.

p	Buffer Requirement
22	391 KB when $k = 1$ and $d = 50$ Kb
23	734 KB when $k = 1$ and $d = 50$ Kb
24	1.9 MB when $k = 2$ and $d = 300$ Kb
25	2.9 MB when $k = 3$ and $d = 450$ Kb
26	4.9 MB when $k = 3$ and $d = 700$ Kb
27	9.4 MB when $k = 5$ and $d = 1350$ Kb
28	22.6 MB when $k = 7$ and $d = 2400$ Kb
29	41.6 MB when $k = 7$ and $d = 3150$ Kb

now present a scheme—*vertical partitioning* algorithm that partitions the $p \times n$ super-clip matrix vertically among the consecutive zones in the sense that each zone stores a number of consecutive columns (the first and last column stored within a zone may be partial). The main difference between the horizontal and vertical schemes is that in the former, data is laid out such that the data retrieval from disk for p streams can be done by k sequential retrievals (k is the number of horizontal partitions) whereas in the latter, data is laid out such that the data retrieval from disk is done by one sequential retrieval similar to the case under the matrix-based allocation scheme. Furthermore, the vertical partitioning algorithm exploits modifications to the "next" relation of the consecutive tracks.

Disks have a number of surfaces (e.g.,15, 21). Until now, we assumed that a zone is a number of consecutive cylinders, namely a zone assumed to span all the disk surfaces. We refer to this definition as one-dimensional one. In this section, we redefine a zone to be a *two-dimensional* structure which yields lower buffering requirements for the vertical partitioning algorithm. The definition of a one-dimensional zone is a special case of the definition of a two-dimensional zone. Now, suppose that we grouped the surfaces such that there are b groups (i.e., if zones are one-dimensional then b is one). A two-dimensional zone is a number of consecutive tracks on a group of surfaces. We refer to the two-dimensional zone which is the part of the jth one-dimensional zone on a given group s of surfaces as the $[j, s]^{th}$ zone, and denote its storage capacity by $C_j[s]$. Two-dimensional zoning can be implemented either by modifying the geometry of a disk or simply by data layout. If two-dimensional zones are implemented via the first approach, during the retrieval of data one can still take advantage of the features supported by disk drives such as read-ahead buffering. For example, the draft of SCSI-2 standard supports a bit to define whether to allocate progressive addresses to all logical blocks within a cylinder prior to allocating addresses on the next cylinder (i.e., $b = 1$); or to allocate progressive addresses to all logical blocks on a surface prior to allocating addresses on the next surface (i.e., b is equal to the number of surfaces).

The capacity of any two two-dimensional zones that share the same cylinders may be different even if they span the same number of surfaces. This is because of the existence of defective disk tracks. Our model of defect management for disks implies that the transfer rates of two two-dimensional zones that share the same cylinders will be the same. Thus, for any s, $1 \leq s \leq b$, we denote the transfer rate of the $[j, s]^{th}$ zone by r_{disk_j}. Let z be the number zones. We assume that for $1 \leq j < z$, the zones $[j, s]$ and $[(j+1), s]$ are consecutive as well as the zones $[z, s]$ and $[1, (((s+1) \bmod b)+1)]$. Furthermore, the sum of capacities of all the two-dimensional zones that share the same cylinders is equal to the capacity of the one-dimensional zone that spans over the same cylinders, namely, $C_j = \sum_{s=1}^{b} C_j[s]$ holds.

Let k be the smallest integer that satisfies $l \cdot r_{med} \leq \sum_{j=1}^{k} C_j$. The vertical partitioning algorithm stores each column contiguously one after another similar to the matrix-based storage allocation scheme. The initial section of the column-major representation is stored on the first group of surfaces starting from the outermost zone, the next section is stored on the second group of surfaces starting from the outermost zone, and so on. The differences are as follows. First, during data retrieval, more than one column (i.e., more than $p \cdot d$ bits) may be retrieved from a zone of which the transfer rate is greater than $p \cdot r_{med}$ in the time a stream consumes d bits (i.e., $\frac{d}{r_{med}}$ units of time). If this is the case, this additional amount of data is used to compensate for the transfer rates of zones which are less than $p \cdot r_{med}$. Thus, the total size of the video buffers may be larger than $2 \cdot p \cdot d$. Second, a portion of some of the columns may not be stored on disk but in buffer space in a column buffer. The size of each column buffer depends on the values of p and d, and may be different for each column.

6.1 Size of Buffers

We now need to calculate the size of the video buffers. The set of video buffers is a first in first out buffer. Each column is appended at the tail of the buffer while p streams consume data from the head of the buffer. The retrieval starts from the first column which stored at the outermost zone; and the consumption starts $\frac{d}{r_{med}}$ units of time after the beginning of the retrieval. While the transfer rates of the consecutive zones are greater than $p \cdot r_{med}$, the amount that can be retrieved from disk will be more than the amount consumed. Let $h[s]$ be the last zone for which $r_{disk_{h[s]}} > p \cdot r_{med}$. Thus, the maximum extra amount that can be retrieved is

$$\sum_{j=1}^{h[s]} C_j[s] - p \cdot r_{med} \cdot \sum_{j=1}^{h[s]} \frac{C_j[s]}{r_{disk_j}} \tag{6.1}$$

In the above equation, the first term is the amount of data stored in the zones of which transfer rate is greater than the consumption rate $p \cdot r_{med}$.

The second term is the amount of data consumed by all the streams of the super-clip in the time it takes to retrieve data from those zones.

Now, let $e[s]$ be the last zone in the sth group of surfaces. The difference between the amount of data that will be consumed within the time, which is the sum of the time to retrieve the super-clip data stored in zones of which transfer rates are less than or equal to the consumption rate and the time to position the disk head from the $e[s]^{th}$ zone to the first zone, and the amount of the data stored in zones of which transfer rates are less than or equal to the consumption rate is

$$p \cdot r_{med} \cdot \left(\sum_{j=(h[s]+1)}^{e[s]} \frac{C_j[s]}{r_{disk_j}} + t_{seek} \right) - \sum_{j=(h[s]+1)}^{e[s]} C_j[s] \qquad (6.2)$$

In the above equation, the first term is the amount of data that will be consumed in the time it takes to retrieve the super-clip data stored in the zones of which the transfer rate is less than or equal to the consumption rate $p \cdot r_{med}$ plus the time it takes to move the disk arm from the innermost zone of the group of surfaces to the outermost zone of the next group of surfaces. The second term is the amount of data in these zones.

Suppose that there is only one group of surfaces (i.e., b=1). Equation 6.2 is equal to the amount of buffer space required to compensate for the zone transfer rates which are less than the consumption rate $p \cdot r_{med}$. Equation 6.1 is the extra amount that can be retrieved from zones of which transfer rates are greater than the consumption rate. If this amount is greater than the amount in Equation 6.2, then the extra amount that needs to be retrieved from zones of which transfer rates are greater than the consumption rate is only equal to Equation 6.2. Otherwise, all the extra amount is retrieved into the video buffers but also additional column buffers are used to compensate for the remaining bits that need to be consumed but cannot be retrieved from disk in the time it takes to consume all the data retrieved from disk. Thus, the size of the video buffers need to be at least equal to the minimum of these two equations. In the case when there may be more than one group of surfaces (i.e., $b \geq 1$), then the size of the video buffers needs to be at least equal to the the maximum of this value among all the surface groups. Furthermore, additional $p \cdot d$ space is allocated since the consumption is allowed only $\frac{d}{r_{med}}$ units of time after the retrieval has initiated and another $p \cdot d$ bits are allocated since the retrieval of the next column is initiated when the empty buffer space is at least equal to the size of the next column to be retrieved. Therefore, the size of the video buffers is

$$\max_s \{ \min \{ (\sum_{j=1}^{h[s]} C_j[s] - p \cdot r_{med} \cdot \sum_{j=1}^{h[s]} \frac{C_j[s]}{r_{disk_j}}),$$
$$(p \cdot r_{med} \cdot (\sum_{j=(h[s]+1)}^{e[s]} \frac{C_j[s]}{r_{disk_j}} + t_{seek}) - \sum_{j=(h[s]+1)}^{e[s]} C_j[s]) \} \} + 2 \cdot p \cdot d \qquad (6.3)$$

If there are groups of surfaces for which Equation 6.1 is less than Equation 6.2, increasing the size of the video buffers and retrieving more data than needed from the zones of which transfer rates are greater than the consumption rate will not suffice to compensate for the zone transfer rates which are less than the consumption rate. We examine two solutions for such groups of surfaces. The first solution is based on column buffers. For such groups of surfaces, some of the columns or portions of the columns that are to be stored in innermost zones need to be stored in column buffers. The amount of data that needs to be maintained in column buffers for such a group of surfaces is the difference between Equation 6.1 and Equation 6.2. Thus, the total size of the column buffers will be

$$\sum_{s=1}^{b} \max \quad \{(p \cdot r_{med} \cdot (\sum_{j=(h[s]+1)}^{e[s]} \frac{C_j[s]}{r_{disk_j}} + t_{seek}) - \sum_{j=(h[s]+1)}^{e[s]} C_j[s] - \sum_{j=1}^{h[s]} C_j[s] + p \cdot r_{med} \cdot \sum_{j=1}^{h[s]} \frac{C_j[s]}{r_{disk_j}}), 0\} \tag{6.4}$$

The second solution can only be used if the retrieval time of the the entire super-clip is less than or equal to the time it takes a stream to consume $(\frac{1}{p})^{th}$ of the super-clip, namely if the following condition is satisfied:

$$\sum_{s=1}^{b} \sum_{j=1}^{k} \frac{C_j[s]}{r_{disk_j}} + b \cdot t_{seek} \leq \frac{l}{p} \tag{6.5}$$

We refer to the values of p for which there is no need for column buffers as *permissible.* The permissible values of p can be derived from Condition 6.5 as

$$p \leq \frac{l}{\sum_{s=1}^{b} \sum_{j=1}^{k} \frac{C_j[s]}{r_{disk_j}} + b \cdot t_{seek}} \tag{6.6}$$

If p is permissible, then there is no need for additional column buffers. The main idea behind the second solution is to increase the size of the video buffers such that the extra amount that can be retrieved from a group of surfaces for which Equation 6.1 is greater than Equation 6.2 is used for another group of surfaces for which Equation 6.1 is less than Equation 6.2. The simple approach in this case is to store the initial section of the column-major super-clip matrix into groups of surfaces for which Equation 6.1 is greater than Equation 6.2. This approach increases the size of the video buffers by the amount in Equation 6.4. Thus, the buffer requirement of these two approaches will be the same.

The buffer requirement of the second approach can be reduced by careful pairing of the groups of surfaces. The idea is as follows. If there is a group b_1 of surfaces for which Equation 6.1 is greater than Equation 6.2 and another group b_2 of surfaces for which Equation 6.1 is less than Equation 6.2, such

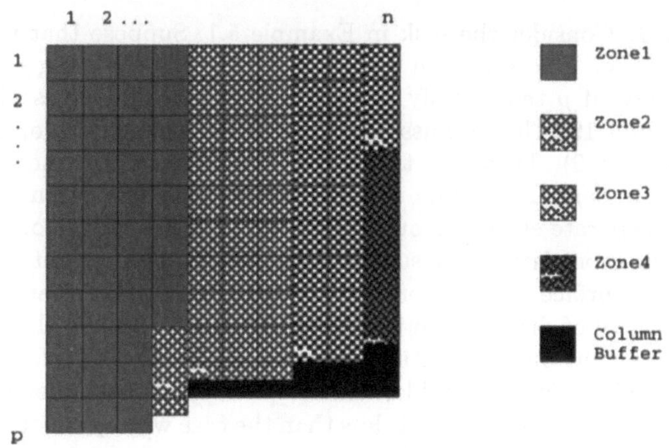

Fig. 6.1. Vertical partitioning of a super-clip matrix.

that the retrieval time of the super-clip data stored in both groups is equal to the consumption time of this amount of data, consecutive bits of column-major representation of the super-clip data can be stored in b_1 and b_2 to reduce the size of the video buffer.

6.2 Data Retrieval

For the permissible values of p, if the second approach is used, then the storage algorithm is nothing more than matrix-based allocation scheme in which the concept of consecutive zones is as defined. However, the data retrieval is not periodic. It is driven by the available space in the super-clip buffers. If there is enough empty space in the super-clip buffers to hold the next column, the retrieval of the next column is initiated.

If the first approach is used, a column is either entirely on disk, or some portion of the column is on disk and its remaining portion is in the corresponding column buffer. Figure 6.1 illustrates the partitioning of a super-clip matrix in the case that there is only one group of surfaces. If p is selected as $p = \lfloor \frac{r_{disk_{min}}}{r_{med}} \rfloor$, then the algorithm reduces to the matrix-based storage allocation scheme in which case there is no need for additional buffer space.

The data retrieval under the first approach is also driven by the available space in the super-clip buffers. If there is enough empty space in the super-clip buffers to hold the next column, the retrieval of the next column is initiated. The retrieval differs from the second approach as follows. Let c be the next column to be loaded into super-clip buffers. If $|\mathsf{col\_buf}|_c = 0$ holds, then the portions of c which are on disk are retrieved from disk and loaded into super-clip buffers and the remaining portions of c are copied from the column buffer $\mathsf{col\_buf}_c$ into the super-clip buffers.

Example 6.1. Consider the disk in Example 5.1. Suppose that there are no defective tracks. The graph in Figure 6.2 plots the buffering requirements for the values of p that satisfy Equation 4.1 when the values of b changes between 1 and 19. The permissible values of p are less than or equal to 30 (see Equation 6.6). These are the values of p under which there is no need for column buffers. The buffer requirement is minimum when each surface becomes a separate surface group (i.e., $b = 19$). This verifies our claim that changing the geometry of disk such that two tracks are consecutive if they are on the same surface on two consecutive cylinders (rather than the conventional geometry of disks where two tracks are consecutive if they are on the same cylinder but on consecutive surfaces) yields better performance. Furthermore, while p is permissible, the rate of increase in buffer requirement with the the number of streams is less than the case when p is not permissible. For example, if the basic matrix-based allocation scheme is used, then the example disk can support at most 22 MPEG-1 streams, whereas the vertical partitioning algorithm can support 30 MPEG-1 streams on the same disk at a cost of 7 MB of additional buffer space. This is approximately 36% increase in the number of streams. □

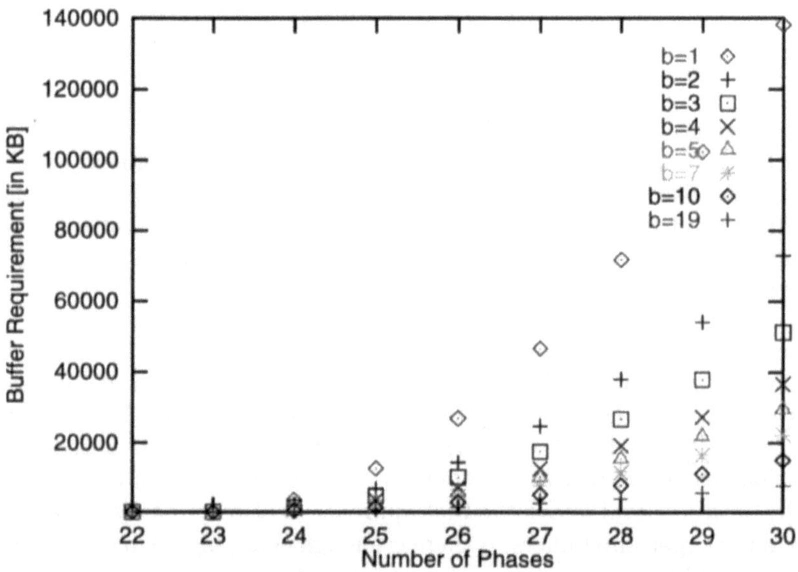

Fig. 6.2. Buffer requirement versus streams

7. Related Work

A number of storage schemes for continuous retrieval of video and audio data have been proposed in the literature [2], [12], [11], [4], [15], [5], [13], [6]. Among these, [2], [12], [4], [13], [6] address the problem of satisfying multiple concurrent requests for the retrieval of multimedia objects residing on a disk. These schemes are similar in spirit to the simple scheme that we presented in Section 2. In each of the schemes, concurrent requests are serviced in rounds retrieving successive portions of multimedia objects and performing multiple seeks in each round. *Admission control* tests based on computed buffer requirements for multiple requests are employed in order to determine the feasibility of additional requests with available resources. The schemes presented in [2], [12], [4] do not attempt to reduce disk latency. In [13], the authors show that the CSCAN policy for disk scheduling is superior for retrieving continuous media data in comparison to a policy in which requests with the earliest deadlines are serviced first (EDF) [7]. In [6], the authors propose a greedy disk scheduling algorithm in order to reduce both seek time and rotational latency.

In [15], in order to reduce buffer requirements, an audio record is stored on optical disk as a sequence of data blocks separated by gaps. Furthermore, in order to save disk space, the authors derive conditions for merging different audio records. In [11], similar to [15], the authors define an interleaved storage organization for multimedia data that permits the merging of time-dependent multimedia objects for efficient disk space utilization. However, they adopt a weaker condition for merging different media strands, a consequence of which is an increase in the read-ahead and buffering requirements.

In [5], the authors use parallelism in order to support the display of high resolution of video data that have high bandwidth requirements. In order to make up for the low I/O bandwidths of current disk technology, a multimedia object is declustered across several disk drives, and the aggregate bandwidth of multiple disks is utilized.

8. Research Issues

In this section, we discuss some of the research issues in the area of storage and retrieval of continuous media data that remain to be addressed.

8.1 Load Balancing and Fault Tolerance Issues

So far, we assumed that continuous media clips are stored on a single disk. However, in general, continuous media servers may have multiple disks on which continuous media clips may need to be stored. One approach to the problem is to simply partition the set of continuous media clips among the various disks and then use the schemes that we described earlier in order to store the clips on each of the disks. One problem with the approach is that if requests for continuous media clips are not distributed uniformly across the disks, then certain disks may end up idling, while others may have too much load and so some requests may not be accepted. For example, if clip C_1 is stored on disk D_1 and clip C_2 is stored on disk D_2, then if there are more requests for C_1 and fewer for C_2, then the bandwidth of disk D_2 would not be fully utilized. A solution to this problem is *striping*. By storing the first half of C_1 and C_2 on D_1 and the second half of the clips on D_2, we can ensure that the workload is evenly distributed between D_1 and D_2.

Striping continuous media clips across disks involves a number of research issues. One is the granularity of striping for the various clips. The other is that striping complicates the implementation of VCR operations. For example, consider a scenario in which every stream is paused just before data for the stream is to be retrieved from a "certain" disk D_1. If all the streams were to be resumed simultaneously, then the resumption of the last stream for which data is retrieved from D_1 may be delayed by an unacceptable amount of time. Replicating the continuous media clips across multiple disks could help in balancing the load on disks as well as reducing response times in case disks get overloaded.

Replication of the clips across disks is also useful to achieve fault-tolerance in case disks fail. One option is to use disk mirroring to recover from disk failures; another would be to use parity disks [3]. The potential problem with both of these approaches is that they are wasteful in both storage space as well as bandwidth. We need alternative schemes that effectively utilize disk bandwidth, and at the same time ensure that data for a stream can continue to be retrieved at the required rate in case of a disk failure. Finally, an interesting research issue is to vary the size of buffers allocated for streams dynamically, based on the number of streams being concurrently retrieved from disk at any point in time.

8.2 Storage Issues

Neither storing clips contiguously, nor the matrix-based storage scheme for continuous media clips is suitable in case there are frequent additions, deletions and modifications. The reason for this is that both schemes are very rigid and could lead to fragmentation. As a result, we need to consider storage schemes that decompose the storage space on disks into pages and then map various continuous media clips to a sequence of non-contiguous pages. Even though the above scheme would reduce fragmentation, since pages containing a clip may be distributed randomly across the disk, disk latency would increase resulting in increased buffer requirements. An important research issue is to determine the ideal page size for clips that would keep both space utilization high as well as disk latency low.

Another important issue to consider is the storage of continuous media clips on tertiary storage (e.g., tapes, CD-ROMs). Since continuous media data tends to be voluminous, it may be necessary (in order to reduce costs) to store it on CD-ROMs and tapes, which are much cheaper than disks. Techniques for retrieving continuous media data from tertiary storage is an interesting and challenging problem. For example, tapes have high seek times and so we may wish to use disks to cache initial portions of clips in order to keep response times low.

8.3 Data Retrieval Issues

The scheme we presented in Section 2. yields low response times but has significantly large buffer requirements. The alternative scheme presented in Section 3., on the other hand, has much higher response times but it eliminates disk latency completely and has low buffer requirements. Further research along the lines of [9], [13], [6] must be carried out in order to reduce disk seek and rotational latency when servicing stream requests while keeping response times low.

In the simple scheme presented in Section 2, a separate buffer is maintained for each stream. Thus, it may be possible that two requests for the same clip retrieve the same data in their own buffers; thus, resulting in disk bandwidth being wasted. A solution that utilizes the disk bandwidth more effectively is one in which streams share a global pool of buffer pages. Furthermore, data belonging to a clip is retrieved into the global pool only if the data is not already contained in it[10]. An important research issue is the buffer page replacement policy. For example, a *least recently used* (LRU) policy may be unsuitable if another stream, in the near future, needs access to the least recently used page. It may instead be more suitable to replace a page that has been accessed by a stream and does not need to be accessed by any other streams. Thus, a buffer page replacement policy that takes into account streams being serviced would result in better performance.

Also, in the extension of the simple scheme to handle clips with different rate requirements, a common period was used to determine buffer sizes for streams. In order to maximize the utilization of disk bandwidth as well as memory, an effective method to determine the common period based on the expected workload, and schemes to dynamically vary the common period if the actual workload is very different from the expected workload, need to be developed.

In the schemes we developed, we made the pessimistic assumption that the disk transfer rate r_{disk} is equal to the transfer rate of the innermost track. By taking into account the disk transfer rate of the tracks where continuous media clips are stored, we could substantially reduce buffer requirements. Also, in our work, we have not taken into account the fact that disks are not perfect. For example, disks have bad sectors that are remapped to alternate locations. Furthermore, due to thermal expansion, tables storing information on how long and how much power to apply on a particular seek, need to be recalibrated. Typically, this takes 500-800 milliseconds and occur once every 15-30 minutes. Finally, in this paper, we have only considered continuous media requests. We need a general-purpose system that would have the ability to service both continuous (e.g., video, audio) as well as non-continuous (e.g., text) media requests. Such a system would have to give a high priority to retrieving continuous media data, and use *slack* time in order to service non-continuous media requests.

9. Concluding Remarks

In this paper, we considered two approaches to retrieving continuous media data from disks. In the first approach, response times for servicing requests are low, but a high latency is incurred, resulting in significantly large buffer requirements. The second approach eliminates random disk head seeks and thus reduces buffer requirements but may result in increased response times. We presented simple schemes for implementing pause, fast-forward and rewind operations on continuous media streams (in case the data is video data). Finally, we outlined future research issues in the storage and retrieval of continuous media data.

References

[1] Scsi-2 draft proposed by american national standard of accredited standards comittee x3 based upon ansi x3.131-1986. Technical report, ANSI.

[2] D. P. Anderson, Y. Osawa, and R. Govindan. A file system for continuous media. *ACM Transactions on Computer Systems*, 10(4):311–337, November 1992.

[3] G. R. Ganger, R. Y. Hou B. L. Worthington, and Y. N. Patt. Disk arrays: High-performance, high-reliability storage subsystems. *Computer*, 27(3):30–36, March 1994.

[4] J. Gemmell and S. Christodoulakis. Principles of delay-sensitive multimedia data storage and retrieval. *ACM Transactions on Information Systems*, 10(1):51–90, January 1992.

[5] S. Ghandeharizadeh and L. Ramos. Continuous retrieval of multimedia data using parallelism. *IEEE Transactions on Knowledge and Data Engineering*, 5(4):658–669, August 1993.

[6] H. M. Vin A. Goyal and P. Goyal. Algorithms for designing large-scale multimedia servers. *Computer Communication*, 1994.

[7] C. L. Liu and J. Layland. Scheduling algorithms for multiprogramming in a hard real-time environment. *Journal of the ACM*, 20(1):46–61, 1973.

[8] B. Özden, A. Biliris, R. Rastogi, and A. Silberschatz. A low-cost storage server for movie on demand databases. In *Proceedings of the Twentieth International Conference on Very Large Databases, Santiago*, September 1994.

[9] B. Özden, R. Rastogi, and A. Silberschatz. *Fellini*—a file system for continuous media. Technical Report 113880-941028-30, AT&T Bell Laboratories, Murray Hill, 1994.

[10] B. Özden, R. Rastogi, A. Silberschatz, and C. Martin. Demand paging for movie-on-demand servers. Technical Report 113880-941028-39, AT&T Bell Laboratories, Murray Hill, 1994.

[11] P. V. Rangan and H. M. Vin. Efficient storage techniques for digital continuous multimedia. *IEEE Transactions on Knowledge and Data Engineering*, 5(4):564–573, August 1993.

[12] P. V. Rangan, H. M. Vin, and S. Ramanathan. Designing an on-demand multimedia service. *IEEE Communications Magazine*, 1(1):56–64, July 1992.

[13] A. L. N. Reddy and J. C. Wyllie. I/O issues in a multimedia system. *Computer*, 27(3):69–74, March 1994.

[14] C. Ruemmler and J. Wilkes. An introduction to disk drive modeling. *Computer*, 27(3):17–27, March 1994.

[15] C. Yu, W. Sun, D. Bitton, Q. Yang, R. Bruno, and J. Tullis. Efficient placement of audio data on optical disks for real-time applications. *Communications of the ACM*, 32(7):862–871, July 1989.

Querying Multimedia Databases in SQL

Sherry Marcus

21st Century Technologies, Inc. 1903 Ware Road, Falls Church, VA 22043

Summary. Although numerous multimedia systems exist in the commercial market today, relatively little work has been done on developing the mathematical foundations of multimedia technology. [5], [6] have taken some initial steps toward the development of a theoretical basis for multimedia information systems. They define a mathematical model of a media-instance. A media-instance may be thought of as "glue" residing on top of a specific physical media-representation (such as video, audio, documents, etc.) Using this "glue", it is possible to define a general purpose logical query language to query multimedia data. This glue consists of a set of "states" (e.g. video frames, audio tracks, etc.) and "features", together with relationships between states and/or features. A structured multimedia database system imposes a certain mathematical structure on the set of features/states. Using this notion of a structure, they are able to define indexing structures for processing queries, methods to relax queries when answers do not exist to those queries, as well as sound, complete and terminating procedures to answer such queries (and their relaxations, when appropriate). Using the [5], [6] work on multimedia database integration systems, we show how their logical based query language can be redefined as an SQL based query language. As there are numerous commercial SQL database systems, a wide and diverse population of users may accesss the Marcus and Subrahmanian work using their SQL interface. Also, there has been a great deal of study of query optimization of SQL based languages[8]. Such optimizations can be applied to "SQL version" of the Marcus and Subrahmanian system.

1. Introduction

Though there has been a good deal of work in recent years on multimedia, there has been relatively little work on multimedia information systems. In [5], [6], the authors have developed a theoretical framework for multimedia database systems. They show how, given a set of media sources, each of which contains information represented in a way that is (possibly) unique to that medium, it is possible to define general-purpose access structures that represent the relevant "features" of the data represented in that medium. In simple terms, any media source (e.g. video) has an affiliated set of possible features. An instance of the media source (e.g. a single video clip) possesses some subset (possibly empty) of these features. Thus, a feature may be "Taurus" or "Mustang". The features associated with a media source may have properties of two types – those that are independent of any single media-instance, and those that are dependent upon a particular media-instance. Thus, for instance, the property `price(taurus,15k)` is true and is independent of any single video-clip. In contrast, the feature `color(taurus,blue)` may depend upon a particular video-clip. [5] develop a general scheme that, given a set of media-sources, and a set of instances of those media-sources, builds additional data structures "on top" of the physical representation of data in that medium. This physical representation allows for the definition of suitable query languages, and database query processing algorithms.

In this paper we present the Marcus and Subrahmanian logical query language as an SQL based language and show that they are equivalent. Hence, we are then able to conclude that the indexing structures for processing queries, methods to relax queries when answers do not exist to those queries, as well as sound, complete and terminating procedures to answer such queries (and their relaxations, when appropriate) may be accessed in SQL as well. Therefore, this greatly expands the user population who may access this system. As well as the query optimization techniques available in SQL[8]. Thus, the Marcus and Subrahmanian framework is not only a logic-based framework, but an SQL-based framework as well. We first present the basic definitions and ideas as outlined in Marcus and Subrahmanian. Suppose a person is interested in purchasing a new car and has access to a mulitmedia database about cars. This database has audio/video, image, and textual information. Below is a sample list of queries a user might want to make to such a system.

1. What kinds of cars can I buy for about 12,000 ?
2. What is the name of the dealer in the state of Virginia who has the cheapest sticker price for a 1994 Ford Taurus?
3. Can I see a video clip of the 1994 Ford Mustang?
4. How much and what are the options of a 1994 Ford Mustang?
5. Describe the basic engine features of the 1994 Ford Taurus.
6. How much is insurance in Northern Virginia for a 1994 Ford Taurus?

Responding to these queries involves multimedia access to audio, video, document, (and possibly) other databases. This media must be indexed in such a way so as to answer queries of the kind listed above. Methods to store and identify features for these diverse media are explored in more depth in [5], [6].

In the next section, we describe a small multimedia database system about automobiles. This system contains video/audio/textual and imagery information pertaining to the newest models of the Ford Taurus and the Ford Mustang. In the subsequent sections, we define the basic Marcus and Subrahmanian data structures and query language. We then use their framework to define an SQL based system.

In many instances, such as large supermarkets, internet services, and real estate shopping, access to a multimedia database systems may expedite whatever decision a user may wish to make. In the following example, we have a collection of a few documents of concerning automobiles. This database contains standard audio/video/text frames containing information about the Ford Taurus and the Ford Mustang.

2. Automobile Multimedia Database Example

1. **Video:** We have eight video-frames $v1, ..., v8$.
   - Frame $v1$ is a picture of a Ford Taurus.
   - Frame $v2$ is a picture of an engine block of the Taurus
   - Frame $v3$ is is a picture shot from the driver's seat of a Ford Mustang.
   - Frame $v4$ is a picture of stereo and cellular phone options.
   - Frame $v5$ is a picture of car alarms and airbag options.
   - Frame $v6$ shows a closeup of the dashboard of a Taurus with all options.
   - Frame $v7$ is a picture the Taurus' dashboard without options.
   - Frame $v8$ is a picture of a mustang.
2. **Audio:** There is one audio-frame $a1$ describing the overall features of the Taurus.
3. **Documents:** There are four documents $d1, d2, d3, d4$.
   - Document $d1$ describes the sticker prices for the Ford Taurus in the Virginia area.
   - Document $d2$ describes the basic specifications for the Mustang
   - Document $d3$ describes optional features of the Mustang.
   - Document $d4$ is a list of average insurance rates for the Ford Taurus in Northern Virginia.

At this point, we may now present the notion of a media instance. A media instance is the "glue" which resides on top the the physical media. The definition of media instance is independent of how the actual media is stored. (Using this technology, Marcus and Subrahmanian are able to define a logical query language and algorithms for processing such queries. The notion of an optimal answer is developed as well. An optimal answer to a query is, informally speaking, a solution to a (possibly) relaxed version of the query – without relaxing the query any more than absolutely necessary.) A media-instance (formally defined below) consists of the actual data represented in the medium, together with a certain 8-tuple which constitutes the desired glue. A *media-instance* is an 8-tuple

$$(\mathcal{S}, \mathbf{fe}, \mathtt{ATR}, \lambda, \Re, \mathcal{F}, \mathbf{Var}_1, \mathbf{Var}_2)$$

where:

- $\mathcal{S}$ is a set of objects called *states*, and
- **fe** is a set of objects called *features*, and
- ATR is a set of objects called *attribute values*, and
- $\lambda : \mathcal{S} \rightarrow 2^{\mathbf{fe}}$ is a map from states to sets of features, and
- $\Re$ is a set of relations on $\mathbf{fe}^i \times \mathcal{S}$ for $i \geq 0$, and
- $\mathcal{F}$ is a set of relations on $\mathcal{S}$, and
- $\mathbf{Var}_1$ is a set of objects, called *variables*, ranging over $\mathcal{S}$, and
- $\mathbf{Var}_2$ is a set of variables ranging over **fe**.

Note that this 8-tuple may be thought of as residing "on top" of a given physical representation of a body of data in a given medium. Thus, for instance, if data is stored on CD-Rom, then there is a 8-tuple of the above form associated with the CD-Rom. Furthermore, each state $s \in S$ is physically represented on the CD-Rom using whatever electronic representation and/or compression scheme is being used. Physical retrieval of a frame from a medium (such as CD-Rom) may be accomplished using whatever (pre-existing) retrieval mechanism is used to access frames on the CD-Rom.

We now show how the Multimedia Database System of an automobile described at the beginning of this section may be expressed as media instances.

Example 2.1. **(Media Instances of Automobile Multimedia Databases)** Let us suppose that we have information about both the Ford Taurus and the Ford Mustang. Let's suppose that both cars have driver's side airbags, but the Mustang is equipped with a passenger airbag as standard. Both cars have as optional features stereos, cellular phones, and car alarms. The video media instance may be described as follows:

1. **(Video Media-Instance)** This is the tuple

$$(\{v1,\ldots,v8\},\mathbf{fe}^1,\mathtt{ATR}^1,\lambda^1,\Re_1,\Re_2,\mathbf{Var}_1,\mathbf{Var}_2)$$

where $\mathbf{fe}^1 = \{$ `taurus`, `taurus_dashboard_options`, `taurus_dashboard_no_options`, `mustang`, `taurus_engine_block`, `taurus_drivers_view`, `car alarm`, `cellular phone`, `stereo`, `air bag`$\}$, $\Re_1 = \{$ `type`, `left`, `right`, `color`, `successor`$\}$, and $\Re_2 = \{$ `earlier`$\}$. λ^1 is the following map:

$$\begin{aligned}
\lambda^1(v1) &= \{\mathtt{taurus}\}.\\
\lambda^1(v2) &= \{\mathtt{taurus_engine_block}\}.\\
\lambda^1(v3) &= \{\mathtt{mustang_drivers_view}\}.\\
\lambda^1(v4) &= \{\mathtt{stereo, cellular\,phone}\}.\\
\lambda^1(v5) &= \{\mathtt{car\,alarm, air\,bag}\}.\\
\lambda^1(v6) &= \{\mathtt{taurus_dashboard_with_options}\}.\\
\lambda^1(v7) &= \{\mathtt{taurus_dashboard_no_options}\}.\\
\lambda^1(v8) &= \{\mathtt{mustang}\}.
\end{aligned}$$

Intuitively, $\lambda^1(v2) = \{\mathtt{taurus\_engine\_block}\}$, means that the `video` frame v2 possesses the feature `taurus_engine_block`. Likewise, the statement $\lambda^1(v5) = \{\mathtt{car\,alarm, air\,bag}\}$ indicates that video-frame $v9$ possesses two features – `air bag` and `car alarm` reflecting the fact that this constitutes a picture of the car alarm and air bag options of Ford products. The relations in $\Re_1$ are relations between features. We assume that the following tuples are contained in $\Re_1$:

```
type(taurus,midsize,S)        type(mustang,compact,S)
type(tempo,compact,S)         left(stereo,cellular phone,v5).
color(taurus,red,v1)
color(mustang,black,v8)
```

Likewise, the relation `earlier` in $\Re_2$ is an inter-state relation; for example we may know that `v3` was an earlier shot than `v8`, in which case the tuple
`earlier(v3 ,v8)` is present. The *attribute values* present in ATR for this media-instance is the set `midsize, compact, red, black` as well as all integers.

2. **(Audio Media-Instance)** This is the tuple

$$(\{a1\}, \mathbf{fe}^2, \mathtt{ATR}^1, \lambda^2, \Re_1, \Re_2, \mathbf{Var}_1, \mathbf{Var}_2)$$

where $\mathbf{fe}^2 = \{\mathtt{taurus}\}$ and $\lambda^2(a1) = \{\mathtt{taurus}\}$.

3. **(Document Media-Instance)** This is the tuple

$$(\{d1, d2, d3\}, \mathbf{fe}^3, \mathtt{ATR}^1, \lambda^3, \Re_1, \Re_2, \mathbf{Var}_1, \mathbf{Var}_2)$$

where $\mathbf{fe}^3 = \{\mathtt{taurus}, \mathtt{t\_interior}, \mathtt{dashboard}, \mathtt{mustang}, \mathtt{m\_interior}, \mathtt{odometer}\}$, and the map λ^3 is defined to be:

$$\begin{aligned}
\lambda^3(d1) &= \{\mathtt{dashboard}\}.\\
\lambda^3(d2) &= \{\mathtt{mustang}\}.\\
\lambda^3(d3) &= \{\mathtt{mustang}, \mathtt{stereo}, \mathtt{car\ alarm}, \mathtt{cellular\ phone}\}.\\
\lambda^3(d4) &= \{\mathtt{taurus}, \mathtt{insurance}\}.
\end{aligned}$$

The above defintion does not account for some very basic feature/ subfeature relationships. For example, if a user wanted an image of the dashboard with options, and there was no such image available, then perhaps the user might be satisfied with a picture of the dashboard with no options and assorted picturess of car stereos. Because of the need for feature/subfeature relationships, the definition of structured multimedia database systems is introduced.

A *structured multimedia database system,* SMDS, is a quadruple $(\{\mathcal{M}_1, \ldots, \mathcal{M}_n\}, \leq, \mathtt{RPL}, \mathtt{SUBST})$ where:

- $\mathcal{M}_i = (\mathcal{S}^i, \mathbf{fe}^i, \mathtt{ATR}^i, \lambda^i, \Re^i, \mathcal{F}^i, \mathbf{Var}_1^i, \mathbf{Var}_2^i)$ is a media-instance, and
- $\leq$ is a partial ordering on the set $\bigcup_{i=1}^n \mathbf{fe}^i$, and
- $\mathtt{RPL} : \bigcup_{i=1}^n \mathbf{fe}^i \rightarrow 2^{\bigcup_{i=1}^n \mathbf{fe}^i}$ such that $f_1 \in \mathtt{RPL}(f_2)$ implies that $f_1 \leq f_2$. Thus, RPL is a map that associates with each feature f, a set of features that are "below" f according to the $\leq$-ordering on features.
- SUBST is a map from $\bigcup_{i=1}^n \mathtt{ATR}^i$ to $2^{\bigcup_{i=1}^n \mathtt{ATR}^i}$.

Intuitively, suppose f_1, f_2 are features. When $f_1 \leq f_2$, then this means (intuitively) that f_1 is deemed to be a subfeature of f_2. The map RPL is used (as we shall see later) to determine what constitutes an "acceptable" answer to a query. For example, if we want a video-state depicting a car `dashboard_with_options`, and if no such video-frame exists, then an alternative answer may be a picture of the `stereo` happens to be a "subfeature" of the `dashboard_with_options`. If this is the desired behavior, then `stereo` should be in the set RPL(`dashboard_with_options`). The map SUBST is used to determine what attribute values may be considered to be appropriate replacements for other attribute values, i.e. if `red` $\in$ SUBST(`black`), then `black` is deemed to be an appropriate attribute value to substitute for `red` . This may be useful because an end-user may request a picture of a red Taurus; if no such picture is available, and `red` $\in$ SUBST(`black`), then the system may present the user with a picture of a `black` Taurus instead. Until we explicitly state otherwise, we will assume, for ease of presentation, that for all attribute constants a, $\mathtt{SUBST}(a) = 2^{\bigcup_{i=1}^{n} \mathrm{ATR}^i}$, i.e. any attribute constant can be substituted for any other attribute constant without restriction. It is possible to remove this assumption. See Marcus and Subrahmanian for more details.

Example 2.2. **(Car Example Revisited)** The structured multimedia database system associated with the car example, as formalized earlier, is the quadruple ({`video`, `audio`, `document`}, $\leq$, RPL, SUBST) where the $\leq$ ordering is the reflexive transitive closure of the following $\leq$ pairs:
`stereo` $\leq$ `dashboard_with_options`,
`dashboard_with_options` $\leq$ `taurus`,
`dashboard_without_options` $\leq$ `taurus`,
`air bag` $\leq$ `dashboard_with_options`,
`celluar phone` $\leq$ `dashboard_with_options`,
`car alarm` $\leq$ `dashboard_with_options`.

Note that in general, the ordering on the set of features must be provided by the designer of the multimedia system and must correspond to the intuition that $f_1 \leq f_2$ means that f_1 is a "subfeature" of f_2.

An example of the replacement map RPL is given by:

RPL(`taurus`)	=	$\emptyset$.
RPL(`enginei_block`)	=	$\emptyset$.
RPL(`dashboard_with_options`)	=	{`stereo`, `car alarm`, `cellular phone`, `air bag`}.
RPL(`stereo`)	=	`dashboard_with_options`.
RPL(`mustang`)	=	`drivers_view_mustang`.
RPL(`car alarm`)	=	`dashboard_with_options`
RPL(`air bag`)	=	`dashboard_with_options`
RPL(`cellular phone`)	=	`dashbaord_with_options`

For instance, the statement $\mathtt{RPL(mustang)} = \{\mathtt{drivers\_view\_mustang}\}$ says that if we are looking for a particular type of frame depicting the `mustang` and if no such frame exists, then finding a frame of the same type depicting the feature `drivers_view_mustang` serves as an acceptable alternative to query.

In the next section, we outline the Marcus and Subrahmanian logical query language. The next section after that, we show how SQL queries can be used to express the exactly the same kind of queries.

3. Logical Query Language

In this section, we recapitulate the logical query language developed by Marcus and Subrahmanian to express queries addressed to a structured multimedia system

$$\mathtt{SMDS} = (\{\mathcal{M}_1, \ldots, \mathcal{M}_n\}, \leq, \mathtt{RPL}, \mathtt{SUBST})$$

where

$$\mathcal{M}_i = (\mathbf{ST}^i, \mathbf{fe}^i, \mathtt{ATR}^i, \lambda^i, \Re^i, \mathcal{F}^i, \mathbf{Var}_1^i, \mathbf{Var}_2^i).$$

they developed a logical language to express queries that is briefly described here. This language will be generated by the following set of non-logical symbols:

1. **Constant Symbols:**
   a) Each $f \in \mathbf{fe}^i$ for $1 \leq i \leq n$ is a constant symbol in the query language. (For convenience, we will often refer to these as "feature-constants.")
   b) Each $s \in \mathbf{ST}^i$ for $1 \leq i \leq n$ is a constant symbol in the query language. (For convenience, we will often refer to these as "state-constants.")
   c) Each integer $1 \leq i \leq n$ is a constant symbol.
   d) For each medium $\mathcal{M}_i$, $\mathcal{M}_i$ is a constant symbol. (Thus for instance, if $\mathcal{M}_1 = \mathtt{video}$, then `video` is a constant symbol, etc.)
   e) A finite set of symbols called *attribute-constants*. (Intuitively, these are constants such as `red`, `blue`, `midsize`, 2, 3, etc. that are neither features, nor states, but reflect attribute-values.)
2. **Function Symbols:** `flist` is a binary function symbol in the query language. `flist` is a list of features that is associated with a given frame. In the automobile example, the `flist` of $v1$ contains the feature taurus.
3. **Variable Symbols:** We assume that we have an infinite set of logical variables $V_1, \ldots, V_i, \ldots$.
4. **Predicate Symbols:** The language contains
   a) a binary predicate symbol `frametype`, where `frametype` describes the physical type of media. In the automobile example, the `frametype` of $v1$ is video.

b) a binary predicate symbol, $\in$,
c) for each inter-state relation $R \in \Re^i$ of arity j, it contains a j-ary predicate symbol R^*.
d) for each feature-state relation $\psi \in \Re_2^i$ of arity j, it contains a j-ary predicate symbol ψ^*.

As usual, a term is defined inductively as follows: (1) each constant symbol is a term, (2) each variable symbol is a term, and (3) if η is an n-ary function symbol, and $t_1, \ldots, t_n$ are terms, then $\eta(t_1, \ldots, t_n)$ is a term. A ground term is a variable-free term. If p is an n-ary predicate symbol, and $t_1, \ldots, t_n$ are (ground) terms, then $p(t_1, \ldots, t_n)$ is a (ground) atom. A *query* is an existentially closed conjunction of atoms, i.e. a statement of the form

$$(\exists)(A_1 \,\&\, \ldots, A_n).$$

Hence, informally expressing the query "Is there a picture of a white Taurus ?", can be formally expressed in the logical query language as:

$$(\exists \mathtt{S})(\mathtt{frametype}(\mathtt{S}, \mathtt{video}) \,\&\, \mathtt{taurus} \in \mathtt{flist}(\mathtt{S}) \,\&\, \mathtt{color}(\mathtt{taurus}, \mathtt{white}, \mathtt{S})).$$

In the next section, we will show how the logical query language may be replaced by an SQL based query language.

4. Querying Multimedia Databases in SQL

Recall the definition of the extraction map, λ, as a map from a given state S, to a set of features. We redefine λ in terms of the the binary relation L as follows:

$$L(statename, featurename) \iff featurename \in \lambda(statename)$$

The definition of a video media instance is exactly the same except that λ is replaced with L. For completeness, we state the defintions of video, audio, and document multimedia instances in terms of the new notation.

1. **(Video Media-Instance)** This is the tuple

$$(\{v1, \ldots, v8\}, \mathbf{fe}^1, \mathtt{ATR}^1, \mathtt{L}^1, \Re_1, \Re_2, \mathbf{Var}_1, \mathbf{Var}_2)$$

where $\mathbf{fe}^1$ = {`taurus`, `taurus_dashboard_options`, `taurus_dashboard_no_options`, `mustang`, `taurus_engine_block`, `taurus_drivers_view`, `car alarms`, `cellular phones`, `stereos`, `air bags`}, $\Re_1$ = {`type`, `left`, `right`, `color`, `successor`}, and $\Re_2$ = {`earlier`}. And L^1 is defined as:

$L^1(v_1, taurus)$

$L^1(v_7, taurus\_dashboard\_without\_options)$
$L^1(v_2, engine\_block)$
$L^1(v_3, drivers\_view\_mustang)$
$L^1(v_4, stereo)$
$L^1(v_4, celluar\ phone)$
$L^1(v_5, car\ alarm)$
$L^1(v_5, air\ bag)$
$L^1(v_6, taurus\_dashboard\_with\_options)$
$L^1(v_8, mustang)$

Thus, $L(v_1, taurus) \iff taurus \in \lambda(v_1)$.

2. **(Audio Media-Instance)** This is the tuple

$$(\{a1\}, \mathbf{fe}^2, \mathtt{ATR}^1, \text{Ł}^2, \Re_1, \Re_2, \mathbf{Var}_1, \mathbf{Var}_2)$$

where $\mathbf{fe}^2 = \{\mathtt{taurus}\}$ and

$$L^2(a_1, taurus)$$

3. **(Document Media-Instance)** This is the tuple

$$(\{d1, d2, d3\}, \mathbf{fe}^3, \mathtt{ATR}^1, \text{Ł}^3, \Re_1, \Re_2, \mathbf{Var}_1, \mathbf{Var}_2)$$

where

$\mathbf{fe}^3 = \{\mathtt{taurus}, \mathtt{t\_interior}, \mathtt{dashboard}, \mathtt{mustang}, \mathtt{m\_interior}, \mathtt{odometer}\}$

and L^3 is defined to be

$L^3(d_1, dashboard)$ $L^3(d_2, mustang)$
$L^3(d_3, mustang)$ $L^3(d_3, stereo)$
$L^3(d_3, car\ alarm)$ $L^3(d_3, cellular\ phone)$
$L^3(d_4, taurus)$ $L^3(d_4, insurance)$

We can now redefine the logical based queries into SQL based queries using the L relation and the small relational database used in section 1 of this paper. Thus, the informal query of the last section "Is there a picture of a white Taurus ?" expressed as the formula:

$$(\exists \mathtt{S})(\mathtt{frametype(S, video)} \,\&\, \mathtt{taurus} \in \mathtt{flist(S)} \,\&\, \mathtt{color(taurus, white, S)}).$$

is translated to the SQL query:

```
1. SELECT Statename
   FROM Frametype, Color, L
   WHERE Media.type = 'video' and
         L.Statename = Frametype.Statename and
         Color.Featurename = 'taurus' and
         Color.Type = 'white' and
```

```
            Color.Statename = L.Statename
```

Frametype is a binary relation defined on (*Media_Type* x*Statename*) where $Media\_Type = video, audio, image$, etc., and $Statename = v_1, \ldots, v_8, a_1, d_1, \ldots, d_4$. Color is a relation defined on (*Featuretype* x *type* x *statename*).
In this case, the answer will be NO, as there is no picture of of a white Taurus in our database. However, by using the notion of an "optimal answer" it is possible in the Subrahmaninan and Marcus framework to express to the user that there is a picture of a red Taurus. In this situation, the user may respond affirmatively or negatively depending on his/her requirements. Similiarly, we may redefine the logical query
"Is there an audio description as well as a picture of a midsized car ?"
This can be expressed as logical the query

$$(\exists S_1, S_2, S_3, C)(\mathtt{frametype}(S_1, \mathtt{audio})\,\&\,\mathtt{frametype}(S_2, \mathtt{video})\,\& \\ C \in \mathtt{flist}(S_1)\,\&\, C \in \mathtt{flist}(S_2)\,\&\,\mathtt{type}(C, \mathtt{midsize}, S_3)).$$

can be rewritten as

```
2. SELECT  L_1,Statename
   FROM Frametype t_1, Frametype t_2, Frametype t_3,
        Type L L_1, L L_2,
   WHERE Media.type ='video' and
         t_2.Type = 'audio' and
         L_1.Statename = t_1.Statename  and
         L_2.Statename = t_2.Statename  and
         L_1.Featurename = L_2.Featurename =t_3.model and
         t_3.size = 'midsize'
```

In this example, we are trying to select a property on different media types. In the first example, we were trying to select a feature and a property on one media type. In the following example, we are trying to select multiple features on one media. Informally, this query asks, 'Does there exist a video of the interior of a mustang?' In the logical query language this is expressed as,

$$(\exists S)(\mathtt{frametype}(S, \mathtt{video})\,\&\,\mathtt{mustang} \in \mathtt{flist}(S)\,\& \\ \mathtt{m\_interior} \in \mathtt{flist}(S)).$$

which can be rewritten in SQL as

```
3. SELECT Statename
   FROM Frametype  L L_1, L  L_2
   WHERE Media.type = 'video' and
         Frametype.Statename = L_1.Statename and
         Frametype.Statename = L_2.Statename and
         L_1.Featurename = 'mustang' and
         L_2.Featurename = 'm_interior'
```

Suppose that we are given the following extension to $\Re_1$, a relational database which contains more specific information about cars.

```
engine(taurus,v6,S).          engine(mustang,v8,S).
engine(tempo,v4,S).           price(taurus, 1993, 15k).
price(mustang,1993,18k).      price(tempo,1993,12k).
airbags(taurus,1,S).          airbags(mustang,2,S).
airbags(tempo,0,S).
```

The designer of the Car multimedia system may wish to define a predicate called `diff` which takes two arguments `Car1` and `Car2` and returns a list of differences between `Car1` and `Car2` (as far as certain designated predicates are concerned). This predicate, `diff`, is a derived predicate defined as follows:

```
diff(Car1, Car2, L, S)  ←  diff_engine(Car1, Car2, L1, S) &
                           diff_price(Car1, Car2, L2, S) &
                           diff_airbags(Car1, Car2, L3, S) &
                           append(L1, L2, L4) &
                           append(L4, L3, L).

diff_engine(Car1, Car2, [enginedif(E1, E2)], S)  ←  engine(Car1, E1, S) &
                                                    engine(Car2, E2, S) & E1 ≠ E2.

diff_engine(Car1, Car2, [], S)  ←  engine(Car1, E1, S) &
                                   engine(Car2, E2, S) & E1 = E2.

diff_price(Car1, Car2, [pricedif(P1, P2)], S)  ←  price(Car1, P1, S) &
                                                  price(Car2, P2, S) & P1 ≠ P2.

diff_price(Car1, Car2, [], S)  ←  price(Car1, P1, S) &
                                  price(Car2, P2, S) & P1 = P2.

diff_airbags(Car1, Car2, [airbagsdif(A1, A2)], S)  ←  airbags(Car1, A1, S)
                                                      airbags(Car2, A2, S) & A1 ≠ A2.

diff_airbags(Car1, Car2, [], S)  ←  airbags(Car1, A1, S)
                                    airbags(Car2, A2, S) & A1 = A2.

L = [enginedif(v6, v8), pricedif(15k, 18k), airbags(1, 2)].
```

The above definition of the predicate `diff` enables an end-user to be able to ask queries such as "What is the difference between the Ford Taurus and the Ford Mustang ?" This can be expressed as the query

$$(\exists \mathrm{L}, \mathrm{S})(\mathtt{diff}(\mathtt{taurus}, \mathtt{mustang}, \mathrm{L}, \mathrm{S}).$$

The answer to this query consists of

$$\mathrm{L} \ = \ [\mathtt{enginedif}(\mathrm{v6}, \mathrm{v8}), \mathtt{pricedif}(15\mathrm{k}, 18\mathrm{k}), \mathtt{airbags}(1, 2)].$$

This query may also be easily represented in SQL.

5. Expressing User Requests in SQL

In this section, we show how certain requests that the user may wish to make can be expressed in SQL. Suppose that a user is looking at a certain state or frame s. Suppose also that there is an alogrithm which, given a user interrupt, will identify the feature F is state s. This may require signal processing and/or statistical pattern recognition techniques which are studied in other papers (e.g. [7], [3], and [4]). The scenario we envision in the next section is that the user is in state s and wishes to obtain further information on one or more of the features in the current media-event.

Query I. Suppose the user wishes to find all states (irrespective of the medium involved) in which feature F occurs. This can be expressed in the logical language as the query $\mathtt{info}(F)$ defined as:

$$(\exists S)F \in \mathtt{flist}(S).$$

This is a relatively "vague" query in that it asks for a list of all states in which F is a feature. The system may respond with a menu of possible answers (in different media such as audio, video, document, etc.) that satisfy the given query.

This may easily be rewritten in SQL as

```
SELECT Statename
FROM Frametype , L
WHERE Frametype.type = 'video' or
      Frametype.type = 'audio' or
      Frametype.type = 'document' or
      L.featurename = 'F'
```

Query II. Suppose the user wishes to ask a more specific query where s/he is only interested in information about F on a particular medium. This can be expressed as the query $\mathtt{info}(F, M)$ defined as:

$$(\exists S)\mathtt{frametype}(S, M) \,\&\, F \in \mathtt{flist}(S).$$

Thus, when the user asks the query $\mathtt{info}(\mathtt{mustang}, \mathtt{audio})$ s/he is asking for audio-clips containing information about the Mustang. These may include sound clips reflecting engine noise of the Mustang, as well as an audio sales-pitch for the Mustang.

This query may be rewritten in SQL as :

```
SELECT Statename
FROM Frametype,  L
WHERE Frametype.type = 'M' and
L.featurename = 'F' and
L.Statename = Frametype.Statename
```

Other user request queries as outlined in Marcus and Subrahmanian may similiarly be written in SQL.

Subrahmanian has developed a theory of annotations which has been used to reason about time and uncertainty. For example, a user may which to view a series of video clips in a certain order and having each video clip a certain time length. Or a user may wish to view an image in which the quality of the scanned image must be very high. In order to implement these annotation in SQL the field of the L relation would need an additional field called "annotation". Using this extended language, these annotations are easily incorportated into SQL. An example of how these annotations may be expressed in SQL is provided below.

Find all pictures of Bill Clinton where the "quality" of the picture of Bill Clinton exceeds 75% and where he is pictured with a statue of Lincoln. This can be expressed as follows:

$$(\exists \texttt{Picture})(\texttt{frametype}(\texttt{Picture}, \text{"}\texttt{picture}\text{"}) \;\&\; \texttt{feature}(\text{"}\texttt{BillClinton}\text{"}, \texttt{Picture}) : \texttt{0.75} \;\&$$

$$\texttt{feature}(\text{"}\texttt{LincolnStatue}\text{"}, \texttt{Picture})).$$

In this query, the atom `feature("Bill Clinton",Picture)` is *annotated* with the real number 0.75. Any picture in which Bill Clinton appears with over 75% "goodness" is considered to satisfy that annotated atom `feature("Bill Clinton",Picture):0.75`. When a `feature` atom is not annotated, then this implicitly represents an annotation of 1.

We rewrite this query in SQL as:

```
SELECT STATENAME
FROM FRAMETYPE L L_1, L L_2
WHERE FRAMETYPE.TYPE = PICTURE and
FRAMETYPE.STATENAME = L_1.STATENAME = L_2.STATENAME and
L_1.FEATURENAME = 'BILL CLINTON' and
L_1.ANNOTATION = '0.75' and
L_2.FEATURENAME = 'LINCOLN STATUE'
```

However, if we wanted to the query , 'Show me a picture of Clinton, directlly followed by a picture of Gore.' Using the Marcus and Subrahmanian framework, we could first write down the logical query,

$$(\exists S_1, S_2)\texttt{frametype}(S_1, \texttt{picture}) \;\&\; \texttt{frametype}(S_2, \texttt{picture}) \;\&$$

$$\texttt{Clinton} \in \texttt{flist}(S_1) \;\&\; \texttt{Gore} \in \texttt{flist}(S_2)$$

followed by the constraint,

$$\texttt{start}(S_2) \geq \texttt{end}(S_1) + 0.001.$$

In this case, SQL is not powerful enough to represent this query because '$\texttt{start}(S_2)$' and '$\texttt{end}(S_1)$' would be need to represented as functions. Hence,

SQL only represents a subset of the extended language in [6], but can fully represent the entire logical query language in [5].

The equivalence between the logical based queries of Marcus and Subrahmanian and the SQL based queries is apparent. Hence, SQL queries may be used in their framework with the corresponding access structures and algorithms remaining the same.

6. Conclusions

There is now intense interest in multimedia systems. These interests span across vast areas in computer science including, but not limited to: computer networks, databases, distributed computing, data compression, document processing, user interfaces, computer graphics, pattern recognition and artificial intelligence. In the long run, we expect that intelligent problem-solving systems will access information stored in a variety of formats, on a wide variety of media. The work done in this paper develops on the the work of Marcus and Subrahmananian who have developed a unified framework to reason across these multiple domains.

The major contribution of this paper is the development of an SQL based layer on top of the logical query language developed by Marcus and Subrahmanian. SQL based queries provide a greater ease of use than logical based ones. More importantly, there are numerous commercial SQL databasse systems who could be used as a layer to access the Marcus and Subrahmanian framework. Query optimization techniques may also be used in satisfying SQL queries. Hence, the Marcus and Subrahmanian system, is not only a logical based one, but may also be expressed in an SQL-based language.

There is now a great deal of ongoing work on multimedia systems, both within the database community, as well as outside it. All of these works, without exception, deal with integration of *specific types of media data*; for example, there are systems that integrate certain compressed video-representation schemes with other compressed audio-representation schemes. However, to date there seems no unifying framework for integrating multimedia data which is independent of both the specific medium and it's storage. The work of [5], [6] allow in principle the integration of multimedia data without knowing in advance what the structure of the this data might be. Further, this integration can now be done with an SQL layer developed on top of this framework.

References

[1] S. Adalı and V.S. Subrahmanian. (1993) Amalgamating Knowledge Bases, III: Distributed Mediators, accepted for publication in: Intl. Journal of Intelligent Cooperative Information Systems.

[2] A. Brink. (1994) M.S. Thesis, George Mason Univ., in preparation.
[3] Y. Gong, H. Zhang, H.C. Chuan and M. Sakauchi. (1994) *An Image Database System with Content Capturing and Fast Image Indexing Abilities*, Proc. 1994 Intl. Conf. on Multimedia Computing and Systems, pps 121-130, IEEE Press.
[4] A. Gupta, T. Weymouth and R. Jain. (1991) *Semantic Queries with Pictures: The VIMSYS Model*, Proc. 1991 Intl. Conf. on Very Large Databases, Barcelona, Spain, pps 69–79.
[5] S. Marcus and V.S. Subrahmanian. (1995) *Towards a Theory of Multimedia Database Systems*, this volume.
[6] S. Marcus and V.S. Subrahmanian. (1994) Foundations of Multimedia Database Systems, submitted for publication.
[7] W. Niblack, et. al. (1993) *The QBIC Project: Querying Images by Content Using Color, Texture and Shape*, IBM Research Report, Feb. 1993.
[8] A. Silberschatz, M. Stonebraker and J. D. Ullman. (1991) *Database Systems: Achievements and Opportunities*, Comm. of the ACM, 34, 10, pps 110–120.
[9] V.S. Subrahmanian. (1992) *Amalgamating Knowledge Bases*, ACM Transactions on Database Systems, 19, 2, pp. 291–331, 1994.
[10] V.S. Subrahmanian. (1993) *Hybrid Knowledge Bases for Intelligent Reasoning Systems*, Invited Address, Proc. 8th Italian Conf. on Logic Programming (ed. D. Sacca), pps 3–17,
[11] G. Wiederhold. (1993) *Intelligent Integration of Information*, Proc. 1993 ACM SIGMOD Conf. on Management of Data, pps 434–437.

Multimedia Authoring Systems

Ross Cutler and Kasım Selçuk Candan

Department of Computer Science, University of Maryland, College Park, Maryland 20742

Summary. In this paper we survey three multimedia authoring systems (Multimedia Toolbook 3.0, Director 4.0, and Authorware 3.0). Each system uses a different metaphor (book, movie, and icon-based flowchart) for creating multimedia applications. A sample application is developed in each MAS and the effects of the corresponding metaphors are compared. We also discuss current technologies like *ODBC*, *OLE*, *DDE*, *DLL*, and *MCI*, and describe how MAS's are benefiting from them. In the last section of the paper, we look at the limitations of current systems, and discuss the future of the research in this area.

1. Introduction

Multimedia software applications have become a multi-billion dollar business. Typical multimedia applications include:

- Product demos (e.g. Multimedia Toolkit demo)
- Kiosk applications (e.g. concert ticket ordering)
- Computer Based Training (CBT) (e.g. Microsoft Excel tutorial)
- Games (e.g. Iron Helix is written in Director)
- Multimedia References (e.g. MS Encarta, 747 repair manual)
- Education (Multimedia textbooks and courseware)

However, the growth of the multimedia software market didnot keep up with the hype that multimedia gets in the press. This slowness was in large part due to the inadequacies of the tools supplied to multimedia software developers. For example, it is only within the last two years that cross platform tools became available, and it is even more recent that these tools started to provide interprocess communication and database connectivity.

Multimedia applications can also be developed using traditional tools, such as C++ (if provided with graphics, sound, hypertext, animation, video, and database libraries). However, the number of tools that a developer would have to learn in order to write even a simple multimedia application is quite daunting. Obviously, use of a multimedia authoring system (MAS) is a better alternative.

MAS's are high-level systems providing unified environments for creating multimedia applications. A major advantage of MAS's is the ease of use they provide to non-programmers (e.g. domain experts) too. Still, most systems come with programming languages for more advanced applications. A typical MAS includes tools for hypertext, pictures, animation, video, sound, database connectivity, and interprocess communication.

In this paper we will concentrate on three MAS's:

- Asymetrix's Multimedia Toolbook 3.0
- AimTech's IconAuthor 6.0
- Macromedia's Director 4.0

These systems are chosen because (1) each has proved to be very successful in the market, and (2) each uses a different metaphor to create multimedia applications. More specifically, Toolbook uses a *book* interface, Director uses a *movie* metaphor, and IconAuthor uses an icon-based *flowchart*. Director and IconAuthor are cross-platform systems, and run on Microsoft Windows and MacOS systems (Director applications also run on the 3DO which is an inexpensive multimedia game system). Toolbook only runs on Windows platforms, but because of its popularity and the predominance of Windows in the marketplace, we have prefered to include it in our paper as the representative of the *book* metaphor.

In order to evaluate and compare each MAS, we have built a simple application in each system. The application is one that you might find in a video tape rental store (or in a video-on-demand system). It allows users to query a database of available movies. For example, the user could search for all in-stock movies that are dramas, cast Gary Cooper, and won an Oscar. For each such movie, the user would be able to receive a short review and a small video clip. The user can also check out the movie using the application, which would notify a clerk to get the movie from storage and hold it at the checkout desk.

Before getting to the details of each MAS, we first discuss some of the common technologies: *ODBC*, *OLE*, *DDE*, *DLL*, and *MCI*(note that Director does not support *OLE*, *DDE*and *ODBC*).

2. Underlying Technology

2.1 ODBC

The Open Database Connectivity (*ODBC*) interface allows applications to access data in database management systems (DBMS) using the Structured Query Language (SQL). The interface permits maximum interoperability – a single application can access different database management systems.

This technology allows an application developer to prepare, compile, and ship an application without targeting a specific DBMS. Users, then, can use some modules (database drivers) to link their choice of database management systems to their application.

As a result, developers do not have to write database specific code for connections or communications of queries and results.

2.2 OLE

Object Linking and Embedding (*OLE*) is a technique that is extensively used in Windows and MacOS that enables users to create an object in one application (the server application), and then incorporate it into a file from another application (the client application).

There are three types of *OLE* objects:

- **Linked Object**: An object that is stored in a separate file called the source file.
- **Embedded object**: An object that is a copy of the original object but stored within your document.
- **Static object**: An object that is originally imported into a document as an *OLE* object, but whose connection to the server application has been severed to ensure that it cannot be edited.

Using *OLE*, it is possible to create applications that integrate the capabilities of many different *OLE* compliant programs. For instance, Toolbook does not include an equation editor, so to include equations in an application one needs to pick an equation editor (e.g. EquationEdit) and write/edit the equations through *OLE*. If one wishes to prevent the readers from modifying the resulting equations, then s/he can convert them into static objects.

A future version of *OLE* is expected to let applications share objects across a network.

2.3 DDE

Dynamic Data Exchange (*DDE*) is a Windows and MacOS communication protocol used for exchanging data between applications or for executing commands in other applications.

A *DDE* conversation consists of two or more applications. The client application initiates the conversation, while the server application responds to the client's requests.

DDE has also been extended to *NetDDE* allowing conversations across networks.

2.4 DLL

Dynamically Linked Libraries (*DLL*'s) is a technology that allows libraries to be dynamically loaded at runtime. *DLL*'s can be used to add libraries of routines to MAS's. For example, if one wants to add a MPEG-2 video player to a MAS that does not come with one, s/he can do so via a *DLL*. The MPEG video player can then be called in a similar fashion as other (built-in) library calls.

2.5 MCI

The Multimedia Control Interface (*MCI*) is a communications standard that is used to control multimedia devices like video disks, CD players, camcorders, etc. For example, a multimedia application can use a video disk player to provide video clips, or a CD jukebox player to provide sample sound bites.

3. Sample Application - "Find-Movie"

We now discuss the sample application that we have implemented in all three systems. The application mainly consists of three screens: *title*, *query*, and *result* screens.

The *title* screen is what is displayed when the application is idle. It contains a moving text string ("Press any key") and random movie stills (which fade in and out in random locations on the screen). When a key is pressed, the query screen is activated.

The *query* screen allows a user to construct a query using the following criteria:

- Movie Title
- Director
- Genres
- MPAA Rating
- Actor/actress
- Star Rating (1-4)
- Release Date (range)
- In Stock (Y/N)
- Awards

Attribute	Type
title	char[]
director	char[]
release_date	date
movie_id	int
genres	char[]
mpaa_rating	char[]
num_in_stock	char[]
star_rating	int
clip_filename	char[]

Table 3.1. Movies table

Once a query has been constructed, the user can press the "Search" button to send an SQL query to a movie database system through *ODBC*. In all likelihood, there would be one database server per store, which would be accessible via a network from each kiosk. The sample database consists of the following three tables: `Movies` (table 3.1), `Actors` (table 3.2) and `Awards` (table 3.3).

Attribute	Type
movie_id	int
actor	char[]

Table 3.2. `Actors` table

The *result* screen displays a list of movies satisfying the given query. When the user selects a movie from this list, a short review and video clip of the movie is displayed. Video clips and reviews are stored on a central file server. The format for the video is MPEG, and the format for the reviews is Rich Text Format (RTF). If a user decides to check the movie out, the application sends a *NetDDE* message to the clerk's computer (which runs a *DDE* server) to inform the clerk.

Attribute	Type
movie_id	int
award	char[]

Table 3.3. `Awards` table

4. Multimedia Toolbook 3.0

Multimedia Toolbook uses a book metaphor to build multimedia applications. The components of a book include

- graphic objects,
- fields,
- viewers,
- pages,
- buttons, and
- backgrounds.

A book is built by creating pages, placing objects on the pages, and writing scripts in Toolbook's OpenScript language to perform actions (see Figure 4.1).

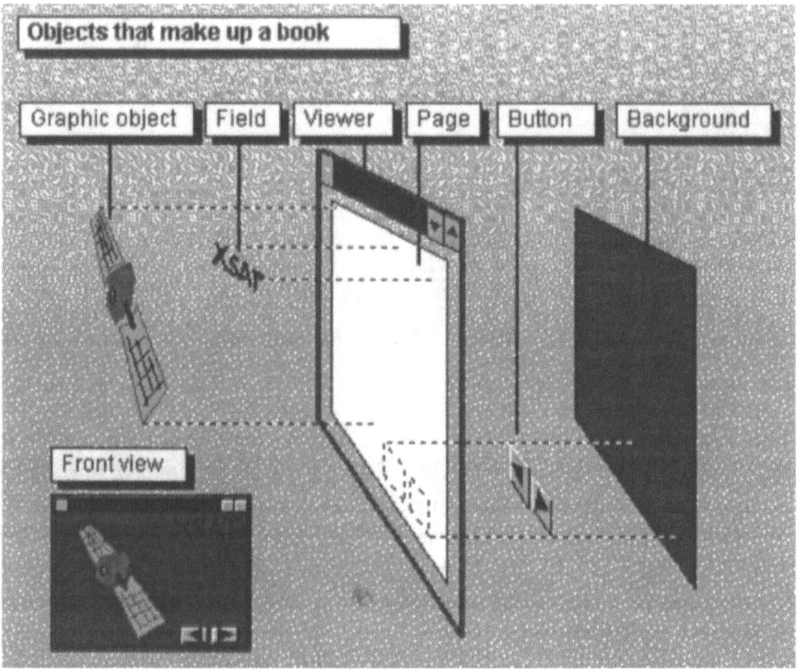

Fig. 4.1. Toolbook book components

Toolbook provides an object-oriented event driven programming environment; however the scripting language is not object oriented (i.e., it doesn't provide classes, inheritance, or encapsulation).

In our sample application, the *title* page is expected to display random movie stills and a scrolling text ("Press any key to continue") across the bottom of the screen. Figure 4.2 shows a snapshot of this screen. The text label that scrolls in this page is a *Field* object with the following attached script:

```
-- on idle, makes text scroll horizontally
notifyBefore idle
        x = item 1 of my position
        y = item 2 of my position
        dx = item 1 of my size
        width = item 1 of size of this book

-- wrap the text to the left hand side of the screen
        if x > width
             x = -dx
        end
        set my position to x + 30, y
end
```

The text label is animated simply by changing its position by 30 units to the right each time the idle handle is called. Note that the idle handle is activated whenever no other events are being processed.

A *Paint* object is used to display a series of movie stills. Unfortunately, it is very difficult (but still possible) in Toolbook to dissolve individual items, so in our sample application no special effects are performed when the stills are changed.

Finally, to handle the *key press*, the following script is attached to the *Page* object (which is called "titlePage"):

```
to handle keyDown
        fxDissolve fast to page ''queryPage''
end
```

When a key is pressed, the *title* page dissolves and the *query* page appears instead (page transition special effects are easy to handle in Toolbook).

Fig. 4.2. Title page

The *query* page (Figure 4.3) uses a series of *ComboBox* and *Button* objects to build a query. Once the user constructs the query and presses the "Search" button, a SQL statement is generated (using the *ComboBox* and *Button* objects). This SQL statement is then sent to the store's database server via *ODBC*. The results are read into a global array[1] with elements of

[1] The array is created global because it is the most efficient way to transfer data between event handlers.

the form {movie title, review file, MPEG filename}. These results are then displayed on the *Results* page (Figure 4.4).

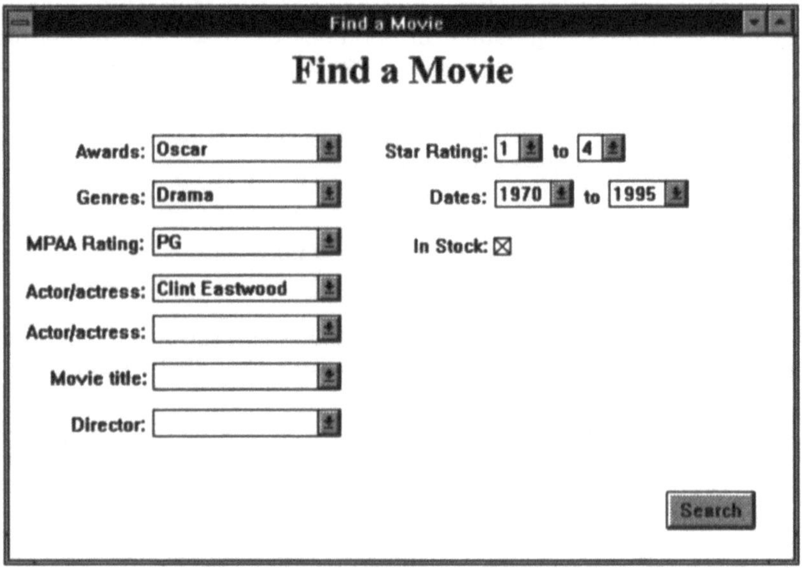

Fig. 4.3. Query page

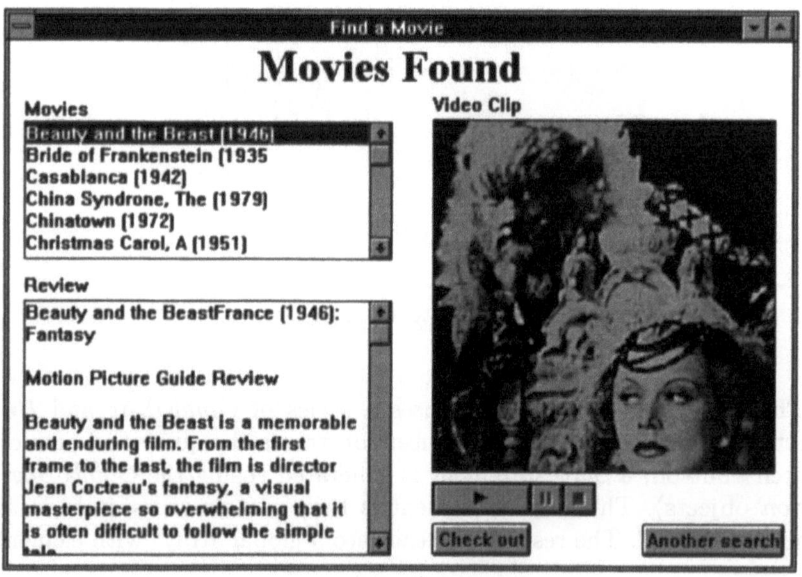

Fig. 4.4. Results page

If the user clicks on a particular movie in the *movies* field, an *OLE* connection is made with the application "QuickTime Player" to play the associated MPEG file. The *play*, *stop*, and *pause* buttons can be used to communicate with the "QuickTime Player" to control the movie.

If the user wants to check out a movie, s/he can do so by pressing the *Check-out* button, which has the following script:

```
to handle buttonClick
        -- check out the selected tape
        tape = selectedText of field ''moviesField''
        executeRemote ''send checkout'' & tape application
                ''clerk''
end
```

This script uses *NetDDE* to communicate with the clerk's Toolbook program which acts as a *DDE* server. When this server recieves a "checkout tape" message, it adds the name of the tape to a scrolling field object on the clerk's screen and beeps to notify the clerk. Note that there is no need to specify what computer the clerk is at on the network, this flexibility is achieved by using a network administrative program to setup a *DDE* "*share*" (which is similar to a disk or printer share used in Microsoft networks).

As one can see, Toolbook is quite a powerful tool for authoring multimedia applications. Unfortunately, even our simple application required significant programming.

5. IconAuthor 6.0

Unlike Toolbook, IconAuthor does not include a programming language. Instead, applications are described using an icon-based flowchart called a structure (see Figure 5.1). An icon is a small picture that represents a function that can be performed. An application starts off at the *Start* icon and executes the icon immediately below it; each subsequent icon executes the icon immediately below or the the right of itself (depending on the type of the icon and the state of the program).

It is important to note that the flow of control is procedural and not event driven. IconAuthor is geared for non-programmers, and procedural control flow is probably easier for non-programmers to conceptualize.

Figure 5.1 shows the implemention of the *title* page for our application. The "Scrolling text" icon is a *Display* icon used for displaying bitmap graphics, animation scripts, or SmartObject files (a collection of user interface objects). In our case, we display a simple animation script which brings the scrolling text "Press any key to continue" to the screen. This script is very similar in concept to a Toolbook script, but it is described using icons instead of words.

Fig. 5.1. Title page structure

IconAuthor supports both scalar and array variables. In the icon "Load @still", we load an array named "@still" and fill it with values from a text file. In particular, @still contains a list of path names to bitmap files containing the stills that we want to display on the *title* page.

The next icon starts a loop, which can be terminated by an *Exit* icon. The "LoopStart" and "LoopEnd" icons are nothing but two dummy icons, automatically included to delimit the loop.

The next three icons in the figure assign random numbers to the variables @i, @x, and @y. The range of @i is $[1,N]$, where N is the number of stills. The range of @x and @y are $[1,dx - px]$ and $[1,dy - py]$, respectively. Here, dx, dy are the dimensions of the screen and px, py are the dimensions of the stills.

The "Display @still[i]" icon displays the still @still[@i], with the dissolving effect. This is followed by the "Check for event" icon waiting for an event (e.g. key press or mouse click). If no events occur in five seconds, the icon times out and sets the appropriate system variable. If one wishes to have a reverse dissolve effect on the still, then s/he can do so by adding "Display @still[i]" icon below the "Check for event" icon.

The "If no event" icon is an *If* icon which checks whether an event is received (via the mentioned system variable) or not. If a time-out occured then then the icon below the *If* icon is executed; otherwise, the other icon (which is located to the right) is executed. In the latter case, the "Subroutine" icon is executed, and as a result the *query* page is displayed and the execution is continued from a new event loop.

IconAuthor uses icons to describe the flow of the program; objects are used for creating the user interface and providing connectivity (via *ODBC*, *OLE*, *DDE*, *DLL*, and *MCI*). For the query page, *Combo* and *CheckBox* objects are used (as in Toolbook) to generate a page very similar to Figure 4.3. These objects are used to build an SQL query string, and a *Database* object uses this SQL string to query the database via *ODBC*. The results are stored in a *List Box* object in a page very similar to Figure 4.4. IconAuthor was the only MAS to directly support MPEG among the ones that we have studied, hence an *OLE* was not necessary for implementation of the *result* page.

6. Director 4.0

Director uses a *movie* metaphor to create applications. This metaphor consist of

- a stage,
- cast members (e.g. graphics, animation, video, text, and sound), and
- a score.

A score can be thought of as a virtual piece of film. It is described by a score window (see Figure 6.1), which contains a matrix of cells; the matrix columns represent individual frames of the movie, and rows represent layers on the stage where cast members can appear. A cell can contain scripts, special effects, timing instructions, color palettes, and sound control. The score window allows up to 48 interactive media elements or 32,000 static objects to be onstage simultaneously.

Director uses an object oriented scripting language (Lingo) to enhance the power of the movie metaphor. Each cast member can have a script associated with it. Objects can catch events and modify the control flow of the application by jumping to a particular frame.

In the remaining part of this section, we describe how to implement our sample application in Director.

For the scrolling text, Director provides a Banner animation which does just what we want (with no programming). A Banner animation is a cast member, so we include that member in the score whenever the *title* page is visible. For example, Figure 6.1 shows cast member 2 (which is the Banner

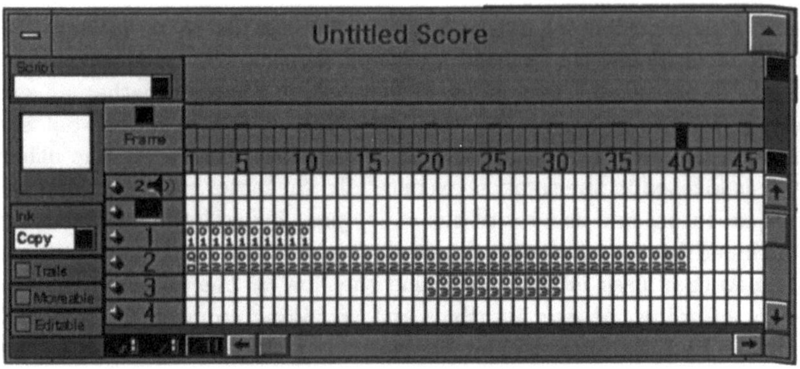

Fig. 6.1. Director score window

animation) in frames 1-40. We also wish to display a series of movie stills (in this case the movie stills are not random). Each movie still is included in the score as a cast member. For example, in Figure 6.1, two stills (cast members 1,3) are displayed in frames 1-10 and 20-30, respectively. By modifying the blend attribute for these members, we can make them fade in and out (other special effects are also possible). The next thing to do is to include more movie stills in the score, put a loop at the end of the score so that it repeats, and add an event handler to the stage which will cause a jump to the *query* page when a key is pressed.

During the implemention of our sample application, we ran into some major deficiencies of Director: it does not support *ODBC*, *DDE*, or *OLE*; and it cannot import RTF (or any formated text). In fact, it does not have any built in database support. It does, however, support *DLL*'s, and an extension mechanism to Lingo, XObject, which allows us to use a third party solution for database connectivity (e.g. *ODBC*). In theory, *DDE* could also be implemented, since it is provided as *DLL*'s (at least on the Windows platform). But the fact that these essential items are not standard, causes a detraction from one of the main goals of MAS's: "minimizing the number of tools to be learned".

7. MAS's and Current Technology

As discussed in the previous sections, multimedia authoring tools are getting more sophisticated everyday. They are becoming more attractive to both naive users and experts as they are enhanced with:

- the portability of the applications to multiple hardware/OS platforms,
- the development of GUI's which make MAS's very easy to learn and use,
- the introduction of application independent structures allowing a large range of users to benefit from them,

– the use of technologies like *ODBC*, *OLE*, *DDE* and *DLL* which let the users fit their MAS's to their own needs.

In this section we study both how the current research in multimedia technologies can be helpful in increasing the strength of the multimedia authoring tools, and how MAS's can be used in increasing the efficiency and productivity of the multimedia research.

7.1 How to improve MAS's?

Current research in multimedia technologies can roughly be classified as follows:

- Research in multimedia hardware:
  - Fast and efficient storage devices for multimedia objects (CD-ROM's etc.),
  - Fast and high quality displays,
  - High bandwidth, low delay communication media.
- Research in multimedia software:
  - Efficient data structures for representing multimedia objects,
  - Methods for merging/synchronizing homogeneous/heterogeneous media objects,
  - Indexing/searching of non-traditional data (video, audio etc.)
  - Automatic feature extraction and semantic indexing,
  - Computer vision and image processing,
  - High speed operating systems (especially for mutlimedia),
  - Network protocols which satisfy a given set of quality of service (QoS) requirements such as:
    - low delay,
    - low jitter,
    - low loss rate.
  - Fast compression algorithms.

Although the above list is far from being complete, it is large enough to show that there is a huge number of open problems waiting to be solved in this area. Despite these problems, the demand for sophisticated applications (like *video-on-demand*) is rapidly increasing and this fact gives researchers a strong incentive to concentrate their efforts on multimedia research. Although current technology does not allow very sophisticated applications to be widely used, it is not too optimistic to expect them to be up and running in the near future. Various companies have built prototype *video-on-demand* servers, and they are testing their systems in pilot areas.

The demand for highly sophisticated multimedia software also affects the designers of *Multimedia Authoring Systems*. They also suffer from problems similar to those that multimedia researchers are currently facing. It is clear that any advance in multimedia will help the designers of MAS's in building better systems. For instance, the lack of a well-studied and well-understood knowledge representation for multimedia objects prevents the MAS designers from building a system which can bring various types of media together and which can easily be extended with the addition of new media types. Today, most of the MAS's deal with a fixed set of media types, and do not let users add new ones. To build an extensible MAS, it should be possible to "introduce" new *media types* to the MAS by presenting information about the characteristics of the corresponding media objects:

- the description of the information that may be attached to the objects (i.e. metadata [10], [11], [12]),
- the constraints (time etc.) that should be satisfied when such an object is retrieved and/or displayed (e.g. time constraints [12]),
- the interactions of these objects with other objects of different types (e.g. How can an audio object be linked to a video object? What are the constraints that need to be satisfied when an object of *audio* type is displayed along with an object of *video* type?),
- the interactions of the objects of the same type (e.g. How to play two objects of the *audio* type together? Or is it possible to do so?),
- the preferred indexing and/or storage strategies that should be used with the objects of the new type,

Users of MAS's may also want to describe how different multimedia objects should be composed together (e.g. [12]) to create new types of multimedia objects. Some of the questions that may arise in such compositions are:

- Which characteristics of the parent object types are inherited?
- What are the additional characteristics that needs to be added to the new object?
- How to perform the dynamic merging and decomposition of the objects?

All of the above questions point to the the necessity of a uniform and comprehensive knowledge representation framework for multimedia data. Unfortunately, although MAS users desire high expressive powers from the authoring systems, they and the MAS designers are limited with the status of the current technology.

Most existing MAS's still rely on databases which are well suited for traditional data (such as *text* or *numbers*), for both their internal data representation/storage and for the database capabilities they provide to the application programmers. This fact makes it difficult for MAS's to use the properties of multimedia items for enhancing storage and retrieval efficiency. However, the characteristics of such media (like *video* or *hand writing*) are inherently different from those of the more traditional data, and they require a totally different approach. For instance video data

- has a temporal extent which can not be represented in relational databases in an efficient way,

- contains objects, roles and events which need to be extracted and indexed for content-based retrieval,
- has associated QoS constraints that need to be satisfied for network transmission,
- usually has some associated metadata.

Because of these (and other) properties of video data, it difficult to implement a multimedia application with video capabilities using relational databases. Today, most of the multimedia systems use 'Object Oriented' approach which overcomes some of the deficiencies of the relational approach. Unfortunately, even *OO* databases are not completely suited for all multimedia purposes.

Some of the current MAS's provide a facility called *ODBC* which enables their users to attach their favorite DBMS's to their MAS's. In theory, such systems could be integrated with more advanced multimedia database systems using database specific drivers, solving the problem of storage for multimedia items. These systems usually allow various extensions to SQL so that different types of data can be reached. Since standard *SQL* is not suitable for most multimedia applications, either *SQL* needs be extended or a totally new query language needs be built in *ODBC* to use this paradigm for multimedia databases. In fact, there are various extensions to SQL such as "Spatial SQL" [5] which handle different types of data, and a specially designed *ODBC* driver could be used to link a spatial database to a multimedia application using "Spatial SQL".

Many researchers are working on query languages which will address the requirements of the multimedia databases. However, due to the lack of a solid knowledge representation in which all the properties of the multimedia items, their interactions and their requirements can be fully encapsulated, it is almost impossible to create a comprehensive multimedia query language.

OLE is a technique which enables the creation-exportation-reuse of objects in multimedia applications. The reuse of *OLE* objects requires a search mechanism that will provide access to existing multimedia objects. For instance, such a mechanism would be very useful in applications like "video editing" in which parts of the existing video segments are brought together to create new videos. Such an application, requires the understanding of temporal aspects of video segments as well as the video annotation methods. It also requires a content based or annotation based index which will let the users search for video segments (i.e. video objects) in a video database.

Note that in some applications the objects in question may not be explicitly stored, but they can be extracted dynamically upon need (e.g. the video editting application decribed above). Unfortunately, it is still an open question how such a dynamic extraction can be performed. Furthermore the extracted objects may require to be gathered to create new multimedia objects (e.g. new video segments). If the interactions between multimedia objects can be modeled properly, the merging/synchronizing of them can be done more easily.

Schemes like Dynamic Data Exchange (*DDE*), on the other hand, provide a platform in which communications can be established between external softwares and the MAS's. Data can flow back and forth between MAS's and the external softwares, henceforth MAS's can benefit from the capabilities of these softwares. To design a communication protocol through which MAS's and external softwares can efficiently exchange multimedia information, it is necessary to understand the characteristics of the multimedia objects.

Again, the key to build an efficient distributed multimedia environment is to understand how *QoS* requirements can be satisfied. Current advances in the network area attracts people to distributed computation. Users choose to reach remote data when necessary, instead of storing it at their own sites. Hence, the need for MAS's that are providing platforms for building distributed multimedia systems is increasing. However, the communication characteristics that are applicable to the traditional data are very different from the characteristics of those of the multimedia information. These characteristics needs to be fully explored, and efficient protocols need to be developed for providing fast and high quality multimedia communication.

One of the uses of *DDE* is to exchange data among software packages that are geographically distributed. As mentioned above it is still an open question how to guarantee *QoS* requirements in multimedia environments, and *DDE*'s are usually slow in this regard. Today, most MAS's provide their users the power of building distributed systems by the use of network file systems which may not be the most suitable way for multimedia communication. Note however that, there are lots of networking problems to be solved to be able to use the networks in the most efficient way for multimedia communication.

As you can see, although the current technologies like *ODBC*, *OLE*, *DDE* and *DLL* are capable of providing various nice properties to MAS's, in practice they lack a lot of crucial aspects. There is a large amount of research going on in multimedia technologies, and it is clear that MAS's will highly benefit from the results of these researches.

7.2 How to Benefit from MAS's in Multimedia Research

One of the biggest problems that multimedia researchers face today is the lack of time and manual power. In order to build a complete multimedia system, many researchers devote a large portion of their time in building and integrating unrelated components of their systems.

Preparing GUI's and creating databases in which multimedia objects will be stored are usually among the crucial steps of building a multimedia system. However, designing such a multimedia environment from scratch is usually very cumbersome and sometimes impossible.

Multimedia authoring tools, on the other hand, provide a framework in which many desired properties of such multimedia systems can be built very easily. For instance, a researcher who uses a MAS does not need to design a whole database; instead s/he can integrate an already existing database with the system and use it along with the tool s/he has designed. Similarly MAS's let researchers build GUI's for their multimedia systems with great ease and in addition, they increase the portability of the resulting systems.

These properties of MAS's help researchers in minimizing the time spent for research-unrelated issues, and let them concentrate on more relevant problems.

8. Conclusion

In this work, we have studied three popular MAS's and we have implemented a sample multimedia application in each of these systems.

Among the three systems we have studied, we have found that, Multimedia Toolbook is the best for developers with programming experience. Toolbook also turned out to be the most powerful and elegant MAS we have studied. The only real deficiency of this tool is its lack of portability (it is available for Windows only).

Although IconAuthor's *icon-flowchart* metaphor is easy to learn, and the procedural control flow is suitable for non-programmers, it can be quite awkward for experienced users. Furthermore, procedural control flow is not nearly as concise as event programming in many cases. On the plus side, it has excellent OS connectivity, and superb special effects and media support (much better than Toolbook). For non-programmers, this would probably be the tool of choice.

Finally, although Director was not suited for our sample application, it is very well suited for many others (it is the single most popular MAS in use). For example, Director excels in animation and video control.

We have also looked at the deficiencies of the current MAS's and we have discussed how the reserach in the multimedia area will effect the design of future MAS's. It appears that there are various properties that would be nice to have in MAS's, but that are not currently provided.

Acknowledgements

This research was supported by the Army Research Office under grant DAAL-03-92-G-0225, by the Air Force Office of Scientific Research under grant F49620-93-1-0065, by ARPA/Rome Labs contract Nr. F30602-93-C-0241 (Order Nr. A716), and by an NSF Young Investigator award IRI-93-57756.

References

[1] *Microsoft Windows for Workgroups Resource Kit.* Microsoft Press, Chapter 11.
[2] *Multimedia Toolbook 3.0 Users Guide.* Asymetrix
[3] *IconAuthor 6.0 User's Guide.* AimTech

[4] *Director 4.0 User's Guide.* Macromedia

[5] M.J. Egenhofer *Spatial SQL: A Query and Presentation Language.* In *IEEE Transactions on Knowledge Engineering*, Vol.6, No. 1, pages 86–94, February 1994.

[6] L.E. McKenzie and R. Snodgrass *Evaluation of Relational Algebras Incorporating the Time Dimension in Databases.* In *ACM Computing Suirveys*, Vol.23, No. 4, pages 501–543, December 1991.

[7] T.-S. Chua, S.-K. Lim and H.-K. Pung *Content-based Retrieval of Segmented Images.* In *ACM Multimedia Conference*, October 1994.

[8] N. Dimitrova and F. Golshani *Px for Semantic Video Database Retrieval.* In *ACM Multimedia Conference*, October 1994.

[9] D. Woelk and W. Kim *Multimedia Information Management in an Object-Oriented Database System.* in Proc. of the 13th VLDB Conference 1987

[10] K. Bohm and T.C. Rakow *Metadata for Multimedia Documents.* In *SIGMOD Record*, Vol. 23, No. 4, pages 21–26, December 1994

[11] R. Jain and A. Hampapur *Metadata in Video Databases.* In *SIGMOD Record*, Vol. 23, No. 4, pages 27–33, December 1994

[12] S. Marcus and V.S. Subrahmanian *Foundations of Multimedia Database Systems.* submitted for publication (1994).

[13] R. Hjelsvold and R. Midstraum *Modelling and Querying Video Data.* in Proc. of the 20th VLDB Conference 1994

[14] S. Adali, K.S. Candan, S.-S. Chen, K. Erol and V.S. Subrahmanian *Advanced Video Information System: Data structures and Query Processing.* submitted for publication (1995).

Metadata for Building the MultiMedia Patch Quilt

Vipul Kashyap[1,3], Kshitij Shah[2,3], and Amit Sheth[1]

[1] LSDIS, Department of Computer Science
University of Georgia, 415 GSRC, GA 30602-7404.
[2] Bellcore, 444 Hoes Lane, Piscataway, NJ 08854.
[3] Department of Computer Science, Rutgers University, New Brunswick, NJ 08903

Summary. Huge amounts of data available in a variety of digital forms has been collected and stored in thousands of repositories. However, the information relevant to a user or application need may be stored in multiple forms in different repositories. Answering a user query may require correlation of information at a *semantic level* across multiple forms and representations. We present a three-level architecture comprising of the *ontology, metadata* and *data* levels for enabling this correlation. Components of this architecture are explained by using an example from a GIS application.

Metadata is the most critical level in our architecture. Various types of metadata developed by researchers for different media are reviewed and classified *wrt* the extent they model data or information content. The reference terms and the ontology of the metadata are classified *wrt* their dependence on the application domain. We identify the type of metadata suitable for enabling correlation at a semantic level. Issues of metadata extraction, storage and association with data are also discussed.

1. Introduction

In recent years, huge amounts of digital data in a variety of structured, unstructured (e.g., image) and sequential (e.g., audio) formats has been collected and stored in thousands of repositories. Significant advances in managing textual, image, audio, and video databases support efficient storage and access of data of a single type in a single repository. Affordable multimedia systems and a variety of internetworking tools (including the current favorite, the World Wide Web [2]) allow creation of multimedia documents, and support locating, accessing and presenting such data.

However, information relevant to a user or application need may be stored in multiple forms (e.g., structured data, image, audio, video and text) in different repositories. Answering a user query typically requires correlation of such information across multiple forms and multiple representations. Correlating various pieces of information at the physical level by pre-analysis and establishing explicit hypertext/hyper-media links is not an attractive option. For example, there could be thousands of objects that could be recognized in an image, but linking all of these objects to relevant textual or structured data would be a very time consuming and unrewarding process.

We believe that it is necessary to represent semantic information to support the correlation of heterogeneous types of information. Humans are able to abstract information efficiently from images, video or audio data displayed on the computer. This enables them to correlate information at a higher *semantic level* with other forms of representation such as the symbolic representation of data in structured databases. This capability of correlating information at a semantic level across different representations such as symbolic, image, audio and video is lacking in current multimedia systems, and has been characterized as a "semantic bottleneck" [11] – a problem that we are working on. Among recent examples of visual information management in a semantically meaningful manner is the VIMSYS approach to support semantic queries on images [10]. Chu et al. [5] have also adopted a semantic modeling approach for content-based retrieval for medical images.

In the InfoQuilt project, we visualize the related information in heterogeneous media types as a "patch quilt" of digital data. To enable correlation of information across heterogeneous digital media types at a semantic level, we propose a three-level architecture (Figure 1.1). The three main levels of this architecture are described below.

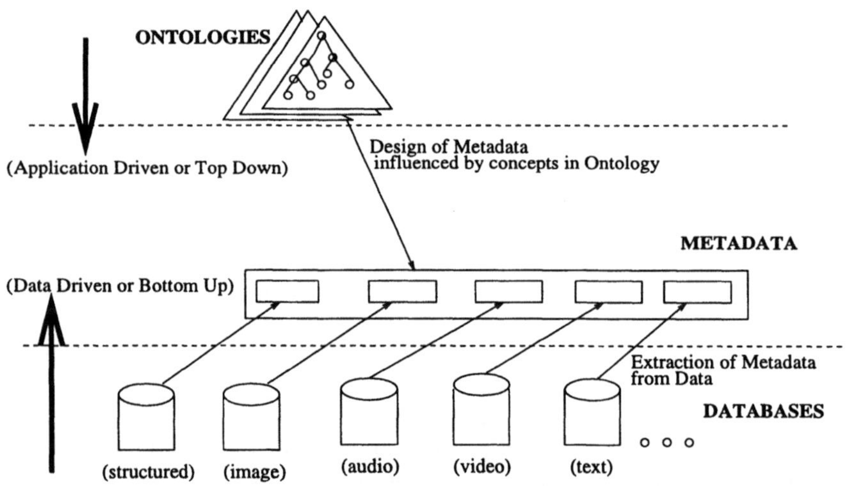

Fig. 1.1. Three level architecture for information correlation in Digital Media

Ontologies: These refer to the terminology/vocabulary which characterizes the content of information in a database irrespective of the media type. We shall capture this vocabulary in a symbolic representation (as opposed to, e.g., an image or audio representation). The vocabulary in general shall contain both domain-independent and domain-specific terms. The domain-independent terms may or may not depend on the characteristics of the media type.

Metadata: These represent *information* about the data in the individual databases and can be seen as an extension of the concept of schema in structured databases. They may describe, or be a *summary* of the information content of the individual databases in an intensional manner. They typically represent constraints between the individual media objects which are implicit and not represented in the databases themselves. Some metadata may also capture content-independent information like *location* and *time of creation*. Typically, however, metadata would capture content-dependent information like *the relief of a geographical area.*

Data: This is the actual (raw) data which might be represented in any of the media types. Examples of what we consider media types are structured data (data in relational or object-oriented databases), textual data, images (maybe of different modalities like X-Ray, MRI scan), audio (maybe of different modalities like monoaural, stereophonic) and video.

From the perspective of answering queries which require correlation of heterogeneous data in different repositories, the most critical level of the above architecture is the **metadata level**. For enabling semantic correlation, the metadata should be able to model the *semantics* of the data. Semantics of an object include both the "meaning" and "use" of an object [16]. Researchers in the area of multidatabases have investigated the issues of semantic heterogeneity [21] and the issues of semantic similarity and structural differences [22]. To compare and combine information from the various media types, we need to view them independent of their representation medium [11]. The metadata level represents the level at which we shall view the information from the various media types and compare and combine them.

Some of the significant recent work in developing metadata for digital media is compiled in [17]. Böhm and Rakow have provided a classification of metadata in the context of multimedia documents [3]. Jain and Hampapur have characterized video metadata and its usage for content-based processing [12]. Kiyoki et al. have used metadata to provide associative search of images for a set of user-given keywords [13]. Anderson and Stonebraker have developed a metadata schema for management of satellite images [1]. Grosky et al. have discussed a data model for modeling and indexing metadata and providing the definition of higher abstractions [7]. Glavitsch et al. have demonstrated how a common vocabulary suffices to develop metadata for integration of speech and text documents [9]. Chen et al. describe automatic generation of metadata to support mixed media access [4].

In this chapter, we have reviewed the work done by the researchers on different media types and classified the metadata designed by them. The criteria we use to classify the metadata is the extent to which they are successful in capturing the data and information content of the documents represented in various media types. The level of abstraction at which the content of the documents is captured is very important. As suggested by others (e.g. Wiederhold [26] and Gruber [8]), we believe that to capture the content at a level of abstraction closer to that of human beings, it is important for the metadata to model *application domain-specific* information.

It is in this context that the terms/vocabulary used to design the metadata assumes special significance. We believe that in order for the metadata to model information at a level of abstraction closer to human beings the choice of terms to construct the metadata should be domain-specific. The terms chosen should be influenced by the application in mind or user needs. Information of this type is captured at the ontology level. We categorize the vocabulary based on whether the terms are data or application-driven and whether they are domain-dependent or domain-independent.

An important component in being able to query across multiple, heterogeneous representations of related information is to be able to design and store associations of the metadata with the actual data stored in the databases. This might mean relating domain-specific terms in the metadata (e.g., cloud-cover in an image) to media-specific domain-independent terms characterizing the data (e.g., color, texture, shape of image objects). Issues of metadata extraction and storage are also discussed.

We have presented a three-level architecture to support correlation of information stored in different digital media at a higher semantic level. We review the state of art in different digital media and analyze the types of metadata used and the vocabulary from which they are constructed. We identify the types of metadata and the nature of vocabulary required to achieve semantic correlation. Where appropriate, we shall discuss examples from a GIS application to illustrate components of our three level architecture.

The organization of this chapter is as follows. We discuss issues related to the vocabulary/ontology from which the metadata are constructed in Section 2.. Issues related to construction, design, storage and extraction of metadata are discussed in Section 3.. Issues related to the association of data with metadata are discussed in Section 4.. Conclusions and future research directions are presented in Section 5..

2. Characterization of the Ontology

We believe that for effective computer-based *correlation of related information* between heterogeneous digital media, it will be necessary to take advantage of knowledge pertaining to the application domain. The key to utilizing the knowledge of an application domain is identifying the basic *vocabulary* consisting of terms (or concepts) of interest to a typical user in the application domain and the interrelationships among the concepts in the ontology.

In the course of collecting a vocabulary or constructing an ontology for information represented in a particular media type, some concepts or terms may be independent of the application domain. Some of them may be media-specific while others might be media-independent. There might be some application-specific concepts for which interrelationships may be represented. They are typically independent of the media of representation.

Information represented using different *media types* can be associated with application-specific concepts and then be appropriately correlated. This forms the basis for a *semantic correlation* of information stored in heterogeneous repositories.

2.1 Terminological Commitments: Constructing an Ontology

An ontology may be defined as the specification of a representational vocabulary for a shared domain of discourse which may include definitions of classes, relations, functions and other objects [8]. We assume that media types presenting *related information* share the same domain of discourse. However, different database designers might use different terminology for the identification and representation of various concepts. There have to be agreements on the terms used by the different designers. These agreements can be the basis of the construction of the ontology and are called *ontological commitments*. We view ontological commitments as a very important requirement for domain-dependent terms.

Typically there may be other terms in the vocabulary which may not be dependent on the domain and may be media-specific. Further it may be necessary to translate between descriptive vocabularies that involve approximating, abstracting or eliminating terms as a part of the negotiated agreement reached by the various designers. It may also be important to translate domain-dependent terms to domain-independent media-specific terms by using techniques specialized to that media type.

Research in the area of Multidatabases has typically used concept hierarchies to represent the vocabulary of the domain of discourse [27], [25], [20], [19]. Let us consider the domain of a GIS application. An important problem in the GIS area is Site Location and Planning. We illustrate fragments of the concept hierarchies used in developing the ontology in Figure 2.1.
In the process of construction, we view the ontology from the following two different perspectives.

- The *data-driven vs* the *application-driven* perspectives.
  Data-driven approach: This refers to the concepts and relationships designed by interactive identification of objects in the related information stored in the databases corresponding to different media types.
  Application-driven approach: This refers to the concepts and relationships inspired by the class of queries for which the related information in the various media types is processed. The concept Rural Area in Figure 2.1 is an example of a concept obtained from the application-driven approach.
- The *domain-dependent* and the *domain-independent* perspectives.
  Domain-dependent perspective: This represents the concepts which are closely tied to the domain of the application we wish to model. Most

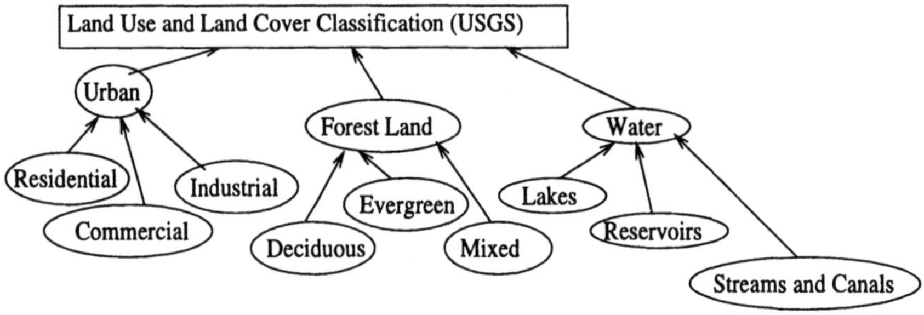

A classification using a generalization hierarchy

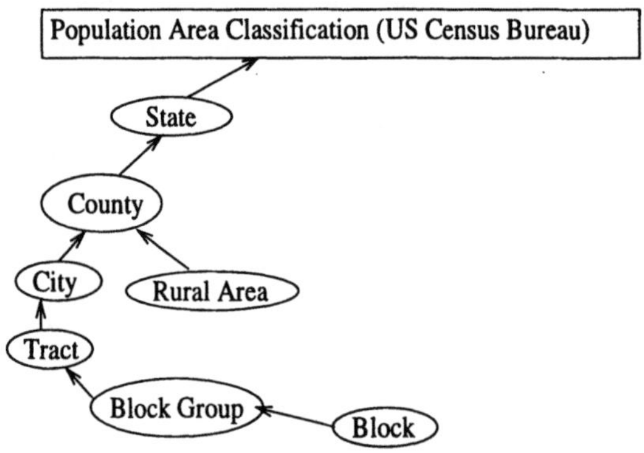

A classification using an aggregation hierarchy

Fig. 2.1. Examples of Generalization and Aggregation hierarchies that may be used for Ontology construction

of the concepts are likely to be identified using the application-driven approach.

Domain-independent perspective: This represents the concepts required by the various media types (e.g., color, shape and texture for images, such as R-features [12]) to identify the domain-specific concepts. These are typically independent of the application domain and are generated by using the data-driven approach.

2.2 Controlled Vocabulary for Digital Media

In this section we review the discussion in [17] on extracting metadata. We focus on the terminology and vocabulary identified by the various researchers for characterizing the information content of the data represented in a particular media type. We identify how the various terms relate to the perspectives discussed above.

Jain and Hampapur [12] have used domain models to assign a qualitative label to a feature (such as *pass*, *dribble* and *dunk* in basketball) and are called

Vocabulary Feature	Media Type	Domain Dep. or Indep.	Appl ication or Data Driven
Q-Features (Jain and Hampapur)	Video, Image	Domain Dependent	Application Driven
R-Features (Jain and Hampapur)	Video, Image	Domain Independent	Data Driven
English Words (Kiyoki et al.)	Image	Domain Dependent	Data Driven
ISCC and NBS colors (Kiyoki et al.)	Image	Domain Independent	Data Driven
AVHRR features (Anderson and Stonebraker)	Image	Domain Independent	Data Driven
NDVI (Anderson and Stonebraker)	Image	Domain Dependent	Data Driven
Subword units (Glavitsch et al.)	Audio, Text	Domain Dependent	Data Driven
Keywords (Chen et al.)	Image Audio Text	Domain Dependent	Application and Data Driven

Table 2.1. Controlled Vocabulary for Digital Media

Q-Features. Features which rely on low level domain-independent models like object trajectories are called R-Features. We consider Q-Features as an example of the domain-dependent, application-driven perspective and R-Features as an example of the domain-independent, data-driven perspective.

Kiyoki et al. [13] have used 850 basic words from the "General Basic English Dictionary" as features which are then associated with the images. We consider these features as examples of domain-dependent, data-driven perspective. They also use the color names defined by ISCC (Inter-Society Color Council) and NBS (National Bureau of Standard) as the features. We consider these as examples of the domain-independent, data-driven perspective.

Anderson and Stonebraker [1] model some features that are primarily based on the measurements of the five channels of the Advanced Very High Resolution Radiometer (AVHRR) sensor. Other features refer to spatial (latitude, longitude) and temporal (begin date, end date) information. We consider these examples of domain-independent, data-driven perspective. However there are features like the normalized difference vegetation index (NDVI) which are derived from different channels. We consider this as an example of the domain-dependent, data-driven perspective.

Glavtisch et al. [9] have determined from experiments that good indexing features lay between phonemes and words. They have selected three special types of subword units: VCV-, CV- and VC-. The letter V stands for a maximum sequence of vowels and C for a maximum sequence of consonants. They process a set of speech and text documents to determine a vocabulary for the domain. The same vocabulary is used for both the speech and text media types. We consider these as examples of the domain-dependent, data-driven perspective.

Chen et al. [4] use the keywords identified in the text and speech documents as their vocabulary. They have discussed issues of restricted *vs* unrestricted vocabulary. If the set of keywords is fixed, metadata based on keyword locations can be pre-computed and stored later for indexing. In general, unrestricted vocabulary produces better results than restricted vocabulary searching. They support the search by spotting keywords "on the fly". We consider these as examples of the domain-dependent, data and application-driven perspectives.

A summary of the above discussion is presented in Table 2.1.

The summary of the vocabulary used in digital media illustrated in Table 2.1 does not bring out the contribution of the media type in determining the features to characterize the information content of the databases. We recognize the fact that constructing a vocabulary with domain-independent perspective would entail both *media-specific* and *media-independent* features. We may also be able to write programs for automatic extraction of some media-specific features from the digital data. We discuss metadata extractors in further detail in Section 3.3. The role played by the media types is illustrated in Figure 2.2.

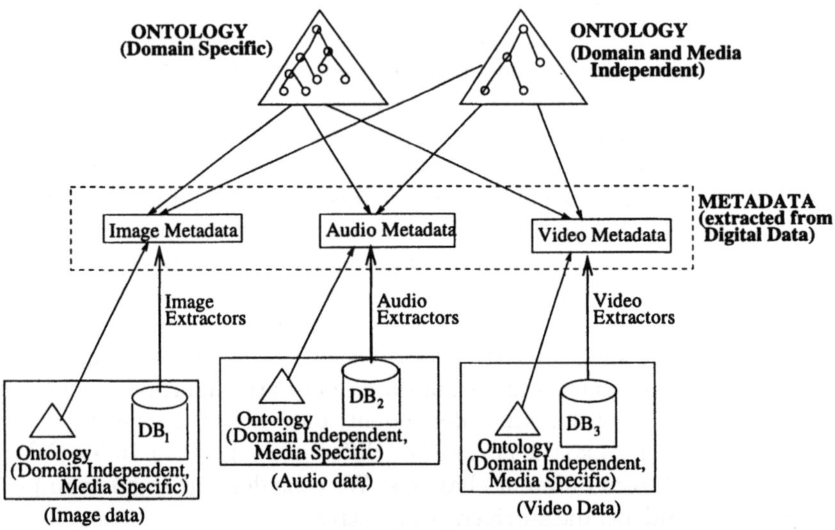

Fig. 2.2. Role of the Media Type in determining the metadata features

2.3 Better understanding of the query

When the terms used in a user's query are not expressive enough, or cannot be mapped by the system to the ontological concepts, the user may guide the construction of the query metadata with the help of the ontology (that may be graphically displayed). The query metadata may typically represent application-specific constraints which the answer should satisfy. We assume the representation of metadata as a collection of meta-attributes and values. For the discussion in this chapter see [16], [18] for further details.

Let us consider the Site Location and Planning Problem referred to earlier. This requires correlation of related information represented in two media types, structured databases and images. A typical query that may be asked by a decision maker trying to determine a desirable location of a shopping mall is:

Get all blocks with a population greater than five hundred with an average income greater than 30,000 per annum, that have moderate relief with a large contiguous rectangular area and are of an urban type of land use.

The metadata for the query can be constructed as follows. Let the variable X refer to the final output unified with the regions in which a mall may be built in a geographical region characterized above.

```
[ (region X) (population [> 500]) (contiguous-area [large])
(relief [moderate]) (average-income [> 30,000])
(shape [rectangular]) (land-use [Urban]) ]
```

These metadata are designed from the domain-specific ontology as its basis, and are later described as *content-descriptive domain-dependent metadata.* The current state of art in multimedia databases does not support querying at this level of abstraction. In Section 3. we survey the state of art in this area and propose the research efforts required to support the above level of abstraction.

2.4 Ontology Guided Extraction of Metadata

The extraction of metadata from the information in various media types can be primarily guided by the domain-specific ontology though it may involve terms in the domain-independent ontology. Both content-dependent and content-independent metadata may be extracted (as discussed in Section 3.).

Let us consider again the GIS application discussed earlier in the section. For this application we model the metadata as a collection of attribute value pairs. The meta-attributes can be derived from concepts in the domain-specific ontology. The values of the meta-attributes can be the set of constraints imposed on the class of domain objects represented by the set of regions. These constraints are qualitative descriptions of the spectral (i.e., color, intensity), morphological (i.e., shape related) and textural properties of the objects. For example, the meta-attribute *vegetation* can have as values, a set of image regions with the qualitative spectral constraint *green* and with the qualitative textural constraint of being either *grass-like*, *forest-like* or *shrub-like*.

Kiyoki et al. [13] describe the automatic extraction of *impression vectors* based on English words or ISCC and NBS colors. The users when querying an image database then use English words to query the system. One way of guiding the users could be to display the list of English words used to construct the metadata in the first place. However, because this is inconvenient the vocabulary is typically not displayed to the user.

Glavitsch et al. [9] describe the construction of a speech feature index for both text and audio documents based on a common vocabulary consisting of subword units as discussed earlier. Given a query, the features can be evaluated easily because the canonical forms of the features (vowel and consonant sequences like VCV-, CV- VC-) are well defined.

Chen et al. [4] describe the construction of keyword indices, topic change indices and layout indices. These typically depend on the content of the documents and the vocabulary is dependent on the keywords present in the documents. A query can be a set of spoken keywords which might result in the retrieval of documents containing those keywords.

In the above cases, the vocabulary is not pre-defined and depends on the content of the documents in the collection. Also, the interrelationships between the terms in the ontology is not identified. We believe that identifying these relationships would result in the reduction of the size of the vocabulary. A typical set of relationships have been identified in [19]. A controlled vocabulary with terms and their interrelationships can be exploited to create metadata which model domain-dependent relationships as illustrated in the case of the GIS application discussed earlier in this section.

3. Construction and Design of Metadata

In this section, we identify and classify various kinds of metadata which are mandatory, or could facilitate, the handling of different media types, including multimedia. The way in which the documents of different media types is used will be directly affected by the metadata. We classify metadata based on whether they are based on the data or information content of the documents. We also identify the type of metadata suitable for enabling correlation at a *semantic level.*

The extraction of metadata from data is highly influenced by the media type of the data. Our definition of **media type** is explained as follows. The American Heritage Dictionary defines *Medium* as a means of mass communication. This is generally determined by the way in which the information would be presented based on the original intention of the information creator. Of course, the same information could be stored in different physical formats and could be subjected to various transformations between creation and storage and between storage and presentation. We thus differentiate between what is meant by a data type, as used in conventional database technology, and media type, which depends on the presentation as opposed to the former. Issues of metadata extraction are discussed in Section 3.3. Metadata storage and organization is a very relevant issue and is discussed in Section 3.4.

3.1 Classification of Metadata

In this section we review the different kinds of metadata used by researchers in different digital media types [17]. We classify the various kinds of metadata based on whether they are based on the data or information content of the documents or not. The basic kinds of metadata we identify are:

- Content-dependent metadata.
- Content-descriptive metadata (Special case of Content-dependent metadata).
- Content-independent metadata.

Content-dependent metadata, as the name suggests, depends only on the content of the original data. When we associate metadata with the original data, which describes the contents in some way, but cannot be extracted automatically from the contents themselves, we call it content-descriptive metadata. This kind of metadata relates to characteristics, which could be determined exclusively by looking at the content (i.e., by the cognitive process), or derived intellectually with the support of tools and which could not have been derived on the basis of content alone.

A text index, like the document vectors in the LSI index [6] and the complete inverted WAIS index [14] are examples of content-based metadata. The index is determined by the content, e.g., the frequency and position of text units in the document.

Content-descriptive metadata, itself, can be classified as domain-dependent and domain-independent. Domain-dependent metadata uses domain-specific concepts. These concepts are used as a basis to determine the actual metadata created. An example of domain dependent metadata would characterize the set of images in a GIS database containing forest land cover. Domain-independent metadata, on the other hand, relies on no such domain-specific concepts. A typical example of a domain-independent metadata would be the one which describes the structure of a multimedia document [3].

Content-independent metadata, on the other hand, does not depend on the content. This kind of metadata can be derived independently from the content of the data. This is like attaching a tag to the data irrespective of the data contents. Examples of content-independent metadata about a text-document are its date of creation and location.

Most of the work, so far, has concentrated on issues related to content-based and content-descriptive domain-independent metadata. These are not adequate for capturing the semantics of the domain. Content-descriptive domain-dependent metadata is needed to characterize the meaning and usage of the underlying objects.

We have proposed the use of content-descriptive domain-dependent metadata for structured data [15]. We believe that the techniques for structured data can either be extended to or inspire analogous techniques for digital data. Image and visual data are inherently rich in semantic content. These objects can be better interpreted in the context of a given domain. Methods exist in advanced image analysis systems exist for low-level pattern recognition, image processing and segmentation and object recognition. Similarly various tools and techniques exist for other media types. We need to build upon these techniques to achieve correlation across different media types at a *semantic level* by associating these methods with content-descriptive metadata.

Jain and Hampapur [12], have used video and image metadata for content-dependent access of videos in a video database. The Image and Video R-feature value pairs (e.g. the Object Track feature associated with a Set of image positions) may be considered as content-dependent metadata. The Image and Video Q-feature value pairs (e.g., the Video Class feature with associated values such as *News*, *Sports*) may be considered as content-descriptive metadata whereas the Meta feature value pairs (e.g., the Producer Info feature with the associated producer name) may be considered as examples of content-independent metadata.

Kiyoki et al. [13], have demonstrated a method for associating users' impressions of images with the images themselves. They create a semantic metadata space which is used to dynamically compute similarity between keywords and metadata items of the image. These may be considered as content-descriptive metadata.

Anderson and Stonebraker [1] propose a metadata schema for satellite images. They lay emphasis on content-descriptive metadata for supporting temporal and geographic queries. These are primarily domain-independent.

Glavtisch et al. [9] discuss the use of subword units for speech documents for indexing. They use these indices to integrate speech documents in an information retrieval system. These may be considered as examples of content-dependent metadata.

Chen et al. [4] identify keyword locations, conversation segmentation by speaker and regions of speakers speaking emphatically, and index these for speech. Similarly they index features like keywords and layout for text image documents. These features are derived either in advance or at retrieval time. These may be considered as examples of content-dependent metadata.

Böhm and Rakow [3] have suggested a classification of metadata for multimedia documents. The different types of metadata they identify and their relationship to our classification are:

- *Metadata for the Representation of Media Types.* This includes format, coding and compression techniques that may have been applied. These may be considered as content-independent metadata.
- *Content-descriptive Metadata.* A list of persons or institutions having some relation to a particular multimedia document's content are examples of these. We have also classified these metadata in a similar manner.
- *Metadata for Content Classification.* These refer to a classification of the content of a document. One way of classifying the content of a document is to identify the subject domain of the document. These are examples of domain-dependent content-descriptive metadata.
- *Metadata for Document Composition.* These refer to the logical components of multimedia documents. They may be considered as content-descriptive domain-independent metadata.
- *Metadata for Document History.* These metadata record the status of multimedia documents like approvedByEditor and notApproved. These may be considered as content-independent metadata.
- *Metadata for Document Location.* This may be considered as content-independent metadata.

A summary of the above discussion is presented in Table 3.1.

Looking at the classification in Table 3.1, we observe that the Speech feature index and Impression vector are statistical correlations of the various terms of interest in the vocabulary. They do not represent semantic relationships. Also, R-feature value pairs, Grid and Metadata for Representation of Media Types, represent metadata influenced by the media type. Hence they cannot be used to correlate information *independent of the medium.* Spatial registration, keyword index, topic change indices, layout indices and metadata for document composition are domain-independent in nature. For semantic correlation, we should be able to capture domain-specific information independent of the medium of representation. This facilitates the representation of the meaning and use of the data in the documents. The metadata which satisfy this criteria are Q-feature value pairs and Content classification metadata. We believe that it is these types of metadata which provide the key for *semantic correlation.*

Our initial investigation on content-descriptive metadata which characterize the domain of GIS applications for the Site Planning Problem is discussed next.

3.2 Meta-correlation: The Key to Media-Independent Semantic Correlation

In this section we discuss with an example how related information represented in different digital media can be combined by making use of metadata. The relation between information in different media may be represented using

Metadata	Media Type	Content Dependence
Q-Feature Value pairs (Jain and Hampapur)	Image, Video	content-descriptive
R-Feature Value pairs (Jain and Hampapur)	Image, Video	content-dependent
Meta Feature Value pairs (Jain and Hampapur)	Video	content-independent
Impression Vector (Kiyoki et al.)	Image	content-descriptive
Grid (Anderson and Stonebraker)	Image	content-dependent
Spatial Registration (Anderson and Stonebraker)	Image	content-descriptive
Temporal Information (Anderson and Stonebraker)	Image	content-independent
Speech feature index (Glavtisch et al.)	Audio	content-dependent
Keyword index (Chen et al.)	Text	content-dependent
Topic change indices (Chen et al.)	Audio	content-dependent
Layout indices (Chen et al.)	Image	content-dependent
Metadata for Representation of Media Types, Document History, Location (Böhm and Rakow)	MultiMedia	content-independent
Content Descriptive, Content Classification Document Composition Metadata (Böhm and Rakow)	MultiMedia	content-descriptive

Table 3.1. Metadata Classification

meta-correlations as illustrated in Figure 3.1. In Section 3.1 we have identified the content-descriptive domain-dependent metadata as being suitable for information correlation across multiple representations. In this section we discuss an example from the GIS domain to illustrate information correlation across structured data and images. We can view the problem of correlating the information across different types of digital media from two perspectives:

3.2.1 A Partial Schema for Digital Data. We can consider the metadata which captures the information represented in a particular media type as an *elementary schema* for the information. Consider an example of the GIS database which contains images on land use and land cover. One representation of the metadata for such a database is as follows.

```
[(region [ block (bounds [33N <= latitude <= 34N,
        84W <= longitude <= 85W])]) (relief [moderate,steep])
        (contiguous-area [large, medium])
        (shape [rectangular,square]) (land-use [urban,forest])]
```

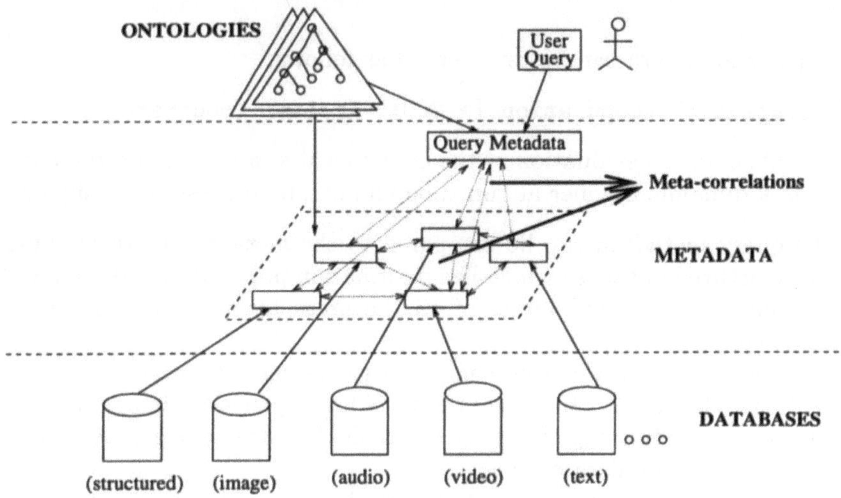

Fig. 3.1. Meta-correlations: correlating information using metadata

This metadata entry for the image database states that all the images within it contain blocks with the following characteristics:

- All blocks fall within the latitudes 33N and 34N and longitudes 84W and 85W.
- All blocks have either moderate or steep relief.
- All blocks have large or medium contiguous areas.
- All blocks have rectangular or square shapes.
- All blocks are either of the urban or forest land use type.

This can be used as a starting point for representations of correlations with information represented in heterogeneous repositories. For instance, having identified areas of *moderate relief* one might establish a correlation with metadata associated with a structured database modeling population information for that region. This may then be considered as an example of a rudimentary *inter-schema correlation.*

The correlations described above can be exploited for browsing through related information represented in different media. For instance, in the example mentioned above, the user can decide to browse population information about a region after having determined its relief from the image database.

3.2.2 Query Processing. The other perspective is to model the information need of a user as metadata guided by a domain-specific ontology. The *query metadata* then acts as the basis for correlation between the metadata for different digital media. Consider a query based on the browsing example discussed above.

Get me all regions having moderate relief and population greater than 200

The query metadata can be represented as follows:

```
[(region X) (population [> 200]) (relief [moderate])]
```

In this case the evaluation of the query results in computing the correlations in a dynamic manner at run time and can be processed as follows:

- The query metadata can be compared to the metadata corresponding to the structured database which has information population and retrieve the latitude and longitude values of all the areas having population greater than 200.
- The query metadata can be compared to the metadata corresponding to the image database. This results in invoking appropriate image processing routines and retrieving the images and the latitudes and longitudes of all areas having a moderate relief.
- The intersection of the latitude-longitude pairs can be computed. This correlation is illustrated in Figure 3.2.

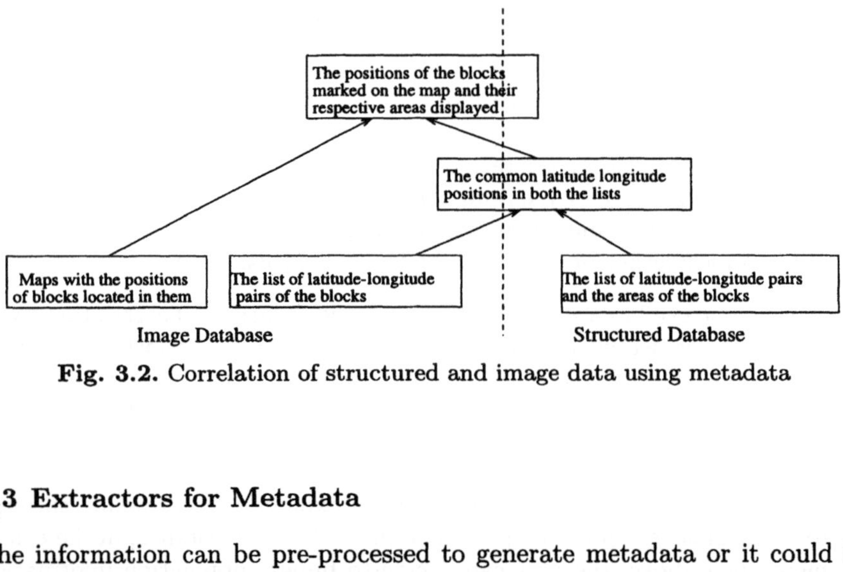

Fig. 3.2. Correlation of structured and image data using metadata

3.3 Extractors for Metadata

The information can be pre-processed to generate metadata or it could be subjected to access time metadata extraction. Extracting content-dependent metadata is entirely media type dependent. The extractors would automatically generate metadata based on the media type, e.g., an extractor for *TEXT* would filter out relevant words and index them. Metadata like sender, date, and subject could be generated from mail messages by an extractor for *MAIL* type which would look for lines starting with the keywords like *SUBJECT:* and *DATE:*, and return those lines. We could have extractors for *C* or *C++* [24] type which would recognize features such as functions, classes and subclasses. The extractors for this type of metadata would require knowledge of the type of the underlying objects. They may also make use of magic tables that are reference tables which map patterns appearing in files or peculiar file names to data types.

Extracting content-dependent metadata for images would involve anticipating the range of user queries and is generally not feasible. Instead, some information like color and shapes could be extracted during pre-processing and others like patterns and outlines could be extracted at access time.

Content-independent metadata like size and location can be determined during pre-processing. We could view the media type itself as metadata. Metadata like container hierarchies for multimedia can either be explicitly supplied or extracted. Extraction of content-descriptive domain-dependent metadata involves associating semantics with the contents. The generation of such metadata involves automatic and semi-automatic approaches and is discussed at length in the previous section.

The extraction of any type of metadata depends on the range of user queries. Querying itself should then be independent of the metadata although the metadata could be used as a factor during querying. For example a query might utilize the size of the data as a retrieval criterion when transport costs have to be taken into account. Also, metadata could control the presentation and dynamic composition of retrieved information. If, based on content-descriptive metadata like type and size, the information is not presentable to the requester of the information, then, it would not be transported to the requester.

Jain and Hampapur [12] have described various methods to extract content-dependent as well as content-descriptive metadata for their video database system. Content-dependent metadata, like the raw Image and Video Features, are extracted by the respective Feature Extractors which have low-level image and video processing routines. These would, for example, extract features like regions and lines from images. To generate content-descriptive domain-independent metadata, Image and Video Classifiers are employed which use a set of domain models to generate qualitatively labeled features for the image or video, like image brightness and texture. Users can also label, or annotate, images or videos with a unit called the Annotator. This would provide content-descriptive domain-dependent metadata. An Object Linker is used to maintain metadata regarding the temporal relationships between sets of frames, which denote a time-interval in video.

Kiyoki et al. [13] use different techniques to generate metadata for the orthogonal, semantic metadata space. The techniques relate to extracting content-descriptive metadata. The generation of domain-dependent metadata is done manually, where a small set of words are used to weigh an image. If a word corresponds to an image, as perceived by the metadata creator, a value of 1.0 is assigned for that word. Similarly, -1.0 is assigned if the word corresponds negatively and 0 is assigned otherwise. Domain-independent metadata is generated automatically by recognizing the colors in an image and using these to annotate the images based on some psychological models of correlating colors and words.

The extraction of metadata from satellite images [1] follows the same basic principles. Content-dependent and content-descriptive domain-independent metadata are extracted automatically from the satellite images using operating system scripts and SQL triggers. Domain-dependent metadata, like keywords describing an image, are inserted manually into the database and associated with the respective images.

An interesting method of metadata generation is implemented by Grosky et al. [17] to support intelligent browsing of structured media objects. User navigation patterns are captured and used to build relationships amongst the web of objects for individual users. This metadata is used for future user navigation. They call this metadata mediated browsing.

Glavitsch et al. [9] use speech recognition routines to extract sub-word features which are then used for indexing. Chen et al. [4] employ a wide array of automatic metadata extractors. These locate user-specified keywords and phrases in images of text and audio streams. The located keywords and their locations are used as metadata. Other derived metadata include partition information in audio streams for different speakers, emphatic speech detection and sub-topic boundary locations.

3.4 Storage of Metadata

Metadata can be stored in a variety of formats. The simplest would be as plain text files. Object-relational database systems could also be employed to manage the metadata. This would provide more flexibility with respect to querying the metadata itself and allowing the browsing of stored metadata prior to query building. Metadata in different media types could also be manipulated in an intuitive manner in such systems. We might relate unstructured data, e.g. images, and their structured data representations using metadata. In such cases it would be advantageous to store the metadata alongwith the original information. Metadata can be easily modified to reflect changes in the information contents or the content descriptions (e.g. location) if the metadata is stored in such database systems. Type specific functions could also be encapsulated alongwith the metadata to perform associative searches for unstructured information by using the metadata representing its features. Storing content-descriptive metadata, like container hierarchies, for multimedia objects determines the way in which the information can be browsed.

Query processing can be done off-line, as a pre-processing stage, if the vocabulary allowed in the query is of manageable size. Metadata based on this finite set of keywords and their locations could be pre-computed and stored for indexing. This is quite restrictive in most cases and searching provides better results if the vocabulary is unlimited. In this case metadata cannot be pre-computed and stored, but will have to be generated at run-time. Query processing on multimedia objects can be optimized if we store statistical metadata and metadata about logical structure.

Another issue in metadata storage is the location of the metadata for cases where the queries are submitted at a site remote to the site from where the information has to be retrieved. In most cases metadata is stored locally. Systems exist where metadata is stored at the remote sites, or could be pre-fetched for a query, and this is then used to intelligently analyze the query. For example, if we can determine from the metadata that the size of the query results could not be handled by the site where they are to be presented, appropriate action could be taken rather than retrieving the information and then failing.

4. Association of Digital Media Data with Metadata

As a result of query processing, the associated digital data also may be required to be displayed to the user (e.g., displaying the regions suitable for site location). Thus it is very important for associations to be stored between the extracted metadata and the underlying digital data. As discussed earlier, the type of metadata suitable for information correlation at a semantic level are the content-descriptive domain-dependent metadata. The main issues in associating these type of metadata to the actual data in the underlying digital media is to relate the domain-specific terms in the metadata to the domain-independent media-specific terms which might characterize the digital data.

4.1 Association of Metadata with Image Data

Consider once again our GIS application. Here we associate content-descriptive domain-dependent metadata with the underlying image data. This may be brought about by mapping the domain-dependent terms used to construct the metadata (e.g., moderate relief) to the domain-independent media-specific terms from the ontology (e.g., shape, color, texture, etc.). The mapping can be implemented as follows.

- Static embedding in an appropriate index/hash structure. For example, the value *green* for the meta-attribute[1] *vegetation* contains the qualitative spectral attribute *green* which could be mapped to a range of color coordinates (R,G,B) which conform reasonably to the notion of greenness (*wrt* the application domain). This can then be mapped to a set of images containing the regions of interest.

[1] We are modeling domain-dependent content-descriptive metadata as a collection of meta-attribute value pairs.

- The mapping of the meta-attribute to image object attributes could be done using a set of parameterized precompiled plans. The initial retrieval of the images containing the regions corresponding to the meta-attribute could be conducted by indexing/hashing on a subset of the image object attributes. The parametric plans can then be used to verify whether the mapping is successful by invoking the plan on the retrieved images and verifying whether the remaining image object attributes satisfy the constraints specified in the metadata.

4.2 Association of Symbolic Descriptions with Image Data

We have seen the different kinds of content-dependent and content-descriptive metadata for images. We can perform semantic associative search on an image database if we could associate these two kinds of metadata. Kiyoki et al. [13] propose a "mathematical model of meaning" which provides functions for performing this kind of a search by using the metadata representing the image features. Here the abstract information about the images is used for their indirect retrieval. In such systems, an orthogonal semantic space is maintained which could consist of the users' impressions as given by keywords with words describing their context and the image contents. The associative search is carried out in this orthogonal space.

4.3 Metadata for Multimedia Objects

When we consider multimedia as a separate media type, we need additional metadata beyond the ones we maintain for the component objects. We might have metadata associated with objects of media type text, images, audio or any other which we might see in the future, but a multimedia object will also have information about how these different objects are related to each other. This kind of metadata is not dependent on the contents of the constituent objects themselves, but we might think of it as being dependent on the content of the multimedia object itself. Thus, we could view these multimedia objects as composite objects and the relationship or structural metadata could be generated manually or automatically on the basis of predefined rules as in [23].

We could also take a deeper view at this kind of metadata which holds information about the relationships between multimedia objects. When we think of multimedia objects as representing some real-world entities, we can say that the content of such objects are the real-world entities that they represent. This then becomes content-dependent metadata as we can use the media object to infer information regarding the real-world entity. Thus we might associate the identity of a person appearing in an image with the image. Grosky et al. [7] present a schema to support this notion. This schema allows intelligent associations between media objects and decides the way in which the user could browse through the database. Their architecture is capable of involving the user's navigation to form higher order clusters from this metadata using neural nets and genetic algorithms. This provides higher level concepts to the users which they can then modify. These clusters provide the user with a modified view of the metadata without actually modifying the metadata itself. Also, each user can maintain their own view of the metadata.

5. Conclusion

When the information relevant to a user resides in heterogeneous repositories and is stored in multiple representations, correlation of information at a higher *semantic level* may be required. As discussed in [11], we also believe that correlation of information across various media types is possible only if we view them independent of their representation medium. We have presented a three level architecture comprising of the *ontology, metadata* and *data* to support such correlation. We used examples of a GIS application to explain components of this architecture.

We have also reviewed the use of vocabulary by various researchers to construct and design their metadata. We identify the domain-specific terms chosen with the application in mind as the most promising to support design and construction of metadata for semantic correlation. An important issue identified is the association of the metadata with the data stored in the various media. Typically this would involve relating the domain-specific, media-independent terms in the ontology to domain-independent, media-specific terms characterizing the data in a particular media type. We illustrate this with an example of the GIS domain mentioned above.

We have identified the *metadata level* as the most critical level in the three level architecture. The metadata should be able to model the *semantics* of the data which we characterize as the *meaning* and *use* of the data. We have reviewed the metadata designed for different media types by various researchers and analyzed them based on factors such as whether they model information specific to the domain of the data and whether they are specific to the media type. For the metadata to model the meaning of the data, it is important for it to capture as much domain-specific information as possible. Also, the metadata should be able to view the data independent of the medium of representation. Thus, we identify the domain-dependent, content-descriptive and media-independent metadata to be the best suited to support semantic correlation. We also discussed the type of metadata we support for semantic correlation in the example GIS application.

However for the state-of-the-art to overcome the "semantic bottleneck" [11] the following research challenges should be met.

- The design of domain-dependent, media-independent metadata, and the constraints about the data that should be represented to capture the semantics of the data.
- The use of the metadata in comparing and combining information independent of the representation medium. This might involve combining and propagating constraints represented in the metadata for related data stored in different representation media.
- Determining a good set of terms and relationships among them to characterize the application domain and capture the semantic content of the data stored in the various media types.
- Determining a good set of terms that are media-specific and can characterize the information content of the data stored in that media type.
- Design of media-specific routines and indexing strategies to map the domain-dependent, media-independent terms to media-specific terms. This is important in the context of associating domain-specific metadata to the actual data.

Acknowledgements

We thank Wolfgang Klaus for his collaboration in preparing the special issue [17] on which some of the work in this chapter is based. The GIS example is based on ongoing collaboration with Dr. E. Lynn Usery at UGA.

References

[1] J. Anderson and M. Stonebraker. Sequoia 2000 Metadata Schema for Satellite Images, in [17].
[2] T. Berners-Lee et al. World-Wide Web: The Information Universe. *Electronic Networking: Research, Applications and Policy*, 1(2), 1992.
[3] K. Böhm and T. Rakow. Metadata for Multimedia Documents, in [17].
[4] F. Chen, M. Hearst, J. Kupiec, J. Pederson, and L. Wilcox. Metadata for Mixed-Media Access, in [17].
[5] W.W. Chu, I.T. Leong, and R.K. Taira. A Semantic Modeling Approach for Image Retrieval by Content. *The VLDB Journal*, 3(4), October 1994.
[6] S. Deerwester, S. Dumais, G. Furnas, T. Landauer, and R. Hashman. Indexing by Latent Semantic Indexing. *Journal of the American Society for Information Science*, 41(6), 1990.
[7] W. Grosky, F. Fotouhi, and I. Sethi. Content-based Hypermedia - Intelligent Browsing of Structured Media Objects, in [17].
[8] T. Gruber. A translation approach to portable ontology specifications. *Knowledge Acquisition, An International Journal of Knowledge Acquisition for Knowledge-Based Systems*, 5(2), June 1993.
[9] U. Glavitsch, P. Schauble, and M. Wechsler. Metadata for Integrating Speech Documents in a Text Retrieval System, in [17].

[10] A. Gupta, T. Weymouth, and R. Jain. Semantic Queries with Pictures: The VIMSYS Model. In *Proceedings of the 17th VLDB Conference*, September 1991.

[11] R. Jain. Semantics in Multimedia Systems. *IEEE MultiMedia*, R. Jain, ed., 1(2), Summer 1994.

[12] R. Jain and A. Hampapuram. Representations of Video Databases, in [17].

[13] Y. Kiyoki, T. Kitagawa, and T. Hayama. A meta-database System for Semantic Image Search by a Mathematical Model of Meaning, in [17].

[14] B. Kahle and A. Medlar. An Information System for Corporate Users : Wide Area Information Servers. *Connexions - The Interoperability Report*, 5(11), November 1991.

[15] V. Kashyap and A. Sheth. Semantics-based Information Brokering. In *Proceedings of the Third International Conference on Information and Knowledge Management (CIKM)*, November 1994. http://www.cs.uga.edu/LSDIS/infoquilt.

[16] V. Kashyap and A. Sheth. Semantics-based Information Brokering: A step towards realizingthe Infocosm. Technical Report DCS-TR-307, Department of Computer Science, Rutgers University, March 1994. http://www.cs.uga.edu/LSDIS/pub.html.

[17] W. Klaus and A. Sheth. Metadata for digital media. *SIGMOD Record, special issue on Metadata for Digital Media*, W. Klaus, A. Sheth, eds., 23(4), December 1994. http://www.cs.uga.edu/LSDIS/pub.html.

[18] V. Kashyap and A. Sheth. Semantic and Schematic Similarities between Databases Objects: A Context-based approach. Technical report, LSDIS Lab, University of Georgia (http://www.cs.uga.edu/LSDIS/infoquilt), January 1995.

[19] D. McLeod and A. Sheth. Interoperability in Multidatabase Systems. *Tutorial Notes - the 20th VLDB Conference*, September 1994.

[20] D. McLeod and A. Si. The Design and Experimental Evaluation of an Information Discovery Mechanism for Networks of Autonomous Database Systems. In *Proceedings of the 11th IEEE Conference on Data Engineering*, February 1995.

[21] A. Sheth. Semantic issues in Multidatabase Systems. *SIGMOD Record, special issue on Semantic Issues in Multidatabases*, A. Sheth, ed., 20(4), December 1991. http://www.cs.uga.edu/LSDIS/pub.html.

[22] A. Sheth and V. Kashyap. So Far (Schematically), yet So Near (Semantically). *Invited paper in Proceedings of the IFIP TC2/WG2.6 Conference on Semantics of Interoperable Database Systems, DS-5*, November 1992. http://www.cs.uga.edu/LSDIS/pub.html.

[23] L. Shklar, K. Shah, and C. Basu. The InfoHarness Repository Definition Language. In *Proceedings of the Third International WWW Conference*, May 1995.

[24] L. Shklar, A. Sheth, V. Kashyap, and K. Shah. Infoharness: Use of Automatically Generated Metadata for Search and Retrieval of Heterogeneous Information. In *Proceedings of CAiSE '95*, June 1995. http://www.cs.uga.edu/LSDIS/infoharness.

[25] P. Tsai and A. Chen. Concept Hierarchies for Database Integration in a Multidatabase System. In *Advances in Data Management*, December 1994.

[26] G. Wiederhold. Interoperation, Mediation and Ontologies. In *FGCS Workshop on Heterogeneous Cooperative Knowledge-Bases*, December 1994.

[27] C. Yu, W. Sun, S. Dao, and D. Keirsey. Determining relationships among attributes for Interoperability of Multidatabase Systems. In *Proceedings of the 1st International Workshop on Interoperability in Multidatabase Systems*, April 1991.

Contributors

Walid G. Aref, Matsushita Information Technology Laboratory, Panasonic Technologies Inc., Two Research Way, Princeton, NJ 08540, USA.
aref@mitl.research.panasonic.com

Manish Arya, IBM Almaden Research Center, San Jose, California, USA.

Daniel Barbará, Matsushita Information Technology Laboratory, Panasonic Technologies Inc., Two Research Way, Princeton, NJ 08540, USA.
dpl@mitl.research.panasonic.com

A. Belussi, Dipartimento di Elettronica e Informatica, Politecnico di Milano, P.zza da Vinci 32 20133 Milano, Italy.

E. Bertino, Dipartimento di Scienze dell'Informazione, Università degli Studi di Milano, Via Comelico 39/41, 20135 Milano, Italy.

A. Biavasco, Dipartimento di Scienze dell'Informazione, Università degli Studi di Milano, Via Comelico 39/41, 20135 Milano, Italy.

Kasım Selçuk Candan, Department of Computer Science, University of Maryland, College Park, MD 20742, USA.
candan@cs.umd.edu.

William Cody, IBM Almaden Research Center, San Jose, California, USA,

Ross Cutler, Department of Computer Science, University of Maryland, College Park, MD 20742, USA.
rgc@cs.umd.edu

Christos Faloutsos, University of Maryland, College Park, MD 20742, USA.
christos@cs.umd.edu

Shahram Ghandeharizadeh, Department of Computer Science, University of Southern California, Los Angeles, CA 90089, USA.

Venkat N. Gudivada, Department of Electrical Engineering and Computer Science Ohio University, Athens OH 45701, USA.

H.V. Jagadish, AT&T Bell Labs, Murray Hill, NJ 07974, USA.
jag@research.att.com

Vipul Kashyap, Department of Computer Science, University of Georgia, 415 GSRC, GA 30602-7404, USA.

Daniel P. Lopresti, Matsushita Information Technology Laboratory, Panasonic Technologies, Inc., Two Research Way, Princeton, NJ 08540, USA.
andrewt@mitl.research.panasonic.com

Sherry Marcus, 21st Century Technologies, Inc. 1903 Ware Road, Falls Church, VA 22043, USA.
sem@cais.com

Banu Özden, AT&T Bell Laboratories , 600 Mountain Avenue , Murray Hill, NJ 07974, USA. ozden@research.att.com

Vijay V. Raghavan, The Center for Advanced Computer Studies, University of Southwestern Louisiana, Lafayette, LA 70504, USA.

Rajev Rastogi, AT&T Bell Laboratories, 600 Mountain Avenue, Murray Hill, NJ 07974, USA.
rastogi@research.att.com

Joel Richardson, The Jackson Laboratory, Bar Harbor, Maine, USA.

S. Rizzo,, Dipartimento di Scienze dell'Informazione, Università degli Studi di Milano, Via Comelico 39/41, 20135 Milano, Italy.

Kshitij Shah, Department of Computer Science, University of Georgia, 415 GSRC, GA 30602-7404, USA.

Amit Sheth, Department of Computer Science, University of Georgia, 415 GSRC, GA 30602-7404, USA.

Avi Silberschatz, AT&T Bell Laboratories, 600 Mountain Avenue, Murray Hill, NJ 07974, USA. silber@research.att.com

A. Prasad Sistla, Department of Electrical Engineering and Computer Science, University of Illinois at Chicago, Chicago, Illinois 60680, USA.
sistla@surya.eecs.uic.edu

V.S. Subrahmanian, Department of Computer Science, University of Maryland, College Park, MD 20742, USA.
vs@cs.umd.edu

Arthur Toga, Dept. of Neurology, UCLA School of Medicine, USA.

Kanonluk Vanapipat, The Center for Advanced Computer Studies, University of Southwestern Louisiana, Lafayette, LA 70504, USA.

Clement Yu, Department of Electrical Engineering and Computer Science, University of Illinois, Chicago, Illinois 60680, USA. `yu@dbis.eecs.uic.edu`

Springer-Verlag and the Environment

We at Springer-Verlag firmly believe that an international science publisher has a special obligation to the environment, and our corporate policies consistently reflect this conviction.

We also expect our business partners – paper mills, printers, packaging manufacturers, etc. – to commit themselves to using environmentally friendly materials and production processes.

The paper in this book is made from low- or no-chlorine pulp and is acid free, in conformance with international standards for paper permanency.